DESIGNING
RESILIENCE

DESIGNING RESILIENCE

PREPARING FOR EXTREME EVENTS

Edited by Louise K. Comfort, Arjen Boin,
and Chris C. Demchak

University of Pittsburgh Press

Published by the University of Pittsburgh Press, Pittsburgh, Pa., 15260

Manufactured in the United States of America

Printed on acid-free paper

10 9 8 7 6 5 4 3 2 1

ISBN 13: 978-0-8229-6061-4

ISBN 10: 0-8229-6061-3

Library of Congress Cataloging-in-Publication Data

Designing resilience : preparing for extreme events / edited by
Louise K. Comfort, Arjen Boin, and Chris C. Demchak.

    p. cm.

Includes bibliographical references and index.

ISBN 978-0-8229-6061-4 (pbk. : alk. paper)

1. Emergency management.   2. Preparedness.   3. Disasters.

I. Comfort, Louise K. (Louise Kloos), 1935–   II. Boin, Arjen.

III. Demchak, Chris C.

HV551.2.D47 2010

 363.34′7—dc22   2010011784

CONTENTS

TABLES AND FIGURES

Tables

Figures

PREFACE

This project has its origins in two small international workshops organized around the intriguing topic of resilience. The University of Pittsburgh hosted the first workshop, Managing Extreme Events: Transatlantic Perspectives, held on March 3–4, 2006, sponsored by the European Union Center of Excellence and the Graduate School of Public and International Affairs, University of Pittsburgh, with financial support from the Swedish Emergency Management Agency. The second workshop was held in Leiden in June 2007, with support from the Department of Public Administration, Leiden University, the Dutch National Science Foundation, and the Swedish Emergency Management Agency. The discussions and papers presented in Pittsburgh and Leiden inspired the participants to rewrite their papers and bring them together in this volume.

We incurred our debts along the way and want to take a moment to acknowledge some key players who were instrumental in the process of putting together this volume.

We thank all participants in both workshops for creating an exciting atmosphere, delivering sharp comments, and being such nice colleagues. We are particularly indebted to our long-standing friend Todd R. LaPorte, who provided us with a lengthy set of comments after the Leiden workshop. Being an editor could not be easier or more fun than it is with such a wonderful group of colleagues.

All this was possible because of the generous funding of the Swedish Emergency Management Agency, the Dutch National Science Foundation, the Department of Public Administration at Leiden University, the European Union Center of Excellence (EUCE), and the Graduate School of Public and International Affairs (GSPIA) at the University of Pittsburgh. We thank Alberta Sbragia, the director of EUCE; Timothy S. Thompson, the associate director of EUCE; Carolyn Ban, the dean of GSPIA; and Thomas

Haase, Joyce Valiquette, and Sue Sawyers, who assisted with the arrangements for the Pittsburgh workshop. We also thank Wieteke Zaalberg and Maaike Schaap for their assistance during the Leiden workshop. Finally, we are grateful for the support of the editors at the University of Pittsburgh Press, Peter Kracht and Joshua Shanholtzer. We also wish to acknowledge the anonymous reviewers for their constructive comments, which helped to improve this manuscript.

1 THE RISE OF RESILIENCE

Arjen Boin, Louise K. Comfort, and Chris C. Demchak

The Advent of Resilience

Resilience has become a fashionable buzzword in recent years. The term is frequently found in many different discourses, ranging from the sports pages (resilient teams overcoming late-game deficits) to the international news (the war in Iraq), from reports of natural disasters (Hurricane Katrina) to policy papers on the protection of critical infrastructures (the 2001 California blackout). It appears that everything (organizations, cities, nations) and everybody (from schoolteachers to the U.S. president) can and should be resilient.

This advent of the resilience concept in popular and professional discourse can be viewed as a function of a rising need for resilience. If we accept that dominant trends such as globalization, increasing interdependence and complexity, the spread of potentially dangerous technologies, new forms of terrorism, and climate change create new and unimaginable threats to modern societies, it is only a small step to recognizing and accepting the inherent shortcomings of contemporary approaches to prevention and preparation. If we cannot predict or foresee the urgent threats we face, prevention and preparation become difficult. The concept of resilience holds the promise of an answer.

Hurricane Katrina and its aftermath demonstrated the need for such an answer. The televised sight of stranded masses, people utterly helpless and without assistance, hammered home the message that modern, large-scale sociotechnical systems have become vulnerable to shocks. The technical system of levees, pumping stations, and canals designed to protect the vulnerable city of New Orleans from the intrusion of water failed, and as a result the people depending on the stable functioning of the system suffered. In this case, the political-administrative system and the people it governs were unable to prepare for and cope with a *predicted* disaster. The toll of a *surprise* disaster, such as the Boxing Day tsunami of 2004 or the 2008 earthquake in China, can only be higher.

The Katrina disaster, in other words, exposed the lack of resilience in New Orleans, in its citizens, and in the wider disaster management system designed to mitigate such destructive events. This often-heard statement may seem fair, but it also begs the question: what is meant by resilience? The word *resilience* evokes images of governments that spring back into action after a blow, of resilient people who make the best of their situation with the little that they possess. These are without doubt the qualities a stricken society must possess if it is to rebound.

But is it really fair to expect this? How much can we expect after a devastating onslaught of natural or man-made forces of destruction? How fast and how far does a city have to rebound before it earns this honorary descriptor? We may broaden the inquiry by asking which factors cause some organizations or cities to be resilient, whereas others apparently are not (cf. Vale and Campanella 2005). We may even ask how important resilience really is—maybe the role of government or the state of the economy is a much more important determining factor for the fate of postcrisis systems. The blossoming literature with *resilience* in its titles does very little to answer these questions.

This book seeks to fill the void. The authors in this volume inquire into the characteristics, causes, consequences, and measurement of resilience. They plough very different conceptual and theoretical fields, but their collective harvest presents us with a clear understanding of what resilience is—and what it is not.

Resilience and the Vulnerable Society

Terrorist attacks, water shortages, critical infrastructure failures, a looming energy crisis, a continuing flow of illegal immigrants, the effects of climate change, the threat of a pandemic: societies face an array of potentially devastating threats. These are not "routine emergencies" such as fires, traffic accidents, and hostage takings. These are so-called *low-chance, high-impact* events: urgent threats to societal core values and life-sustaining systems that typically require governmental intervention under conditions of deep uncertainty (Rosenthal, Boin, and Comfort 2001a; Boin et al. 2005).

The prevention and mitigation of these potential catastrophes have traditionally been a national government responsibility. It is a responsibility that has proven difficult to uphold: crises and disasters tend to pose "impossible" challenges to the political-administrative elites who are called upon to deal with them (Boin et al. 2005). To help us understand the scope and intensity of these challenges, the four-phase model that is used in practice proves analytically useful (Comfort 1988; Rosenthal, Charles, and t'Hart 1989).

Mitigation/prevention. Most communities have experienced threats and hazards and have at least some knowledge of the risk to which they are exposed. Mitigation means moving that "common-sense" awareness of risk based on historical experience to a systematic assessment of the risks to which communities are exposed, engaging in scientific inquiry into the conditions that generate risk. It includes mapping the interdependencies among the physical environment that gives rise to destructive events; the built environment that may be vulnerable to risk; and the social environment, or populations and their practices that are affected by severe events. Mitigation was long considered a "bottom-up" approach, engaging citizens, businesses, nonprofit organizations, and communities in the shared task of increasing their capacity to reduce risk and respond effectively to potential hazards. This approach, recognized as fundamental in the 1990s, was overshadowed by the concept of prevention following the terrorist attacks of September 11, 2001.

The concept of prevention enhances the role of government in preventing disasters from happening.[1] In the United States, prevention traditionally justified a "top-down" approach to disaster in which governments are expected to design proper prevention mechanisms for known risks. These mechanisms typically include regulation and inspection regimes and detailed lists of tasks that are mandated for each level of government, building on lessons from previous disasters and emergencies. In putting such mechanisms into place, governments must weigh the potential benefits of strong prevention policies against the cost that excessive regulation may exert on social habits, economic activities, and civil liberties.

The difficulty is that not all incidents and breakdowns can be prevented, as this would require a level of foresight and understanding that governments simply do not possess (Wilensky 1967; Turner 1978; Kam 1988; Parker and Stern 2005). This tension between mitigation and prevention underlies the continuing debate regarding resilience and informs the various approaches toward disaster preparation. If all disasters cannot be prevented, preparation becomes essential. The question becomes whether policies of mitigation will increase the capacity for communities to reduce the scope of damage and recover quickly from damaging events. Developing resilience to potential hazards offers a reasoned strategy to cope with uncertain threats.

Preparation. If incidents, breakdowns, and periodic catastrophes are inevitable, preparation for such disturbances becomes preeminent. The right policies, organizational structures, and resources must be in place to deal with emerging breakdowns. Responders must be trained and facilities ready. A major obstacle to planning and training, however, is the unknown nature of the next contingency. It is one thing to prepare for routine incidents (a fire, a hostage situation, a major traffic incident), but it is much more difficult to plan for biological weapons attacks, long-term energy failures, or extreme weather. The real challenge, as impossible as it sounds, is to prepare for the unknown (Weick and Sutcliffe 2001). Careful assessment of potential risks and informed calculation of the interdependencies among organizations that share those risks contribute significantly to effective investments in planning and preparedness actions. Yet society should also prepare for unimaginable contingencies.

Response/consequence management. Once a crisis or disaster occurs, administrative and governing elites are widely expected to avert or contain the threat, minimize the damage, and prevent critical systems from breaking down. Several problems are sure to emerge.[2] There will be deep uncertainty as to the causes of the incident and the immediacy of the necessary response strategies. Communication among actors in the response network will be hampered by time pressures and uncertainty. Coordination will be a problem: it is never clear who among the many actors involved should make which decisions (Brecher 1979; Drabek 1985; Janis 1989). The capacity to mobilize rapid response operations depends critically on the actions taken previously in the mitigation/prevention and preparedness/ preparation phases and the degree to which a community has invested in the resources, training, and interorganizational skills necessary to muster a "surge capacity" in response to a major threat. After critical decisions are made, implementation hurdles pose yet another set of problems. All these challenges must be met under the glaring lights of an ever-present media.

Recovery/aftermath politics. The aftermath of an energy- and emotion-consuming event is marked by the desire for a quick return to normalcy. Lessons must be learned about the causes and effects of the chosen response (Stern 1997); governmental responses will likely be subjected to some sort of accountability process. Both learning and accountability processes tend to be heavily affected by the "politics of crisis management" (Boin, t'Hart, and McConnell 2008). Different stakeholders will seek to impose their definition of the situation upon the collective meaning-making process that takes place in the aftermath of any crisis. The stakes are high, as decisions made to avert recurrence of a specific crisis often lead to unintended consequences that create a different crisis. Political dynamics can prolong a crisis even after operational challenges have dissipated. If political-administrative elites fail to defend and explain their actions and intentions, the crisis aftermath can carry painful surprises.

Conventional policy-making and bureaucratic organizations are not well designed to manage threats that emerge rapidly in unforeseen and often undetectable ways. The nongovernmental members of society—think of businesses, schools, and citizens—may be even less prepared to deal with these contingencies. In fact, it may be those modern societies enjoying rising levels of economic welfare whose members are least prepared (the so-called vulnerability paradox). Given the inadequacies of governmental performance in reducing the frequency, costs, and consequences of disaster, the call for "resilience" increases in volume as managers seek to balance the shortcomings of existing policies with the reality of increasing exposure to risk.

Modern Challenges

A crisis—almost by definition—is difficult to manage. There are clear signs, however, that such challenges are becoming even harder to meet. Three trends seem particularly relevant. First, the transboundary nature of modern threats widens the range of the contingencies that can besiege a society. Second, modern societies have become increasingly vulnerable to threats new and old. Third, the changing political climate has made it harder for public leaders to deal with crises. These trends, which we briefly discuss below, add up to the "perfect storm" that can paralyze national governments and cause untold damages.

Nation-states have always confronted crises and disasters, most of which tend to visit in known guises and follow familiar if destructive patterns. Yet today's threats appear to be fundamentally different in their disregard of geographical and functional borders. The classic, biblical threats that states have traditionally confronted now carry unprecedented capacity to wreak havoc because their potential "reach" has extended. Dealing with both the causes and the impact of these potential disasters is becoming increasingly impossible for national bureaucracies, as disasters lurk beyond reach and strike with overwhelming force.

To make things worse, nation-states have become ever more vulnerable to these modern manifestations of old-fashioned threats. Modern states have become tightly linked economically, politically, and socially. People, goods, and services now cross borders with relative ease (Friedman 2005). The same pathways that convey people and goods also enable risks to travel across borders. Nation-states thus become susceptible to what were once considered "foreign" or "local" problems in distant places (Schwartz 2003; Sundelius 2005; Missiroli 2006). A crisis in one corner of Europe can now turn into a crisis for the entire continent: think of the Chernobyl explosion or the breakout of "mad cow" disease, which affected multiple countries. Hurricane Katrina originated as a "local" crisis but soon reached beyond geographical and functional boundaries to affect the nation and, indeed, many other countries and industries.

Today's threats change shape as they jump from one system to another (OECD 2003; Missiroli 2005; Quarantelli, Lagadec, and Boin 2006). A glitch in one system can cross over to other systems, snowballing and cascading into a much bigger crisis (Turner 1978; Jervis 1997; Rochlin 1999). Integration is one force to blame: critical systems have become tightly coupled as the result of increasing cooperation (see Perrow 1999). The "life-supporting" systems that sustain basic societal functions (energy infrastructures, transport networks, financial flow structures) are no longer confined to national borders. Nor do they operate independently. The Internet relies on energy grids to power it; energy grid controls are accessed by the Internet.

Modern societies have also become more complex (see Perrow 1999). Cities have expanded rapidly, long-standing social traditions have disappeared, and large immigrant populations have structurally altered Western societies. Governments have retooled following New Public Management principles and have pooled decision sovereignty in certain policy areas. Nongovernmental organizations (NGOs) and multilateral organizations such as the European Union take a greater role in what were traditionally national policy competencies (Wallace 2005; Boin, Ekengren, and Rhinard 2006). As a result, it is harder to recognize an impending threat and unclear who "owns" a transboundary crisis.

There is, of course, a more optimistic note to sound about all this (Baer et al. 2005). It is true that modernization—the sum of technology development, improved infrastructure and transport systems, financial and information efficiencies, and globalization—increases the vulnerability of social systems. These same forces, however, also boost the capacity of social systems to deal with adversity. Because of these forces, many types of incidents that used to bring societies to a grinding halt—from city fires to smallpox epidemics—no longer pose a real threat in modern societies. The underlying question, then, is whether the increased capacity to deal with modern contingencies is sufficient to offset their potential damage.

In this book, we study the societal capacity to deal with emerging contingencies in terms of resilience. As it is impossible to prevent or foresee each and every catastrophe, we assume that all societies will have to face one sooner or later. Their capacity to absorb these events and to emerge from them with their core institutions intact is at the core of resilience.

The Concept of Resilience

The idea of resilience has a firm footing in the fields of engineering, biology, and psychiatry. Engineers apply the concept to materials and technical systems, biologists study resilience in organisms and life systems, and psychiatrists seek to understand the resilience of individuals and their interactions with social systems. In all these fields, the concept of resilience conveys the capacity of a material, person, or biotope to survive sudden shocks. Can a bridge withstand extreme cold and hurricane gales? How does a colony of rabbits deal with the invasion of a predatory species? How does someone reclaim life after the unexpected death of a loved one?

Aaron Wildavsky was one of the first to provide the resilience concept with firm footing in the social sciences. In his now-classic book, *Searching for Safety*, Wildavsky (1988) introduced the concept as an intellectual and instrumental counterweight to the obsession with risk prevention (a logical product of Cold War doom, intended to guard against the environmental and technological disasters that were prevalent during the 1970s and 1980s). The treatise earned much praise but never inspired much empirical work and generated only modest theoretically oriented discussion. It is fair to say that we have not moved very far beyond the territory staked out by Wildavsky.

In recent years, we have witnessed a surge in articles and books on what may be called societal resilience: these works consider how organizations, cities, and societies "bounce back" in the face of a disturbance. Once we begin to work with this rather generic definition, however, deep-running tensions manifest themselves in at least three dimensions (Boin and van Eeten 2007).

The first dimension pertains to the *moment* of resilience: does it come after or before the onset of a major occurrence? Students of disaster tend to "situate" the concept after the shock. This line of thought leads to questions such as, why did Chicago and San Francisco quickly recover after the Great Fire and the Great Earthquake (Vale and Campanella 2005), whereas

New Orleans has yet to emerge from the devastation wrought by Hurricane Katrina? In this conception, resilience is the last line of defense separating a stricken community from structural demise or even extinction.

Students of organizations in flux tend to place resilience before a disturbance. In this view, resilient organizations recognize, adapt to, and absorb variations, changes, disturbances, disruptions, and surprises (Hollnagel, Woods, and Leveson 2006, 3). A resilient organization scans its environment, monitors impending changes, and rolls with the punches. A true mark of resilience is thus the ability to negotiate flux without succumbing to it.

This tension between *speedy recovery* and *timely adaptation* helps us map the extreme poles of the continuum (Westrum 2006). One end is marked by the ability to prevent something bad from happening, the opposite end by the ability to recover once something bad has happened. Somewhere in the middle we find the capacity to prevent something bad from becoming worse. A strict definition of resilience pertains to one of the poles; a wide definition encompasses the entire dimension. In this book, we will adhere to the wider definition of resilience, which captures the capacity to adapt, improvise, and recover.

Before settling on a definition, we should consider a second tension that may divide common ground. This tension pertains to the *severity* of the disturbance. Should we consider resilience as the capacity to deal with rare but devastating events, or is it the capacity to deal with the much wider range of "disruptions that fall outside of the set of disturbances the system is designed to handle" (Hollnagel, Woods, and Leveson 2006, 3)? The first position reserves the term *resilience* for a clearly recognizable disturbance, whereas the second broadens the concept to include all types of routine (and foreseeable) disturbances. The first relegates resilience to the category of rare events, whereas the second waters the concept down to a sloppy synonym for flexibility (see Sheffi 2005). In this book, we begin by staking out the middle ground (although chapter authors may adopt more "extreme" positions).

A third tension that needs to be negotiated is the *state of return* that resilience would need to accomplish (or at least aspire to). What may we reasonably expect from a resilient system that is facing a relatively outsized disturbance? Is a system resilient when it returns to its preshock state? This would amount to backtracking in time, which is, of course, impossible (a return to the status quo is really the emergence of a *new* status quo). Or is it good enough to make the system function again? (New Orleans may then be more resilient than we assumed.) Does resilience refer to the capacity to remain functioning in the face of a serious disturbance? Or should a system emerge stronger and better before we can speak of resilience?

This discussion should take into account the severity of the disturbance in question (the second dimension). If we focus on catastrophic events, a rapid resumption of key functions would be impressive. Routine disturbances, on the other hand, should inform and enhance societal functions before we can speak of resilience.

By staking out an integrative and middle ground along the three conceptual continuums, we can formulate a first definition of resilience:

> *Resilience is the capacity of a social system (e.g., an organization, city, or society) to proactively adapt to and recover from disturbances that are perceived within the system to fall outside the range of normal and expected disturbances.*[3]

It is clear that this definition does not solve all our problems, but it does allow us to bring together empirical chapters that deal with the various dimensions of resilience. After settling on this definition for the time being, we will now consider which research questions flow from our definition.

Questions about Resilience and Theories for Answering Them

The issue of resilience may be connected with other fields of inquiry by formulating a set of research questions that carry both academic and practical relevance and identifying the most promising research perspectives that might allow us to answer these research questions. It should be reiterated that the following list of research questions and perspectives is not an exhaustive one. It merely helps us organize the chapters in this book and allows us to assess the findings presented by the chapter authors.

The first research challenge involves the identification of resilient systems. What are the characteristics of a resilient system? How do we recognize one? This challenge is harder to meet than it might at first seem. It is, after all, easier to recognize the *absence* of resilience, clearly demonstrated by breakdown and long-term demise. But how do we recognize a resilient system that—because of its vaunted qualities—does persist in the face of disturbance and continues unperturbed? How do we separate "lucky" systems that came away with a near-miss from resilient systems that steered clear of an impending breakdown? To complicate matters, how do we recognize a system that has done reasonably well in light of the shock (because of its resilient nature) but has suffered a breakdown all the same?

These questions regularly emerge—but are rarely addressed—in discussions about the quality of crisis management (the reports of postdisaster committees of inquiry provide countless examples). The very fact that a disaster has occurred tends to predispose members of inquiry committees to search for the factors that caused the disaster. Tracing the disaster back to its possible sources, the event easily comes to be perceived as an inevitable outcome of factors that are endogenous to the system (Turner 1978; Perrow 1994). It then becomes difficult to assess whether the organization or city in question really could have prevented the event or was the victim of an unprecedented set of interacting factors. Resilience can then denote the valiant efforts of otherwise failing organizations to recover quickly; it can also become the tombstone epitaph of a city heroically battling the forces of nature (hundreds of people died, but the figure would have been much higher if it were not for the resilient characteristics of the city government).

Once the characteristics of resilient systems have been properly defined, the question of origin imposes itself. How does a system become resilient (and why are so many organizations and cities not resilient)? This question is known in other fields as one of institutional design (Goodin 1996). Is resilience the outcome of smart architecture, heroic leadership, evolutionary adaptation processes, abundant resources, external regulation, sheer coincidence, or a combination of the above?

This is an urgent question, especially for those who believe that modern systems need a dose of resilience in light of contemporary and future threats. If resilience can be engineered into social systems, research should be focused on identifying the variables, strategies, and constraints that can help bring this about. If resilience is a characteristic developed over time and through the seemingly random processes of trial and error, we may have to divest our interest in resilience (focusing instead on risk management and prevention). Taking our cues from the research on public and private institutions, it seems fair to conclude that core characteristics of resilient organizations (e.g., values, ways of working, reputation) can be affected by long-term leadership strategies—for better or worse (Selznick 1957; Wilson 1989). For those who seek to build resilient systems, there is hope.

A complementary research question addresses the potential consequences of resilience and resilient systems. In the fields of crisis and disaster management, resilience is overwhelmingly viewed as a desirable characteristic of social systems. There is another, potentially less attractive side to resilience, however, as organization sociologists have pointed out (Perrow 1986). Resilience may come at a severe cost. Moreover, it may protect a system from external stimuli such as democratic oversight and accountability. This realization urges researchers to consider the normative implications of resilience.

Four Theoretical Perspectives

Our proposed definition and set of core research questions can be addressed with the benefit of many theories. Given the relatively young age of this budding field of inquiry, variety in theoretical approach may not be a bad thing.

The bodies of literature we will discuss here are the emerging field of resilience studies, the slightly more seasoned field of crisis and disaster studies, the very mature field of organization and policy theory, and an interdisciplinary approach to measurement of performance in sociotechnical systems. These fields are, of course, very broadly defined, consisting of many schools and subschools. It is not our intention to provide an authoritative overview of these fields; we simply want to highlight the potential that can be found in each.

An obvious start is the emerging field of resilience studies (Longstaff 2005). We refer here to the work of scholars who, while operating from a variety of academic disciplines, are making an interdisciplinary effort to further our knowledge about resilience. This literature is brimming with ideas on how to conceptualize resilience. It harbors a distinct theoretical approach that is inspired by biological-systems thinking and complexity theory. This literature provides us with a good sense of how resilience functions in complex systems.

The crisis and disaster literature, perhaps surprisingly, has paid little attention to resilience. Much of the research effort has been invested in understanding the causes of these adverse events, their dynamics, and the challenges they pose to political-administrative elites and citizens. One of the key findings in this field, however, helps us explain why resilience is crucial: crisis and disaster researchers have consistently shown that there is very little political leaders and public administrators can do during the immediate aftermath of a catastrophe (especially when they lack accurate knowledge of the unfolding event). It turns out that disaster plans do not work, communication fails, and command-and-control doctrines backfire—only after some time can skilled or talented crisis managers impose some kind of order. Ultimately, the quality of response critically depends on the capacity to enhance improvisation, coordination, flexibility, and endurance—qualities that we typically associate with resilience.

We can draw on the fields of organization theory and policy studies (especially the nexus between the two disciplines) to understand the possibilities and constraints when it comes to building resilience into social systems. Policy scholars explain how hard it is to elevate these types of issues to the top of the decision-making agenda (Baumgartner and Jones 1993; Birkland 2006). Organization theorists offer helpful insights with regard to creating cultures that may enhance and sustain resilience (LaPorte 2007; Schulman and Roe 2007).

A critical approach that distinguishes this book from other discussions of resilience is its inquiry into sociotechnical systems. The literature on social cognition (Hermann et al. 2007), cognitive anthropology (Hutchins 1995), and sociotechnical systems (Coakes, Willis, and Clark 2002) carefully examines what humans do and how they do it in relation to the technical systems they operate. In this perspective, the transition from perception to action at individual, group, organizational, and systemic scales of operation is critical to understanding the dynamics of resilience. Developing metrics of resilience in actual environments exposed to risk represents a critical task that is only beginning.

The interaction between increasingly advanced technical systems and the human organizations that design, build, operate, and manage them has been studied by researchers at the Tavistock Institute for Social Research since it opened in 1946 (Trist, Emery, and Murray 1997). The impact of technology on social organizations is, of course, continually unfolding (Coakes, Willis, and Lloyd-Jones 2000). The modern-day exponential increase in the use of information technology across the world is presenting ever more complex and surprising dynamics in social action and organizational performance (Coakes, Willis, and Clarke 2002). Such changing conditions require considerable integrative efforts to understand the dual nature of these technologies. They can be harnessed to effective decision support in large-scale events, but they also impose new or enhanced constraints on organizational action.

2 RESILIENCE

EXPLORING THE CONCEPT AND ITS MEANINGS

Mark de Bruijne, Arjen Boin, and Michel van Eeten

The term *resilience* has many meanings in academic discourse. It is derived from the Latin word *resilio,* meaning "to jump back" (Klein, Nicholls, and Thomalla 2003, 35; Manyena 2006, 433). In physics and engineering, resilience refers to "the ability of a material to return to its former shape after a deformation" (Arsenault and Sood 2007, 90; O'Rourke 2007, 25; Sheffi 2007, 33) and is considered more or less synonymous with adaptability or flexibility (e.g., Redman and Kinzig 2003; Woods 2006, 21).

When applied to social entities such as societies or organizations, resilience refers to "the ability to resist disorder" (Fiksel 2003, 5332), to an organization's capacity "to continue its existence, or to remain more or less stable, in the face of surprise, either a deprivation of resources or a physical threat" (Longstaff 2005, 27). Resilience can then be considered "the flip side of vulnerability," as it emphasizes the ability of systems or persons to cope with hazards and provides insights on what makes a system more or less vulnerable (cf. Handmer and Dovers 1996, 487; Manyena 2006, 439–43).[1]

In the past decades, research on resilience has been conducted at various levels of analysis—the individual level, the group level, and the organizational or community level (cf. Longstaff 2005; Vogus and Welbourne 2003)—in a wide variety of disciplines including psychology (e.g., Jacelon 1997; Luthar, Cicchetti, and Becker 2000; Luthar, Sawyer, and Brown 2006; Masten and Powell 2007; Olsson et al. 2003), ecology (e.g., Fiksel 2003; Gunderson et al. 2002), organization and management sciences (e.g., Carroll 1998; Crossan et al. 2005; Greenley and Oktemgil 1998; Sheffi 2005; Weick and Sutcliffe 2001), group/team literature (e.g., Bunderson and Sutcliffe 2002; Edmondson 2003), and safety management (e.g., Cook and Woods 1994; Hollnagel, Woods, and Leveson 2006; Krieger 2005).

In recent years, resilience has emerged as a key concept in various academic disciplines that have taken an interest in the capacity of social systems to "resist" adversity and deal with uncertainty and change (Davidson-Hunt and Berkes 2003, 64). As a result, resilience has become a multifaceted concept "full of contestations, especially regarding its affinity with and lucid usage by a multiplicity of disciplines" (Folke 2006; Gallopin 2006; Klein, Nicholls, and Thomalla 2003, 40; Manyena 2006, 433). Some even argue that "both conceptual clarity and practical relevance are critically in danger" (Brand and Jax 2007). An examination of the various disciplines that have used and researched resilience should allow us to evaluate the overall worth of the concept itself.

Psychology and the Resilient Individual

Arguably the first discipline to study resilience (mostly in children) was psychology (cf. Luthar 2007; Schoon 2006). Studies in the 1940s and 1950s aimed to distinguish how individual competence influenced the history and prognosis of children with mental disorders. Many kids with high-risk parents did not develop mental disorders, and research in the 1970s aimed to investigate the underlying conditions that facilitated children "developing well despite their risk status or their exposure to adversity" (Masten and Powell 2007, 2; Olsson et al. 2003, 2). Researchers set out to identify what caused this remarkable adaptation and identified a range of "potential assets or protective factors associated with resilience" (Masten and Obradovic 2006, 14; Olsson et al. 2003).

Two specific strands of research developed from this study. Research initially focused on the individual competences that may have suffered from such exposure, such as intelligence and high self-esteem. Scholars focused on factors that sought to explain the "amazing stories" that involved children overcoming hardships and "succeeding" in life—the epitome of the American dream.[2] This focus on resilience as a "personality trait" unearthed characteristics that enable individuals to overcome hardship: "correlates or predictors of positive adaptation against a background of risk or adversity" (Wright and Masten 2005, 22). This school of thought is also known under the heading "resiliency" (Coutu 2002; Luthar and Cicchetti 2000; Luthar, Cicchetti, and Becker 2000; Tarter and Vanyukov 1999).

A second approach found that resilience derives from factors external to the child (i.e., aspects of families and wider social environments). This has led psychologists to conclude that resilience is not so much an individual trait, but should be considered a *process* (Jacelon 1997; Luthar, Cicchetti, and Becker 2000; Olsson et al. 2003; Wright and Masten 2005). Here the study of resilience distinguished itself from notions of positive adjustment or simply competence that were characteristic in resiliency research, which studied *"how* resilience occurs" (Riley and Masten 2005, 15). This second approach to the study of resilience "takes into consideration the circumstances and processes under which positive adjustment takes place" (Schoon 2006, 8). Resilience was subsequently defined as "a dynamic process encompassing positive adaptation within the context of significant adversity" (Luthar, Cicchetti, and Becker 2000, 543).

Psychology research on resilience has been severely criticized for its lack of clarity and the lack of consensus among researchers (Curtis and Cicchetti 2003; Glantz and Sloboda 1999; Kaplan 2005; Luthar, Cicchetti, and Becker 2000; Roosa 2000; Tarter and Vanyukov 1999; Wright and Masten 2005). Much of the research is vague about the definition of resilience, which makes it difficult to assess whether researchers define resilience as an outcome or as an influential quality or process. Other questions have been raised about the measurement of resilience (Luthar and Cushing 1999), the comparable nature of the risks to which individuals are exposed, and the relationship between adversity and resilience (Bonanno 2004). Critics point out that resilience is a multidimensional construct, meaning that successful coping with adversity at the individual level (i.e., contributing to the well-being of individuals) is something different from the resilience of a group, community, or society (Riley and Masten 2005). Furthermore, being resilient in the face of certain experiences (i.e., competent to overcome a certain type of risk) may not mean that the individual is automatically resilient enough to overcome other negative experiences in life (Kaplan 2005; Luthar, Cicchetti, and Becker 2000; Masten and Obradovic 2006). In fact, it is widely assumed that no single individual is completely resilient.

Consequently, psychologists have concluded that there is a "lack of a unified theory of resilience capable of guiding more structured and empirically based approaches to the development of the construct" (Olsson et al. 2003, 2)—so much so that "some researchers and clinicians despair of ever being able to resolve these various issues" (Kaplan 2005, 45), going so far as to suggest that the concept should not be used anymore. Despite this criticism, resilience research is engaged in what is considered "a third wave," which, based upon past findings, now seeks to "create" or stimulate resilience in individuals and groups of people by focusing on preventive interventions, thereby strengthening the ties with practice and policy (Luthar

2007; Luthar and Cicchetti 2000; Luthar, Cicchetti, and Becker 2000; Olsson et al. 2003; Peters, Leadbeater, and McMahon 2005; Rolf and Johnson 1999; Wright and Masten 2005).

Ecology

Until the 1970s, thinking about ecology was rooted in a scientific tradition that sought to explain the natural world as a stable system. In the 1970s, this focus shifted to understanding instability and dynamics in nature (Scoones 1999). An influential new way of thinking around natural systems and ecology management thus evolved.[3]

As early as 1973, ecologists identified resilience as a way to cope with the dynamics, surprise, and complexity that are generated in abundance in biological environments (cf. Folke 2006). One of the fundamental assumptions of Holling (1973) was that ecosystems may be characterized as complex systems and that the dynamics in the system are never as smooth and linear (i.e., predictable) as traditional models seemed to presume (Berkes, Colding, and Folke 2003a, 5).

In order to deal with the ever-changing patterns and surprises in ecological systems, such as storms, droughts, and over- or underpopulation—or even the extinction of entire species—Holling (1973, 17) introduced the concept of resilience as "the ability of a system to absorb disturbance and still retain its basic function and structure" (Walker and Salt 2006, 1). Holling considered resilience as an emergent system property, the result of processes of self-organization of individual agents and their interactions. Consequently, ecosystem management takes a highly "critical view of the notions of control and prediction" (Berkes, Colding, and Folke 2003a, 8).

The concept of resilience in ecosystem management has received enormous attention as a result of the specific feature that resilience promises: the *continuous* ability to manage change and surprises, to meet current demands without eroding future needs—that is, to maintain control. The more resilient a system, the larger the disturbance it can absorb without shifting into an alternate regime (Walker et al. 2006). This means that the system does not have to deplete scarce resources and maintains sufficient resources to deal with any disturbance. Resilience thus became directly linked to survival: "A resilient social-ecological system, which can buffer a great deal of change or disturbance, is synonymous with ecological, economic and social sustainability. One with low resilience has limited sustainability; it may not survive for a long time" (Berkes, Colding, and Folke 2003a, 15).

A. Engineering resilience (r)

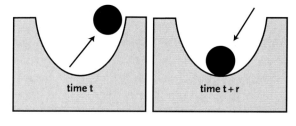

time t   time t + r

B. Ecological resilience (R)

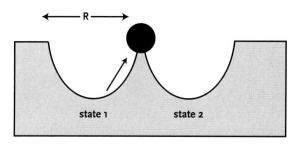

state 1   state 2

Fig. 2.1. Alternative definitions of resilience as represented by a ball-and-cup model. Cups represent the stability domains of the system, the ball represents the system state, and single arrows represent disturbances to the system. (A) Engineering resilience can be depicted by a global equilibrium (ball resting at the bottom of a cup). When the system is disturbed (ball moves up the side of the cup), resilience is defined as the amount of time (r) for the system to return to the equilibrium state. (B) Ecological resilience is defined as the amount of disturbance that the system can absorb without changing state (stable state 1 or 2) and is measured as the width of the stability domain (R). *Source: Gunderson 2003, 35.*

Holling identified two states of resilience and two different types of stability (see fig. 2.1). This distinction between *engineering* resilience and *ecological* resilience is enlightening.

Engineering resilience pertains to "the capacity of something or someone to bounce back to a "normal" condition following some shock or disturbance." This type of resilience may be considered a measure of a system's stability (Brand and Jax 2007; Gunderson 2003, 34; Holling 1996; Walker et al. 2006; Walker and Salt 2006, 62). Stability refers to "the ability of a system to return to an equilibrium state after a temporary disturbance" (Holling 1973, 17). The more rapidly it returns, the more stable the system. Holling and his followers were primarily interested in the *magnitude* of the disturbance the system can tolerate. "Though the time it takes to get back can be important, resilience is *not* about the speed of the bounce back so much as *the ability* to get back." (Berkes, Colding, and Folke 2003a, 15; Gunderson 2003, 34; Walker and Salt 2006, 37; emphasis added).

In trying to control and design systems to behave as stably (i.e., as predictably) as possible, engineers have engaged in elaborate optimization processes. However, according to Holling, "a drive for an efficient optimal state outcome has the effect of making the total system more vulnerable to shocks and disturbances" (cited by Walker and Salt 2006, 9). Consequently, "traditional systems engineering practices try to anticipate and resist disruptions but may be vulnerable to unforeseen factors. An alternative is to design systems with inherent 'resilience' by taking advantage of fundamental properties such as diversity, efficiency, adaptability, and cohesion" (Fiksel 2003, 5330). Ecological resilience refers to "a measure of the amount of change or disruption that is required to transform a system from being maintained by one set of mutually reinforcing processes and structures to a different set of processes and structures" (Bennett, Cumming, and Peterson 2005, 945). This definition assumes that the "structure and function of systems continually change through time" (Walker and Salt 2006, x). A return to a "stable state" becomes irrelevant as ecologists assume there is no such thing as a "stable state" in complex systems, that there is no equilibrium to which the system can "bounce back."

Rather than focusing on the stability of these systems, or the speed with which changes are absorbed, ecological resilience focuses on fluctuation and on what happens when systems are on the verge of moving toward another stable state (near the thresholds that demarcate different regimes). Ecological resilience is all about identifying and understanding these thresholds.[4]

Holling and other ecologists argue that resilient systems thrive on (a limited type of) fluctuation:[5] "The emphasis is not on reaching or maintaining a certain end point or terminal condition, but on staying 'in the game'" (Pickett, Cadenasso, and Grove 2004, 373). Management processes of ecological systems should therefore be improved by making them more adaptable and more flexible, able to deal with uncertainty and surprise, and by building their capacity to adapt to change. This type of *adaptive management* involves strategies such as continuous and close monitoring, iterative learning, learning by doing, and experimentation (cf. Scoones 1999).

The two meanings of resilience reflect fundamentally different conceptions of stability, which frequently clutters debates involving resilience (Holling 1996). Holling distinguishes resilience, the ability to absorb changes and still persist, from stability, which may be defined as the ability of a system to return to a state of equilibrium: "Thus, a very stable system would not fluctuate greatly but return to normal quickly, whilst a highly resilient system may be quite unstable, in that it may undergo significant fluctuation" (Klein, Nicholls, and Thomalla 2003, 39). "Engineering resilience" is primarily based on "maintaining *efficiency* of function" and assumes that a system is close to a stable state, whereas "ecological resilience" tries to

Table 2.1. Development from the Narrow Interpretation of Resilience to the Broader Social Ecological Context

Resilience concept	Characteristics	Focus	Context
Engineering resilience	Return time, efficiency	Recovery, constancy	Vicinity of a stable equilibrium
Ecological/ ecosystem resilience	Ability to buffer capacity, withstand shock, maintain function	Persistence, robustness	Multiple equilibria, stability landscapes
Social-ecological resilience	Interplay disturbance and reorganization, sustaining and developing	Adaptive capacity, transformability, learning, innovation	Integrated system feedback, cross-scale dynamic interactions

Source: Folke 2006, table 1, p. 259; Brand and Jax 2007

accommodate for dynamics and change and "focuses on maintaining [the] *existence* of function" (Holling 1973, 33).

The concept of resilience in ecosystem management has shifted from "an early interpretation of resilience, which focuses on the robustness of systems to withstand shocks while maintaining function, i.e. ecosystem or ecological resilience," to a much wider focus encompassing "social resilience, and a subsequent interpretation, which refers more to the interplay of disturbance and reorganization within a system as well as to transformability, learning and innovation, i.e., social-ecological resilience" (Brand and Jax 2007). With this shift, the concept has gained applicability in the study of social systems

Ecologists differentiate among three types of surprises for which resilience has to be developed, ranging from relatively small-scale surprises, which may be countered through individual action; through medium-sized surprises, which must be countered by coordinated responses in existing institutional settings; down to unprecedented new surprises outside of memory, which require major reorganization, learning, and renewal of institutions (Davidson-Hunt and Berkes 2003, 63–65).

Different types of surprise demand different responses. Small-scale surprises in more "stable" systems (e.g., resource surprises), require "wait-and-see" or "weather-the-storm" strategies, which tend to be less costly and more easily adaptable or reversible alternatives (and may thus be considered a specific form of engineering resilience). In more dynamic and unpredictable systems that operate closer to the edge, an "intensification" strategy may be necessary in which an increased commitment to an investment in one or another mode must be made, albeit at higher costs and less reversible.

Nurturing sources of disturbances and renewal helps maintain the capacity of a system to absorb perturbations and thus prevent regime changes (Davidson-Hunt and Berkes 2003, 65). Resilience theorists have posited that regime changes can be prevented by deliberately creating small disturbances in one part of the system to prevent the occurrence of large disturbances in other parts of the system. For example, ecologists view small-scale wildfires as healthy and even necessary to prevent large-scale uncontrollable wildfires.

Ecologists argue that the inherent dynamics and unpredictability of ecosystem behavior would render a planned, optimized, and rational way of ecosystem management inadequate. Ecosystems should be managed flexibly through learning, adaptation, and self-organization (Gunderson and Holling 2002). "Instead of assuming stability and explaining change," which used to be the dominant way of thinking in ecosystem management, ecosystem resilience emphasizes "the capacity to lead a continued existence by incorporating change" and "stresses the importance of assuming change and explaining stability" (Folke, Colding, and Berkes 2003, 352).

As such, resilience is not so much the actual motion of springing back, but rather the *ability* to spring back. It refers to the capacity of the system to deal with changes, which may be reflected in the technology, knowledge, and social organization of the system under study. Resilience in complex adaptive systems is a dynamic characteristic that changes through time, meaning that "different aspects of resilience assume prominence at particular phases" (Carpenter et al. 2001, 766). In this sense, "resilience incorporates the capacity of social-ecological systems to cope with, adapt to, and shape change and learn to live with uncertainty and surprise" (Brand and Jax 2007).

Despite the abovementioned conceptual clarification of resilience, progress in the empirical domain of resilience research has lagged. Research on social-ecological resilience is still in the explorative phase (Folke 2006, 263). Exactly how institutions and incentives should be designed to sustain and enhance resilience remains unknown (Berkes, Colding, and Folke 2003a, 16). Research to find operational indicators of resilience has received "little attention" (Carpenter et al. 2001, 765), and "there appears to be no consensus on how this concept can be made operational or even how it should be defined" (Klein, Nicholls, and Thomalla 2003, 39). In fact, "most studies that explore resilience-related ideas have used resilience as a metaphor or theoretical construct" (Carpenter et al. 2001, 767).

Resilience in the Social Sciences

Resilience has recently gained popularity within different social science disciplines, "where it is applied to describe the behavioral responses of communities, institutions and economies" (Klein, Nicholls, and Thomalla 2003, 39). This section reviews the state-of-the-art knowledge on resilience in these disciplines

Organization and Management Sciences

Different conceptions of what exactly might be termed (organizational) resilience exist in organization and management literature. One strand clearly springs from the field of psychology (cf. Cho, Mathiassen, and Robey 2006; Coutu 2002; Rerup 2001; Sutcliffe and Vogus 2003), while the other may be linked with the ecological perspective (cf. Gittell, Cameron, and Lim 2005; Wildavsky 1988). Consequently, the study of resilience in organizations and organizational literature has remained more fragmented and even more devoid of empirical studies than in both "maternal" disciplines discussed above (Sutcliffe and Vogus 2003, 99).

Among the first to use the concept in the social sciences was Aaron Wildavksy (1988), who introduced "resilience" in his classic *Searching for Safety* as one strategy or "solution" for decision makers dealing with risk and uncertainty. Wildavsky contrasted resilience with the strategy of anticipation, which is "a mode of control by a central mind; efforts are made to predict and prevent potential dangers before damage is done" (Wildavsky 1988, 77). Anticipation often is effective in coping with known threats and problems. It pushes decision makers to optimize the efficiency of their systems and make them resistant and robust to specific threats. Anticipatory policies seek to sink resources into specific defenses to counter specific threats.

This strategy becomes ineffective when uncertainty, dynamics, and volatility increase. The information and knowledge requirements that allow for this strategy are relatively high and have become increasingly problematic in the field of public policy making and management in general as the complexity and dynamics of problems in our society have increased dramatically. Wildavsky argues that managing risks and uncertainty through anticipation has become increasingly difficult. Nevertheless, many policies focused on managing safety or the environment (i.e., sustainability) through the use of so-called precautionary principles in effect demand full

Table 2.2 Appropriate Strategies for Different Risk/Information Conditions

		Amount of Knowledge	
		Small	Large
Predictability of Risk	High	More resilience, less anticipation (4)	Anticipation (1)
	Low	Resilience (3)	More resilience, less anticipation (2)

Source: Wildavsky 1991, 122

anticipation as they seek to eradicate the risk of harm, failure, or damage (cf. Handmer and Dovers 1996).

Under circumstances of great uncertainty and risk, resilience is the more successful management and decision-making approach: "Resilience is the capacity to cope with unanticipated dangers after they have become manifest, learning to bounce back" (Wildavsky 1988, 77). This notion of resilience closely resembles the concept of "ecological resilience" and stresses the virtues of flexibility and adaptability of decision-making and policy-making strategies. Wildavsky argues that decision makers will have to increasingly rely on risk-tolerant, flexible decision-making strategies that allow for trial-and-error and learning as society's capacity to anticipate risks and dangers fails to keep up with the growing complexity and dynamics of the world in which we live (cf. Homer-Dixon 2001).

Wildavksy identifies different strategies for different conditions and surprises. He proposes to create "a balance of 'anticipation' and 'resilience' as a strategy for reducing risk in uncertain conditions" (Comfort, Sungu, and Johnson 2001, 145). These strategies appear in table 2.2.

Anticipatory strategies work best for risks that can be predicted and are well understood (cell 1). The other extreme, where knowledge of effective measures is lacking and threats are unpredictable (cell 3), calls for resilient strategies. The availability of preventive measures, coupled with the unpredictability of risk (cell 2), suggests a mixed strategy with an emphasis on resilience. When we know what is coming but not how to make things better (cell 4), an anticipatory strategy has some merits. We must, however, chiefly rely on resilience, argues Wildavsky, "because otherwise we are likely to do far more harm than good" (1991, 123).

Wildavsky's views have been taken up and applied by organizational scholars studying the reliable management of large-scale technologies (Summerton and Berner 2003). Their body of knowledge, which has come to be known under the heading of High Reliability Theory (HRT), focuses on a class of organizations that manage complex and tightly coupled technologies (Perrow 1984) and maintain extraordinary levels of safety and reliability (LaPorte and Consolini 1991; K. H. Roberts 1990a, 1990b; Rochlin 1999; Rochlin, LaPorte, and Roberts 1987). Theorists of high-reliability organizations (HROs) found that, among other characteristics, a combination of anticipation and resilience helps to explain their success (LaPorte 1999, 221; Weick and Sutcliffe 2001). HROs sink "resources into specific defenses against particular anticipated risks," but they also have the capacity to retain "resources in a form sufficiently flexible—storable, convertible, malleable—to cope with whatever unanticipated harms might emerge" (Wildavsky 1988, quoted in Weick and Sutcliffe 2001, 178n25).

Resilience is about the ability to improvise, the ability to "bounce back" (Weick 1998). Unlike specific defenses, resilience requires the use of generic resources such as "knowledge, communication, wealth and organizational capacity, the resources that enable us to craft what we need, when we need it, even though we previously had no idea we would need it" (Wildavsky 1995, 433).

Organization and management literature has identified a range of strategies that contribute to resilience: structural flexibility, redundancy, or slack (Grabowski and Roberts 1999; K. H. Roberts, 1989, 1990a, 1990b); high-performance relationships (Gittell, Cameron, and Lim 2005; Sheffi 2005); sense-making (Weick 1995, 2001; Weick, Sutcliffe, and Obstfeld 2005); a culture of reliability (Levinthal and Rerup 2006; Weick 1987; Weick, Sutcliffe, and Obstfeld 1999); and improvisation (Crossan et al. 2005; Rerup 2001; Weick 1998). Resilience "involves more than simply knowing how to regroup during a crisis and keep going. To be resilient also means being able to come away from the event with an even greater capacity to prevent and contain future errors" (Weick, Sutcliffe, and Obstfeld 2002, 14). These organizations must learn how to learn, which enhances their capacity to adapt.

The nurturing of this capacity comes at a price. Resilience competes with traditional notions of efficiency and profit maximization (see van Eeten, Boin, and de Bruijne's chapter in this volume). These principles are mostly found in classic high-risk systems, the traditional HROs. What distinguishes HROs from normal organizations is that the reliability demands are so intense and the failures so potentially disastrous that little trial-and-error learning—the usual way organizations learn—is possible (LaPorte and Rochlin 1994, 222; Schulman 1993, 35). These organizations continuously face the possibility that "their first error may be their last trial" (Rochlin 1999, 1552).

It has become harder to maintain such characteristics, however. HROs increasingly find themselves part of *networks of organizations* as a result of institutional fragmentation, automation, and liberalization processes (de Bruijne 2006, 2007; Roe et al. 2005; Schulman et al. 2004). As a result, many conditions that once allowed for anticipation have been removed. Network forms of organizations have demoted many HROs to mere "managers," which lack information and control over vital resources.[6] In a networked setting, resources are accessed and brought together "just in time" to respond to specified contingencies. Reliability in networks of organizations therefore depends on real-time resilience rather than anticipatory long-term planning (de Bruijne and van Eeten 2007; Roe et al. 2005; Schulman et al. 2004).

Since the early 1990s, the concept of resilience is also featured in organization and management literature as a strategy to defy the complexity, uncertainty, and volatility of today's business environment (e.g., Hamel and Välikangas 2003; Neilson and Pasternack 2005; Riolli and Savicki 2003; Sheffi 2005; Starr, Newfrock, and Delurey 2003). Some industries are starting to respond to increased uncertainty and volatility by seeking to achieve agility rather than leanness, where agility is achieved through organizational flexibility and less static organizational structures and the organization therefore becomes more adaptable to future change (C. J. Miller et al. 2007, 72–73).

A second, related strand of research in organizational resilience draws heavily upon research in psychology. By drawing a parallel between resilience in families and resilience in business systems, these studies have sought to identify the concept of resilience in organizations as a specific form of adaptability (Vogus and Welbourne 2003, 97). Similar to those studying HRT, these researchers view resilience as a process that enables an organization to develop a capacity to continuously cope with the unexpected that can be "managed" and developed over time. Resilience in the context of these studies refers to "the capability of individuals, groups, or organizations to adapt quickly to changes in their environments" (Cho, Mathiassen, and Robey 2006, 25).

However, large differences exist among what researchers consider to be the *sources* of organizational resilience (Cho, Mathiassen, and Robey 2006, 25). Some consider organizational resilience as a systemic property that is closely related to humans in the system or builds on their resilient capacities (Flin 2006; Mallak 1999; Riolli and Savicki 2003).[7] Others consider resilience a strategic characteristic that rests partially on situational factors and resources such as financial reserves (Gittell, Cameron, and Lim 2005). According to these studies, the nurturing of this resilient capacity becomes more important as business environments become more unstable and success increasingly requires change (Hamel and Välikangas 2003, 2).

Despite these various strands of research, organizational-resilience research has made little headway in the identification of conditions that foster resilience in organizations: "Resilience is still best thought of as an art as well as the application of scientific knowledge and techniques" such as coping skills, creativity, improvisation, and leadership (Burke 2005, 633).

The Safety Sciences

Resilience has recently emerged in the engineering field of safety management "as the logical way to overcome the limitations of existing approaches to risk assessment and system safety" (Hollnagel, Woods, and Leveson 2006, xi). Westrum (2006, 59) defines resilience as "the ability to prevent something bad from happening, or the ability to prevent something bad from becoming worse, or the ability to recover from something bad once it has happened." Within their field of study, known under the heading "resilience engineering," safety scientists seek to "develop engineering and management practices to measure sources of resilience, provide decision support for balancing production/safety tradeoffs, and create feedback loops that enhance the organization's ability to monitor/revise risk models and to target safety investments" (Woods 2005, 302).

Safety scholars argue that resilient systems are not conditioned for the optimized execution of a single task. This means that safe systems can prevent or deal with many types of failures, yet once a certain threshold has been passed, they become very brittle and collapse, resulting in accidents.

One could argue that resilience engineering seeks to achieve or maintain a stable, accident-free end state. To achieve this goal, Hale and Heijer (2006, 40) propose to broaden the resilience concept in resilience engineering *to include anticipation* because "if resilience is used with its common meaning of survival in adversity, we do not see it to be of interest to us." Consequently, "the focus on system resilience emphasizes the need for proactive measures in safety management: tools to support *agile, targeted, and timely* investments to *defuse emerging vulnerabilities* and sources of risk before harm occurs" (Woods 2005, 302).[8]

Consequently, resilience engineering scholars have extended the resilience concept to the point where it contrasts or even conflicts with resilience concepts in other disciplines such as ecology and the organization and management sciences, leading organizational scholars to remark that "resilience has been used to describe the ability of an organization to absorb shocks in order to maintain a steady state, and also the ability to rebound back from shocks to a new steady state. At this rate, what isn't resilience[?]" (Roe and Schulman 2008, 163).

Disaster and Crisis Management

In the domain of crisis and disaster management, resilience is defined as "the measure of a system's, or part of a system's, capacity to absorb and recover from the occurrence of a hazardous event" (Janssen et al. 2006; Warrick 1982, 209). A distinction is made between "resilience" and "reliability": "'Reliability' refers to a continuous strategy of protective shielding designed to create reliable systems, whereas 'resilience' is the ability of a system to absorb and bounce back if the protective shielding fails" (Warrick 1982, 209).

Another distinction is made between "reactive" and "proactive" resilience in response to hazards and natural disasters: "A society relying on reactive resilience approaches the future by strengthening the status quo and making the present system resistant to change, whereas one that develops proactive resilience accepts the inevitability of change and tries to create a system that is capable of adapting to new conditions and imperatives" (Klein, Nichols and Thomalla 2003, 39). As in ecology and the organization and management literature, this has linked the resilience concept firmly to issues of adaptation and management (also known as adaptive management; cf. Wise 2006). Based upon these contrasting perspectives, Handmer and Dovers (1996, 494–95) introduce a classification of resilience, defined in terms of responses to a threat or disturbance:

Key characteristics
Type 1   Resistance and maintenance
Type 2   Change at the margins
Type 3   Openness and adaptability (Handmer and Dovers 1996,
          p. 496, table 1)

In another attempt to link resilience to disaster management, Comfort (1994a, 1999) applies concepts from Complex Adaptive System Theory to crisis and disaster management, along with Wildavsky's concepts of anticipation and resilience. Comfort (1999, 21) conceptualizes resilience as "the capacity to adapt existing resources and skills to new situations and operating conditions." In her research, Comfort argues that both anticipation and resilience are needed to create a dynamic tension that, if managed appropriately, can produce an effective strategy for risk reduction and response.

It is here that opinions within disaster management begin to differ.

Some consider disaster management and the emergencies that precede it as *"the predictable result* of interactions among three systems: the physical environment, which includes hazardous events; the social and demographic characteristics of the communities that experience them; and the buildings, roads, bridges and other components of the constructed environment" (Mileti 1999, cited in Bosher et al. 2007, 236; cf. Jones 2001). Others tend to characterize such events according to the "unexpectedness" with which they occur, the severity of the threat, and the level of uncertainty that they produce (McConnell and Drennan 2006, 60).

Another debate rages about whether or not crisis and disaster management includes hazard prevention and/or mitigation. Taking a more reactive stance is more or less associated with the "traditional practice" of disaster management (Manyena 2006, 438). More traditional studies of responses to disasters "tend to embrace the 'engineering' version of resilience" (Pendall, Foster, and Cowell 2007, 4). For instance, some scholars argue that "resilience applies to the minimization of losses and damages when a disaster occurs, thereby indicating similarity to the term 'resistance'" (McEntire et al. 2002, 269). Over the long run, disaster studies have tried to judge resilience based on whether a society recovered from a crisis (e.g., Vale and Campanella 2005).

It has become clear that not only is disaster planning fallible, but so is centralized crisis management through crisis management responders. Crisis preparation involves not just anticipatory measures such as planning, but the development of "strategies to ensue operational resilience" to be able to deal with crises as they occur (McConnell and Drennan 2006, 60).

Broadly conceptualized, resilience refers to "both the ability to adjust to 'normal' or anticipated stresses and strains and to adapt to sudden shocks and extraordinary demands. The concept spans both pre-event measures that seek to prevent disaster-related damage and post-event strategies designed to cope with and minimize disaster impacts" (Tierney 2003). Especially in the research conducted after the 9/11 (Kendra and Wachtendorf 2003) and Katrina disasters, researchers have found that much of the capacity to mitigate the effects of disasters may be found at the decentralized, local level. Research revealed some remarkable community responses and coping behaviors in the sense of "non-linear, adaptive response" (Rose 2004, 308). In the face of imminent physical harm and danger, the capacity for resilience in disaster management shifts radically to the local level (i.e., groups of people or communities). Furthermore, "a trusted source of information is the most important resilience asset that any individual or group can have in times of surprise" (Longstaff 2005, 59).

In the wake of Hurricane Katrina, efforts have been aimed at shifting disaster management from a focus on protecting critical infrastructures toward the creation of "resilient communities" (O'Rourke 2007, 25; cf. Paton and Johnston 2001, 2006).[9] The attention of policy makers and scholars has shifted from anticipation, and a focus on how to organize rescue services to prevent and deal with crisis, to the question of how to increase the capability of communities to deal with disasters. Further, the concept of "resilient communities" acknowledges the use of local knowledge and experimentation and flexibility to deal with local circumstances. Being there on the ground enables a better grasp of system threats and the nature of surprises and perturbations. In other words, it allows for the accumulation of specified knowledge or expertise.[10]

Some even consider the resilience concept part of a new paradigm in disaster and crisis management (Manyena 2006; McEntire 2001; McEntire et al. 2002): "Resilience captures what should underpin holistic risk management. By this we mean a paradigm that includes adaptation to climate change, hazard mitigation and sustainable human development" (O'Brien et al. 2006, 71). Resilience thus encompasses both resistance and recovery and the creativity resulting in "a resilient community [that] predicts and anticipates disasters; absorbs, responds and recovers from the shock; and improvises and innovates in response to disasters" (Maguire and Hogan 2007, 17). Thus, "the resilience of a community is an overarching attribute that reflects the degree of community preparedness and the ability to respond to and recover from a disaster" (Godschalk 2003; O'Rourke 2007, 25; cf. Paton 2006, 9–10; Vale and Campanella 2005).

Nevertheless, the concept of crisis and disaster management is not without its critics. Clear guidance as to how resilience can be promoted is lacking, and resilience remains a conceptual construct. Consequently, "debate is likely to continue about the concept of resilience, and refinements and elaborations of the term are to be expected" (O'Rourke 2007, 25).

Resilience has not been converted into an operational tool for policy and management purposes. Instead, the definition of resilience has become so broad as to render it almost meaningless (Klein, Nichols, and Thomalla 2003, 41–42). Resilience has become an umbrella concept for a range of system attributes that are deemed desirable. This leads to considerable confusion. Some have exhibited doubts as to the use of the concept in social systems, versus physical items, and have concluded that resilience is too vague a concept to use in disaster risk reduction (Manyena 2006).

Sociotechnical Systems

The study of sociotechnical systems offers a more rigorous approach to identifying and measuring resilience in system performance, as it addresses the interdependencies among the technical systems that provide key functions, such as electrical power, communications, transportation, and water, gas, and sewage distribution, essential to daily operations in complex human communities and the organizational systems that design, build, operate, and manage them. The study of the interactions among organizational and technical systems developed largely after World War II as damaged societies began to rebuild their industrial sectors and to do so in more humane yet efficient ways. The research in this field initially began with a focus on the individual in the workplace, and the Tavistock Institute in London became an early center for examining human interactions in work environments (Trist, Emery, and Murray 1997).

As the industrial economy regained strength in the 1950s through the 1970s, researchers focused on interactions between large-scale technical systems and the fragility of these systems under stress. For example, the advent of nuclear power brought both the promise of plentiful, inexpensive energy and the danger of technical systems failing catastrophically (Commoner 1990). Researchers sought to balance the risk of these technologies with the benefits they promised by designing organizational structures to minimize the uncertainties of technical failure (Short and Clark 1992). Resilience was measured in terms of the organization's capacity to maintain continuity of operations, despite sudden disruptions or unexpected failures in technical functions. The "system" was considered to be a single entity—with both social and technical components (Goodman, Sproull, and Associates 1990).

Research on sociotechnical systems changed markedly in the 1980s and 1990s as the world economy shifted to the information age. The impact of information technologies and instantaneous transmission of information via advanced telecommunications networks radically altered the form and function of organizational performance, enabling rapid adaptation to emerging events but also precipitating sudden disruptions (National Research Council 2001). Computational systems became central to organizational performance (Hoschka 1996), facilitating cooperative work among individuals in distant locations (Coovert and Thompson 2001). In this shift, managing information became a critical component of building resilience, as the organization of knowledge to support collective effort in complex tasks required investment of time and attention (Coakes, Willis, and Clarke 2002). Yet issues of reliability and robustness continued to limit the performance of computational systems, despite substantive success (Rochlin 2000).

Current research on sociotechnical systems examines the networks of information and action that are required to sustain them (Newman, Barabasi, and Watts 2006). The meaning of resilience is consequently redefined in these systems as the capacity of the system to function in fused patterns of sociotechnical performance. Without the technology, the organization is severely limited. Without the organization, the technology will inevitably fail. Resilience in sociotechnical systems depends upon a more calibrated measurement of performance, as it represents the threshold between function and failure under stress.

Revisiting the Resilience Concept

The conclusion of this necessarily short and incomplete literature review must be that the concept of resilience is far from clearly defined and must be understood as a concept with different meanings in different disciplines. Whereas in the world of engineers resilience may be considered an inherent property that can be called upon indefinitely, nothing could be further from the truth in the social world. By contrasting these differences, we hope to make the reader cognizant of this very important notion and its often neglected consequences.

Three types of resilience arise from our overview: "emotional resilience," "engineering resilience," and "ecosystem resilience." "Emotional resilience" considers resilience as a character trait in a person, organization, or community. "Engineering resilience" considers resilience as a systemic attribute that allows the system to return to its original stable state as quickly as possible, whereas "ecological resilience" considers the return to a new stable regime through learning and adaptation. Different scholars from different disciplines have argued that in order to deal with complexity, systems should be characterized by a combination of these types (de Bruijne 2006; Comfort 1994a; Handmer and Dovers 1996; Wildavsky 1988).

Nevertheless, and perhaps unavoidably, different disciplines manifest a different emphasis in each of these definitions, resulting in different assumptions with regard to the aspects that constitute resilience. It could be argued that the notions of resilience in all the disciplines share an emphasis on the *ability* of the object under study (human systems) to "bounce back" from a disturbance, rather than some output variable. The initial sharp distinctions and definitions in the various disciplines have been complemented with broader and more nuanced notions of resilience as academics have sought to apply the resilience concept and focused on the management of resilience and the broader notion of adaptability. Scientists in all disciplines have come to conclude that "the resilience of 'natural' systems, though complex, pales in comparison with evaluation of human systems, largely because humans have foresight and creativity and can adapt in advance to anticipated future states" (Pendall, Foster, and Cowell 2007, 15).

The various definitions and notions of resilience in the different disciplines contrast at three levels. First, the different disciplines and definitions clearly emphasize different aspects of this ability to "bounce back." Although the different disciplines seem to converge on the notion that the way in which systems react to shocks becomes increasingly important, some academics still pay considerably more attention to the prevention or anticipation of disturbances than to the reactive aspects of the resilience concept. This notion is still particularly strong in the safety sciences. Thus, the resilience definitions and notions of safety science and disaster management seem to conflict with the initial notion of resilience as provided by Wildavksy (1988). In fact, some recommendations refer to what Wildavsky would have considered "anticipation."

A second distinction concerns the types of disturbances to which the various disciplines argue the resilience concept may be applied. Critics and proponents of the concept throughout the disciplines argue that (too) much variation and too little clarity exist with regard to what should be considered resilience (Carpenter et al. 2001; Glantz and Sloboda 1999, 116). Is resilience the ability to recover from a natural disaster (i.e., a tsunami or a terrorist attack) but also the ability to deal with "disruptions that fall outside of the set of disturbances the system is designed to handle" (Woods and Hollnagel 2006, 3), such as safely landing a plane without engines? Or is resilience even broader—the ability to deal with every nonroutine event that may characterize rather "simple" yet tightly coupled supply chains (cf. Sheffi 2005)? Still others in psychology and the organization and management sciences consider that the conditions under which we may attribute resilience to social entities are "exhibited quite rarely." Consequently, "one can speak of a latent property of organizations, rather than a continuous capability" (cf. Kaplan 2005; Luthar, Cicchetti, and Becker 2000; Masten and Obradovic 2006).[11]

A third distinction among the disciplines, closely related to the second, concerns the explication of the state in which the system bounces back. Resilience to what (cf. Carpenter et al. 2001)? How does one define a "stable" state, which would indicate that ("engineering") resilience has taken place? This problem is especially noticeable in psychology, disaster studies, and safety science, fields that seek to understand why and how people and social systems recover from disturbances (cf. Manyena 2006, 438; Pendall, Foster, and Cowell 2007). What is the safety envelope that distinguishes safe from unsafe systems in safety science? What is the "back to normal" level that is assumed in disaster and crisis management? And how and when do we consider a new state to be stable enough to consider the motion resilience?

3 DESIGNING ADAPTIVE SYSTEMS FOR DISASTER MITIGATION AND RESPONSE
THE ROLE OF STRUCTURE

Louise K. Comfort, Namkyung Oh, Gunes Ertan, and Steve Scheinert

The concept of resilience, defined here as the "capacity for collective action in the face of unexpected extreme events that shatter infrastructure and disrupt normal operating conditions," is characterized by experienced researchers as involving the mental processes of sense-making (Weick 1995), improvisation (Mendonça, Beroggi, and Wallace 2001), innovation (see Demchak's chapter in this volume), and problem solving (Comfort 1994b). Each of these processes involves the exercise of mental skills that depend upon keen observation and access to real-time information in changing conditions. Together, they represent the wider interpretation of resilience that is discussed earlier, in chapters 1 and 2.

This chapter argues that a further process, cognition, is central to increasing resilience in the capacity of communities to manage recurring risk and to respond to, and recover from, disaster. Interpreting cognition in terms of its contribution to resilience—the main theme of this book—requires reconceptualizing the relationship between perception and action and determining when in the sequence of an organization's performance resilient behavior occurs and what factors contribute to its emergence in practice.

Cognition in the context of disaster is defined as the capacity to recognize the degree of emerging risk to which a community is exposed and to act on that information. When risk is not recognized by those who are legally responsible for protecting communities and no action—or inadequate action—is taken, the situation can rapidly escalate into a threatening, imminent disaster. Retrospective analysis of the response to an actual disaster can provide insight into the role of cognition among responders to disaster operations.

With a clear focus on the role of cognition, we reframe the concept of intergovernmental crisis management as a complex, adaptive system. That is, the system adjusts and adapts its performance to fit the demands of an ever-changing physical, engineered, and social environment. The terms of cognition, communication, coordination, and control are redefined in ways that fit the reality of practice more accurately in extreme events (Comfort 2007b). In this process, a framework emerges for analysis. This conceptual framework is used to assess the performance of the intergovernmental system that evolved in response to Hurricane Katrina (2005) and the ensuing flood in New Orleans. The goal of this analysis is to determine more specifically the structure and processes within organizations and among jurisdictions that build resilience to extreme events.

An effective intergovernmental crisis management system is a dynamic interorganizational system characterized by a cumulative sequence of decisions that leads to a coherent response system. This sequence includes four subsets of decisions that define an evolving strategy of action: (1) detection of risk; (2) recognition and interpretation of risk for the immediate context; (3) communication of risk to multiple organizations in a wider region; and (4) self-organization and mobilization of a collective, community response system to reduce risk and respond to danger.

Each subset of decisions involves the search for and exchange of information across organizations and jurisdictions, underscoring the shared responsibility of decision makers in mobilizing a coherent response to an extreme event. With each decision, the responsible managers may choose to reduce, share, or ignore the risk. The cumulative record of decisions taken across organizations and jurisdictions represents the collective capacity of a region to manage the risks to which it is exposed. This capacity is documented by a region's reduction in loss and adjustment in allocation of resources and attention to create an effective balance between immediate demands and long-term goals. Resilience in practice means maintaining this balance between short-term needs and long-term goals of safety and security for the community.

The tension between structure and process in organizing collective action represents a classic problem in organizational design and performance. This tension is especially critical in disaster environments, where the goal is to maintain continuity of operations in communities shattered by destructive events. Organizations and institutions provide structure, order, and predictability in stable communities. The difficulty occurs when the established order no longer fits the requirements for managing risk to the community. The challenge lies in maintaining a sufficient balance between structure, or clear rules for conducting the operations needed to protect a community, and process, the urgent demands of the environment that may require novel approaches and flexible adaptation to support action.

Risk Assessment and Response in Disaster Management

Resilience differs from standard conceptions of emergency management. Emergency management has largely focused on local events. More difficult and less frequent, but far more devastating, are large, multijurisdictional regional events. Hurricane Katrina, for example, crossed the jurisdictional boundaries of multiple municipalities and counties in nine states; three federal regions; and the international borders of Caribbean island nations, Mexico, and Canada.[1] Managing disasters on such a scale exceeded the capacity of the Federal Response Plan and the National Incident Management Plan, which detailed the procedures governing disaster operations in effect when Katrina struck on August 29, 2005.

The challenge to researchers and disaster managers lies in determining how to recognize the emerging threat in sufficient time to take informed action to reduce the risk and to mobilize an effective response. This capacity to assess the indicators of risk and comprehend the threat before it becomes a full-blown danger distinguishes resilience from standard emergency management, which is primarily reactive. For example, fire trucks respond only after a fire has already started.

Disaster management systems require the rapid mobilization of a dynamic interorganizational system that moves from individual to organizational to system levels of action, analysis, and aggregation of information. These different scales of action require different types of information and different means of communication to create a "common knowledge base" to support collective action against threats at each jurisdiction, and successively for the response system. It is at these transition points of escalating requirements for action that human cognitive, communicative, and coordinating skills frequently fail. Six propositions developed from prior research in disaster response and recovery (Comfort et al. 2009; Comfort 2006b) present a conceptual framework for building resilience in communities exposed to recurring risk. The basic argument is that human capacity to act collectively and constructively in risky, uncertain environments can be significantly enhanced through appropriate uses of information technology.

Detection of Risk

Detection of risk involves a complex process of assessing both the vulnerability and the capacity of a region exposed to threat. In detection of risk, scientific data are transmitted through a network of scientists who review and validate the data and then forward their assessment to decision makers. For example, the National Hurricane Center first identified a tropical depression forming off the Bahamas as a potential risk to the Gulf Coast on August 23, 2005. Meteorologists at multiple weather stations on the Gulf Coast tracked the intensifying storm to monitor its direction and intensity before transmitting their collective assessment to policy makers, emergency managers, and the public. Engineers in the urban center of New Orleans checked the status of the built infrastructure; hospitals in the region at risk reviewed procedures for managing patient care. Yet the cumulative assessment of risk across sectors and jurisdictions was not integrated to provide a detailed assessment of threat to the region from the imminent storm.

The process of risk detection is vulnerable to the fragilities of human organization and performance. Responsible decision makers may be watching separate conditions for indicators of vulnerable performance but miss the interaction among these conditions that may intensify the potential destructive impact for the whole community. The design of appropriate networks of sensing technologies to assess performance in a core set of interacting conditions and operational systems critical to the community could augment the early detection and validation of risk. These data, reported as thresholds of risk across a set of critical conditions—such as the status of the levees in New Orleans, the number of households without means of transportation, the status of evacuation planning, and contingency plans for power generation—would provide a more integrated and timely assessment of risk to human decision makers responsible for risk reduction.

Proposition 1. Human capacity to detect risk increases with the timeliness, accuracy, and validity of data transmitted in reference to a core set of thresholds of risk to conditions critical for continuity of community operations.

Recognition and Interpretation of Risk

Prior research has found that an individual's capacity for problem solving drops under increasing complexity (LaPorte 1975) and stress (G. Miller 1967; Simon 1996). This drop in capacity is the result of the increased number of risk factors, the degree of unfamiliarity with new information, and the degree of uncertainty that characterizes extreme events. In these contexts, appropriate uses of information technology offer a means of extending human problem-solving capacity in uncertain conditions. A key question for investigation is the extent to which a sociotechnical information infrastructure, designed to detect and transmit risk information quickly and accurately, can facilitate the rapid recognition of risk within a community and lead to more informed, timely action.

> *Proposition 2. Human capacity to recognize risk conditions can be increased by focusing risk data through notifications or selected views that are directly relevant to the responsibilities of each major decision maker in the system, thus reducing the overload of less relevant information and time required for information processing and facilitating the rapid absorption of threatening information by individual decision makers.*

Communication of Risk

The prevailing method of communicating risk in disaster environments relies largely on command-and-control processes executed through a carefully defined hierarchical order. For example, the National Response Plan (FEMA 2004) and the National Incident Management System (FEMA 2005b), adopted by the Federal Emergency Management Agency (FEMA) and the Department of Homeland Security as the authoritative policies governing emergency operations at the time of Hurricane Katrina, follow a serial format for communicating risk and requests for assistance from lower to upper jurisdictional levels. An analysis of communication patterns among emergency response agencies in the hours and days leading up to, and following, Hurricane Katrina as the storm made landfall on August 29, 2005, illustrates the breakdown of this design in practice (Comfort 2005, 2006b). Building the awareness of risk to support collective action is a cumulative process. If the first two steps of risk detection and communication have not been carried out successfully, the effort to engage organizations from a wider arena in the emergency response system is likely to flounder or fail.

Our model for achieving this task of communicating critical information to focused audiences is the "bowtie" architecture for decision support (Csete and Doyle 2004; Comfort 2005). As shown in figure 3.1, this design identifies key sources of data that "fan in" simultaneously to a central processing unit (or "knot") where the data are integrated, analyzed, and interpreted from the perspective and performance of the whole system. The new information is then "fanned out" to the relevant actors or operating units that use the information to make adjustments in their specific operations, informed by the global perspective. This design fits well with an emergency operations center, where status reports from multiple agencies are trans-

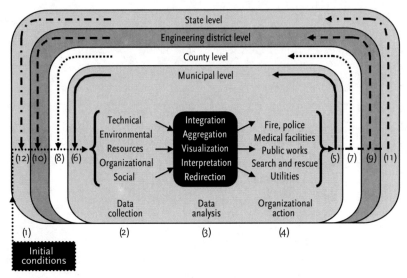

Fig. 3.1 Bowtie architecture for the iterative flow of information within a disaster management system

mitted to the service chiefs, who review the data from the perspective of the whole community. The set of service chiefs collectively integrate, analyze, and interpret the data to adjust performance reciprocally among multiple organizations based on timely, valid information. This process represents self-organization (Axelrod and Cohen 1999) in emergency response, guided by the shared goals of protecting lives and property, and maintaining continuity of operations for the whole community (Comfort 1994b).

This theoretical framework acknowledges the importance of both design and self-organizing action in guiding coordinated action in a complex, dynamic environment. It can be modeled as a set of networks that facilitate the exchange of incoming and outgoing information through a series of analytical activities that support systemic decision making. The information flow is multiway, but decision support gains efficiency through integrated analysis and coordinated action toward a clearly articulated goal for the whole system. The system operates by identifying the key sources of information, the key processes of analysis and interpretation of incoming data, and the key routes of transmission for updated status reports on critical thresholds of risk. It maintains self-organizing functions in that personnel with informed knowledge adjust their own actions to achieve the best performance for the whole system. Design, self-organization, and feedback are central to the effective performance of distinct organizational units within the global response system.

> *Proposition 3. The capacity of a set of organizational managers, each with specific responsibilities and operating at different locations, to coordinate their actions can be increased by the simultaneous transmission of relevant risk information to each manager, creating a "common operating picture" of risk to the region for all managers.*

Self-Organization and Mobilization

The collective capacity of a community to take informed, coherent action in the face of danger is a measure of that community's resilience. This capacity depends upon the cumulative set of cognitive, communicative, and adaptive processes outlined above. If any one of the preceding steps fails, the capacity of the community for collective action is weakened. If all of the preceding steps are performed effectively, the capacity for collective action is strengthened. Further, instances of negative feedback can have the reverse effect of weakening the whole system's performance in response to danger.

Disaster management involves multiple governmental, nonprofit, and private entities with different structures and organizational models. The interest of each organization in gathering information and disaster management data derives directly from its own mission. In current disaster management systems, these organizations are vulnerable to information overload caused by the transmission of large amounts of irrelevant information. As the number and variety of sensors, or monitoring instruments, continue to grow, so does the volume of data generated by these sociotechnical sources of information. The capacity for multiple managers at different levels of responsibility to view the relevant information for their specific arenas of action simultaneously enhances their ability to adapt and adjust their performance to the emerging threat more quickly, efficiently, and effectively. Setting the thresholds of risk for participating agencies, exposed to threats of different degrees of severity and limited by different levels of resources, requires the judgment of experienced emergency managers, as well as timely, valid information. The model of an executive dashboard, or a visual display of real-time information using bowtie architecture, offers a mechanism for building a "common operating picture" among responsible actors in a complex disaster management system for a community at risk.

> *Proposition 4. The collective capacity of a community to act in coherent ways to reduce risk can be increased through information search and exchange,*

focused views, and feedback processes to create an interorganizational learning system that adapts its behavior to fit available resources to changing conditions of risk more appropriately.

Vulnerability to Systemic Failure

In each of the four decision processes identified above, human capacity for informed action is enhanced by access to appropriately designed and functioning information technology. The interaction between organizational performance in coordinating action and the availability of and access to a functioning information infrastructure has a fundamental effect upon a community's capacity to manage the risk to which it is exposed. Without access to such a technical information infrastructure, the organizational capacity to mobilize collective action in a region will likely fail. The collapse of the emergency response system in New Orleans after the city lost its communications aptly illustrates this argument (Comfort 2006b).

> *Proposition 5. Without a well-defined, functioning information infrastructure supported by appropriate technology, the collective response of a community exposed to serious threat will fail.*

Designing a Resilient Disaster Management Network

A disaster response system functions largely as a network of organizations that are focused on a common goal: risk reduction and continuity of operations for the community exposed to threat. The capacity of organizations to recognize risk may be affected by the structure of the network. If an organization performs a bridging function between two unrelated organizations (Burt 1992) in the network, it will gain more influence in the operation of the whole system. If an organization is isolated from other units in the system, it will likely lose influence in the operation of the whole system. The performance of the whole system depends upon the collective capacity of its members to recognize risk and the degree of collaboration they are able to achieve in adjusting their actions reciprocally to one another in order to manage their risk effectively.

> *Proposition 6. The performance of the entire disaster management system depends on the iterative functions of scanning the environment for risk, detecting it accurately, verifying the degree of risk, analyzing the information from the perspective of the whole system, and transmitting the results in a timely manner to the multiple actors to serve as a basis for coordinated action.*

These six propositions, taken together, constitute a conceptual framework regarding the evolution of the capacity for collective action in communities exposed to recurring risk. The test of the framework is whether it provides insight into the strengths and weaknesses of practice.

Disaster Response in Practice

Can actual disaster operations be analyzed to determine whether the decision processes that characterized them correspond to, or vary from, the model of decision making represented in the propositions outlined above? The situation reports recorded by the Louisiana Office of Homeland Security and Emergency Preparedness (LOHSEP) offer an unusual source of empirical data against which to test a theoretical model of an evolving disaster management system. Since the performance of this intergovernmental system following Hurricane Katrina has been evaluated and discussed extensively in other studies (U.S. House of Representatives 2005; Farber et al. 2007; Brookings Institution 2005; Comfort 2005, 2006a), the descriptive context of this disaster will not be repeated here. Rather, the focus of this analysis will be to assess the actual stages of an evolving disaster system, documented by actions recorded in the situation reports (sitreps) maintained by LOHSEP. The sitreps were recorded under the tense, urgent conditions of a major disaster and are subject to human error. Yet this set of reports is likely the most complete record of the disaster operations undertaken by the state of Louisiana. This dataset documents the types of state-level transactions undertaken in disaster operations, with interactions and exchanges reported among municipality, parish, and federal levels of response operations.

The analysis that follows is based on the situation reports that were prepared and maintained by LOHSEP for twenty-three days, from August 27 through September 19, 2005, during the two days preceding and twenty-one days following landfall of Hurricane Katrina on August 29, 2005.[2] The situation reports represent the official record of disaster operations undertaken at the state level in Louisiana in reference to Hurricane Katrina. The reports identify the organizations within the state of Louisiana that initiated requests for assistance (initiating organizations), including the date and the time of each request. They also identify the type of assistance requested (transactions) and the organizations to which each request was assigned for action (assigned organizations). Finally, they identify the status of each request in the response process, specifying the date and time that any change was made.

Each of the six propositions presented above will be examined in reference to the situation reports to assess the record of actual performance against the theoretical model. A critical condition for effective performance in disaster management is the emergence of a "common operating picture" among the organizations participating in response operations. This condition is facilitated by the simultaneous transmission of relevant risk information among the set of participating organizations. Examining the situation reports recorded by LOHSEP, the record shows the status of interactions among organizations with key responsibilities in disaster operations in the period of time immediately before and after the storm.

Detection of Risk

In the evolving conditions prior to Hurricane Katrina's landfall on August 29, 2005, the National Weather Service (NWS) detected a tropical storm off the Bahamas on August 23, 2005, and tracked the storm as it moved across Florida and into the Gulf of Mexico over the next five days, intensifying to a category 5 hurricane (D. L. Johnson 2006). The NWS predicted landfall in Louisiana and Mississippi on August 29, 2005, as a category 4 hurricane. The NWS reported the scientific evidence documenting the storm and its increasing severity to the news media on a daily basis (*Times Picayune*, August 24–29, 2005). Scientific institutions had detected the storm and made this information publicly available

Yet other thresholds of risk were not detected or reported as the hurricane was approaching landfall. These risks included the weakened status of the levees in New Orleans (Seed et al. 2005) and the evacuation needs of a large number of low-income residents of New Orleans who had no means of transportation (GAO 2006b; Brookings Institution 2006). While different agencies, such as the Louisiana State University Hurricane Center (van Heerden et al. 2005), were aware of the status of these conditions, there was no integration of data from multiple sources that would have identified a broader threshold of risk for the Gulf Coast region, particularly the City of New Orleans. This lack of integration of risk data from different sources inhibited the emergence of a "common operating picture" for the public agencies responsible for emergency management agencies. Without a common understanding among agencies of the severity of the hurricane and its potential impact on communities directly in its projected path, the scientific information did not trigger coordinated action critical to a resilient response at the federal, state, and local levels. Inaction at this point in the evolving event affected all subsequent decisions in the process.

Recognition and Interpretation of Risk

Analysis of the situation reports confirms that the public agencies responsible for disaster preparedness at local, state, and federal levels of authority did not adequately recognize the threat to the vulnerable infrastructure and population of New Orleans and consequently did not interpret the risk in time to mobilize action. Table 3.1 reports the number of requests for assistance that were registered in the LOHSEP situation reports, by jurisdiction and date. Only fifteen requests for assistance from parishes were registered on August 27, 2005, two days before landfall. That number increased to eighty requests on August 28, 2005, with twenty-five requests from state agencies. Only on August 30, 2005, the day after Katrina made landfall, was there a significant increase in the number of requests for assistance initiated by parish, state, and regional jurisdictions, with a modest number of requests—thirty-six—initiated by agencies at the federal level. Figure 3.2 shows the graphic distribution of the number of requests by date and jurisdictional level. The data in table 3.1, corroborated graphically in figure 3.2, show that little more than 10 percent of the actions taken in response to Hurricane Katrina were taken prior to landfall on August 29, 2005. These findings demonstrate the widespread lack of recognition of the severity of the risk and consequent inaction by responsible agencies in the face of impending danger. Failure at the initial point of detecting risk was compounded by failure in interpreting the gravity of that risk for the region, especially for the vulnerable City of New Orleans.

The LOHSEP situation reports document the pattern of requests for assistance that came to the State Emergency Operations Center (EOC), the sequence used in processing the requests, and the actions taken in response. Table 3.2 reports the total number of requests for assistance that were submitted to LOHSEP by the fourteen major types of response functions for the period, August 27 to September 6, 2005. The top row of the table shows the number of requests for each type of response function. The lower rows show the status of the requests as they entered the system and the subsequent actions taken. The status categories represent the phases of the dispatch process. "No response" means that a request was received at the LOHSEP EOC, but no response was given. "Action required" means that a request was received and registered for action. "Pending" means that the request was assigned to a responsible agency for action. "Canceled" means that the request was aborted and no action was taken. "Ongoing" means that the request was received and that the urgent situation reported as requiring assistance was continuing. "En route" means that a unit had been dispatched to a specific location to provide assistance. "On scene"

Table 3.1 Number of Requests for Assistance Registered in LOHSEP Situation Reports by Date and Level of Jurisdiction

	Aug. 26	Aug. 27	Aug. 28	Aug. 29	Aug. 31	Sept. 1	Sept. 2	Sept. 3	Sept. 4	Sept. 5	Total
City											
N	0	0	0	7	2	13	18	20	3	12	75
%	0.00	0.00	0.00	9.30	2.70	17.30	24.00	26.70	4.00	16.00	100.00
Parish											
N	15	80	106	319	163	71	96	179	38	264	1,331
%	1.13	6.01	7.96	23.97	12.25	5.33	7.21	13.45	2.85	19.83	100.00
Regional											
N	0	0	2	5	3	2	3	7	2	7	31
%	0.00	0.00	6.50	16.10	9.70	6.50	9.70	22.60	6.50	22.60	100.00
State											
N	0	25	105	466	198	83	103	240	80	264	1,564
%	0.00	1.60	6.70	29.80	12.70	5.30	6.60	15.30	5.10	16.90	100.00
Federal											
N	0	0	4	36	26	8	18	34	21	58	205
%	0.00	0.00	2.00	17.60	12.70	3.90	8.80	16.60	10.20	28.30	100.00
International											
N	0	0	0	0	0	1	1	2	1	1	6
%	0.00	0.00	0.00	0.00	0.00	16.00	16.70	33.30	16.70	16.70	100.00
Total											
N	15	105	217	833	392	178	239	482	145	606	3,212
%	0.47	3.27	6.75	25.92	12.20	5.54	7.44	15.00	4.51	18.86	100.00

Source: Situation reports, Louisiana Office of Homeland Security and Emergency Preparedness, Baton Rouge, LA. August 27–September 6, 2005.

means that the unit had arrived at the scene and that assistance was being given. "Released" means that the unit had completed its task and returned to service. The total number of requests less the number classified as "no response" equals the number of active requests. "On scene" + "en route" + "released" equals the number of completed actions that constructively contributed to disaster operations.

By this classification, four categories of requests for assistance represent the largest share of the total number of reported transactions. These categories include requests for supplies, shelter, security, and equipment. Surprisingly, the category that received the fewest requests was evacuation, indicating that those residents who could leave did and that those who could not were likely more in need of supplies, shelter, security, and equipment. The most sobering finding represented in this table is the high number of actions that remained pending across all categories of response functions—38.7 percent—and the low number of actions, again across all categories, that were successfully completed—0.6 percent—during the eleven-day period for which status reports were recorded. These data document again the heavy burden of demands placed on the state agency in the first days after the storm and its inability to meet them in a timely manner. This situation indicates a lack of dynamic exchange among jurisdictional levels. Given a lack of recognition of risk prior to the storm at all jurisdictional levels, the interorganizational system of disaster response outlined in policy and procedures was not effectively mobilized in the first eleven days after landfall.

Communication of Risk

Communicating the risk that has been detected and recognized as a threat to the community focuses the next set of decisions that are essential to resilient response. The legal framework of the National Response Plan (FEMA 2004) and the National Incident Management System (NIMS) (FEMA 2005b) outlines a formal process for communicating risk among the jurisdictions. This framework specifies that when municipal jurisdictions are overwhelmed in extreme events, they request assistance from the next level of jurisdiction, parish or county. If the parish or county is overwhelmed, it requests assistance from the next level of jurisdiction, the state. In turn, when the state is overwhelmed, it requests assistance from the federal level. The design of NIMS is to facilitate a smoothly functioning transition of as-

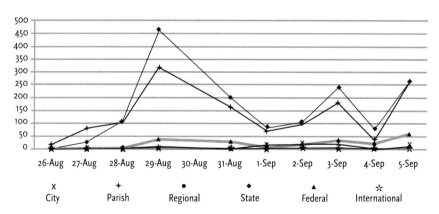

Fig. 3.2   Number of requests for assistance registered in LOHSEP situation reports by date and level of jurisdiction. *Source:* Situation reports, Louisiana Office of Homeland Security and Emergency Preparedness, August 27–September 6, 2005. Situation reports were not available for August 31, 2005.

Table 3.2 Frequency Distribution of Requests for Assistance by Mission Status Reported to Emergency Operation Center, State of Louisiana

	No response	Action required	Operation pending	Canceled	Ongoing	En route	On scene	Released	Total trans- actions
Search and Rescue									
N	27	95	98	15	0	5	0	0	182
%	14.80	52.20	53.80	8.20	0.00	2.70	0.00	0.00	6.00
Damage Assessment									
N	3	7	2	1	0	0	0	0	8
%	37.50	87.50	25.00	12.50	0.00	0.00	0.00	0.00	0.30
Supplies									
N	166	414	248	37	0	9	0	3	665
%	25.00	62.30	37.30	5.60	0.00	1.40	0.00	0.50	21.90
Transportation									
N	40	99	65	26	2	5	7	1	186
%	21.50	53.20	34.90	14.00	1.10	2.70	3.80	0.50	6.10
Evacuation									
N	8	12	3	1	0	0	0	0	14
%	57.10	85.70	21.40	7.10	0.00	0.00	0.00	0.00	0.50
Shelter									
N	45	115	83	28	0	12	36	0	237
%	19.00	48.50	35.00	11.80	0.00	5.10	15.20	0.00	7.80
Security									
N	104	207	248	36	9	27	51	2	505
%	20.60	41.00	49.10	7.10	1.80	5.30	10.10	0.40	16.60
Emergency Response									
N	21	45	36	4	0	5	2	0	84
%	25.00	53.60	42.90	4.80	0.00	6.00	2.40	0.00	2.80
Medical									
N	63	141	26	21	0	1	3	1	178
%	35.40	79.20	14.60	11.80	0.00	0.60	1.70	0.60	5.90
Utility									
N	58	115	100	35	0	28	1	8	226
%	25.70	50.90	44.20	15.50	0.00	12.40	0.40	3.50	7.40
Heavy Equipment									
N	130	245	157	60	7	9	24	1	459
%	28.30	53.40	34.20	13.10	1.50	2.00	5.20	0.20	15.10
Light Equipment									
N	16	36	38	5	0	2	7	0	81
%	19.80	44.40	46.90	6.20	0.00	2.50	8.60	0.00	2.70
Personnel									
N	28	71	47	27	0	4	0	1	134
%	20.90	53.00	35.10	20.10	0.00	3.00	0.00	0.70	4.40
Communication and Coordination									
N	20	38	24	4	1	0	10	1	75
%	26.70	50.70	32.00	5.30	1.30	0.00	13.30	1.30	2.50
Totals									
N	729	1,640	1,175	300	19	107	141	18	3,034
%	24.00	54.10	38.70	9.90	0.60	3.50	4.60	0.60	100

Source: Situation reports, Louisiana Office of Homeland Security and Emergency Preparedness, Baton Rouge, LA. August 27–September 6, 2005.

sistance and authority across jurisdictions to activate a truly national response system of support and assistance to extreme events. Under this legal framework, the situation reports submitted to LOHSEP can be interpreted as requests for assistance from parishes and, in the case of New Orleans, a parish/city. Consequently, one measure of resilience in the communication of risk to wider arenas of response and resources is the timeliness of response to these requests.

Table 3.3 presents the data regarding the change in status categories as requests for assistance were processed by LOHSEP. The data show the number of hours that requests were held in each action status category before moving to the next and provide a profile of the pace of disaster operations and the amount of delay involved in meeting requests for action. The profile shows the slow evolution of the Katrina response system over the period of eleven days for which status data were reported.

Again, the data document the sizeable delay in assigning the requests to an agency for action—the change from "action required" to "pending"—for even the most urgent requests. For example, the delay for search and rescue (mean = 48.2 hours) was more than two days, and that for emergency response (mean = 33.7 hours) was more than a day. For less immediate requests, such as utilities, the time delay was 3.6 days, and for supplies, the time delay was even longer, an average of 7.2 days. Clearly, the EOC at LOHSEP was overwhelmed. The categories with the largest number of requests—"Security," "Search & Rescue," and "Supplies"—had significant delays, indicating disconnected linkages in the interdependent disaster response network.

Two types of requests for assistance made to LOHSEP reveal a higher rate of completion than the others, "Security" and "Utilities." Given the primary need for both types of assistance in the badly damaged environment left behind by Hurricane Katrina, this finding documents the priorities set by the response agencies. While the requests detailed in the situation reports were initially intended for Louisiana state agencies, the cumulative delay in response indicates the inability of the state to meet these requests without federal assistance. This finding further indicates the state emergency preparedness system's low capacity to absorb threatening information and communicate it effectively among its members.

Comparing the response time among the fourteen response function categories, we calculated an analysis of variance (ANOVA) to determine whether there is any significant difference among the means of categories. The results of the ANOVA show a significant difference in mean time spent in moving from "Action required" to "Released" or completed action

Table 3.3   Change in Status of Requests for Assistance, Louisiana Office of Homeland Security and Emergency Preparedness

	No. of requests, required to pending	Total no. of hours in status	Mean no. of hours in status	Median no. of hours in status	Standard deviation	Range	Minimum	Maximum
Search and Rescue	26	1,254.0	48.2	12.0	122.8	627.0	0.0	627.0
Damage Assessment	1	107.0	107.0	107.0	N/A	N/A	N/A	N/A
Supplies	30	5,208.0	173.6	192.0	48.6	179.0	67.0	246.0
Transportation	6	112.0	22.4	15.5	15.1	38.0	6.0	44.0
Evacuation	1	4.0	4.0	4.0	N/A	N/A	N/A	N/A
Shelter	9	290.0	32.2	27.0	32.9	105.0	2.0	107.0
Security	30	981.0	32.7	37.0	14.1	72.0	0.0	72.0
Emergency Response	3	101.0	33.7	32.0	20.6	41.0	14.0	55.0
Medical	2	52.0	26.0	26.0	5.7	8.0	22.0	30.0
Utility	20	1,740.0	87.0	93.0	33.2	124.0	20.0	144.0
Heavy Equipment	6	128.0	21.3	17.0	14.6	35.0	4.0	39.0
Light Equipment	4	156.0	39.0	42.5	29.5	67.0	2.0	69.0
Personnel	5	256.0	51.2	39.0	53.1	130.0	14.0	144.0
Communication and Coordination	N/A	N/A	N/A	N/A	N/A	N/A	N/A	N/A
Raw totals	143							

	No. of requests, required to (pending) to canceled	Total no. of hours in status	Mean no. of hours in status	Median no. of hours in status	Standard deviation	Range	Minimum	Maximum
Search and Rescue	7	79.0	11.3	4.0	16.9	41.0	0.00	41.0
Damage Assessment	1	50.0	50.0	50.0	N/A	N/A	N/A	N/A
Supplies	12	568.0	47.3	39.5	29.3	111.0	3.0	114.0
Transportation	8	344.0	43.0	21.0	51.4	136.0	4.0	140.0
Evacuation	1	108.0	108.0	108.0	N/A	N/A	N/A	N/A
Shelter	10	468.5	46.9	40.8	40.3	138.0	6.0	144.0
Security	19	494.0	26.0	26.0	25.5	94.0	0.0	94.0
Emergency Response	2	89.0	45.0	44.5	60.1	85.0	2.0	87.0
Medical	12	721.5	60.1	8.5	82.2	188.5	4.0	192.5
Utility	15	1,004.0	66.9	46.0	51.8	148.0	2.0	150.0
Heavy Equipment	28	2,141.5	76.5	61.0	57.5	188.0	2.0	190.0
Light Equipment	2	130.0	65.0	65.0	83.4	118.0	6.0	124.0
Personnel	11	365.5	33.2	29.0	19.7	71.0	6.0	77.0
Communication and Coordination	2	41.0	20.5	20.5	16.3	23.0	9.0	32.0
Raw totals	130							

(table continues)

Table 3.3 *(Continued)*

	No. of requests, required to completed (en route + on scene + released)	Total no. of hours in status	Mean no. of hours in status	Median no. of hours in status	Standard deviation
Search and Rescue	2	2.0	1.0	N/A	N/A
Damage Assessment	N/A	N/A	N/A	N/A	N/A
Supplies	6	112.0	37.3	25.0	39.0
Transportation	3	8.0	2.7	2.0	3.05
Evacuation	N/A	N/A	N/A	N/A	N/A
Shelter	11	370.0	33.6	19.0	38.8
Security	35	762.0	21.8	19.0	24.6
Emergency Response	2	56.0	28.0	28.0	12.7
Medical	1	37.0	N/A	N/A	N/A
Utility	28	1,810.0	64.6	39.0	47.5
Heavy Equipment	6	193.0	32.2	24.5	34.5
Light Equipment	1	2.0	2.0	2.0	N/A
Personnel	N/A	N/A	N/A	N/A	N/A
Communication and Coordination	1	14.0	14.4	14.0	N/A
Raw totals	96				

Source: Situation reports, Louisiana Office of Homeland Security and Emergency Preparedness, Baton Rouge, LA. August 27–September 6, 2005.

among categories of transactions (p = 0.000). A post-hoc test (the Games-Howell, because of its heterogeneity) indicates that the mean time for response to requests classified as "Utilities" differs significantly from that for the categories of "Security," "Transportation," and "Emergency Response." Response to requests for assistance regarding "Utilities" was especially slow in comparison to other categories. These findings indicate the points of decision making in the response process where additional staffing and personnel would have increased the resilience of the response system. The means plot shows the ANOVA results graphically in the appendix at the end of this chapter.

Self-Organization and Mobilization

The fourth proposition in the model for a resilient community refers to its capacity to engage in self-organizing action and to mobilize collective action in the response system to reduce risk. Importantly, the data document the rate of change for the whole system, as well as identify the status categories and types of transactions for which the delay in response was the greatest. The high ratio of requests that remained "pending" and "canceled" in the categories of "Search & Rescue" and "Evacuation" documents the difficulty in mobilizing support for these critical functions in disaster operations.

The role of LOHSEP, under the Louisiana Emergency Plan, was to provide backup support to the local municipalities and parishes. The low rate of completion for these tasks indicates a serious lack of coordination among the federal, state, parish, and municipal agencies engaged in disaster operations. In contrast, although the length of time spent in meeting requests for assistance regarding utilities was substantially greater than in the other types of transactions, the ratio of task completion (16.7 percent) for this category was relatively high.

The findings presented in table 3.4 corroborate the substantial delay reported in table 3.3 (above) in moving requests for assistance from one phase of the response process to the next in the overall disaster operations system for the state of Louisiana. Table 3.4 also documents significant differences in demand among the fourteen categories of response transactions. The data presented in both tables 3.3 and 3.4 indicate apparent bottlenecks in moving information and action through the network of the organizations that participated in disaster operations at the state level. The overall performance of the response system reveals substantial delays in managing operations at the state level among state agencies, between state agencies and parishes, and between state and federal agencies. These findings suggest points at which well-designed changes in the process of managing requests for assistance could improve the resiliency of the intergovernmental response system.

Vulnerability to Systemic Failure

If the four decision phases identified in a disaster management system—(1) detection of risk, (2) recognition and interpretation of risk as a basis for action, (3) communication of risk to wider arenas of response and resources, and (4) self-organization and mobilization of action to reduce risk—are not carried out effectively, the system is vulnerable to failure. Data from the LOHSEP situation reports indicate serious weaknesses at each decision phase, revealing vulnerability to failure in catastrophic events not only for the communities exposed to risk but for the entire nation. The analyses document that there was no systematic, reliable information system that could provide decision support to LOHSEP. Without that infrastructure, the communications processes—and therefore the potential for managing collective action in response to this event—largely failed.

Redesigning a More Resilient Disaster Management Network

The analysis of the Louisiana situation reports documents the overloaded response system at the state level for Hurricane Katrina, but the larger question is how these findings can be used to inform the redesign of a dynamic intergovernmental system that can adapt quickly to reduce risk from extreme events. The results from the preceding analyses lead to further research questions: (1) Where are the bottlenecks in the network? (2) Why is there delay in the transmission of critical information among the participating agencies? (3) Why is there a difference in rate of response among the types of transactions?

Examining the record of time spent in each phase of the response process, two types of bottlenecks appear to occur in the system. The first is defined as a jamming point in the process of mobilizing response operations, and the second is a jamming of the interaction of one organization with another in the system. One possible explanation for the delay in response activities may be the existence of bottleneck organizations in the system. If participating organizations cannot scan, validate, and process the appropriate information and resources in an efficient and effective way, they create a domino effect of escalating delay in task completion for all other organizations that are dependent upon that first step.

What Is a Bottleneck Organization?

A bottleneck is a critical point that can cause delay in the interdependent process of emergency response, hindering the operations of the whole system. In seeking to improve the resiliency of the response system, it is essential to identify points in the evolving process where delay by one organization may trigger a cascade of delay throughout the set of organizations participating in response operations. The source of the delay could be either technical or organizational, and it is often both. But if these "bottlenecks" can be identified in an actual response system, the response process can be redesigned to operate more efficiently in future disaster operations.

The situation reports from LOHSEP provide four data points that can be used to track a request for assistance through the response process: (1) initiating organization, (2) transaction, (3) assigned organization, and (4) status

Table 3.4 Types of Ratio for Changes in Status, Requests for Assistance in Disaster Operations, Louisiana Office of Homeland Security and Emergency Preparedness

	Search and Rescue	Damage Assessment	Supplies	Transportation	Evacuation	Shelter	Security
No response ratio							
Number of "no response"	27	3	166	40	8	45	104
Number of total requests	182	8	665	186	14	237	505
Ratio of "no response" to requests	14.84	37.50	24.96	21.51	57.14	18.99	20.59
Holding ratio							
Number of "action required to pending"	26	1	30	6	1	9	30
Number of total requests— no response	155	5	499	146	6	192	401
Ratio of action required to pending	16.77	20.00	6.01	4.11	16.67	4.69	7.48
Cancellation ratio							
Number of "action required to canceled"	7	1	12	8	1	10	19
Number of total requests—no response	155	5	499	146	6	192	401
Ratio of action required to canceled	4.52	20.00	2.40	5.48	16.67	5.21	4.74
Completion ratio							
Number of "action required to en route, on scene, and released"	2	N/A	6	3	N/A	11	35
Number of total requests— no response	155	5	499	146	6	192	401
Ratio of action required to en route, on scene, and released	1.29	N/A	1.20	2.05	N/A	5.73	8.73

Note: "No response ratio" = number of "no response" / number of total requests by transaction category; holding ratio = number of "action required to pending" / (number of total requests by transaction category—number of no response); cancellation ratio = number of "action required to pending or canceled" / (number of total requests by transaction category—number of no response); completion ratio = number of "action required to en route, on scene, and released" / (number of total requests by transaction category—number of no response).

Source: Situation reports, Louisiana Office of Homeland Security and Emergency Preparedness, Baton Rouge, LA. August 27–September 6, 2005.

Emergency Response	Medical	Utility	Heavy Equip-ment	Light Equip-ment	Personnel	Communication and Coordin-ation	Total
21	63	58	130	16	28	20	729
84	178	226	459	81	134	75	3,034
25.00	35.39	25.66	28.32	19.75	20.90	26.67	24.03
3	2	20	6	4	5	N/A	143
63	115	168	329	65	106	55	2,305
4.76	1.74	11.90	1.82	6.15	4.72	N/A	6.20
2	12	15	28	2	11	2	130
63	115	168	329	65	106	55	2,305
3.17	10.43	8.93	8.51	3.08	10.38	3.64	5.64
2	1	28	6	1	N/A	1	96
63	115	168	329	65	106	55	2,305
3.17	0.87	16.67	1.82	1.54	N/A	1.82	4.16

of interaction. To identify the bottlenecks, we focused on the assigned organizations because they receive requests from the initiating organizations and are responsible for taking the next stage of action. If they accept and act on the request, they also distribute incoming information and resources to other organizations in the system.

To identify bottlenecks in the "process," we counted the total number of hours that a request for assistance spent in one phase before it was shifted to the next phase in the response process. As shown in table 3.5, the total number of hours for the entire system to shift from "action required" to "pending" is 10,389 hours, with the mean of 72.7 hours and a standard deviation of 30.0 hours. Although there are no data for the status change from "on scene" to "released," the recorded time delay was very severe in shifts from "action required to pending" and "pending to cancellation." After LOHSEP received initial and unverified requests from initiating organizations, agency staff needed to verify each incoming request and assign it to a response agency. This procedure was established to validate each request and to ensure that scarce resources were allocated appropriately. During this period of verification, the request was classified as "pending." In an event of the scope and scale of Hurricane Katrina, the workload of LOHSEP staff in processing the incoming requests for assistance quickly increased to the point that the requests were stalled in the pending phase. Quick and effective decision making was severely limited. In this time-dependent process, the time lag in the subsequent status shifts decreased dramatically. Apparently, once a request had been assigned to an action agency, and further accepted by that agency, the delivery of services was relatively efficient. This level of performance may reflect the considerably lower number of tasks that were assigned for action out of the total number of requests.

Managing disaster response operations is a very complex, interdependent process. Ironically, the very structure of the process designed to ensure efficient management of resources in disaster operations likely contributed to the substantial delays in mobilizing action and the ineffectiveness of the overall performance of the disaster response system following Hurricane Katrina. The role and location of an organization in the disaster response system can affect substantially the performance of other participating organizations in the system. Clearly, a new model for increasing effectiveness in mobilizing disaster operations is needed, one that acknowledges the capacity of the organizational system to anticipate, adapt, and reallocate its resources according to the demands from its operational context.

To identify the organizations that created bottlenecks, we counted the accumulated time period in hours for each responding organization to es-

Table 3.5 Summary, Total Time Delay in Hours Reported for Each Change of Status

	Number of Trans- actions	Total Time Elapsed (hours)	Mean	Median	Standard Deviation	Maxi- mum	Mini- mum	Range
Action required to pending	143	10,389	72.7	32.0	30.0	150.0	0.0	150.0
Pending to en route	23	938	40.8	39.0	47.0	150.0	0.0	150.0
En route to on scene	21	353	16.8	19.0	7.6	43.0	8.0	35.0
On scene to released	N/A	N/A	N/A	N/A	N/A	N/A	N/A	N/A
Action required (pending) to released	13	893	68.7	44.0	54.3	150.0	2.0	148.0
Action required to cancellation	88	5,031	57.2	39.0	51.2	192.5	0.0	192.5
Pending to cancellation	42	1,569	37.4	15.5	46.4	162.0	0.0	162.0

Source: Situation reports, Louisiana Office of Homeland Security and Emergency Preparedness, Baton Rouge, LA. August 27–September 6, 2005.

timate the length of time it took for these organizations to shift to the next stage in response operations. For example, if it took 35 hours for FEMA to shift from "action required" to "pending," and 10 hours to shift from "pending" to "on scene," and again took 12 hours to shift from "on scene" to "released," then the total accumulated number of hours in this case is 57 hours, and the mean is 19 hours. One possible criticism of this approach is that if any one organization has a lot of interactions with other organizations, then the accumulated time would increase accordingly. By dividing the accumulated number of hours over the response process by the number of interactions, we calculated the mean time of the delay between an initial report of "action required" and the shift to the next stage of action. The results are reported in table 3.6.

None of the organizations reported rapid mean response records, but compared to the others, the Louisiana National Guard, the Louisiana Office of Homeland Security and Emergency Preparedness, and the Louisiana

Table 3.6   Total Time Lag for Each Responding Organization

Name of Organization	Accumulated Total Delay, When Responding (hours)	Number of Transactions	Mean (hours)
Department of Health and Hospitals, Louisiana	730.5	5	146.1
American Red Cross: Louisiana Southeast Chapter	144.0	1	144.0
Department of Transportation and Development, Louisiana	152.0	2	76.0
Army Corps of Engineers	4,571.0	64	71.4
Louisiana Emergency Operations Center	283.0	4	70.8
Federal Emergency Management Agency, United States	1,477.0	25	59.1
Department of Agriculture and Forestry, Louisiana	955.0	18	53.1
Department of Wildlife and Fisheries, Louisiana	791.5	20	39.6
Parish of East Baton Rouge	39.0	1	39.0
Civil Air Patrol—Louisiana Wing	76.0	2	38.0
Emergency Management Assistance Compact	37.0	1	37.0
Louisiana State Police	145.4	4	36.4
Homeland Security Division of LOHSEP	64.0	2	32.0
Louisiana Office of Homeland Security and Emergency Preparedness	862.0	27	31.9
Louisiana Army National Guard	312.5	10	31.3
Louisiana National Guard	2,915.5	105	27.8
Louisiana Air National Guard	183.0	10	18.3

Source: Situation reports, Louisiana Office of Homeland Security and Emergency Preparedness, Baton Rouge, LA. August 27–September 6, 2005.

State Police were more efficient in playing their roles. These findings document the lower time lag for the organizations responsible for security at the state level in comparison to the other categories. Other organizations that received a significant number of requests, such as the U.S. Army Corps of Engineers and FEMA, were much slower to respond.

The next question concerns what causes the bottlenecks for these organizations. Are bottlenecks related to managerial problems in each organization? Or to the position of these organizations in the emergency response process? Or both? With current data, it is difficult to determine whether managerial failure really existed, but it is possible to check the structure of the disaster response network by using network analysis to determine what might affect the delay of the responding organizations. Network measures of degree centrality, betweenness centrality, density, and distance were calculated to see whether there exists any significant correlation between these measures and mean time lag.

The organizations listed in table 3.6 represent the set of organizations identified in the situation reports as the primary actors in the disaster response system that emerged following Hurricane Katrina. Each organization interacted with other organizations in the performance of the fourteen categories of response actions. These fourteen categories represent subsets of actions taken within the entire disaster response system. Table 3.6 presents a summary of the accumulated time, the total number of requests for assistance, and the mean response time for each organization.

Network analysis measures confirmed a high degree of fragmentation among the organizations participating in response operations. The set of 181 organizations that were identified as interacting in the first eleven days reported a total degree centralization of .193, low for a coherent response system. Out of 181 organizations, 54, or 29.8 percent, were isolates—organizations that were unconnected with others. Network analysis offers several further measures of this disaster response system, but these findings will be presented in a subsequent paper.

Further evidence of bottlenecks is given by a regression analysis of the hours of delay time in interactions initiated between jurisdictions. Table 3.7 presents findings that report regression coefficients for mean hours of delay for jurisdictions initiating interactions with other jurisdictions against the dependent variable, the duration of time spent in a mission phase. The first column indicates the number of cases for each pair of interacting organizations. The second column reports the regression coefficient, and the third column reports the significance level, with $p < .05$ considered statistically significant.

Interestingly, the findings document that the response operations were largely performed at the parish and state levels of jurisdiction. The largest category of interactions, 125, or 32.9 percent, initiated by parish organizations to the state, had a significant delay time, $p < .03$. The next largest category of interactions, state organizations interacting with other state organizations, 120, or 31.6 percent, also showed a delay time, but it was not significant. All categories including federal interactions, except city to fed-

Table 3.7 Regression Coefficients for Mean Hours of Delay against Duration of Time Spent in Mission Phase by Jurisdictional Relationship

Jurisdictional Relationship[a]	Number of of Cases	Coefficient[b]	Significance Score
City organization interacting with state organization	4	17.70	0.52
City organization interacting with federal organization	3	14.03	0.08
Parish organization interacting with either parish or regional organization	2	65.20	0.09
Parish organization interacting with state organization	125	12.66	0.03
Parish organization interacting with federal organization	44	44.97	0.00
State organization interacting with state organization	120	8.22	0.11
State organization interacting with either federal or regional organization	43	34.36	0.00
Federal organization interacting with state organization[c]	23	26.30	0.00
Federal organization interacting with federal organization	3	74.86	0.01
International organization interacting with state organization	1	12.70	0.00

Dependent variable: duration   N = 380 R^2 = 0.1226

a. These ten relationships are the only relations observed with an identifiable mission duration.

b. All coefficient scores reported here refer to the score on federal to state durations, since that case was used as the reference case.

c. The case of federal organizations interacting with state organizations was taken as the reference case, since it had the lowest mean duration time. Values listed here are formally presented as the constant in the regression analysis results.

eral, reported statistically significant delay times. These findings document the slow response of jurisdictional agencies generally, but the particularly slow federal response to any jurisdictional level except city. The city to federal relationship must be viewed cautiously, as there were only four such cases reported in the situation reports.

Intergovernmental Disaster Response as a Learning Process

The analysis of the situation reports of actual disaster operations conducted through LOHSEP documents the degree to which the intergovernmental system was overwhelmed in the Katrina disaster. The data show that four of the six propositions listed above as essential for a resilient intergovernmental response system were not present in the response system that evolved in Louisiana after Hurricane Katrina. Regarding Proposition 1, the situation reports documented delays in the data transmission that reduced the capacity of state managers to comprehend the full extent of losses to the communities affected by the hurricane and the flood.

In reference to Proposition 2, the extensive delays in moving requests for assistance through the different steps in the process of allocating response personnel and resources provided clear evidence of overload for the system. Regarding Proposition 3, the evidence showed that managers at different locations—parishes, other state agencies, federal agencies—did not have a common understanding of risk to the region. Concerning Proposition 4, the sitrep data reveal little capacity for participating organizations to act collectively and coherently. There is little evidence of information exchange or feedback among the organizations participating in the response system.

Propositions 5 and 6 indicate how an intergovernmental response system could be strengthened by investing in information infrastructure that would facilitate communication and feedback within and between parishes, within and between state agencies, among state agencies and parishes, and between state and federal agencies. Extending a well-designed information infrastructure across intergovernmental boundaries, including federal agencies, was presumably the intent of NIMS, but this goal was not realized in the response operations following Katrina. Without a well-functioning information infrastructure, communication and coordination fail, and the response system is compromised. As data from disaster operations in Katrina demonstrate, the system was essentially a scattered set of organizations that performed in an erratic manner under severely compromised operating conditions.

The initial lack of regionwide recognition of the threat posed by the advancing storm in the days prior to landfall on August 29, 2005, inhibited the emergence of a common consensus on strategies to minimize risk among the many jurisdictions and organizations operating in the region. The technical failure of the communications system in the days immediately after landfall left the state organizations without direct contact with the parishes and municipalities most at risk. Without that "common operating picture" clearly communicated to the relevant actors, the delays among this large set of interdependent actors increased, and the emergency response system outlined on paper cascaded into failed actions.

The challenge, of course, is to use findings from this analysis to assess more accurately the points of possible intervention that could have reversed the downward spiral of failure in the intergovernmental response system.

Clearly identified, these points could serve as the basis for redesigning an effective intergovernmental crisis management system. Returning to the propositions specified in the theoretical model, a major investment of time, effort, and talent in building an analytical knowledge base for the vulnerable Gulf Coast region is a primary first step toward increasing its capacity to manage the recurring risk of hurricanes and water-related hazards. Disaster plans that are bounded by jurisdictional constraints limit the vision needed to recognize the risk of catastrophic events that threaten wide geographic areas or span decades in their return rates.

Second, the human capacity of managers and organizations to learn new strategies, try new approaches, and rigorously evaluate failed policies offers the strongest potential for constructive change in the region. Yet this is a learning process, and it needs to be structured for timely, valid information exchange and nurtured to elicit candid feedback to achieve significant results. Information technology, carefully designed to function in extreme events and deployed with consistent standards for operation, offers a substantial technical advantage in coping with complex, interdependent, large-scale catastrophic events. But this strategy requires a consistent commitment of time and effort to maintain a current knowledge base and to train personnel to use the technology appropriately. The alternative—not to take advantage of appropriately designed information technology to facilitate management of both risk and related technologies at a regional level—is starkly clear in the sobering losses in lives and billions of dollars in damage following Hurricane Katrina.

Third, clear evidence of bottlenecks in the response process is revealed in the status data reported in the situation reports maintained by the Louisiana Office of Homeland Security and Emergency Preparedness. Based on these findings, the highest priority in redesigning an effective system for disaster mitigation and response is reducing the impact of such obstacles to managing the efficient flow of information within and among participating agencies. This task requires a sociotechnical approach, given the volume of requests in a major disaster, and the need for response organizations to build surge capacity before an extreme event occurs.

Appendix: Means Plot of ANOVA

The results of the analysis of variance (ANOVA) show a significant difference in means among the nine categories of response functions by transactions: F $(8,394)=7.181$ P-value $=0.000$ $(a=0.05)$. Because equal variances are not assumed, this analysis used the Games-Howell post-hoc test to check which category is different from other categories in mean difference. According to this post-hoc test, the category of "Utility" has a longer mean time lag compared to the other categories, and "Security" has a significantly shorter mean in response time. (The mean difference is significant at the .05 level). The transaction categories of "Damage Assessment," "Evacuation," "Communication & Coordination," "Emergency Response," "Light Equipment," and "Others" have not been included in this ANOVA because of the small number of cases in these categories.

Table 3.8   Network Measures for Disaster Management Categories

	Search and Rescue	Security	Transportation	Emergency Response	Utility	Supplies	Personnel	Equipment	Medical	Communication	Shelter	Evacuation	Aggregate Network
Row count	35	88	80	35	49	102	37	76	44	31	55	11	217
Column count	35	88	80	35	49	102	37	76	44	31	55	11	217
Edge count	58	169	151	55	78	194	49	144	70	33	83	6	625
Density	0.049	0.022	0.024	0.046	0.033	0.019	0.037	0.025	0.037	0.036	0.028	0.055	0.013
Isolate count	3	6	6	0	3	4	2	3	4	4	3	3	15
Component count	4	8	8	2	4	6	4	7	6	8	5	5	16
Characteristic path length	1.851	2.023	2.93	1.538	2.13	2.189	2.079	2.481	1.963	1.775	1.448	1	2.611
Krackhardt connectedness	0.834	0.826	0.809	0.889	0.880	0.886	0.794	0.777	0.744	0.458	0.826	0.236	0.866
Degree centralization	0.245	0.301	0.203	0.123	0.335	0.314	0.225	0.221	0.266	0.194	0.250	0.117	0.521
Betweenness centralization	0.047	0.037	0.081	0.015	0.087	0.040	0.079	0.062	0.054	0.032	0.020	0.000	0.045
Closeness centralization	0.013	0.001	0.004	0.018	0.004	0.001	0.011	0.003	0.009	0.010	0.004	0.035	0.001
Fragmentation	0.166	0.174	0.191	0.111	0.120	0.115	0.206	0.223	0.256	0.542	0.174	0.764	0.461

Source: Situation Reports, Louisiana Office of Homeland Security and Emergency Preparedness, Baton Rouge, LA. August 27–September 6, 2005.

4 LESSONS FROM THE MILITARY

SURPRISE, RESILIENCE, AND THE ATRIUM MODEL

Chris C. Demchak

> *Military strategists are sometimes accused of planning and spending for the worst case and least likely scenarios. Given the difficulty of accurate forecasting and the gravity of failure in war, it would be negligent to do otherwise.*
>
> Captain George Kastens, *Building a Beehive: Observations on the Transition to Network Centric Operations*

Nations run as effectively as their underlying critical systems. Deleterious surprises can trigger breakdowns as unexpectedly linked events cascade into catastrophes. The continuous operation of these critical infrastructures in the face of surprise and disruption depends on collective knowledge systems and the willingness to act in concert.

Critical infrastructures are best defined in terms of complex sociotechnical systems. Their complexity imposes an inherent "knowledge burden" on the operators of critical infrastructures. It is hard to provide knowledge in the form and frequency operators need to employ a single complex system or an array of such systems.

This chapter investigates lessons in how to collectively and organizationally assure the resilience of critical infrastructures. It does so by closely investigating the experiences of a particularly prominent, large, and complex modern institution designed to take on catastrophic surprises and yet be resilient—the military. Centuries of military history provide a plethora of trial-and-error lessons. Military failures underscore the difficulties in developing a capacity for collective action in the face of surprise. Often enough, otherwise routinely functional organizational designs miss critical but obtainable knowledge in spectacularly consequential ways.

Military history is a history of repeated experiences, providing a large set of natural experiments in how an organization may or may not successfully demonstrate the capacity for collective action in the face of unexpected extreme events. More focused than any civilian government on successfully neutralizing surprise from a deliberate or nature-based enemy, modern militaries emphasize knowledge acquisition and an internally socialized, resilient form of collective action. And yet these organizations have still been surprised in foreseeable circumstances. Their actions intended to solve problems in advance and to improvise under urgent conditions have often enough resulted in local and widening crises with unexpected rippling effects.

The discussion will include a brief review of such knowledge-based failures, which will result in an institutional design proposal for a seamless sociotechnical system of knowledge. Called the "Extreme Event (EE) Atrium," the model draws on the axioms of several literatures, including the large-scale technical systems field, the emerging collaboration studies field, organization theory, information systems and applications, and complexity. Designed to facilitate resilience in a networked age, this organizational structure directly sustains the necessary mechanisms within and across organizations that have to work together when their members are surprised, scared, and endangered.

The Military Experience

Knowledge is critical to effectively respond to surprise. It is, however, not easy or necessarily inexpensive to obtain knowledge in complex systems. Public and quasi-public organizations vary greatly in their sense of urgency about the collective need to understand the surprises possible in these systems and then to act on that knowledge in concert. It is generally exceptionally difficult to get relatively sovereign agencies to reciprocally reach out beyond their borders to share knowledge.

Militaries offer a rich history of organizations and leaders both fearing surprise and taking steps in advance to nullify its effects. In recent decades, modern armies and navies have altered their organizational structure, socialization, knowledge focus, information content, training, technology, and employment practices to prepare for—and respond to—rippling surprises while operating. The military's term equivalent to resilience is continuity of operations. Its lessons have been largely ignored outside of military history communities.

Crisis Management in the Modern Military Operation

Dealing with catastrophic surprise across different organizations and critical infrastructure protection is inherent in the modern military operation. Leaders of large-scale militaries have always struggled with coordinating vast numbers of differentially talented and trained people with a variety of mostly operational equipment. For modern military leaders and force planners, protecting critical systems in operations is intrinsic to their job.

Critical systems cannot be rapidly or easily replaced if suddenly disrupted. A sudden disruption can cause immediate or escalating, unavoidable, and nontrivial harm; it can ripple through connected systems with escalating, deleterious effects.

The classic military critical path element is ammunition in battle, or water in the desert, or fuel in a major advance. Logistical breakdowns have determined a significant portion of military outcomes, and this history is rich with leaders who did not see disruption coming. As military knowledge accumulation and analysis resources have deepened and matured, more and more efforts are made to recognize the starting signs of a disruption. Ultimately, successful armies intuitively engage in the precautionary steps analyzed in Sunstein's (2006) "Irreversible Harm Precautionary Principle" and "Catastrophic Harm Precautionary Principle."

The very properties that define critical systems also describe the characteristics of breakdown. Routine critical path functions are disrupted. There is no immediate restoration of functionality. Dysfunctional deviations emerge across connected systems. It is not possible to immediately dampen the rippling deviations across the wider network of connected nodes. The rippling effects are often the most devastating for a large-scale system that survives the first major event or bounces back from a surprise attack, much like aftershocks from an earthquake. With that in mind, modern militaries actively seek to design their organizations to face surprise through extreme emphasis on gaining knowledge in advance and then acting quickly at the first signs of surprise.[1]

To this effect, military organizations strive to use structure to create resilience via interchangeable expertise across their organizations, rather than relying on individual experts. This process entails widespread (sometimes universal) in-house training (lifetime socialization and retraining), research (extended external consulting), planning (highly detailed projections), and anticipation (built-in slack and redundancy). Militaries also use knowledge enhancements such as sensors, spies, and field-level intelligence units with a very clear focus on importing data from the environment. These are so associated with military operations that modern corporations seeking information on competitors routinely refer to these efforts in terms of "business intelligence." The structures, doctrine, and processes of a modernized military can be taken to express a set of organizational hypotheses about what it takes to embrace surprise. These "fixes" may be compared against historical results.

Military Failures, Successes, and Lessons for Resilience

Cascading Collective Ignorance Dooms Improvisation

Everyone is familiar with Napoleon's lack of supplies, which crippled and ultimately destroyed his attack on Russia in 1813. Few realize what an aberration this outcome was. The French logistique system was exceptionally advanced for its time and supported extraordinary speed and many successful campaigns. The Russian fiasco emerged more like today's modern rolling failure of highly integrated systems. An accumulation of small events profoundly exacerbated by leading generals produced irremediable circumstances by the time of the march across the steppes (Seymour 1988). None of these small events alone would have produced the catastrophe; together they were devastating.

The logistical failures in more recent and mechanized militaries evidence the same sort of cascading collective ignorance of ground truths at middle and higher levels of the organization, despite all efforts to avoid these kinds of outcomes. Rommel's dash to control North Africa in 1942 skidded to a halt as a result of fuel shortages, insufficient port capacity (unchecked in advance), and his subordinates' dedication (despite the time lost due to fatigue and back-and-forth travel) to personally assuring lines of communication. The long distances that supply staff and fuel trucks shuttled over alone consumed nearly 25 percent of an already too small fuel supply. So devastating was this disregard for a basic and well-known shortfall that not even heroic efforts by the Italians (for their own reasons) could reverse the situation (van Creveld 1977).

The timing of the Allies' attack on the heartland of Nazi Germany was cumulatively stalled by a nasty technical surprise stemming from even less predictable systemic ignorance. Poorly trained factory workers and inaccurate equipment back in the United Kingdom "made do" with what they had in rushing the manufacture of fourteen hundred British lorries, essential to the Allies' movement of fuel and irreplaceable for imminent operations. When they arrived at the North African port just prior to the major operation, they were found to be so defective that they could not be repaired in time. All available alternatives were already in use, and even individual units that still had some fuel could not be reallocated. As a result, a lightning thrust to end the war in 1944 was halted on the ground and then canceled. Instead, critical Allied forces crawled forward, allowing German forces time to regroup and defend locations that otherwise would have been abandoned (van Creveld 1977).

Even in an institution focused on being prepared for surprise, leaders may contribute to a lack of resilience by being unaware of their own ignorance of "ground truths." Particularly inexcusable is the senior leader uninformed about the basic real-time conditions of locations in which forces are about to engage in potentially hostile operations. For example, the American rescue of the U.S. Merchant Marine crew kidnapped by Cambodian guerrillas in 1975 cascaded into error after error. The failure began with a simple lack of island maps of the area, despite twenty years of operating there (Gabriel 1985). Similarly, the disastrous U.S. effort to rescue the U.S. embassy hostages in Iran in 1979 suffered from absent knowledge about the region and from planners imposing a joint approach without having laid the foundations of knowledge, redundancy/slack, skills, and trust that would have been necessary for success. Most of the military pilots engaged in the rescue mission were not prepared to fly their helicopters in sandstorms, even though the staging ground for the raid was in a region known for horrific sandstorms. No reasonable buffers were available in case of surprise. The loss of several critical helicopters left competing service leaders jockeying for control. The operation quickly spiraled into an internally embarrassing catastrophic failure (Gabriel 1985).

Resilience Lessons in Near-Failure Successes

Even overall successes contain lessons about acquiring knowledge and sensibly accommodating possible surprise. In 1982, just after announcing in a white paper that no war was expected for the next ten years, the British government found itself shipping marines thousands of miles away to retake an island group in the South Atlantic, the Falklands. The operation, though overall successful, was a near catastrophe. Almost no internal governmental knowledge existed that could be provided to political leaders about operational needs in the South Atlantic. Most Falkland losses are today attributed to the military's lack of maps of the terrain on which the marines would need to fight and even lack of knowledge of the likely military capabilities of the armed forces of Argentina—one of the two largest continental powers of South America (Keegan 2003).[2]

Escaping defeat by the inadvertent mitigation of a nasty surprise is a consistent theme in the history of military resilience. Only a few years after the

Falklands war, the U.S. invasion of Grenada was launched without recognition of pending failures in critical infrastructure, resulting in otherwise avoidable deaths. A shortage of functioning airlift systems led to a cascade of workaround decisions to parachute in soldiers who were sent in planes rigged to land, not to drop troops. Fixing this problem in-flight so delayed the soldiers' arrival that it was fully daylight when the assault began. The lightly armed parachute troops were then belatedly and slowly airdropped, in full sunshine, in front of Cuban-prepared firing positions. When the first wave of soldiers received the inevitable heavy fire, panicking officers at headquarters diverted the rest of the limited planes away from the original troops to pick up heavier backup forces. Two-thirds of the original Ranger force stayed behind in the United States for lack of transport, leaving the first assault forces to scramble as best they could (Gabriel 1985).

Causes of Failure

Modern militaries over time, because of such experiences, have built into their leadership goals and supporting structures many characteristics of effective crisis management (cf. Boin et al. 2005). They have the capacity to "make sense" of complex, evolving threats. The modern and usually westernized officer corps is vigorously prepared to use worst-case scenarios, follow-up plans, and analysis after analysis of enemy options. Critical decision making is the sine qua non for effective modern military leadership. Military leaders excel at "shaping the overall direction and coherence of the collective efforts to respond to the crisis" (Boin et al. 2005, 140). Learning from adversity is firmly embedded in mechanisms such as after-action briefings, doctrinal schools, manuals, required professional education, and constant practice of skills deemed critical to future survival in combat operations. A strong domain consensus and acceptance of the varying roles and responsibilities in or out of crises are well institutionalized in most military organizations.

How, then, do failures happen in organizations self-consciously preparing for surprise? A review of the twenty most significant battles or wars lost provides a set of "lessons in resilience" (Seymour 1988), focusing on whether and which of the three process metrics of Cohen and Gooch (1990)—absorbing, forecasting, or adaptation—occurred when surprise emerged.[3]

Absorbing is the process of internalizing the knowledge essential for resilience that is already available to the organization across disparate units. Forecasting is the process of accurate and timely anticipation and accommodation of the uncertainties of operations and possible surprise. Adapting is the process of recalibrating one's expectations on the spot, with the surprise at hand, and then acting exactly and speedily to mitigate, improvise, or innovate out of a failure.

Of the eighteen significant failures in military resilience, eleven of them occurred after the advent of the telegraph, which enabled unprecedented communications among dispersed units. Acting in concert should therefore in principle have been eased considerably, compared to prior eras. Of these eleven failures, five were due to knowledge shortcomings in forecasting what would be needed and five to neglect in absorbing previously held knowledge across the losing organization. Failure to adapt was responsible for only one of the eleven (see the appendix at the end of the chapter).

This very limited analysis suggests that militaries are possibly very good at adapting, through improvisation and innovation, if they survive long enough to reach the point at which adaptation is necessary. More often, however, the lack of resilience has its origins in the knowledge shortcomings already in place before the surprise surfaces. Again, and important for the later discussion of tacit knowledge collection, ten of the eleven modern and significant military failures are equally attributable to design and management issues of knowledge forecasting and absorption.

Collective problem solving appears to occur for two main reasons. The first might be thought of as an organization doing its homework: using shared knowledge systems to identify and analyze preventable and nonpreventable failures. Without this information, an organization cannot fully use its skills to compensate for surprises. The second centers on an organization's relative willingness and flexibility to act adaptively in concert on the basis of that information. Civilian organizations and, even more so, wider emergency response communities tend to experience problems in knowledge acquisition, collaboration, and trust. For militaries, lack of action is less often the issue than is lack of knowledge at hand, collectively created and integrated before an operation begins. Militaries share this shortcoming with their civilian counterparts. They offer many lessons in socializing groups to act in concert, but they also offer equally many cautionary tales about seeking and implementing in advance knowledge essential for resilience.

Based on these insights, we can further structure the problem and propose a model (the "Atrium") that deals directly with the shortcomings in tacit knowledge acquisition and employment suggested by military history, particularly such failures of forecasting and absorption. This model provides a way to accommodate the particular collaborative resilience difficulties of jointly operating organizations facing enormous uncertainties and inevitable surprise. First, we establish a foundation for understanding how complex systems can confound efforts at resilience.

Knowledge Burdens and Devilish Surprises

We begin by characterizing the general resilience problem as a lack of a good system fit between the collective "knowledge burden" and the organizations involved (Demchak 1991). Crisis managers know by hard experience that complexity can produce surprise in extensive, networked systems (Casti 1994). Knowledge and crises are directly related through the surprise felt by systems' operators. A complex system is one that exhibits high levels of numbers of components or nodes, differentiation between them, and interdependence among them, and thus a large need for knowledge (LaPorte 1975). The more complex the system, and the more precision in the transactions necessary for its operations, the larger the knowledge requirements are both initially and over time for successful operation and resilience when surprised.[4]

These knowledge requirements comprise what I call the knowledge burden. Here knowledge is more than information carried by an individual or contained in human learning. Its variations are embedded in the design, operation, parts, and demands of the sociotechnical system at risk. Surprise, then, emerges as one's models of reality—one's knowledge inventory and use and search structures—diverge from one's experience of reality itself (Casti 1994, 268). We speak of a crisis emerging when this surprise contains a threat to the functioning of one or more critical systems. Many surprises are partially knowable in advance in form or frequency, and some crises are open to limitation by preparatory accommodations.

Knowability and Crisis Potential

For any set of interrelated systems, there is a universe of unknown deleterious outcomes. Their knowability in advance ranges from knowable (form or frequency can be determined with sufficient research) to completely unknowable (there are no indications). Their crisis potential ranges in extent from accommodated (deterrence, dampening, mitigation, or reconstitution in place) to unaccommodated (no preparations in place). This parsing of outcomes may be sorted into quadrants labeled for an organization's knowledge search processes that accommodate knowable and unknowable unknowns. These quadrants represent "tolerable" outcomes that are both knowable and accommodated; "fortunate" outcomes that are unknowable but accommodated; "neglected" outcomes that are knowable but not accommodated; and "rogue" outcomes that are neither knowable or accommodated. The following discussion explains the distinctions that create the crisis potential.

First, outcomes range across knowable and unknowable according to the dynamics of the level of complexity. At a base level, outcome warnings may be discerned in their form or frequency, preferably both. Irrespective of how much research is performed, some subset of outcomes will remain mysteries because a system cannot evaluate itself (Hofstadter 1980, 1999). Every system has some "unknowable unknowns," but complexity encourages these unknowns (Perrow 1984).[5] The greater the number of essential relations among a large number of components, the greater the likelihood of improbable events—"deviant amplitudes"—rippling through the system and producing an unpredictable outcome (or "dynamic instabilities") (Sproull and Kiesler 1991; Casti 1994).

Second, unknowns also range in accommodation according to human decisions about risk, the costs in time and resources to research missing knowledge, and the cost-versus-benefits of applying methods of accommodation to forestall, diminish, dampen, mitigate, and compensate for knowable unknowns and nasty outcomes. Sometimes an effort to accommodate a knowable outcome inadvertently and serendipitously also accommodates an unknowable outcome.

The outcomes are clustered according to the complexity designed into the system (knowable and unknowable) and the responses of the system to the risks (accommodated and unaccommodated). Deleterious outcomes that are foreseeable and accommodated are tolerable and fortunate if prepared against without foreknowledge. Outcomes that could be known in either form or frequency but are not accommodated are neglected. The worst cases are the unaccommodated outcomes that were unknowable from the outset. These outcomes, called rogues, capture the sense of surprise humans feel when significantly negative events seem to emerge out of nowhere to disrupt operations.[6]

All societies have a notion of rogue outcomes, some kinds of "acts of God," but complex systems increase their chances of occurring and raise the costs of accommodating the knowledge burden commensurately. It is harder to move bad surprises into less disruptive quadrants by having the correct knowledge precisely when and where needed in order to immediately compensate for either neglected or rogue outcomes at precisely the moment undesirable events occur (i.e., the "point of surprise"). For the study of resilience in complex critical infrastructures, therefore, the goal is to have conditions in place so that unforeseen outcomes can nonetheless be accommodated accurately and immediately through collective problem solving with improvisation and innovation. What would have been a rogue outcome then moves into the fortunate category. If only form or frequency is knowable, but the outcome has nonetheless been researched and accommodated by preparations against a related, likely set of outcomes, then the neglected outcome also may move toward a more tolerable quadrant.

Accommodating Knowledge Burdens

The worst of all possible worlds for managers is being constrained by operational, resource, and theoretical limits, rendered unable to flexibly guide subordinates, while facing a suddenly turbulent environment where it is exceptionally difficult to acquire the knowledge needed to maintain complex sociotechnical systems at effective levels. The necessary sensitivity analysis across masses of data is always difficult, but it becomes even more troubling if catalyst events—say, a lack of port-capacity knowledge, of maps of islands, or of skills for flying in sandstorms—are clearly knowable in advance.

When the critical knowledge-burden requirements are not met (in redundancy or slack), the missing knowledge and the difficulty of acquiring it undermine the resilience of the whole sociotechnical system (LaPorte 1975; Galbraith 1977). For example, before both the attack on Pearl Harbor on December 7, 1941, and the attack in New York on September 11, 2001, indicators of these attacks were in the "intelligence pipeline." In both cases, the data were not recognized as critical or absorbed quickly enough to provide warning and possible preparations (Wirtz 2006).

Cascades in negative event paths emerge more easily in systems with large knowledge burdens and tighter coupling. The "amplifying deviations" that avalanche surprisingly into crisis begin when research is shortchanged or accommodation neglected. Somebody locally ignored, did not report, or misunderstood a warning; some critical complex equipment exceeded its own precision tolerances, and the knowledge needed to compensate was not at hand (Sproull and Kiesler 1991, 2). Such breakdowns can occur suddenly, as in an earthquake or a terrorist bomb; they can also happen emergently, as in the slowly rising but uninterruptible levels of a devastating flood or the unstoppable advance of an overwhelming force.

Overwhelmed, many organizations retreat to focus on locally predictable outcomes. Managers often ratchet up their control of local deviations in operations in compensation, tightening the coupling of the organization over time (Weick 1979). If this greater control tendency is not accommodated, the resulting tighter coupling creates a positive feedback loop. More and more baffled managers react locally to produce conditions that ripple outward, spreading the surprise throughout the system. While local adaptations can indeed bring local benefits, their presence alone adds to the structural intricacy of a system and increases the knowledge needed in order for the system to function according to some desired pattern and to demonstrate resilience.

A resilient system is accommodated against knowable unknowns and is more likely to serendipitously accommodate unknowable unknowns. What is physically required in accommodation often depends on whether missing knowledge is largely in the specific form or on the actual frequency of a disruptive occurrence. Often the difference between sudden versus emergent breakdowns may not matter broadly if the effects, spread avenues, dampening options, mitigation requirements, or reconstitution costs are the same. What does matter universally is how the tradeoff between time and resources is spent on sensors to detect indications in advance (find knowable outcomes) and to integrate the systems' experiences internally over time (accommodate outcomes). For example, if the undesirable outcome is destruction of traveling food-supply trains—if the uncertainty is merely whether hobos or rats get into the railcars at rail yards—then obstacles or deterrents that work at least once against each uncertainty and can be replaced easily are necessary. If, however, the outcome feared is solely rats, and rats could arrive unexpectedly throughout the year, then the obstacles or deterrents will have to be tailored for the possible range of rat attacks and reinforced for multiple, unforeseeable events.

If the form is known, then redundancy in the inventory of knowledge relevant to outcomes is preferred. If only the frequency of disruptions is known, then slack—which entails loosening the coupling among elements and may include redundancy—is preferred as an initial accommodation mechanism (Gleick 1987). It is, of course, most difficult to accommodate undesirable outcomes when both form and frequency are unknown.

Militaries have routinely tried to prepare for both, and the nitty-gritty details of their failure experiences suggest redundancy has been historically more powerful in allowing improvisation and innovation in the face of systemic surprise. But there is a limit to how much can be kept around just in case or even created quickly and collectively in response to shock. Slack operates as a dampener in operations, often facilitated by trust and flexible rapid reallocation of resources to buffer the system, and is essential as a bulwark for when rogue outcomes dominate and redundancy fails.

Slack in a sociotechnical system is exquisitely tied to human organizational decisions. The more complex and resilient a system is, the more likely it is that its designers and managers have appreciated the knowledge burden. They have probably used trial and error to embed appropriate levels of redundancy and slack to accommodate unknowns in the critical infrastructure. The downside (cost) of knowing more is much lower than the disruptive costs of knowing less.

Designing for Resilience

Two presumptions are directly relevant to resilience in organizations and societies. First, we do not routinely know what we know collectively. Second, if we did, such knowledge would help accommodate the surprises and the knowledge burdens of complex systems. The lessons of military history, complexity theory, large-scale technical systems, and the emerging field of computational organization science support both of these assertions well. Modern forms of organizational collaboration are, at their core, tools for resilience in a world of "fundamental socio-technical problems that are so complex and dynamic that they cannot be fully addressed by traditional techniques" (K. M. Carley 2003, 253; 2002). The emerging, generally virtual collaborative means of productive sharing provide the arenas in which to gather and refine the ground truths—the tacit knowledge and creative skills—currently fixed in the heads and unrecorded conversations of an organization's experienced, creative, and/or observant members.

Tacit knowledge matters because in the natural and orchestrated trials and errors of a system's life, it provides surprise's warning lights (Rochlin 2000; Roe 1998). Suddenness does not mean that an event is impossible to anticipate; suddenness is subjectively felt by humans, not objectively present in all cases that we would accept as surprising. Often the design of a system discourages a broad scanning of events for new knowledge; the path-dependent culture of an organization reinforces inaccurate valuation of unusual sources of information. For example, technical rationality influences many organizations, but often, "a rational-scientific way of sense making...does not allow for 'unscientific' reasoning....Early signals of impending crises may be simply put aside [pending]...hard proof rather than gut feeling" (Boin et al. 2005, 21–22).

The design of a system meant to embrace and survive surprise needs to recognize the value of making resilience part of its routine. The useful capture of tacit knowledge occurs in streams, not occasional collections, and then in persistent application and validation in system actions. Equally critical within as well as outside of organizations, processes blending the social and technical need to coevolve over time (Haytthornwaite 2005).

Unfortunately and quite frequently, the knowledge needed to prepare for surprise is undervalued for efficiency purposes or because of simple managerial ignorance. Such knowledge is expected to emerge from only occasional exercises of short duration across mass groups of people. It is commonly and mistakenly assumed that collaborative learning processes need only a minor social stimulus and the proper technical tools to persist and succeed. The field research, however, says otherwise (Kreijns, Kirschner, and Jochems 2003).

To succeed, collective problem solving must be made easy, useful, and routine (Mühlenbrock and Hoppe 1999). In large organizations, routine procedures matter greatly in their influence on crisis decisions. Practicing collaboration as a procedure embedded in shared daily practices provides legitimacy, the sound development of group cohesion, opportunities to tailor the tools to local needs for knowledge, and a widened base of known actors whose trust attributes are experientially tested. Interestingly enough, in a study of cross-cultural collaboration for problem solving, the participants who communicated the most frequently were seen by both cultures as being more effective at knowledge transfer (Sarker 2005). Repeated interactions are necessary to build the foundations for resilience, blending the social with the technical for collaborative knowledge development (Kreijns, Kirschner, and Jochems 2003).

Embedded collaboration is not easy, even if great similarity in socialization, motivation, context, and mission exists, as in the modern militaries of Westernized nations. The tacit knowledge and trust benefits of joint operations, often called "combined arms," have proven time and again extremely difficult to maintain between deployments, even when promotions are tied to demonstrating time spent in joint operations, as in the U.S. military (D. E. Johnson 2002). The continuing difficulty of militaries in collaboration, despite their historical interest in collective action, strongly underscores the need to socially construct a positive view of collaboration.

Participants must be helped to see the value in providing missing and needed knowledge in any collaboration. For effective collective problem solving and action, collaborators must recognize the holistic aspects of this process in terms of social acceptance, endorsement, and return for effort (Dirckinck-Holmfeld and Sorenson 1999). Without this nurtured openness to mutually agreed-upon change, collective improvisation may be delayed for time-consuming negotiations that then doom effective responses to surprise. Innovation—the more permanent response to surprise—usually requires even more goodwill among actors and hence is even more hampered when collective knowledge development is not valued.

Toward a Resilient Organization

The Atrium model of "computer as colleague" deliberately seeks to make routine, easy, and useful the processes and means for tacit and collaborative knowledge development across otherwise disparate communities. It was originally designed for use by modernizing militaries engaging in network warfare and apparently unwittingly walking into an enormously enlarged knowledge burden for which they were unprepared. The Atrium model is a sociotechnical organizational design adapted specifically to accommodate the emerging complexity of rapid reaction organizations. The model could conceivably apply to any large-scale system expecting to face surprise and confront situations in which subordinate units must respond.

The basic Atrium organization incorporates the computer as a colleague, not as a library or controller.[7] Rather, the knowledge base of the organization is actively nurtured both in humans and in the digitized institutional structure. Writing for the commercial world, the system's original designers, Nonaka and Takeuchi, attempted to reconcile the competing demands and benefits of both matrix and hierarchical organizational forms. Their "hypertext" organization intermingled three structures: a matrix structure in smaller task forces, specifically focused on innovative problems at hand and on answering to senior managers; a second hierarchical structure, the core, that supports the general operational systems but also contributes and then reabsorbs the members of task forces; and finally a large underlying knowledge base, called the Atrium here, that is intricately interwoven throughout the activities of both matrix and hierarchical elements.

Ten years later and integrated with the emerging Web 2.0 and its three-dimensional next evolution called Web 3.0, the Atrium model knowledge base is interactive, visually accessible, and ubiquitous. It is a constantly emergent structure in and of itself, integrating applications. Data is being shaped, employed, and extended by its participating organizations and their needs. Task forces use it for data mining, while also sustaining general operations, sharing information broadly. Public administrators do not have the time or resources to look for published information, let alone to gather the kind of tacit experience-based information available through personal observation. The Atrium model explicitly seeks to provide participants with a familiar place in which to learn such lessons and also, more important, to share their own experiences, intermixed with those of others, thus shaping and testing collective knowledge for ground truths and possible future scenarios.

The Atrium is a model for the emerging virtuality, a blend of realistic but remote graphical and rapid knowledge exchanges and physical reality, in which each affects events in the other.[8] It creates the psychologically safe communication and knowledge development environment (C. B. Gibson and Gibbs 2006). Entering into and interacting with the Atrium is essentially interacting with another major player in the institution, coconstructing a virtual productive work space with others. The term Atrium captures the sense that this is a place to which people can go, virtually or otherwise, to contribute and acquire essential knowledge and also a place of refuge in which participants can work out solutions. Both kinds of cognitive environments are essential for effective, online, and cross-organizational collaboration, nurturing the intricacies of sense-making needed for individuals and organizations to sniff out impending surprises (Gasson 2005).

Routinely interacting in the Atrium rationalizes organizational costs that might otherwise be used to argue against collaborative tacit knowledge-development activities. Efforts to ensure implicit knowledge are integrated into long-term analyses of the system, such as the time task-force members spend in downloading experiences and information before they return to more hierarchical circumstances. The procedures embedded in the Atrium model are designed to overcome the inherent cognitive conflicts of most modern remote collaborative tools. In particular, the Atrium's design and procedural requirements directly address the lack of shared contextual knowledge and coordination costs from different member groups' localized priorities, the need for stabilizing structures allowing members to share knowledge and work together, the absence of venues allowing early compromise over conflicts in deep institutions and cultural preferences, and the disabling distrust and automatic out-group evaluation discounts so common among near strangers (C. B. Gibson and Gibbs 2006).

The Atrium model described here is intended for rapid-reaction organizations, providing them with a blueprint for an organic, immersive, and useful knowledge-management system.[9] In this work, the model is interchangeably called the Extreme Events (E²) Atrium for emergency management settings or the Joint Atrium for deployed military settings. Both types of situations demand readiness for surprise amid complex dynamic environments and readiness to improvise and innovate.

Cycling Tacit Knowledge into Virtually Reinforcing Resilience

One "goes into" the Atrium as a consumer, contributor, or producer: each organization or individual cycles through roles. Key to this model is the stabilizing locus of institutional memory and creativity in human-Atrium networks. Everyone, according to primary and secondary career specialties, rotates among the main set of organizations, task forces, and Atrium support activities. Often sitting at their normal desks, everyone—from senior leaders on down—cycles through all three Atrium roles.

As a consumer, each individual experiences the Atrium daily, and these interactions alone provide knowledge for the rest of the system. At scheduled or timed intervals according to his or her job patterns, each person is also formally assigned to be a contributor. As each person transfers into a new position, becomes accustomed to the new office and work, and then moves on, each spends several weeks initially doing a tacit data dump, including frustrations about process, data, and ideas, into his or her organization's share of the Atrium files. Noncritical identifying tags may be masked to encourage honesty, and then the knowledge is added to the central pools. Some of these data will be captured implicitly as contributors are encouraged to "act out" or "play through" their concerns in the form of challenges or changes to game-based simulations played through by themselves or others in the system. System members elsewhere can then apply data-mining or other applications to this expanding pool of knowledge elements to guide their future processes. Explicit and implicit comparative institutional knowledge thus becomes instinctively valued and actively retained and maintained for use in ongoing or future operations.

While everyone cycles through the Atrium routinely to download experiences, every so often, perhaps once every six months, each person also spends an additional week or so as a producer, setting up questions and looking at the data for the benefit of the system as a whole. Compiling tacit knowledge is thus not a task outsourced to those far from the day-to-day needs, experiences, and challenges of a particular Atrium's active community. In militaries, police forces, or other emergency services, organizational members with shared experiences review the words or simulation behaviors of others like themselves. They also read the inputs of others with whom they may have to work. In this role, these individuals try to define the kinds of questions they or people like them would like to have answered. The producers try to incorporate new data into the kinds of questions that data might answer, questions that may yet be unasked. The goal is for producers to understand what knowledge is out there, beyond what they have requested so far, and to see new patterns they had not perceived before. Technological support for this kind of cross-fertilization lies not only in the field of visualization but also in conceptual mapping, such as the emerging field of "coterm" network analysis (Jacobs 2002). The effect is a broadening of understanding of other organizational dilemmas, as well as of other approaches to solutions.

This commonality in experience also permits easier cycling through collaborative task forces, the kind of coordinated behaviors critical for emergency operations and thus dependent on trust and interactor knowledge. For the members of an emergency management system, this cycling needs to be both routine and concretely useful in their work. Hence emergency service members in New York, as well as police officers, need to find in the Atrium something of use when they share their tacit experiences in the E² Atrium.

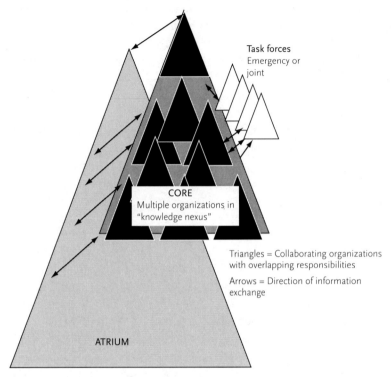

Task forces
Emergency or
joint

CORE
Multiple organizations in
"knowledge nexus"

Triangles = Collaborating organizations
with overlapping responsibilities

Arrows = Direction of information
exchange

ATRIUM

Fig. 4.1. Conceptual portrayal of an Atrium to support problem solving among agencies interacting in knowledge exchange and collaboratively refining experience for operational innovation

Cocreating Actionable Knowledge and Resilience

With this new social construction of what one does with information, each organization in the E² Atrium system creates, stores, refines, connects, weights, shares, and nurtures its own knowledge, while common applications blend the tacit information into wider knowledge queries and lessons. Doing what is needed for their own organizations in capturing tacit knowledge and searching for comparative lessons, individuals learn how to engage the Atrium as a trusted colleague. Plenty of tasks will routinely be performed singly in organizations that may be associated with the Atrium, both in the initial creation of applications, elements, processes, and uses but also in the coordination and integration of these evolutions.

In a Joint Atrium, the core exists virtually among the participating organizations, shepherded by the cadre element, located wherever emergency management coordination would normally be housed. Individuals serving in the core come to understand the Atrium as an intelligent world of knowledge and experimentation, rather than as a mindless amalgamation of individual databases. In short, the vibrancy of the Atrium in providing knowledge to accommodate surprise is due not to the professionalism of the small permanent core party but to the freshness of perspective and, importantly, the rising familiarity of both active and part-time participants.

Surrounded by complex systems, as well as itself being a complex system, the core and its Atrium denizens will constantly face emerging problems beyond normal operations. Some of these will be physically dangerous and immediate. Some will be prospective, such as determining the future evolutionary paths of neighboring political units and their likely ability to allocate sufficient budgetary amounts to tools necessary for operations or preventative programs. Some problems will come from beyond national borders, fed by cloaked actors seeking financial or political gains by operating violently in the surrounding society. Some will be long-term, such as rechanneling the design goals of key data-chunk allocations within the Atrium or retargeting some of its uses in the light of wider global trends. For these kinds of challenges, structurally collective problem solving is necessary, making a matrix organization imminently preferable. Hence we come to the final element of the Atrium, task forces.

Implementing Knowledge-Driven Response to Surprise

Extreme events surprise organizations so much that they often form their own response units, tending to produce emergency units that are small, unique, and specialized. Each of them develops a broad and deep array of implicit knowledge that the Atrium model would be able to capture and put to good use. In an extreme event, with some prior knowledge of form or frequency and considerable interorganizational trust and consensus, these many divergent units could be equipped to function jointly as task-force structures with a clearer definition of what needs to be done. The key is frequent and easy interorganizational operations under nonemergency situations. If the four stages of sense-making in task forces are to occur rapidly when responders are surprised, the preparatory process requires considerable social and technical practice.[10]

The knowledge creation in the E[2] Atrium not only serves the needs of member institutions but allows an empirical dataset to be accrued for use in online high-fidelity trial-and-error scenarios, as well as speculative routine exercises for each organization. The more virtual, realistic, flexible, and easily used this dataset is, the more participants would instinctively incorporate what they know well. Thus, routine use of the E² Atrium would capture the implicit information currently lost or buried after each related event or emergency experience. As members are tagged to be on call as first responders, they rotate into online virtual simulations, experiment with choices in scenarios constructed through the experiences of like others, and play out decisions jointly with others who are also online testing their decisions. The developing research into online multiuser gaming suggests that this kind of frequent exercise, in combination with real-time operations, is exceptionally valuable in developing both expertise and trust across partners (Jay, Glencross, and Hubbold 2007).

As the emerging "augmented reality gaming" develops and is adapted into the Atrium environment, it will become possible, for example, for police officers in New York City to walk through graphically realistic, surprising, and demanding missions while seeing what kinds of help they can expect or extract from state and federal individuals who are also online, experiencing these same situations (Liarokapis 2006). Periodic physical mass-casualty or disaster exercises will still be necessary to cement lessons learned or to reintegrate some physical constraints as yet not incorporated into the virtual world.[11] Exercises that are now held in real time with the individuals or organizations on call as first responders can more easily be orchestrated by coordinators in the emergency management system through Atrium venues. And of course, after a real-world experience—routine or not—each individual would reflect his or her interpretation of what had happened back into the Atrium for the use of his or her organization and the wider emergency responder community.

Once an emergency begins, each participating organization would leap into surprise-response activities that had been enhanced in virtual spaces, along with social trust, respect, cohesion, and credibility. Through the Atrium, member-organization decision makers would be more aware of the roles and likely actions of other agencies in their grand alliance. Through the simulations, they would also be more likely to know many of their corresponding actors in other organizations. The key here is that all members, including leaders, cycle through each section—the Atrium, core duties, and first responder task forces.

Final Thoughts

When decision makers cycle through the Atrium in order to truly know their organization and the wider system's players, their shared experiences widen the chances of domain consensus; role acceptance; trust; shared contextual knowledge; and innovation across organizations, individuals, and environments. Even rogue outcomes may be less catastrophic when Atrium institutions respond because of the human ownership of systemic resilience. Tacit knowledge collection is organically constructed from common experiences through institutionally and cognitively sensitive virtuality aimed at trust across disparate actors, as well as solutions.

The "socio" part of sociotechnical systems cannot be overstated. The history of war is replete with examples of how personal trust across unexpected lines enabled the survival of a set of units. When that trust was disrupted by the departure of some players, the units began to fail. An E^2 Atrium provides all leaders with what they need to gain more holistic knowledge of their own organizations, as well as of other partners on whom their people will depend in anticipating and responding to an emergency. Since one uses or cycles "into" the Atrium at one's desk, ubiquitous sharing is possible at smaller time increments, increasing the chances of an accurate picture of events emerging before memories deteriorate and are reconstructed rationally by other pressing needs. At the end of the day, leadership in crisis situations is made easier by this common ubiquitous colleague, presenting as much knowledge as possible. The E^2 Atrium's holdings, thanks to the producing process and the source filters on contributors, are politically neutral. In an Atrium, both sensitive and proprietary knowledge can be source masked, while the lessons set in response to queries can still be shared, reducing the value of hoarding knowledge because of distrust.

Knowledge development aimed at resilience in the Atrium model does not depend on absolutes in operations or predictions. In complexity across large-scale, diversely composed systems under active threats—the environment faced by extreme-event responder forces today—only trends, not specifics, can be perceived in advance. The best preparation for an organization is to have the knowledge base and the willingness to act in creative combinations ready and waiting for the elements of the trend to take concrete shape.

Resilience is profoundly collective, and as such, it will always be subject to interorganizational conflicts. A key distinction between the Atrium model and others is the Atrium's insistence on the formal and automatic cycling of all assigned participants before and after any operations, to download implicit knowledge, update their understanding of the Atrium's holdings and possible insights, and contribute to the community's ability to improvise or innovate as a whole. Positive social constructions and the evident use of this knowledge in new simulations testing solutions, in alterations in operations, or in the wider group discussion will make inherent conflict more of a creative stimulus for resilience than a hindrance. In addition, sensible data mining of these experiences over time—even if the data are frustrated tirades—will allow in- and out-negotiations to respond with a wider view of trends in the system. Sometimes with organizations, as with humans, doing something clearly positive in response to a critique brings participants creatively on board for further developments. The Atrium model encourages resilience sensibly across multiple mutually dependent organizations, using technology and a cognitively sensitive common socialization of individuals and organizations cycling in and out of the Atrium. In the process, each person and organization both benefits locally and contributes broadly. Tacit knowledge incorporating the "wisdom of cooperative strangers," collected and developed in this fashion, is more likely to allow the adaptive, improvised, and innovative dampening of the cascading rogue outcomes affecting all.[12] It does so by spreading familiar forms of knowledge access, contribution, development, and use among all members, including leaders. Its design presumes that surprise during operations is normal in complex systems and that only slack built through knowledge mechanisms can really accommodate, mitigate, or dampen the knowledge-burden effects on a large-scale organization.

Hence, the Atrium concept encourages independent thinking as well as trust, while permitting widespread coordination and integration across the organization, time, and operations. Importantly, this knowledge-enabled response can take place at any scale. For task forces in particular, the Atrium makes it possible to experiment before deleterious surprises hit and to set up an array of possible responses that are currently too cumbersome to enact. Implementing an Atrium moves work from localized relationship-based "controlled hoards" to web-based "trusted-source" structures. The intent is to balance the social and technical aspects of human responses to surprise. This model is designed to provide consistent, accessible, useful, and rewarded virtual workspaces, necessary for the "support, openness, trust, mutual respect, and risk taking" essential to effective innovation across remote, culturally diverse, yet reciprocally dependent organizations. (Gibson and Gibbs 2006, 462). From the Atrium, one could conceivably find new combinations virtually integrating different kinds of resources across first responder forces, by using novel reordering of information accumulations and reality expectations and then checking them against real experiences and the instincts of the real individuals who had those experiences. Clearly, more work is required to explore this possible design for surprise-embracing resilient institutions.

Appendix: Major Military Failures

Seymour (1988) identifies twenty major military failures that were responsible for a major cost in life, resource, or strategic objectives. At critical moments, institutional actors in key positions chose not to seek, recognize, or use knowable unknowns to accommodate likely surprise. Eleven of his examples occurred after the advent of the telegraph, in documented failures to forecast (seek knowable unknowns) or absorb/adapt (accommodate knowable unknowns). The table below summarizes the results.

Only one failed due to an inability to take new data and alter operations. In our sample, therefore, most failures were set on their course before battle by shortcomings in the collective knowledge systems in the organizations.

Table 4.1   Major Military Failures to Forecast, Adapt to, or Absorb Critical Infrastructure Knowledge

Failure Event and Location	Year	Dominant Type of Failure
Battle of Manzikert, Anatolian plain	1071	Failure to forecast
Battle of Bosworth, England	1485	Failure to forecast
Naseby Campaign, England	1645	Failure to adapt
Battle of Leuthen, Prussia	1757	Failure to adapt
Battles of Freeman's Farm and Bemis Heights, Saratoga Campaign	1777	Failure to forecast
Battle of Borodino, Russia	1812	Failure to absorb
Battle of Ligny, Belgium	1815	Failure to absorb
Battle of Waterloo, Belgium	1815	Failure to absorb
Battle of the Alma, Crimean Peninsula in the Black Sea (Ukraine)	1854	Failure to absorb
The Seven Days of Battle for Richmond, Virginia	1862	Failure to forecast
Campaign for Vicksburg, Virginia	1863	Failure to absorb
Battle of Gettysburg, Pennsylvania	1863	Failure to forecast
Battle of Isandhlwana, South Africa	1879	Failure to absorb
Battle of Tannenberg, Russia-Poland border area	1914	Failure to absorb
Disaster at Gallipoli, Turkey	1915	Failure to adapt
Battle of Warsaw	1920	Failure to forecast
German submarine successes, U.S. Atlantic Coast	1942	Failure to absorb
Battle of Dien Bien Phu	1954	Failure to forecast
Yom Kippur surprise attack on Israel	1973	Failure to forecast

5 BUILDING RESILIENCE

MACRODYNAMIC CONSTRAINTS ON GOVERNMENTAL RESPONSE TO CRISES

Alasdair Roberts

The Macrodynamics of Resilience

When societies suffer substantial losses as the result of some calamity, it is natural to wonder whether the harm might have been avoided and how similar harms can be avoided in the future. In this volume, the problem is expressed in terms of societal resilience—that is, the capacity of communities to rebound after unanticipated shocks or at least to "fail gracefully," with a slow degradation of essential functions (Wildavsky 1988, 77; Boin and Smith 2006, 301). The question, then, is how communities acquire the quality of resilience.

There is a strong temptation to regard the improvement of resilience as a problem in engineering (see chapter 2 of this volume). We can think of this both literally and metaphorically. In many instances, communities do enhance their resilience by building better infrastructure—such as earthquake-proof buildings, floodwalls, or emergency radio systems. This is engineering in the literal sense. In addition, though, we seek to design and implement policies that dictate how organizations and individuals will behave in moments of crisis. This is engineering in the metaphorical sense.

Once it is expressed in this way, we can see that attempts to improve resilience are susceptible to the same complaint that is lodged against many other efforts at "social engineering." That is, we may greatly overestimate the ease with which organizational and individual behavior can be changed. Societies (including their governmental systems) are highly complex; in some respects deeply resistant to change; and in other respects shaped by long-term trends that are difficult to resist. Attempts to design policies that do not accommodate these realities are likely to fail or to produce wholly unexpected results (Merton 1936).

This point can be put more positively. A proper understanding of the reasons why governmental systems achieve (or fail to achieve) resilience cannot be attained by looking narrowly at the design of specific policies or at the qualities of particular organizational leaders. This is because there is a set of larger considerations—political, economic, cultural, and technological—that defines the set of feasible policies and heavily constrains the range of possible actions available to even the most talented leaders. It is necessary to build a way of explaining resilience that accommodates the operation of these larger forces, which have been elsewhere described as the "macrodynamics" of institutional development (A. Roberts 2009).

This chapter attempts to undertake this sort of analysis in an effort to understand the U.S. federal government's response to two events that caused profound disruption to American life—the first on September 11, 2001, when Islamist terrorists attacked New York City and Washington, D.C.; and the second on August 29, 2005, when Hurricane Katrina made landfall on the U.S. Gulf Coast.

The administration of President George W. Bush was widely criticized for its handling of the response to both crises. The federal government, it was said, had not taken the steps needed to improve the country's capacity to rebound quickly from such catastrophes. Federal authorities were reproved for their failure to improve coordination among federal civilian agencies or to coordinate properly with state and local agencies; for their failure to invest properly in organizational capacities needed for emergency preparedness and response; and for putting key responsibilities in the hands of ill-qualified officials. In both cases, problems in federal administration contributed to a lack of resilience in the system as a whole: the costs incurred by the systemic shock were unnecessarily large.

How do we explain these failures? There was a strong temptation, in the aftermath of both crises, to look for explanations that dwelt heavily on the foibles of particular individuals (such as Michael Brown, the unlucky director of the Federal Emergency Management Agency at the time of Katrina) or weaknesses in the design of particular policies (such as procedural weaknesses in the Federal Bureau of Investigation prior to the 9/11 attacks). The implication is that simple changes in personnel or policies are likely to yield significant improvements in resilience. But the story is not so simple. The weaknesses in the federal response to these two crises were also consequences of the operation of large societal forces that are not easily countered.

One of these large trends consists of a dramatic change in the mechanisms by which information about crises is disseminated among the American public. Crises, although they may be triggered by natural phenomena, are not themselves natural phenomena. A community must agree, through some process of information sharing and deliberation, that an event constitutes a crisis—that is, that the event profoundly threatens some valued state of affairs and demands an urgent response by specific actors (Schneider 1985). The premise is that profound changes in information and communication technologies now transform *events* into *crises* more rapidly. Moreover, this technological transformation has the effect of federalizing the problem of crisis management. That is, more pressure is put on the U.S. national government to take the lead in managing the response to major crises. In other words, a *technological* change is shifting opinion on the *constitutional* question of where the primary responsibility for crisis management should lie.

This technological transformation is a distinctly postmillennial trend. However, it collides with a second reality of contemporary governance: that the U.S. central government is ill-suited to respond authoritatively to crises, because of a combination of ideological and institutional constraints on federal action. Deeply entrenched constitutional choices mean that the civilian component of the federal executive branch is prone to fragmentation, underinvestment in key capabilities, and politicization. Americans remain hostile to measures that threaten to expand the authority and budget of their central government. Indeed, the dominant trend in American politics in the quarter century preceding the 9/11 attacks was toward *restricting* the role of the federal government in Americans' daily lives.

The predicament, therefore, is the collision between the effects of technological shifts that place new demands on the federal government and ideological and constitutional constraints that make it difficult for the federal government to manage these new demands effectively. Other countries may not suffer equally from this predicament. This may be an illustration of the extent to which distinctive national considerations—relating to constitutional and legal traditions, as well as political culture—shape the capacity of a governmental system to assure resilience in the aftermath of catastrophe.

The U.S. federal government, as a superpower, is able to manage this predicament in ways not available to most other governments. Faced with significant limitations within the federal civilian bureaucracy, the president has strong incentives to enlist the national security apparatus, which has greater capacity and legitimacy than its civilian counterpart. Crises are militarized so that the federal government is able to execute a quick and firm response. This is expedient in the short term, as a way of accommodating the public expectation of a federal response to crisis. The long-term consequences of militarization are more severe. One long-term cost is the diversion of attention from measures that are more likely to promote societal resilience, such as investments to improve coordination among networks of civilian agencies at different levels of government.

The Postmillennial Infosphere

Changes in information technology have had a profound effect on the way in which the American people react to crises and on their attitudes about the responsibility of different levels of government for responding to crises. The purpose of this section is to sketch the character of these technological changes and to show how they have shaped views on the constitutional question of where the burden of leadership in crisis response should lie.

We must begin with an acknowledgment that information technologies play a critical role in determining whether a polity regards an event as a crisis at all. It is often argued that disasters such as the 9/11 attacks or Hurricane Katrina function as powerful "focusing events"—that is, as phenomena that profoundly shape public and elite attitudes about issues that demand immediate attention by government (Birkland 1997). Strictly speaking, however, it is not the phenomenon itself—the actual attack on the Twin Towers or the flooding of New Orleans—that influences the policy agenda. Rather, it is the *representation* of the phenomenon, conveyed by mass media or other information technologies, that has this effect. Most of the U.S. polity does not acquire knowledge of a catastrophe directly. What we know of a crisis—and whether we regard a particular phenomenon as a crisis—depends largely on the information and imagery that are conveyed to us through these technologies. As Boin et al. observe, the media have "a central role in creating and modulating crises" (Boin et al. 2005, 72–75).[1]

It follows from this observation that the extent to which governments are compelled to engage in "crisis management" hinges largely on the structure of information technologies. To take an extreme example, a government would not face any public pressure to manage crises at all if methods of communication were primitive or nonexistent. If there is no widely shared knowledge that an event has occurred, there cannot be any shared perception that it constitutes a crisis or any public demand for government to respond authoritatively to it.

At the dawn of the twenty-first century, this may seem to be an absurd hypothetical. But it is not; on the contrary, these are roughly the circumstances under which the United States government operated for most of its history. Two examples, almost exactly one century old, may help to make this point. The 1900 storm that devastated Galveston, Texas, killing over six thousand people, failed to become a *national* calamity largely because communication technologies available at that time proved incapable of disseminating information about the disaster quickly and broadly. Most Americans simply did not know what had happened in Galveston. The storm knocked down telegraph lines, leaving state and federal officials largely ignorant of conditions in the city. (The next day, the *New York Times* reported only "a suspicion that an awful calamity rests behind the lack of information from the Gulf coast" [New York Times 1900b].) For days, Galveston remained "entirely isolated" from the outside world (New York Times 1900a).

The San Francisco earthquake of 1906 was equally devastating, causing almost one thousand deaths and leaving over two hundred thousand homeless (NOAA 1972). But national consciousness of the disaster was again limited by technological capabilities. Telegraph lines remained operational but strained to convey news even to Washington (New York Times 1906). In major urban areas, the first brief reports about the disaster (but not images) traveled principally through newspapers published the following day. The majority of Americans, still living in rural areas, received their first news of the disaster much later.[2]

The speed with which these communication gaps were bridged in the United States is often overestimated. The Japanese attack on Pearl Harbor in December 1941 is often said to have shocked the United States, but even in the age of radio, information diffused slowly and imperfectly. Driving across the United States after the Hawaiian attack, the British journalist Alistair Cooke found "a lot of people sitting in their homes not 'stunned' as the newspapers have it but fuzzily wondering where Pearl Harbor was" (Cooke 2006, 6). Americans were compelled to rely on their imaginations to envisage the Japanese assault. Film footage of the attack was not released by government censors and distributed through newsreels until November 1942.

These examples illustrate the central point: that the manner by which crises are constructed in popular opinion hinges significantly on the structure of the technologies that are relied upon to convey news about catastrophic events. Moreover, social technologies—that is, the norms and routines that govern the business of news dissemination—matter as much as technical capacities. Newspapers, for example, rely heavily on text and for most of their history were incapable of conveying high-resolution, full-color imagery. This reliance on textual communication was often said to encourage more deliberate and rational responses to messages conveyed by newspapers, because readers must concentrate on the text, which in turn compels them to follow a linear mode of exposition (McLuhan and Fiore 1967; Postman 1986). The professional ideology of the mainstream print and broadcast media—which emphasized reportorial detachment, fairness, and balance (Kovach and Rosenstiel 2001)—also encouraged audiences to take a restrained response to news reports.

The "whole informational environment" that surrounds any individual or organization might be described as an *infosphere* (Floridi 2007). The print and electronic media comprise a major part (but not the whole) of this infosphere. We can restate our main point by saying that perceptions of the significance of crises, and the obligations of governments in relation to crises, are largely shaped by the structure of the infosphere. Moreover, it is clear that the infosphere has changed radically in the last three decades.

One obvious shift is the decline of the print and broadcast media. The daily newspaper was once the dominant source of news about current affairs in the United States: on the eve of World War II, 90 percent of Americans read a daily newspaper, according to the Gallup poll. However, the average circulation of U.S. daily newspapers has been dropping steadily for years. Broadcast television networks, which supplanted the print media as a major news source in the post–World War II era, have also lost influence. Viewership of evening news programs produced by the major U.S. broadcast networks eroded from over fifty million viewers in 1980 to twenty-five million in 2006 (Project for Excellence in Journalism 2007).

In the 1990s and early 2000s, these older media faced competition from cable news networks, such as CNN, Fox News, and MSNBC, which proved capable of providing vivid reportage on a round-the-clock basis. By 2002, Americans were as likely to say that they obtained their news from cable news networks as from newspapers or broadcast networks, according to the Gallup poll. The cable news networks played a critical role during the Bush presidency, as figure 5.1 shows: average viewership roughly doubled from the last years of the Clinton presidency, with remarkable spikes in moments of crisis.

Nor is this the end of the convulsions in the infosphere. The whole edifice of institutionalized news production—whether in print, broadcast, or cable media—has been challenged by the advent of the Internet and the dramatic reduction in barriers to entry into the business of news dissemination. The Internet has growing significance as a news source, although

Viewers in
millions

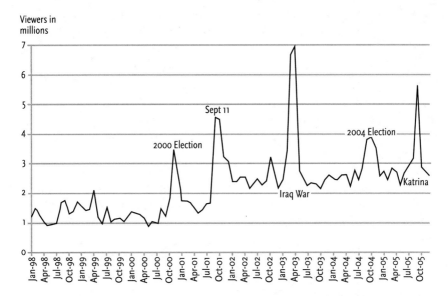

Fig. 5.1. Total prime-time viewership for the major cable news networks, by month. *Source:*
Nielsen Media Research.

it does not yet rival other media as a principal source for Americans (Project for Excellence in Journalism 2007). While many online resources are still controlled by traditional offline media, a large number are not. Over seventy million weblogs were created during the Bush presidency; between 2004 and 2007, the number of daily postings to these blogs quadrupled, to an average of 1.4 million a day. The task of news production is being broadly decentralized. Many Americans now prefer to extract and interpret information directly from newsmakers, rather than relying on intermediaries to do this for them.

These changes in the structure of the infosphere have had profound consequences for the character of news production and dissemination. The field is more competitive and faster paced than it was only a few years ago. Technological changes have produced a "never-ending news cycle" in which stories emerge and spread at "warp speed" (Kovach and Rosenstiel 1999). "The media is fracturing into more choices and more diversity," said Ari Fleischer (2005, ix, 8), President Bush's first press secretary: "In the modern media world, marked by the Internet and three all-news, all-the-time cable networks that compete furiously with one another, the ability to digest news slowly when facts emerge and sometimes change is seriously hindered. Gone forever are the days when news would break, reporters and sources would discuss ongoing developments throughout the day, and most Americans would first hear the news in a carefully digested story hours later on the evening news. For reporters now, it's an immediate need to tell and a rush to air. The need for the public to 'know' hasn't changed, but the urgency for reporters to 'tell' has grown more intense." In the view of many journalists, such competition has had a corrosive effect on professional ethics. As profit margins have narrowed, and the pace of news production has intensified, media outlets have placed less emphasis on thoroughness and more emphasis on sensationalism. A national survey of journalists taken in 2004 found mounting concern that reporting had become more sloppy and simplistic. Half of the journalists surveyed thought that the 24/7 news cycle had weakened their profession (Pew Research Center 2004).

Academic studies of crisis management have given inadequate attention to the ways in which the infosphere has changed and the manner in which it alters the task of responding to catastrophes.[3] Furthermore, the "mass media" are treated as a fixed variable. But the infosphere is clearly being transformed and in the process is profoundly altering the American public's awareness and perception of crises. Two obvious changes are in *immediacy* and *vividness* of awareness: Americans now become alerted to crises more quickly, and have a stronger appreciation of the human costs of a crisis, than ever before.

Consider, for example, the public's response to the attacks of September 11, 2001. As figure 5.1 suggests, an unprecedented number of Americans watched live reportage on the attacks on the three cable news networks. (Figure 5.1 shows prime-time viewership, but daytime viewership shows a similar pattern.) The major broadcasters, struggling to compete against their cable rivals, each provided roughly ninety hours of live coverage in the four days following the attacks, drawing a viewership of eighty million (C. Baker 2001). As a result, the nation's apprehension of the crisis was immediate, unmediated, and graphic. Five years later, 95 percent of Americans said that they could remember exactly where they were at the moment of the attacks, according to a Pew Research Center poll. "Unlike any news I can remember, news of September 11 was almost exactly simultaneous with the events themselves," recalls novelist Jonathan Raban (2005, 4): "Somehow, in the eighteen minutes since the first strike on the north tower, everybody knew, and everybody was watching CNN.... If you happened to live in Seattle, or Portland, or San Francisco, you were not excluded.... September 11 was unique in this: other shocking and violent events in the American past were relatively specialized and local—the assassinations of presidents, the destruction of a naval fleet, the mass murder of children at a school, the fiery annihilation of an eccentric cult, the blowing-up of a federal building. Except when they occurred in your neighborhood or line of work, they were about other people. September 11 was different."

September 11 may have been different from earlier crises, but it presaged the manner in which popular understanding of later crises would be constructed. Hurricane Katrina was also an information-age crisis. *MediaWeek* reported that the cable news networks "racked up stunning ratings" for their nonstop coverage of the disaster (Crupi 2005). (Indeed, cable news viewership actually exceeded levels for the 9/11 attacks: see figure 5.1.) As on 9/11, Americans were "drawn together ... by the shared response of living together through a searing event, moment by moment" (A. Brinkley 2003, 454).

The nonstop coverage was also marked by the further decline of the journalistic ethos of detachment and balance. This was most clearly evidenced by the reporting of CNN's Anderson Cooper, who came close to tears on camera as he interviewed victims and attacked Republican senator Mary Landrieu for defending the federal response to Katrina (Foer 2005). CNN was one of several media outlets that explicitly challenged the "official version" of events in New Orleans proffered by federal officials (Shafer 2005).

Media coverage of Katrina was not only intense and preoccupied with deficiencies in the federal government's response. It also dwelt heavily on the apparent breakdown of social order in New Orleans in the aftermath of the storm. Images and reports of looting and violence saturated the media (Waugh 2006, 15). Katrina was not distinctive in this respect; the tendency of mass media to exaggerate lawless behavior has been observed in earlier crises as well. However, this perceptual bias was aggravated during Katrina because of changes in the structure of the infosphere: "Anyone who watched or read [the new electronic media] in the aftermath of Katrina can only conclude that the images of looting and looters these media conveyed were even more extreme" than those presented in traditional media (Tierney, Bevc, and Kuligowski 2006, 68).

This intense coverage had the effect of drawing the federal government directly into the eye of the controversy surrounding the response to Katrina, whether it wished to be there or not. Activity on the Internet had the effect of amplifying pressure on federal authorities. Traffic on the Web sites of the White House and the Federal Emergency Management Agency (FEMA) surged during the Katrina disaster. The White House had not seen so much traffic on its site since the invasion of Iraq two years earlier.[4] Queries about Katrina also dominated the major Web search engines. Blog postings doubled, from a midsummer level of thirty thousand postings per hour to a record high of sixty thousand per hour.[5] Much of this Web activity had the effect of reinforcing perceptions of federal incompetence. The beleaguered head of FEMA, Michael Brown, briefly found himself a popular object of searches on Google, before resigning in mid-September 2005.[6]

One of the ironies of Katrina is that the infosphere largely succeeded in accomplishing what the community of emergency responders could not— that is, developing a "common operating picture" of the unfolding disaster (Comfort 2007b). However, this "common picture" was not necessarily accurate—for example, it exaggerated the degree of lawlessness—and certainly was not flattering to government, whose deficiencies were heavily emphasized.

Moreover, the federal government was placed in the center foreground of the quickly emerging picture. The New Orleans broadcaster Garland Robinette recalled that he "kept saying on the air to the U.S. government, 'Where are you? Where the hell are you?'" (D. Brinkley 2006, 530). "A man came up to me today," Anderson Cooper told Senator Landrieu on live television three days after Katrina's landfall. "He asked, 'Don't we pay taxes for the federal government to be protecting us?'" (CNN.com 2005b). By the end of the week, this was a widely shared complaint. Major polling firms began asking Americans about their assessment of the federal government's performance within forty-eight hours of landfall and found that most were deeply disappointed in its response. Many Americans held the federal government, rather than state and local governments, primarily responsible for the failure to respond properly to the disaster.[7] Which level of government should bear primarily responsibility is, of course, an important constitutional question. As a practical matter, however, the answer—that it should be the federal government—was heavily driven by the effect of a transformed infosphere on public opinion.

Constraints on Federal Response to Crises

The Clinton administration may have believed that it was governing in the "information age," but the conditions under which it governed were, in significant respects, simpler than those confronting the Bush administration only a few years later.[8] This postmillennial shift increasingly puts the federal government in the foreground when disaster strikes. At the same time, however, a number of considerations limit the federal government's capacity to meet the new expectations that are thrust upon it. These constraints are not new: on the contrary, they are political, institutional, and cultural factors that have dominated American politics throughout its history, and particularly in the thirty years of the last millennium.

Doctrine about the role of the federal government. One of the principal constraints is popular ambivalence about the expansion of federal governmental authority. Resistance to the growth of central government is a long-standing theme of American political history. This resistance ebbed during the New Deal and in the quarter century following World War II, but by the end of the 1970s, skepticism about federal government was resurgent. This was manifested in a sharp decline in public trust in central government, both in absolute terms and relative to attitudes about state and local government. Polls undertaken in the early 1980s showed that a large majority of Americans believed the balance of responsibilities had shifted too far toward the federal rather than state or local governments (Reeves 1986). Political leaders in both major parties responded to and encouraged this sentiment, promising initiatives that would restrain the federal role in key policy fields (A. Bowman and Krause 2003, 304).

The federal role in emergency response must be understood in the context of this larger debate about the proper role of the federal government. It was often taken for granted during post-Katrina debates that the federal government had a critical, if not leading role to play in the response to major natural disasters. But this is an assumption that would not have been tenable during most of U.S. history. A century ago, the federal role (as in Galveston and San Francisco) was largely confined to expressions of solidarity and the provision of limited material support. The federal role in the Mississippi floods of 1927 was more extensive but still bounded: "not a single federal dollar" was spent to aid victims of the cataclysm (Barry 2005; Kosar 2005).

The federal role in disaster response was only consolidated in the 1970s, with the passage of the Disaster Relief Act of 1974 and the creation of FEMA itself in 1979. However, FEMA was preoccupied with another mission—civil defense against nuclear attacks—throughout the 1980s (Sylves and Cumming 2004). It was the Clinton administration that gave FEMA a higher profile in responding to natural disasters—although even then it was careful not to intervene without the consent of governors. The agency was never intended to hold a "command position" in emergency response (Leonard and Howitt 2006, 4).[9] The Bush administration came to power determined to reappraise the wisdom of the growing federal role in disaster response. In early 2001, the FEMA director, Joe Allbaugh, told Congress that the federal role in disaster management "may have ballooned beyond what is an appropriate level" and that the Bush administration would try to "restore the predominant role of state and local response to most disasters" (Allbaugh 2001). This sentiment was entirely consistent with the broad trend of political rhetoric over the preceding quarter century.

This attitude was fueled by reasonable suspicion about the probity of the Clinton administration's approach to disaster response. Critics complained that the Clinton administration had simply perfected a technique of building political support by offering liberal payments for postdisaster assistance. The General Accounting Office (GAO) reported substantial growth in disaster-assistance costs in the 1990s, caused by an increase in the number of presidential disaster declarations and loosening of the eligibility for aid (GAO 1998). Research showed that disasters were more likely to be declared in states that were politically important to the president (Garrett and Sobel 2003). Along with increased spending came complaints about lack of controls to assure that aid was used properly (GAO 1996). (The weaknesses of Clinton-era policies are also discussed in Thomas Birkland's contribution to this volume.)

In a sense, the Bush administration was caught between the rhetoric of devolution, a legacy of the Reagan-era assault on "big government," and the pressures of the evolving infosphere. The rhetoric of devolution assumed that federal leadership in critical policy areas was at least contestable, if not illegitimate. The "big question" was whether "state or federal authorities [should] be in control of recovery efforts" (Waugh 2006, 37). In the context of disaster itself, however, public opinion tended to regard federal leadership as essential. There is, of course, a fundamental inconsistency here: a public that professes distrust of central government nonetheless expects it to take a critical role in response to major disasters. But there is no requirement for consistency in public attitudes. As a matter of realpolitik, the critical point is that the Reagan-era language of restraint and devolution ceased to be tenable in an age when news about disasters is instantaneously and universally distributed.

Austerity. Budgetary pressures also compromise efforts to build the capacity to respond effectively to domestic emergencies. This was most evident in the case of FEMA. "If you want big capability," a FEMA official told a Senate inquiry in 2006, "you got to make a big investment" (U.S. Senate 2006, 14-8). But even the Clinton administration had declined to do this: with three thousand employees, the Clinton-era FEMA was about one sixth the size of the New York City Fire Department.

Under the Bush administration, fiscal pressures further corroded FEMA's capacity. FEMA reduced the number of its emergency response and medical assistance teams and eliminated funding for training. The response team mobilized for New Orleans was, at the moment of Katrina's landfall, "theoretical": it had never worked together as a unit. FEMA's urban search-and-rescue teams also operated on a shoestring budget, a Senate investigation later found. Funding shortfalls delayed the development of FEMA's plans for the 2005 hurricane season (Block 2005; Select Bipartisan Committee 2006, 151–58; U.S. Senate 2006, 14-6 to 14-12).

The absorption of FEMA into the new Department of Homeland Security (DHS), pitched as a way of bolstering its limited capabilities, largely backfired. "FEMA is really now FEMA on steroids," Michael Brown had boasted in June 2003. "That's the best way to describe us" (Homeland Security Advisory Council 2003). In reality, FEMA staff complained, DHS treated FEMA as an "organ donor," extracting money to pay for central functions not funded by Congress (Rood 2005). Key functions were moved elsewhere in the department. Morale plummeted. In a 2004 survey, a majority of FEMA's career officials said that the agency had deteriorated since its absorption into DHS and that they would prefer to move to jobs elsewhere if possible (Hsu 2005).

Other components of the new DHS were similarly compromised by budget pressures. The new Transportation Safety Administration (TSA), for example, was compelled to cut its research-and-development budget by half in 2003 to meet shortfalls elsewhere in the agency (GAO 2004, 3, 32, 36). TSA's poorly paid screener workforce had a turnover rate of 23 percent in 2005—four times higher than the rate for federal government as a whole. The Government Accountability Office found that funding shortages were the "primary obstacle" to the deployment of more efficient systems for detecting explosives in checked baggage (GAO 2006a, 23, 27). Increases in staffing for the Border Patrol were delayed because the DHS had been cautioned by the White House to "think carefully about spending restraint" (DHS 2005b). The Department of Health and Human Services mounted the same defense of its effort to limit spending on programs to improve the health care system's readiness for bioterror attacks (Leavitt 2005; CDC 2006).

Broadly speaking, the homeland security apparatus was caught in a powerful budgetary vise. On one side, there were strong incentives for the Bush administration to reduce the federal tax burden. In the last years of the Clinton administration, the proportion of national income dedicated to federal taxes had reached levels unprecedented in modern U.S. history. Popular frustration with federal taxes increased at the same time. Surveys showed that the average American believed that the federal government wasted roughly half of the money that it collected in taxes; this held true even after the 9/11 attacks (K. Bowman 2006, 12–13). The Bush administration responded to such sentiments by pursuing a program of tax reductions that returned the overall federal tax burden to its historic average. Although these tax reductions were sharply criticized by the president's opponents, they were broadly supported by the American public. One month after the 9/11 attacks, for example, three quarters of the U.S. public told the Gallup poll that they favored making the first phase of proposed tax reductions effective immediately; 60 percent favored additional cuts (Gallup poll, October 5–7, 2001).

On the other side of the budgetary vise are expenditure pressures elsewhere in the federal budget. One major issue is the rising cost of popular entitlements such as Social Security, Medicare, and Medicaid. The cost of these programs is determined by the size of the over-sixty-five population, which will grow substantially for the next thirty years—a phenomenon that the comptroller general has called a "demographic tidal wave" (D. M. Walker 2000). It is estimated that by 2030 these three programs will consume over 15 percent of the country's gross domestic product (GDP) (Congressional Budget Office 2005). A smaller issue is the cost of the Iraq War, which transpired to be much larger than the administration's estimates in early 2003. The combined effect of growing defense and entitlement spending has been to crowd out expenditures on nondefense government operations, including homeland security programs. The Bush administration sought to relieve the overall fiscal pressures through increased borrowing, but this practice was widely criticized by many of the president's supporters, financial markets, and international financial institutions (IMF 2006).

Bureaucratic fragmentation. A third consideration—bureaucratic fragmentation within the civilian component of the federal government—also compromised the government's ability to meet public expectations on crisis management. This was evident in the preoccupation with the problem of coordination among the many federal agencies that could claim a role in emergency response. The need for improved coordination was recognized even before the 9/11 attacks: in February 2001, the Hart/Rudman Commission on National Security warned that the federal government needed to reshape its homeland security bureaucracy to ensure that it was "coherent and integrated" and that the federal government could say "quickly and surely who is in charge" in a moment of crisis (U.S. Commission on National Security/Twenty-first Century 2001, vii–viii, 10).

Problems of intragovernmental coordination are not peculiar to the U.S. federal government. But there are several reasons why coordination is particularly difficult within the U.S. system of government. Two centuries of rivalry between the executive and the legislative branches has produced a bureaucracy distinguished by its disorder. The executive's capacity to promote coordination is more limited than in other systems of government. Executive-legislative rivalry gives license to bureaucrats who want to resist coordination. All bureaucrats may have an "instinct for autonomy," but the U.S. system gives more freedom for this impulse to be pursued (Nelson 1982, 255; Kettl 2004, 122). In addition, the task of coordination has been made more complicated by the growth and institutional elaboration of the institutions that must be coordinated. Most federal government agencies are larger, and more complex in their internal structures, than they were only a few decades ago.[10]

Two major bureaucratic reorganizations were undertaken in an effort to promote coordination after the 9/11 attacks—one creating the new Department of Homeland Security and the other reorganizing the intelligence community. Both encountered serious problems. "Civil wars" within DHS delayed several initiatives, including efforts to tighten security on the transportation of hazardous chemicals and development of technologies to improve border control (Mintz 2005). DHS had equal difficulty in integrating agency systems for managing money, employees, information, and contracts (DHS 2004b, 2005a). Part of the difficulty stemmed from the inherent complexity of the task: for example, workers in DHS were represented by seventeen unions, laboring under twenty-seven different pay systems (Relyea 2005, 10). However, senior administrators within DHS often lacked the authority to induce cooperation from their lower-level counterparts (Ervin 2006, 19). An immediate consequence of the muddle in DHS reorganization was plummeting morale. In a 2006 study, DHS ranked last among major federal agencies on key measures of organizational health.[11]

The homeland security reorganization was also hampered by Congress's inability to put its own two houses in order. Twenty-six committees and sixty subcommittees in the House of Representatives and the Senate shared jurisdiction over homeland security matters, and they did not respond well to the suggestion that agency rationalization should be accompanied by a comparable clarification of committee responsibilities (Preston and Crabtree 2002; Ornstein and Mann 2003). The 9/11 Commission co-chair Lee Hamilton (2003, 5) complained in 2003 that fractured congressional oversight "sowed confusion" within the executive branch. Only after the commission criticized its inaction did the House of Representatives create a new standing committee on homeland security, still with limited authority (National Commission on Terrorist Attacks upon the United States 2004, 419–21). The Senate took similarly halting steps to reform oversight.

Its committee changes were "limp and inadequate" (Mann and Ornstein 2006, 150–51).

Problems of coordination were also evident as DHS attempted to develop routines for dealing with future crises. In 2002, the Bush administration began to develop a National Response Plan that explained how federal efforts would be synchronized in a moment of crisis. In January 2005, DHS secretary Tom Ridge announced that the plan had been finalized, calling it a "bold step forward in bringing unity in our response to disasters and terrorist threats" (Edmonson 2005). "The end result," Ridge promised, "is vastly improved coordination…to help save lives and protect America's communities" (DHS 2004a, i).

This, a White House advisor later conceded, was "false advertising" (Lipton et al. 2005). The National Response Plan conveyed the impression of rationality in crisis response, but the tendency toward disarray could not be easily suppressed. A training exercise undertaken in April 2005 revealed "confusion at all levels" and "a fundamental lack of understanding" about procedures outlined in the plan. Indeed, key components of the plan were still incomplete when Katrina hit the Gulf Coast five months later. DHS itself did not activate key procedures within the plan for four days after the National Hurricane Center's warning of Katrina's path and devastating power (GAO 2006c; U.S. Senate 2006, 27-12).

A second reorganization, intended to improve coordination within the network of intelligence agencies, encountered difficulties similar to those that plagued DHS. The federal intelligence community is highly fragmented, with responsibilities for collection and analysis of intelligence shared by seventeen agencies (Posner 2005, 50). Attempts to integrate the work of that community before 9/11 were often stymied by bureaucratic resistance to centralization of control and the reluctance of Congress to rationalize its own oversight mechanisms (Zegart 1999). Although the National Intelligence Reform Act passed in December 2004 finally established the post of national intelligence director, this position's powers are still constrained, both formally and by the bureaucratic and political realities that frustrated earlier reforms (DeYoung 2006; Gertz 2006; Lowenthal 2006, 276–79; Shane 2006; Zegart 2006). The first director, John Negroponte, sought a reassignment after only two years, weary of the "total, ongoing food fight" among intelligence agencies (Dinmore 2007).

Politicization. There is, finally, a fourth institutional constraint on the federal government's capacity to meet public expectations for crisis management: that is the practice of staffing critical positions within the bureaucracy with political appointees. The risks associated with politicization of key positions were illustrated by the controversy over the performance of Michael Brown, the head of FEMA at the time of Hurricane Katrina. Brown, a political appointee who had come to the agency from a post at the International Arabian Horse Association, was criticized for exaggerating his experience in the field of emergency management and for incompetence in handling the response to Katrina. But Brown was not an exceptional case. Other key appointees within FEMA were equally inexperienced (Hsu 2005; U.S. Senate 2006, 14-4). Brown's predecessor as FEMA head, Joe Allbaugh, also lacked strong credentials. He had claimed the position after serving as George W. Bush's 2000 campaign manager. Indeed, FEMA has had a long history of poorly qualified leaders; James Lee Witt, the much-lauded leader of FEMA during the Clinton administration, was an exceptional case (Waugh 2006, 33).

Problems caused by politicization of key positions were not limited to FEMA. Its parent department, DHS, also suffered from the inexperience and massive turnover of political appointees during its first years (Mintz 2005). By 2005, DHS had lost its secretary, its deputy secretary, three undersecretaries, six assistant secretaries, its chief security officer, its chief information officer and his deputy, its cybersecurity director and his deputy, and dozens of other key personnel (Dizard 2005). By 2006, two thirds of DHS's senior executives had departed, often taking more lucrative positions as lobbyists for homeland security contractors (Lipton 2006a, 2006b). A 2007 report commissioned by DHS criticized its overdependence on political appointees and urged the Bush administration to begin "supplementing" the department's leadership with career employees to prevent a "Homeland Security 'meltdown'" following the 2008 election (Homeland Security Advisory Council 2007).

Incompetence and discontinuity in leadership are not the only risks associated with dependence on political appointees. Interagency planning may also be jeopardized, because political appointees lack the personal connections to peers in other organizations that would otherwise ease the task of coordination. Such social capital may be particularly important in moments of crisis, facilitating ad hoc coordination and reducing the risk of miscommunication. However, political appointees often do not know or trust one another, even though they may serve the same party and president. Each new crop of political appointees comprises "a government of strangers" (Heclo 1977, 1). The lack of social capital was evident during the Katrina disaster, after which Brown complained about his inability to communicate with other appointees even in his own department.

Heclo's "government of strangers" has grown in numbers throughout the modern era (Volcker 1988; Light 1995; U.S. House of Representatives 2006). Turnover among political appointees has also increased: in the post-Nixon years, average length of service sank to a low not seen since the Jacksonian era (Chang, Lewis, and McCarty 2001, 30). The growth in number of political appointees could be explained by the need for a larger stock of positions to reward supporters in increasingly costly presidential campaigns. It might also be explicable as part of a misguided effort to discipline a bureaucracy that is perceived, particularly in the post-Reagan era, to be resistant to control by elected officials (Pfiffner 1987). The perversity, of course, is that growing dependence on short-term political appointees who lack either skills or social capital actually corrodes the president's capacity to command the administrative apparatus of the executive branch (D. Cohen 1998).

Incentives for Militarization

The federal government has been caught between mounting public pressure to take a leadership role in crisis response—as a consequence of a changing infosphere—and a set of constraints that make it difficult for its civilian bureaucracy to fulfill that role. Twice in the last eight years it has used the same strategy to deal with this predicament: the militarization of crisis response. This is expedient in the short term but arguably undermines systemic resilience in the long run.

The strategy of militarization takes advantage of the fact that the federal government has a dual or bifurcated structure. That is, it combines two systems of governance, organized on distinct principles and operating in discrete policy fields (Wildavsky 1969, 230–45; Draper 1991, 580–98). One system is dedicated to domestic policy. As we have seen, it is prone to bureaucratic fragmentation, dominated by a leadership cadre that consists heavily of political appointees, and vulnerable to austerity measures. Another system, largely dedicated to military affairs, is organized on different principles. While the nondefense sector is highly federalized, and thus dependent on the cooperation of state and local governments, the defense sector is more centralized.[12] Leadership positions of the uniformed services are staffed by career employees. The defense sector also enjoys greater independence from Congress and nongovernmental stakeholders, especially when national security considerations are invoked (Alterman 1998). Added to these attributes is another critical element: legitimacy. While Americans are generally distrustful of governmental institutions, the military is a conspicuous exception.[13] One consequence is that the defense sector is often in a better position to extract funding for its programs. We might also note that the defense sector is also the preponderant part of the federal bureaucracy: it accounts for roughly half of the federal workforce (including uniformed personnel) and two thirds of operating expenditure.

The president faces strong incentives to exploit the advantages of the defense sector—its clearer line of command, relatively stronger capacity for coordination and execution, and higher legitimacy—by relying on it as the primary mechanism for response to crises.

The tendency to militarize response to crises was evident in the wake of the 9/11 attacks. At the very moment he was told of the World Trade Center attacks, President Bush later recalled, "I made up my mind that we were going to war" (Woodward 2002, 15). A "War on Terrorism" was declared by the president within twelve hours of the attacks (Executive Office of the President 2001). By September 13, 2001, Bush had resolved to "hit the Afghans hard" (Woodward 2002, 63). On September 17, Bush instructed the Defense Department to refine its contingency plans for action in Iraq, and by November 2001 the military was planning a full-scale invasion of Iraq (Rothkopf 2005, 433; Gordon and Trainor 2006, 15–23). The 9/11 attacks did not need to be framed in these terms: other countries have dealt with decades-long terrorist threats by framing the problem primarily as one to be dealt with through improved intelligence-gathering, stricter law enforcement, and improved domestic security.[14]

Katrina, which involved no violence by a foreign entity, may provide a better illustration of the tendency toward militarization. As exasperation over the response of the civilian bureaucracy grew, the president faced mounting pressure to restore a sense of order in New Orleans by giving the military a leading role in relief. Perceptions about growing lawlessness within the city, encouraged by media and Internet coverage, also increased demands for military intervention (Tierney, Bevc, and Kuligowski 2006, 77). On September 3, five days after landfall, President Bush ordered the deployment of seven thousand troops to New Orleans. "Basically," said a disaster response expert, "we declared war on Hurricane Katrina" (Gosselin and Hook 2005).

The media and public responded positively to the militarization of disaster response. The *Baton Rouge Advocate* reported that a little girl shouted "Thank you, Mr. Army!" as troops entered New Orleans (Baton Rouge Advocate 2005). The *New York Times* reported: "On streets where gun battles, fistfights, holdups, carjackings and marauding mobs of looters had held sway through the week, the mere sight of troops in camouflage battle gear and with assault rifles gave a sense of relief to many of the thousands of stranded survivors who had endured days of appalling terror and suffering. 'They brought a sense of order and peace, and it was a beautiful sight to see that we're ramping up,' Governor Blanco said. 'We are seeing a show of force. It's putting confidence back in our hearts and in the minds of our people. We're going to make it through'" (McFadden 2005).

The shared desire for a forceful response to the crisis was evidenced in the praise given to Lieutenant General Russell Honoré, the commander of the military task force. Honoré, CNN reported, was a "cigar-chewing, stomping, cussing general" who nonetheless stooped "to pick up babies on the street and take them to safety" (CNN.com 2005c). The New Orleans mayor, Ray Nagin, lauded Honoré as a "John Wayne dude who can get some stuff done" (CNN.com 2005a). "The Department of Defense saved the day," a federal official said later (U.S. Senate 2006, 26-25).

The mobilization of troops was not without complications. The Posse Comitatus Act, adopted shortly after the Civil War, generally prevents federal troops from enforcing law within U.S. borders. President Bush could have relied on another postbellum law, the Insurrection Act, to justify the use of federal troops in restoring order, but the administration was reluctant to risk political controversy by exercising that rarely used authority over the objections of the Louisiana governor, Kathleen Babineaux Blanco (Los Angeles Times 2005). Bush and Blanco negotiated for four days but failed to reach agreement on a command structure that would comprise federal and National Guard troops, who could exercise law-enforcement functions while under state command (U.S. Senate 2006, chap. 26). Fortunately, the political antagonism between Bush and Blanco was offset by a longtime friendship between two career officials—Honoré and Major General Bennett Landreneau, the commander of the Louisiana National Guard—who worked out problems of coordination informally (Los Angeles Times 2005).

The lesson that the Bush administration took from Katrina was that it should push for an expanded military role in domestic crisis response (Waugh 2006, 42). It was clear, the president said, "that a challenge on this scale requires...a broader role for the armed forces—the institution of our government most capable of massive logistical operations on a moment's notice" (Executive Office of the President 2005a). Bush argued that the Defense Department—the only federal organization with the capacity to "marshal resources and deploy them quickly"—could become the lead agency for response to major disasters (Executive Office of the President 2005b; Tyson 2005). His administration asked Congress to amend legislation that limited the domestic role of federal forces and directed military commanders to develop plans for rapid response to disasters (Schmitt and Shanker

2005). In October 2006, Congress altered the Insurrection Act so that federal troops could be deployed more easily to restore order after a natural disaster, epidemic, or terrorist attack.[15]

Militarization is expedient for federal policy makers because it allows them to respond to public expectations by providing a decisive response to crises. But it is arguable that militarization undermines societal resilience in the longer run. Militarization reinforces the notion that crises require a firm response by structures built on the principle of hierarchy and unity of command. It also discourages attention to investment in civilian agencies, as well as the construction of stronger crisis-response networks—that is, a web of strong "horizontal relationships" among the many civilian and military agencies responsible for crisis management (Kettl 2006, 278–79; Comfort 2007b). Such networks may be more difficult to establish, but they are also more likely to assure resilience in moments of crisis.

A Continuing Dilemma

Any study that is intended to consider how governments may contribute to societal resilience must take into account the larger considerations that shape (and constrain) governmental capacities in a particular jurisdiction. This chapter has provided evidence to substantiate this point. Changes in the infosphere that have accelerated the process of "crisis production" and heightened the accountability of central government may be more advanced in the United States than in other countries. Similarly, central government in the United States is affected by constitutional, political, and cultural constraints that may not operate with equal force in other countries. An interesting comparison can be drawn, for example, between the predicament of central government in the United States and that of France, described in Claude Gilbert's contribution to this volume. In the American case, the challenge is marshalling authority at the center; in the French case, it is almost the reverse—that is, an unhealthy concentration of central authority.

The trends that have complicated the position of the U.S. federal government with regard to crisis response are likely to continue. We can reasonably expect that technological changes will further improve the capacity to diffuse information about natural and terrorist-induced calamities and that as a consequence these events will be transformed into full-blown crises with greater efficiency. Increasingly, the public will assume that federal authorities should have a critical role, if not *the* leadership role, in dealing with these crises. In short, expectations with regard to federal performance in crisis management are likely to mount.

At the same time, however, the institutional and political considerations that impair the performance of the federal government's civilian bureaucracy are likely to persist. With time, merged components of the federal bureaucracy might learn to integrate their operations, and morale might rebound. But such progress is likely to be slow and complicated by Congress's reluctance to rationalize its own committee system. Moreover, budgetary pressures will increase as the United States' retired population increases over the next two decades. Nor is there any sign of a change in the number or duration of tenure of political appointees. In 2005 a prominent commentator on homeland security issues suggested that one way to deal with the problems of the civilian bureaucracy—poor coordination, underresourcing, politicization—would be to establish a financially and administrative autonomous structure, akin to the U.S. Federal Reserve (Flynn 2005). This proposal was bold and, as it transpired, completely impracticable. There is no enthusiasm for substantial structural reforms that would ameliorate the long-standing problems of the civilian bureaucracy.

It is possible, however, to imagine countervailing considerations. The U.S. military might balk at the expansion of its responsibilities, as it did when the Clinton administration attempted to broaden the range of "military operations other than war" in the 1990s. Internal resistance to the accretion of functions might be especially acute if the military continues to bear responsibility for extensive overseas engagements, such as those in Iraq and Afghanistan. Respect for the military might also decline as it becomes more actively engaged in domestic crises and its own organizational shortcomings become more obvious. In other words, militarization of crisis response might also have appeal in the short run precisely because it is novel and its defects are not yet obvious.

6 FEDERAL DISASTER POLICY

LEARNING, PRIORITIES, AND
PROSPECTS FOR RESILIENCE

Thomas A. Birkland

Policy Learning and Community Resilience

This chapter considers the extent to which federal-level "learning" from disaster experience yields policy changes that enhance disaster resilience at the local level. There is evidence of learning from experience at the state and federal levels after major natural disasters (Birkland 2006); that is, disaster policy changes and in some ways improves based on disaster experience. However, certain conditions must be in place for successful policy learning, which do not always exist (Gerber 2007). While learning and the capacity for learning might be considered essential aspects of effective disaster policy, I argue that the lessons that are generally learned are not intentionally designed to enhance community disaster resilience and indeed have had little effect in improving resilience.

Even if we settle for more readily assessed aspects of policy—hazard mitigation and disaster preparedness—we still cannot find evidence that resilience occupies many federal policy makers' attention. The overwhelming evidence suggests that most learning has been about the instrumental and political aspects of the quick and generous delivery of disaster relief. Federal and state policies promoting hazard mitigation and disaster preparedness may have the incidental effect of promoting resilience, but even if these policies were explicitly designed to improve resilience, these aspects of disaster policy are such relatively minor parts of federal and most states' policies that in the best case their influence on local resilience would be minimal.

In reality, national policy tends to *undermine* resilience because of its centralizing tendencies—"the feds know best" tendency—and because of its continued focus on disasters after the fact, in the form of sometimes massive amounts of federal aid that constitutes little but pork-barrel spending (Platt 1999), while continuing to encourage development in areas most prone to hazards (Burby 2006; Burby et al. 1999; Burby and Dalton 1994). This lack of attention to resilience and even to mitigation has become more pronounced in the "homeland security" era, in which the federal government has sought to centralize disaster policy under a command-and-control mode (Scavo, Kearney, and Kilroy 2006) that is antithetical to what science has learned about how people, communities, institutions, and the built environment behave in disasters.

Because *preparedness* and *mitigation* are more familiar terms of art than *resilience* (the meaning of which remains contested, at least at the margins), I use *mitigation* and *preparedness* as proxies for policies that are more likely to promote community and regional resilience than are relief policies that have been demonstrated to undermine efforts to promote resilience. I will show that the federal government and Congress, in particular, devote less of their attention to mitigation and preparedness (i.e., to preimpact policies that may promote resilience) than they do to relief and recovery aid (trans- and postimpact) (Kendra and Wachtendorf 2006; Quarantelli 1980). I argue that, from a resilience perspective, preparedness and mitigation—particularly "nonstructural" or "process" mitigation (as described below)—are two aspects of disaster policy that are most associated with resilience because they focus on preimpact capacity, while relief and recovery are simply palliatives that may inject some resources into the community, but with the effect of reducing resilience and increasing hazardous behavior (Burby et al. 1999). I further argue, based on a historic analysis of federal policy, that efforts to engage communities in resilience-promoting activities peaked in the late 1990s with the emergence of Project Impact, a community-based mitigation and resilience partnership initiated by the Federal Emergency Management Agency (FEMA), only to be undermined by the Bush Administration's gutting of FEMA; this gutting began before the September 11 attacks but accelerated rapidly thereafter.

Defining Resilience

There are many ways to define and operationalize disaster resilience (Comfort 1994a; Aguirre 2006; Manyena 2006). Resilient social and constructed systems are described in many ways: as being able to "fail gracefully" or as having "rebound capacity." The editors of this volume define resilience as the capacity for collective decision making both during and immediately after the onset of a crisis. In this definition, the ability of a community to recover or "bounce back" is the essence of resilience.

Researchers at MCEER (formerly the Multidisciplinary Center for Earthquake Engineering Research) at SUNY Buffalo have developed the idea of a "resilience delta" (MCEER 2006), which reflects the fact that there are many systems in a community that have different resilience profiles. Such systems include, as Aguirre (2006, 1) notes, "physical, biological, psychological, social, and cultural systems." Similar thinking has informed research and programs on "disaster-resistant" communities, although 100 percent *resistance* to a disaster is not usually achievable, from an economic, political, or engineering perspective. Rather, a resilient community is one that may not be entirely resistant—that is, things may break during the disaster—but that has the capacity to recover quickly. If we conceive of a community faced with many events—hurricanes or coastal storms, for example—a learning and resilient community would be one that experiences successive but successively less disruptive disasters, even if we hold the physical characteristics of these events constant.

It is noteworthy that the *political* considerations or features of the policy process at the local, state, or regional level rarely feature in analyses of resilience (Kendra and Wachtendorf 2006). Yet the nature and function of politics are as important to community resilience as any other social process (see Alasdair Roberts's chapter in this volume). Politics is that activity that helps societies decide "who gets what, when, and how" (Lasswell 1958). Disasters and the policies that deal with disasters are clearly political in the sense that they imply the distribution of resources through a system of government. Thus, we may offer the hypothesis that most if not all aspects of resilience are influenced by public policy, either by design or by accident.

In the mid-2000s, researchers and practitioners began to take a more active interest in resilience and vulnerability. This interest is driven, in part, by the way catastrophic events such as Hurricane Katrina and the 2004 Sumatra earthquake and Asian tsunami showed that successful disaster policies promote a form of resilience in which a community can begin to recover and provide assistance to victims for an extended time without outside aid (Manyena 2006). This interest may also be driven by a desire to find "all-hazards" terminology to address natural, technological, and purposive hazards in an era of extreme attention to terrorism and reduced concern about natural disasters, a trend that Hurricane Katrina may have reversed. The emerging discussion of resilience is helpful because it might be a way to think more holistically about the disaster cycle: instead of thinking of preparedness, mitigation, response, and recovery as different phases of a cycle, we can think of them as aspects of a system that promotes or retards resilience.

Policies That Promote Resilience

Mitigation has often been divided into two categories: structural mitigation and nonstructural mitigation. A clearer and more useful definition is offered by Philip Ganderton, who divides mitigation measures into "project" and "process" mitigation. Project mitigation involves building things that resist natural forces, such as levees, beach groins, beach nourishment, floodwalls, and the like. Process mitigation involves using policy tools to alter the behavior of actors in the process, so that their actions will promote or at least not undermine community, regional, and national mitigation goals. Process mitigation includes planning, zoning, building codes, and similar regulations intended to reduce a structure's, a site's, or a neighborhood's vulnerability to disasters, thereby enhancing overall community safety. The outcomes of project mitigation are much more easily assessed than are the outcomes of process mitigation (Mason 2006).

The goal of any disaster mitigation program should be community resilience (Godschalk 2003), but promoting mitigation is not the same thing as promoting resilience. Indeed, as currently practiced in the United States, while some forms of mitigation may improve resilience, others may, in fact, undermine resilience over the long run (Burby 2006).

For example, some project-oriented mitigation works, such as levees, might prevent most flooding but may make flooding worse during a catastrophic failure. Such works therefore replace resilience with robustness, but robustness implies strength until a catastrophic failure occurs (the opposite of "failing gracefully"), thereby yielding catastrophic damage in areas where people believed that the mitigation works would protect them. This is generally considered a "false sense of security," particularly when the claimed or perceived level of robustness falls short of actual performance, as happened in New Orleans during Hurricane Katrina.

Process mitigation, such as land-use planning to remove vulnerable property from hazardous areas, may increase resilience simply because the amount of damage—the sharp downward line in the resilience delta— should be less than if no mitigation measures were undertaken and will not be deeper due to a catastrophic failure of a "robust" system. Thus, the depth of the near-vertical line is a function of preexisting mitigation measures that lower the toll of a disaster. Furthermore, process-oriented mitigation programs may engage people and community institutions more directly than will project mitigation, thereby creating knowledgeable and supportive communities that understand and seek hazard mitigation (Burby et al. 1999; Burby and May 1998).

While little was changed in the 1990s to discourage the subsidy for risky activity that Burby and his colleagues identified as the key feature of disaster policy, some efforts were made by the Clinton administration, and by FEMA under James Lee Witt, to support local mitigation initiatives, as well as at the aforementioned Project Impact. Local hazard mitigation became an important element of disaster policy in the 1988 Stafford Act and in the Stafford Act amendments in 1993; the shortcomings of the 1993 amendments—particularly with respect to harmony between state and local mitigation plans—were addressed in the Disaster Mitigation Act of 2000. Project-related mitigation remains important both for substantive mitigation reasons and because projects such as flood-control works undertaken by the U.S. Army Corps of Engineers are broadly popular among members of Congress who actively seek such distributive spending, even as such projects subsidize risky behaviors and do not work particularly well over the long run. These techniques also carry with them substantial environmental side effects that likely diminish the net value of the project to society (Birkland et al. 2003). The efficacy of many of these projects is less important to many members of Congress than is their distributive nature: these projects allow for credit claiming and the distribution of "pork-barrel" projects to individual districts.

Another aspect of resilience is preparedness. While a community that does not engage in effective mitigation may still have a very deep hole to dig out of, preparedness is one of the aspects of emergency management that will shorten the period between the acute phase of the event and a return to something approaching normal. This chapter will consider mitigation more carefully, but I acknowledge that being prepared for a disaster—having the proper response capacity, health and safety facilities, equipment, and the like—will influence resilience.

Policies That Inhibit Resilience

The most popular and most common federal expenditures relating to natural disasters are for relief and recovery. Funding is provided to communities through FEMA's public assistance program. Direct grants of federal aid to individuals are also available from FEMA's individual assistance program in declared disaster areas. The Small Business Administration (SBA) offers disaster loan programs for individuals and businesses. Despite occasional concerns expressed by politicians and journalists, such payments are not wildly munificent—FEMA makes clear in its guide for disaster victims that Individual and Household Relief (IHR) under the Individual Assistance rubric is not intended to supplant insurance, will not cover all losses, and is often secondary to SBA loan programs (FEMA 2005a). The public assistance program helps fund debris removal, infrastructure repair, and similar community costs. Taken together, FEMA disaster relief seeks to compensate disaster victims for what Burby (2006) calls "residual risk"—that is, the risks that remain after flood protection, hurricane protection, beach nourishment, or other project-oriented mitigation actions are taken.

Of course, such policies yield substantial moral-hazard problems, in which individuals, believing that they are somehow protected from risk, take actions that are riskier than they would ordinarily assume if (1) they knew the full extent of the residual risk that they assume and that the mitigation works do not protect against and (2) the engineered works functioned as promised. They often do not work: beach nourishment is a Sisyphean task that involves constant restoration of beaches in the face of continuing demand to restore beaches for the benefit of property owners, even as that very development, and that along the beach throughout the region, has disrupted normal sand-transport mechanisms (Kaufman and Pilkey 1983a; Kaufman and Pilkey 1983b; Dean 1996; Pilkey 1998). Building-elevation and flood-insurance requirements often fail to take into account changes in the floodplain resulting from additional development; these changes include both the extent of the floodplain and the depth of floodwaters. And when engineered flood- and hurricane-protection works fail, they often do so catastrophically, so much so that, for example, the one-hundred-year probability flood might not be the better design standard for such works. A five-hundred-year flood would allow builders and property owners to more clearly understand the consequences of catastrophic losses. Even then, not every hazard-prone community can be protected solely by constructed mitigation. And some hazards, like earthquakes, cannot be mitigated through the building of major public works projects; rather, mitigation is nearly always process oriented and is focused primarily on building codes and on improvements in professional practice (Geschwind 2001).

The shortcomings of federal disaster policy and its distortions of state and local regulation, and of individual behavior, are well-known, and these issues are repeated after every event. If this is the case, and federal effort could be shifted away from relief and insurance payouts (i.e., promoters of moral hazard) toward preparedness and mitigation, it is likely that the rate of growth of disaster losses, if not the absolute value of disaster losses, could be reduced.

Learning from Earthquakes and Hurricanes at the Federal Level

Normatively, it is sensible to say that policy makers *should* learn from experience. Whether they do or do not is not always clear, although often there is little evidence that they do. Specifically, I am interested in what May calls "instrumental policy learning," which is learning about ways to improve the application of policy tools, or instruments. Sometimes the learning yields a change in tool choice, from a more coercive tool to a more cooperative one, or vice versa, while other times the learning may be that the instrument has potential, but that it does not work without rigorous enforcement.

I do not argue here that learning is a feature of a disaster-resilient federal government or federal polity; the United States is far too large for any single natural disaster to test national resilience. The September 11 attacks and the 1941 attack on Pearl Harbor, Hawaii, tested local resilience but did not undermine national resilience. Something on the scale of full-scale nuclear war could truly test national resilience, but I am interested in more common events that are regionally disastrous or catastrophic. In particular, I am interested in federal instrumental policy learning that promotes local resilience, as well as policies that reduce dependency relationships between communities and higher levels of government, thereby undermining local or regional resilience.

I approach the learning question from a policy process perspective (Busenberg 2001; Levy 1994; May 1992; Sabatier 1987, 1991; Sabatier and Jenkins-Smith 1993). Students of the policy process are concerned with "the institutional arrangements and political events that shape individual learning" (Busenberg 2001, 173), not primarily with the organization-theory aspects of learning. I do not approach this from an "organizational learning" perspective because, as Sabatier (1987) argues, organizational learning is "metaphorical."

Peter May's (1992) discussion of learning from policy failure is most useful for this analysis because disasters generate potential evidence of policy failure, thereby triggering learning. May argues that policy failure inspires three different kinds of learning: instrumental policy learning, social policy learning, and political learning. I focus primarily on instrumental policy learning, which describes how accumulated knowledge is applied to improve policy. Social policy learning involves learning about attitudes toward program goals and the nature and appropriateness of government action. Political learning consists of learning about "strategy for advocating a given policy idea or problem," leading potentially to "more sophisticated advocacy of a policy idea or problem" (May 1992, 339).

Historically, community-level resilience as a concept has not been a key feature of federal policy. Instead, project-oriented mitigation—particularly the flood-control works constructed by the U.S. Army Corps of Engineers—played a central role both in flood mitigation and in water policy generally, with the not incidental effect of spreading federal "pork" (distributive spending) throughout the nation (Platt 1999). In more recent years, the limits of project-oriented mitigation have been recognized, and process tools, such as land-use controls, improved building codes, and actuarially sound insurance programs have been recognized as better long-run ways to address hazards than are the usual project-oriented palliatives.

Nevertheless, project-oriented mitigation and postdisaster relief continue to dominate national policy and local expectations, in large part due to the accretion of federal laws promoting such programs and because, as Platt notes, disaster declarations and disaster relief provide the president and Congress with another opportunity (aside from mitigation projects) to distribute federal largesse. Thus, relief is the short-term version of this largesse, project mitigation is the longer-run manifestation, and both streams of money flow to the same hazardous places.

Once a disaster strikes, the immediate interest of local officials and residents is in relief and recovery, not in broader questions of improved mitigation or resilience, despite technical experts' attempts to keep such ideas on the agenda (May 1990; Stallings 1995; Alesch and Petak 1986). This focus on relief and recovery is exacerbated by the dominance of relief in federal policy, which creates few incentives for communities to plan for hazard mitigation and response. And crises do not last long in institutional memory or on the government agenda (Alesch and Petak 1986; Prater and Lindell 2000; Rossi, Wright, and Weber-Burdin 1982). Some communities, and the federal government, have resisted undertaking process mitigation because it is less immediate, less visible, is seen by some as "soft" or "squishy," and is difficult to measure. And many process-oriented mitigation techniques, such as buyouts of hazard-prone land, or more stringent land-use controls, are not undertaken because of fears of "property rights" issues, notwithstanding the constitutionally sound public benefits of such regulation to protect human lives and property. Interest therefore wanes until the next disaster, in which the same relief/recovery cycle repeats. None of this is to suggest that process-oriented mitigation has been entirely ignored. Consider, for example, the National Flood Insurance Program (NFIP), which requires flood-prone communities to adopt building and planning standards before property owners can purchase federally subsidized flood insurance; flood insurance is often required to obtain a mortgage. However, many flood-insurance policies are not actuarially sound, yielding major moral-hazard and adverse-selection problems. While a recent study suggests that 75 percent of flood-insurance policies are actuarially sound, it is highly likely that the other 25 percent constitute the greatest potential for loss, further exacerbating the adverse-selection problem. And if this 75 percent figure is true, this is up only fifteen percentage points since 1994. Finally, some states are more progressive than others in undertaking process-oriented mitigation—California in earthquakes, and North Carolina and Florida in hurricanes, for example—but few states have strong mandates for careful local planning for disasters. Indeed, Burby notes that "fewer than 10% of local governments in the United States have programs to encourage building owners to invest in measures to reduce the risk of damage from natural disasters" (Burby et al. 1999, 252). Furthermore, only about twenty-five states require some sort of municipal planning effort, and fewer than ten require natural-hazards elements in these plans (Burby 2006, 172). Certainly, we cannot say that there are strong mandates or incentives for state governments to engage in the most effective mitigation activities.

The major breakthrough in mitigation policy was the enactment of the Robert T. Stafford Disaster Relief and Emergency Assistance Act of 1988, further strengthened by the Disaster Mitigation Act of 2000 (DMA 2000). The Stafford Act created the Hazard Mitigation Grant Program (HMGP), under which 10 percent of federal disaster relief could be spent on mitigation projects after disasters, if states had prepared mitigation plans under section 409. This section was replaced by a new planning regime under section 322 of the DMA 2000, because there was little relationship between mitigation planning and mitigation projects. Section 322 requires that local and state governments prepare mitigation plans before they are eligible for both HMGP and new predisaster funds. These predisaster funds were never particularly large, nor were postdisaster funds; taken together, the amount of funds spent on disaster relief continues to dwarf efforts at promoting mitigation and resilience.

As HMGP was being implemented, FEMA, under James Lee Witt, a professional emergency manager, created a mitigation directorate to manage the HMGP and to promote mitigation among state and local governments. However, hazard-mitigation funding under the Stafford Act was triggered by an actual disaster, rather than by an appreciation of the hazard. This policy design does not reflect existing scientific and technical consensus that mitigation should occur *before* disasters strike (Burby 1994; Burby and Dalton 1994; Burby, French, and Nelson 1998). Predisaster efforts might well have enhanced community resilience to disaster; while the immediate aftermath of a disaster may be a good time to induce people to pay attention to mitigation, it may be too late, particularly in catastrophic disasters, to promote community resilience after a community, its institutions, and its physical infrastructure has been shattered.

Momentum toward resilience has eroded since 2001 because federal support of mitigation has eroded, in terms of both openness to the idea of mitigation and actual mitigation programs. While many attribute this to FEMA's subordination to "homeland security," the executive branch's indifference or antipathy toward mitigation predates September 11: in early 2001, the FEMA director, Joseph Allbaugh, upbraided Davenport, Iowa, for failing to build a floodwall. Davenport had chosen not to build a floodwall because of aesthetics and because its citizens believed that land-use planning would be a more effective mitigation technique. Indeed, one can argue that Davenport's efforts were sound process-oriented actions that would work to enhance community resilience—actions for which the town was scorned by an agency that should have been promoting effective mitigation and resilience. This incident demonstrates how lessons apparently learned in the 1990s were unlearned in the 2000s, culminating in the rather spectacular failures at all levels in Hurricane Katrina.

Hazards Policies on the National Agenda

To assess the extent to which the national government learns from disasters, particularly through attention to mitigation, we can first consider the influence of these events on Congress's agenda. The measure I use is the substance of ideas discussed by witnesses in congressional hearings; this method is similar to the one employed by Baumgartner and Jones (1993) to assess Congress's agenda, but my unit of analysis is the witness, not the hearing (Birkland 1997). The types of disasters I consider are earthquakes and hurricanes. I assume that a focusing event, such as a disaster, is sometimes a precursor to learning. Thus, learning is more likely if we see substantial attention to hazard mitigation, particularly as related to specific events. Furthermore, it is interesting to compare instances where witnesses before congressional hearings refer specifically to a particular event (i.e., if testimony is event related) versus more generic testimony about the hazard generally.

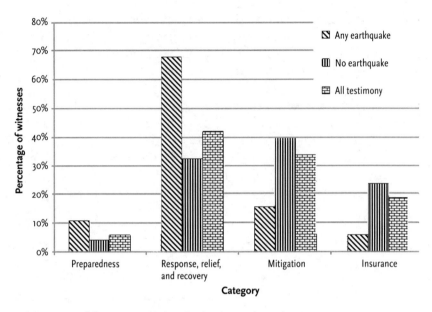

Fig. 6.1. Topics of testimony on earthquakes by topic and agenda status, 1990–2002. *Source:* Birkland 2006, table 4.4, p. 122.

The results of this analysis are shown in figures 6.1 and 6.2. The differences between the attention paid to certain issues in the domains reflect policy-domain differences found in earlier research (Birkland 1997, 2006). In particular, the earthquake domain has a long-standing committed cohort of professionals who actively work to make themselves available to Congress for expert testimony; this is particularly notable when we compare discussions of mitigation, which are usually driven by experts, between the two domains: much greater attention is paid to earthquake mitigation than to hurricane mitigation. The key features of the earthquake domain that lead to greater discussion of mitigation are not evident in the hurricane domain, where Congress is generally more interested in postdisaster relief than in mitigation and where there is no cohesive policy community to press for better policies (Birkland 1997, chap. 4).

Congressional attention, as measured in testimony in hearings, is clearly oriented toward disaster relief and assistance, but in the earthquake case, mitigation is more than twice as likely to be a subject of legislation as it is in hurricane policy. If we include discussions of the National Earthquake Hazards Reduction Act (NEHRA) and its accompanying program, the Na-

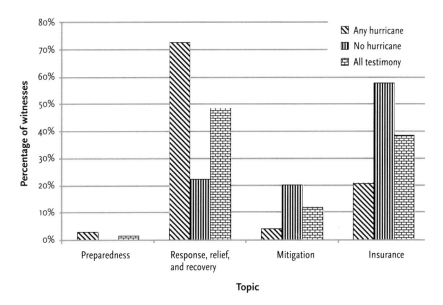

Fig. 6.2. Topics of testimony on hurricanes by topic and agenda status, 1990–2002.

tional Earthquake Hazards Reduction Program (NEHRP), we can say that legislators pay much greater attention to earthquake-hazard mitigation than to hurricane-hazard mitigation. However, we still cannot say that a great deal of attention is paid to mitigation compared with other aspects of earthquakes.

A particularly interesting difference is in the relatively high attention paid to insurance in the hurricane domain compared with earthquake insurance. The problems with creating an insurance regime for earthquakes (which is currently characterized by high premiums and deductibles and low rates of insurance purchases) may be the reason why so much attention has been paid to other forms of earthquake mitigation. By contrast, flood insurance is a popular, federally subsidized program that aids residents of areas prone to inundation from hurricane rains or storm surge, and the existence of flood insurance may have led to less interest in other forms of mitigation.

The NEHRA and NEHRP drive much of the earthquake-mitigation discussion; if a similar program were created focusing on hurricanes, we might well see greater discussion of hurricane mitigation (Birkland 1997). Indeed, the American Association for Wind Engineering (AAWE) and other groups successfully lobbied for passage of the National Windstorm Reduction Act of 2004, a law patterned on the NEHRA and contained as part of the NEHRA's reauthorization (in Title II) (HR 2608, PL 108-360). The real effect of this legislation is yet unclear, although because of much lower levels of funding and the diffuse nature of the risk, it seems that the wind program will not yield the same results as NEHRP.

While there are interesting differences between how Congress addresses earthquakes and how it addresses hurricanes, the key point of this analysis is that *Congress pays much more attention to relief than it does to mitigation or preparedness,* regardless of the type of hazard. While it is true that a major reason for this is that relief is a form of distributive spending, while mitigation and resilience-building efforts are less visible, there is an equally compelling reason why the federal government focuses so much on relief money: constitutionally, this is where it can do the most. Process-oriented mitigation, such as land-use controls and building codes, are primarily state and local functions; while the federal government can support these efforts through funding, it cannot compel action. On the other hand, we would expect, in a rational federal system, for the federal government not to implement policies that undermine local efforts or that largely eliminate local incentives to engage in resilience-building activities.

Thus, we can conclude the federal government did learn from disaster experience during the 1990s and that policy changes reflect this experience. In particular, the Loma Prieta earthquake and Hurricane Andrew "taught" the government—particularly the Clinton administration—that the rapid and generous provision of disaster relief yields political dividends. The government also learned, particularly after the 1993 Midwest floods, that mitigation is an important tool for reducing losses; it didn't directly learn that an incidental effect of appropriate mitigation is to improve community resilience, but in some cases such resilience was enhanced. These lessons were almost entirely unlearned both before and after the September 11 terrorist attacks, particularly when the Bush administration largely abandoned mitigation as an important FEMA function.

Hurricane Policy in Florida and North Carolina

Disasters strike localized areas, not the United States as a whole. It is therefore worthwhile to consider states as the locus of the most important learning from disaster experience and the most important places in which to promote resilience at the regional and local level. In the following discussion, I consider two states—Florida and North Carolina—with reputations for particularly progressive hazard-mitigation policies. Presumably, if there are attempts to promote resilience to be found, they will be found in these states.

Florida

Although Florida is more prone to hurricanes than any other state, its most populated areas had gone years without a severe hurricane until Hurricane Andrew struck in 1992. Hurricane Andrew was a category 5 storm, the eye of which passed about twenty miles south of Miami. Had the storm struck Miami proper, damage and loss of life would likely have been much greater.

Florida was well aware of its hurricane hazard before Hurricane Andrew. Of the five most damaging hurricanes in the United States from 1900 to 1997, three of these storms struck Florida. The recognition of the hazard led to pre-Andrew attempts by the governor and legislature to take steps to be better prepared for hurricanes and to mitigate their damage. Preparedness, response (including evacuation), and recovery appear to have taken a more prominent role in much of this deliberation than did mitigation.

Efforts to coordinate disaster management in Florida began in 1981, when the Florida Department of Community Affairs (DCA) sought to integrate physical and social features of disaster policy into "Comprehensive Emergency Management," or CEM (Mittler 1997). This plan focused more on preparedness than on mitigation. Florida also established several study commissions to examine hurricane policies and make recommendations.

The first annual Governor's Hurricane Conference was held in 1987, after the evacuation of coastal areas in anticipation of Hurricane Elena and at the request of the Florida Emergency Preparedness Association, a group of local emergency managers. To a considerable extent, this conference has become an important learning mechanism; a review of the 2005 conference's agenda reveals a considerable number of workshops devoted to mitigation, including "Building Disaster Resistant Communities," "Promoting Successful Mitigation," and "Mitigation Programs."

The Florida legislature often initiates action rather than waiting for the governor, who is constitutionally weaker than the governors of most other states. In early 1989 (pre-Hurricane Hugo), the speaker of the House created the Speaker's Task Force on Emergency Preparedness. Again, this body was focused more on preparedness and response than on mitigation, although the commission recommended a change to building codes "to require hurricane shutters on multi-unit housing."

Legislation was introduced in 1990, 1991, and 1992 that would have restructured emergency management in Florida, but this legislation was not enacted. In 1990, the chair of the Committee on Emergency Preparedness, Military and Veterans Affairs introduced House Bill No. 3669 to overhaul the emergency management system in Florida (Mittler 1997). Many of these changes were intended to enact the recommendations of the Speaker's Task Force. They included a controversial two dollars per policy assessment on home owners' insurance (four dollars per commercial policy) that would have been deposited into a fund that would improve response, provide for relief after non–federally declared disasters, provide funds to match federal grants, and defray state emergency-management costs. This bill passed in the House but failed in the Senate because senators from North Florida balked at creating a trust fund that appeared solely to benefit South Florida. Similar bills died in 1991 and 1992.

These ideas were resurrected after Hurricane Andrew, particularly in light of both FEMA's and the state's response failures in this storm (Mittler 1997). After Andrew, the governor created the Disaster Planning and Response Review Committee, whose report explicitly acknowledges its formation "to ensure Florida takes advantage of the lessons that can be learned from Hurricane Andrew *to improve emergency preparedness and recovery programs*" (Governor's Disaster Planning and Response Review Committee 1993, 1; emphasis added). This document encapsulated much of what had already been said about emergency management in Florida. The committee, known as the "Lewis Committee," after its chair, former state senate president Philip D. Lewis, made ninety-four specific recommendations intended to improve communications at and among all levels of government; to strengthen plans for evacuation, shelter, and postdisaster response and recovery; to enhance intergovernmental coordination; and to improve training (Governor's Disaster Planning and Response Review Committee 1993, 3). In most contexts, preparedness means de minimus individual preparedness, such as having bottled water, batteries for radios and flashlights, and the like, on hand, as well as instructing citizens how to board up windows. Preparedness also means having the appropriate emergency response assets available; it does not really relate to predisaster capacity and community building. And the key aspects of these efforts were postimpact matters, not preimpact planning or resilience building.

The Florida legislature took up the recommendations contained in the Lewis Committee report, and once again, the House readily passed legislation that implemented much of the committee's legislative agenda, including the two-dollar/four-dollar surcharge on residential and commercial insurance policies, the very issue that was the major sticking point in earlier legislation. Indeed, some northern and central Florida senators continued to balk at the surcharge until "several counties in the central and northern parts of the state were hit by a fierce winter storm on March 13 which convinced Senators in those areas that hurricane threats and emergency management were not just south Florida concerns" (Mittler 1997).

Under the leadership of the Florida Department of Community Affairs and through the Emergency Management, Preparedness, and Assistance Trust Fund (which received policy surcharge funds), the vast majority of the Lewis Committee's recommendations were implemented. In 1995, the DCA recommended that the state should shift priorities to "refocus on mitigation" (Florida Department of Community Affairs 1995, 3; Mittler 1997).

Florida seeks to mitigate hazards through two major programs: the comprehensive planning process and the Florida Building Code. Florida is one of just seven states that require all communities to include hazard elements in their comprehensive plans. The lack of a mandate in other states often means that local governments fail to plan for them, even when the state requires comprehensive plans but does not explicitly specify a hazard element (May 1993; Steinberg and Burby 2002). Florida's mandate is quite strong. Burby describes Florida's planning mandate (in Fla. Stat. 163.3177) as "stringent..., including state review of plans for consistency with state plan" (Burby 2005, 70). Indeed, Florida was well prepared to meet the state and local planning requirements of the Disaster Mitigation Act of 2000.

The second program for mitigating hurricane damage is the Florida Building Code. The code encompasses years of experience with hurricane damage and was for years considered the most stringent in the nation with respect to hurricane hazards. In particular, special provisions for south Florida, contained in the South Florida Building Code (SFBC), made the most hurricane-prone areas of the state subject to the most stringent hurricane building codes in the nation. Still, Hurricane Andrew revealed that a code is only as good as its enforcement (E. J. Baker 1993).

Many interests argued that the more stringent codes added requirements that were unnecessary in some parts of the state, thereby increasing building costs. Even after Hurricane Andrew, builders questioned the need for more stringent codes, particularly in the Panhandle. The insurance industry, on the other hand, cited the huge amounts of damage done by wind and advocated more stringent codes (ISO Properties 2005).

The result of Hurricane Andrew and the politics of building regulation in Florida was ultimately a compromise: the Florida Building Code (FBC). This code incorporated much of the SFBC's provisions for wind resistance. A particular outcome of Hurricane Andrew was new provisions designed to make buildings less prone to damage from wind-driven projectiles; insurance companies were to reduce premiums for buildings so equipped. However, the Panhandle area was excluded from the code; houses in that region need only be built to withstand 120-mile-per-hour winds within one mile of the beach, a much less stringent standard than the rest of the state. Hurricane Ivan, one of three storms that struck Florida in 2004, led to some discussion of improving wind-hazard standards in the Panhandle. The builders' lobby, in particular, continues to believe that there is little difference in damage to buildings built to 2002 building-code standards compared to those that did not comply with the standards (Dunkelberger 2005). In sum, we can say that Hurricane Ivan led to a learning process, in the sense that legislators and others seemed open to taking in new information based on experience gleaned from the 2004 hurricane season. However, there is no evidence of actual instrumental learning because the policy instrument—the building code—has not demonstrably changed.

Did the 2004 hurricane season put post-Andrew changes to the test? While no storm as severe as Andrew has struck the state, it is generally believed that the state and federal officials were well prepared for Hurricane Ivan, that they responded well, and that structures built to more stringent code requirements fared well in the storms that did strike. Indeed, the successful federal response to the 2004 hurricane season may have lulled FEMA into a belief that it could effectively handle Hurricane Katrina, which it manifestly did not do. Ivan demonstrated that no part of Florida was immune from hurricanes. While one might quibble with the FBC's failure to be applied to all of the state, the land-use planning and the high-velocity wind requirements in the one-mile zone did reduce damage and injuries over what would likely have occurred in the absence of these provisions.

In the end, Hurricane Andrew accomplished two things. It revealed the shortcomings in the enforcement of building codes, and it revealed problems with interagency coordination, preparedness, and response. Early indications are that responses to the 2004 storms were much improved over the experience of Hurricane Andrew. It seems unlikely that improved emergency management and mitigation would have been adopted in the absence of Hurricane Andrew. This hurricane led to instrumental policy learning about the substance and enforcement of building codes. It also led to some political learning in that it provided proponents of mitigation with object lessons in hurricane mitigation, or the results of a lack of it, that could be used to promote better hurricane mitigation. And there was some clear social policy learning: Hurricane Andrew taught residents that hurricanes were not freak instances or random acts of nature; Floridians learned that humans and their institutions made decisions that had an important influence on whether a community did or did not suffer substantial damage from hurricanes.

North Carolina

North Carolina's hurricane-mitigation policy is the result of accumulated disaster experience, both in North Carolina and other states; the high costs of one major event; and a reasonably strong commitment to land-use planning and hazard-mitigation activities. The first key milestone in the hurricane-hazard history of North Carolina was the establishment of the Mitigation Directorate in FEMA in 1994, which led to some states emulating FEMA's efforts. North Carolina in particular was an early and relatively enthusiastic adopter of mitigation principles and techniques, but this adoption awaited a catalytic event. Thus, the second of these milestones was Hurricane Fran in 1996, a category 3 storm, with winds of about 115 mph, that caused at least four billion dollars in damage (Whitlock and Williams 1996). This disaster illustrates how even moderately large storms can do substantial damage as coastal areas grow much faster than inland areas, thereby exposing far more people and property to wind, flood, and storm surges. Fran led Governor Jim Hunt to create, in October 1996, the North Carolina Disaster Recovery Task Force, which in the remarkably short period of 127 days issued eighty-four recommendations drafted by seven subcommittees (or "action teams" in the task force's parlance). In a post on an undated Web site, the North Carolina Division of Emergency Management noted that "38 [of the recommendations] are completed, 44 are progressing, and 2 are delayed."[1]

Perhaps the most important policy outcome from a mitigation perspective is the creation of the Mitigation Section in the North Carolina Department of Emergency Management. This commitment to mitigation has been considerably strengthened by legislation enacted in June 2001, popularly called Senate Bill 300. The bill amended North Carolina's emergency-management law to closely parallel federal law; it created a new section, North Carolina General Statutes (NCGS) 166A-6A, under subsections (b)(1)(3), which requires local communities to adopt hazard-mitigation plans to receive state aid, and (b)(1)(4), which requires communities to participate in the National Flood Insurance Program (NFIP) to receive state flood aid. Bill 300 goes far beyond the sort of mitigation planning that was likely associated with, but not directly a goal of, other state environmental and land-use policies. In particular, the Coastal Area Management Act of 1974, as amended, requires each of twenty coastal counties to prepare land-use plans that are consistent with planning goals established by the state of North Carolina.

A third event that occurred between Hurricane Fran and the passage of Senate Bill 300 was Hurricane Floyd (landfall on September 16, 1999), a category 2 storm that became North Carolina's costliest natural disaster because of the extensive flooding it caused. As much as fifteen to twenty inches of rain fell in some places. The Tar and Neuse rivers and their tributaries and creeks flooded, and communities were inundated, with billions of dollars in damage. Inland and estuarine waters were contaminated when the leveelike walls around waste lagoons at hog farms broke or were overtopped, washing waste into rivers, estuaries, and ultimately Pamlico Sound, leading to considerable fears that massive environmental damage would ensue.

Much as the 1933 Long Beach earthquake triggered policy change in California, Floyd triggered much action in North Carolina. The sheer number of hog farms involved—at least forty-six waste lagoons or pits were breached—plus the growing number of such farms in floodplains, led to considerable concern among local residents and environmental officials, particularly because hog farms are "permitted as non-discharge facilities under the assumption that all waste is contained on site" (Wing, Freedman, and Band 2002, 347). The result was a buyout of some hog farms in the one-hundred-year floodplain. North Carolina is among the nation's leaders in using hazard-mitigation funds to purchase flood-prone properties to allow the floodplain to work naturally (Regulatory Intelligence Data 1999). By late 2001, only fourteen of fifty hog farms in the one-hundred-year floodplain had been bought out. After this slow start, the program gained momentum: by 2006, well over one hundred unused hog-waste lagoons had been closed, and the largest corporate hog farmer in the state had agreed to fund additional cleanup and mitigation efforts (News and Observer 2007).

Remarkably, Hurricane Floyd did not lead to what may have been the most obvious policy outcome of this storm: more stringent construction standards in floodplains, for both agricultural and residential construction. Such regulation might have reduced the amount of developed property (a feature of process mitigation), thereby lowering disaster impacts and increasing local resilience. Ultimately, the legislature rejected a requirement that the lowest dwelling floor of a house be built to two feet above the water level expected in a one-hundred-year flood, higher than the less stringent National Flood Insurance Program standard of one foot. That said, the existence of a particular elevation standard might be less important than individual property owners' experiences with flooding and their perceptions of the steps necessary to protect their property (Work, Rodgers, and Osborne 1999). When residents have direct experience with flooding, they will be more likely to take whatever mitigation steps they deem necessary, including building the structure to a higher level above the expected floodplain than required under local or state laws. Indeed, this sort of self-initiated reaction to disaster experience, which improves on minimum standards for mitigation, may be an indicator of resilience and capacity in the face of potential hazards and actual disasters.

In North Carolina, there is evidence of instrumental policy learning, but such learning is more a product of the accumulation of experience in North Carolina and in other states than it is a result of any one individual event, even as Floyd was very important. This is not to say that events do not matter in North Carolina. Rather, no event dominates the policy history of the state the way Hurricane Andrew dominates Florida's hurricane history (and, presumably, as Katrina will dominate Louisiana's and Mississippi's policy making).

Florida also shows considerable evidence of instrumental policy learning. Much of this is associated with one event: Hurricane Andrew. This event also enhanced social policy learning by helping people understand the cause of Andrew's widespread damage: the lax enforcement of building codes and the general low level of preparedness. The resulting damage gave proponents of policy change considerable ammunition to argue in favor of substantive policy change. It is also important to note that, as progressive as North Carolina has become, resilience has not been a central feature of policy change, in large part because one particular form of hurricane damage was the highly visible hog-lagoon problem, which was centered in rural areas and which therefore did not invoke urban areas. Meanwhile, cities like Kinston did make efforts to improve mitigation through buyouts of flood-prone properties, while Princeville, a town founded by African Americans, has not relocated out of the floodplain due to long-standing emotional and cultural ties to the land. In such instances, it is difficult to build resilience in the face of other community goals.

Prospects for Resilience

One of the most difficult aspects of policy design is the choice of the "tools" that government will use to induce desired behaviors (Salamon and Lund 1989). These behaviors are induced in the target populations, be they governments, individuals, or nongovernmental organizations such as businesses or charities. There are several important features to keep in mind in national disaster policy over the past sixty years.

First, national policy in the United States does not and cannot mandate that particular mitigation or preparedness actions take place (Burby and May 1996; May 1993, 1994, 1995; May and Birkland 1994). Rather, national policy can provide some inducements to state and local governments to take actions that would promote disaster preparedness, response, recovery, and especially mitigation in such a way as to promote resilience. There are also few if any guarantees in policy making that any particular policy will be implemented unless there is broad agreement among all parties that the policy should be implemented in a particular way (Goggin et al. 1990). And such agreement is not likely to be forthcoming when other, more visible, and more politically popular policies undermine whatever incentives exist to promote mitigation and resilience.

Second, federal disaster policy is generally piecemeal and does not consider disaster resilience as a major organizing principle. In fact, federal policies undermine resilience-building efforts. Thus, in the Florida and North Carolina case studies, we find that most initiatives to improve mitigation policies (and perhaps incidentally increase resilience) are taken at the state level, often as the result of disaster experience, not at the instigation or the encouragement of the federal government. Other states remain, of course, saddled both with poor state and local planning and with poor federal policy and unsure coordination and response, as was so clearly illustrated in Hurricane Katrina.

Third, disaster policy at all levels of government is remarkably political, in the sense that it represents some sort of vision of the allocation of resources. Starting in the 1990s, decisions on whether to grant disaster relief were apparently driven as much by political concerns as by some objective sense of "need" or "deservedness" (Platt 1999). The Clinton administration, learning from the debacle that was the federal response to Hurricane Andrew, began much more generous grants of relief to communities struck by a "disaster," often with much less regard for whether and to what extent the community had a demonstrable *need* for such assistance. Communities were entirely willing to accept such generous aid. An attempt was made with the 1993 Stafford Act amendments and with the Disaster Management Act of 2000 to encourage greater community mitigation planning, with mitigation funding as an incentive. However, because the program calculated mitigation funding as a fraction of aid granted in a recent disaster, the program required that a disaster take place first; even then, mitigation funding at its peak was no more than 15 percent of the funds spent on disaster relief. Other efforts, such as Project Impact, were cut by the Bush administration, to the point at which federal material *and* rhetorical support for disaster mitigation is even less evident and less effective than it was before Bush took office. Indeed, Project Impact can be viewed as one of the few federal efforts to promote resilience through community capacity building. Project Impact "is based on three simple principles: Preventive actions must be decided at the local level and must be responsive to local hazards; private sector participation is vital; [and] long-term efforts and investments in prevention are essential" (Freitag 2001). These principles were intended to be applied at the local level, not imposed at the national level. At the 2001 Natural Hazards Workshop at the University of Colorado, then–FEMA general counsel Michael Brown defended the elimination of this program, saying that the administration was more interested in programs with demonstrable benefits, rather than funding Cub Scouts and other civic organizations. Clearly, there was little evidence available about the effectiveness, or lack thereof, of Project Impact, given its brief existence, but it is also clear that the administration had little evidence that the costs of the program were so great that it should be cut, and there was emerging evidence that the program was doing some good in building community capacity to address hazards (J. Johnson 1998).

Fourth, state and local policies—and their implementation—are functions of prevailing local conditions, community wealth, experience with disasters, and many other factors that are not amenable to a single set of policy tools or solutions. Communities prepare for disasters with significantly different resources, objective risks, risk perceptions, and hazard profiles (Cutter and Emrich 2006). Because of these differences, federal policy influences state and local disaster policy, but it is not sufficiently prescriptive or coercive as to enforce resilience-promoting policies, such as improved land-use policy backed with real enforcement and a clear commitment to *not* reward risky behavior (Burby 2006). These local features would attenuate some of the effectiveness of these policies even if the federal government were to be more attentive to resilience, in large part because it is unlikely that resilience will replace disaster relief as the focus of federal efforts.

This is particularly true in the new homeland security world in which we live. Prospects for building resilience are quite poor due to the reemergence of top-down, command-and-control techniques for emergency planning and management; such top-down efforts have been a demonstrable failure in hazard mitigation and resilience promotion (Cutter and Emrich 2006) and will likely also fail in a homeland security framework (Scavo, Kearney, and Kilroy 2006).

In the end, some communities may become more resilient than others in spite of, rather than because of, national and state efforts. Because of long-standing political and constitutional biases against the federal government "interfering" in local government decision making, it is unlikely that the federal government will initiate prescriptive policies beyond those existing in federal law. And those prescriptions are focused on mitigation—the planning requirements of DMA 2000, for example—not on changing disaster relief policies so that the proper incentives are provided to people and communities to take risk-reducing actions. Since the federal government is unlikely to take the lead, we will have to look to state and local governments in the United States if we are to promote resilience. This is perhaps less efficient than a wider, all-hazards, national approach, but it is perhaps the only realistic approach, given the federal system of government, the constitutional order, and the political incentives embedded in the system.

.

7 DESIGNING RESILIENCE

LEADERSHIP CHALLENGES IN COMPLEX ADMINISTRATIVE SYSTEMS

Arjen Boin

Catastrophes and the Inherent Limitations of Crisis Management

It is widely perceived, in both academic and practitioner circles, that large-scale systems have become increasingly vulnerable to catastrophic break-downs (Clarke 1999; Rosenthal, Boin, and Comfort 2001b; Quarantelli, Lagadec, and Boin 2006; Perrow 2007). New threats with destructive po-tential—think of climate change, technological revolutions, and evolving forms of terrorism—have emerged on the horizon (OECD 2003; Clarke 2006; Flynn 2007). As critical infrastructure systems have become in-creasingly complex and integrated, relatively small disturbances can rap-idly escalate into compound crises (Turner 1978; Perrow 1984). In addition, modern societies face *transboundary threats and crises,* which play out at large scales and across traditional policy boundaries.

Crisis management—especially early warnings and effective interven-tions—is thus perceived to be of the utmost importance. Societies must be prepared to deal with the impact of transboundary crises and disasters. In-adequate crisis management processes and structures can have enormous consequences.

The response to Hurricane Katrina underscores the importance of cri-sis management. In the wake of Katrina, emergency services did not reach all victims in time, the New Orleans city administration could not take care of its surviving population, police forces lost control over the city, state as-sistance did not materialize in time, the Federal Emergency Management

Agency (FEMA) sat on its hands, and President George W. Bush appeared slow to step in and assume command. The response system, in other words, broke down. As a result, people suffered and lost trust in their government.

Hurricane Katrina exposed a deep truth about the inherent limitations of crisis management in case of catastrophes. This tragic episode, along with the Sumatran earthquake and tsunami in 2004, demonstrated that disaster plans are easily rendered irrelevant by a catastrophe (Clarke 1999); that traditional top-down, command-and-control systems do not work in these situations; and that leaders often fail to understand the dynamics of crisis. Hurricane Katrina serves as a reminder of the many unforeseen and impossible challenges that large-scale crises pose to the response system and the political-administrative elites who govern it.

Catastrophes also pose an intriguing challenge to the research community. If we accept, as many crisis and disaster scholars seem to do, that prevention and planning strategies cannot fully protect modern society from each and every catastrophe, society must be better prepared to respond to, deal with, and recover from these damaging events (Wildavsky 1988; Longstaff 2005). It must, in other words, build resilient response systems.

The big question, then, is whether and how resilience can be engineered into the response systems of large-scale entities such as the United States and the European Union. This chapter contemplates both questions. In doing so, it draws from a variety of sources, including disaster and crisis research, public administration, political science, sociology, psychology, and organization theory.

The aim of this chapter is to see if the "laws" that are thought to govern crisis dynamics can give rise to useful prescriptions for the future (re)designers of public response systems who seek to make their societies more resilient in the face of impending catastrophes. It begins by sketching the state of the art when it comes to understanding government responses to catastrophes. It then outlines the challenges that catastrophes pose to public leaders and sketches the contours of a resilient response system, identifying policy and administrative tools that are feasible and effective.

Defining Adversity

Before we consider the state of preparedness of modern societies, we should clarify what exactly societies should prepare for (after all, societies face very different types of threats). It is helpful in this respect to distinguish among routine, nonroutine, and catastrophic forms of adversity. An *emergency* is a serious yet fairly routine event: it is a complex and urgent problem, but emergency services are usually trained to deal with such events. The details of the situation may be new to them, but emergency workers should have a good idea what should be done and how it should be accomplished. Examples include the sinking of a passenger boat in the Adirondacks and the explosion of a bus during the evacuation preceding Hurricane Rita. These events are a tragedy for those involved. But emergencies are bound in place, have no ripple effects, and are rapidly brought to closure.

A *crisis* poses more complex challenges as it entails a threat to the core values of a system or the functioning of life-sustaining systems, which must be urgently dealt with under conditions of deep uncertainty (Rosenthal, Boin, and Comfort 2001b). As causes and consequences of the threat are unknown, the situation is much harder to manage. Planning and preparation will be only marginally helpful, because the emerging situation was never envisioned. Sometimes crises are contained (the Cuban Missile Crisis serves as a textbook example); in other cases they result in large-scale damage and casualties (Katrina exemplifies this outcome).

In colloquial speech, the terms *crisis* and *disaster* are often used interchangeably. In academic debates, both terms generate ongoing discussions, which we will not repeat here (see Rosenthal, Charles, and t'Hart 1989; Quarantelli 1998; Quarantelli and Perry 2005). For the purposes of this chapter, a disaster is defined as a "crisis with a bad ending" (Boin 2005).

Some disasters are clearly in a league of their own: we refer to these in terms of *catastrophes*. The difference between a disaster and a catastrophe is, of course, merely semantic. The perception of "how bad is bad" is affected by cultural dispositions (what is merely an accident in one country may be perceived as catastrophic in others). Yet it is important to distinguish between the two for analytical reasons. A catastrophe is marked by (1) unprecedented damage (in terms of both finances and lives lost) and (2) a prolonged breakdown of life-sustaining functions in a social system.

Catastrophes are "low-chance, high-impact" events. Some agents of catastrophe—think of asteroids and supervolcanoes—are unlikely to materialize in our life spans, but their occurrence can never be ruled out (Clarke 2006). While improbable, Black Swans or "long-tail" events such as the Asian tsunami or the 9/11 attacks can occur on any given day (Taleb 2007).

Everybody has seen pictures of what catastrophes can do to society, yet the consequences often remain unimaginable—especially in modern societies that have successfully minimized the number of crises and disasters (Clarke 2006). It is hard to imagine what happens—or fails to happen—when nothing works. When a catastrophe paralyzes critical systems (emergency services, electricity, communications, transport) for sustained periods of time, modern society rapidly unravels. And when nothing works, it is hard to get anything working again (the functioning of one critical system often being dependent on the functioning of others).

It takes surprisingly little to cause a complete breakdown in societies with complex and tightly coupled infrastructures (Perrow 1984). When the relatively weak Hurricane Gustav hit Louisiana's state capital, Baton Rouge, in September 2008, it took out the electricity network. The city and its residents remained without power for nearly two weeks. Traffic lights, stores, hospitals, gas stations, schools, cable, Internet, and telephone—nothing worked. The resulting chaos (jammed roads and strained emergency services) made it very hard for crews to fix the power lines. While the storm itself caused very few deaths, its paralyzing effect resulted in a huge bill (totaling hundreds of millions of dollars in damage).

The prospect of societal paralysis should prompt societies to prevent such events from happening in the first place. Societies can and do try to prevent *known* catastrophes—those that have happened before—from happening again. For instance, the Dutch have built an elaborate defense system against the catastrophic potential of the North Sea. Protecting cockpits with steel doors may prevent certain terrorist acts with catastrophic potential. The prohibition of certain gases may prevent sudden and destructive climate shifts.

It is clear that societies cannot prevent *all* catastrophes from happening.[1] Not all terrorists can be stopped. Earthquakes, hurricanes, asteroids, and tsunamis cannot be controlled through human intervention. And while societies can prevent (or minimize) damage from known catastrophic agents (e.g., by building earthquake-resistant buildings), new or unforeseen catastrophes will periodically occur—they cannot be categorically denied. Prevention efforts do not come with a warranty.

If a society may experience a catastrophe at any given time—even if the chances are extremely low—it had better be prepared to deal with the consequences. Preparation then becomes a crucial objective. This becomes especially urgent in societies that depend on modern technologies and infrastructures. Most critical infrastructures appear extremely vulnerable to the effects of natural and man-made catastrophes, an observation that gives rise to the so-called vulnerability paradox: modern societies have become increasingly dependent on critical infrastructures that are likely to fail when we need them most.

Modern societies appear ill prepared for catastrophes. While it is true that "crisis awareness" has risen dramatically since the 9/11 events, and the attacks in Madrid and London, this rude awakening has fed a preoccupation with prevention rather than preparation.[2] Hurricane Katrina demonstrated the importance of preparation and the consequences of its absence. It has been widely observed that Katrina was a "routine catastrophe": foreseeable and preventable. In hindsight, this always seems to be the case. But that misses another, crucial point: even when societies do prepare for the worst, their disaster plans often do not work when a disaster materializes (Clarke 1999). We can only wonder how modern societies will deal with unforeseen catastrophes.

A Leadership Perspective

To prepare a society for the worst is an executive task, a task for public leadership (Boin et al. 2005). It is not easy. The nature of catastrophic events poses a complex set of administrative and political challenges. A close consideration of these challenges makes it clear that there are limitations to what we can expect from public leaders.

In the wake of crisis and disaster, public leaders must make sense of rapidly escalating events, coordinate the response effort, explain to society "what is going on," and restore a sense of order. These challenges are hard enough to meet during a crisis, but they become impossible in the wake of a catastrophe. Leaders quickly find themselves in a Catch-22 situation: they cannot make things happen (as everything has broken down), but everybody looks to them to make things happen.

Moreover, they experience fierce constraints in their attempts to manage the response efforts (Rosenthal, Charles, and t'Hart 1989). Reliable information about the situation or the state of the response network is often unavailable. There are no facts, just stories. Continuing uncertainty feeds the rumor cycle, which in turn deepens uncertainty (Shibutani 1966). The result is undermined trust in governmental capacities to deal with the catastrophe.

Communication becomes impossible when the telecommunications infrastructure is affected (which often happens in the case of natural disasters). Public leaders and their inner circles are likely to experience increased stress levels, which may impair their capacity to make judgments and assess the situation. As a result, a "disconnect" may arise between leaders and citizens. Such disconnects tend to feed on themselves: when Mayor Ray Nagin described New Orleans as a living hell, people started behaving as if they lived in one (arming themselves and barricading themselves in makeshift forts).

The ever-present media feeds these cycles of misperception and overreaction. Somehow they are always ahead of everybody else. They seek official reactions to reports that are often new to leaders, who then treat the media like they are part of the problem. Yet media will report, whether officials speak to them or not. When leaders fail to react, or do so in incoherent ways, they further undermine the legitimacy of their office (already tarnished by the catastrophe).

In short, a catastrophe presents public leaders with a set of "impossible" challenges that they must circumvent in their effort to save lives and minimize damages. It would therefore be unrealistic and perhaps unfair to expect public leaders to effectively "manage" the response to a catastrophe. While all eyes turn to a stricken society's public leaders, the quality of the response may well hinge on another factor. In the immediate aftermath of a catastrophe, the first hours and days, an effective response critically depends on the *resilience* of citizens, first-line responders, and operational commanders.

An effective response system in the face of a catastrophic event is marked by societal resilience, which is facilitated and complemented by long-term design efforts at the public-leadership level. In the immediate wake of a disaster, such a system demonstrates a high level of improvisation, flexibility, and mutual assistance among survivors, first responders, and volunteers. It functions effectively in the absence of formalized leadership structures, detailed planning, and precise protocols. It muddles through on the expectation that outside assistance will arrive in due course, but not necessarily soon.

In such a response system, public leaders make their mark in the long run (days, weeks, or even months after the catastrophe). In the short run, public leaders who seek to play an effective role in the response to a catastrophe begin by *avoiding* a number of often-observed pathologies and concentrate on a very limited set of tasks. Avoidable short-term pathologies that can be derived from the literature include (Quarantelli 1988; Rosenthal, Charles, and t'Hart 1989; Rosenthal, Boin, and Comfort 2001b; Rodriguez, Quarantelli, and Dynes 2006):

- *Clinging to the plan.* There is abundant evidence that disaster plans provide limited guidance at best during unforeseen and unique events. While the planning process is highly valuable, its output (the plan) is less important. Improvisation on the part of first responders is necessary and should be expected. Leaders should refrain from intervening just because the plan suggests different courses of action.
- *Waiting for all facts and figures before making critical decisions.* While it is good practice to make decisions by taking into account all available

information, it should not be the sole guiding principle in the immediate aftermath of a catastrophe. In the first hours and days, it is extremely hard to get all the right information or even to verify all available information.

- *Getting fixated on restoring communication means.* In the wake of disaster, modern technologies such as telephones, television, and Internet often fail due to a lack of power (radio being the exception). Public leaders may be tempted to spend their energy on restoring means of communication to facilitate their search for accurate information (see previous point). This is a frustrating and time-consuming effort that usually proves to be in vain.

- *Acting as if the command-and-control structure still stands.* Plans suggest a clear line of authority, and exercises demonstrate how useful a chain of command is to impose a sense of order in a chaotic situation. Alas, the reality of crisis is different. Neat boxes on the organizational chart rarely match the demands of a crisis situation. Even if they do, leaders find to their dismay that lines of communication, the need for flexibility, and high levels of stress can easily thwart rationally sound lines of command.

- *Waiting for outside help.* Catastrophes create large-scale damage, tax remaining resources, and generally give rise to outside assistance. In view of the devastation and shortage of resources, leaders may be tempted to wait for outside help to arrive. The arrival of this assistance will take time. While it may be hard to accept, leaders will have to do without during the immediate and crucial stages of disaster recovery.

- *Disseminating unverified rumors.* In their eagerness to inform the stricken populace, leaders often share the information they have available to them. With the benefit of hindsight, we can safely predict that much of the initial information available to crisis leaders will prove to be incorrect. By relaying incoming information quickly and without firm, independent information (which usually is unobtainable), leaders run the risk of propagating rumors, which typically come back to haunt them during the later stages of the disaster.

- *Initiating the "blame game."* Crises and disasters become politicized quickly, even in the earliest stages (t'Hart 1993; Boin, t'Hart, and McConnell 2008). The performance of public leaders is subject to intense scrutiny from politicians, media pundits, survivors, and business leaders. The advent of Internet media has facilitated rapid and intensely personal approaches. Astute leaders understand they have to be assertive in the process by which the catastrophe and the response to it are framed. Initiating a blame game, however, tends to create dynamics that easily spin out of control. Finger-pointing typically backfires in the aftermath of a crisis. More important, the blame game tends to have perverse impacts on the effectiveness of interorganizational networks, as it quickly erodes trust.

- *Berating the public.* In their efforts to explain why (so many) people died, leaders may correctly point out to what extent citizens are responsible for their own fate. It is galling to learn that people died unnecessarily, as they ignored clear warnings and behavioral clues. It does not help anyone, however, to make this point all too clearly or loudly. Factually correct observations ("they should have evacuated") can easily be interpreted or framed as evidence of insensitivity to the plight of victims, which can seriously undermine leadership legitimacy in the long run.

- *Treating the media as an enemy.* The media play a key role during and after crises and disasters. Reporters are quick and effective in framing the response to a crisis. Public leaders tend to be very sensitive to these frames, especially if they cast leaders in a negative light. A natural reaction, then, is to shun negative reporters or provide privileged access to favorable reporters. This type of selective outreach initiates and feeds a vicious cycle. Media reporters need to fill screen time and newspaper pages, much more time and space than they usually have available. To provide them with a motive and an opportunity to concentrate on nonresponsive leadership behavior helps to create an image that does not benefit the response.

Key Steps in the First Phase

To be sure, most leaders do not sit on their hands during a catastrophe in order to avoid errors. While the research on crisis and disaster management explains how easy it is to make errors that have serious and sometimes long-term consequences, that same research documents a few constructive activities that public leaders can perform in the wake of a catastrophe. The most important of these activities are:

- *Support and facilitate emerging nodes of coordination.* Emergency services and citizens tend to evolve informal nodes in which information streams come together and actors mutually adjust their response activities. Crisis leaders can try to identify and support these emerging nodes. That is not always easy, because they tend to develop in ways and places typically unforeseen in the disaster planning phase. But the payoff is immediate and substantial: leaders do not have to reinvent the wheel, micromanage, or resort to irrelevant plans. They can strengthen and support what works on the ground.

- *Organize outside forces.* It is hard if not impossible (and usually counter-productive) to try to lead the local response effort from afar. Public leaders can spend their time more effectively by making inventories of what local response networks need (see previous point) and coordinate outside assistance to the catastrophe area. This aid is typically provided by the military, nongovernmental organizations, private businesses, or international actors. Many logistical barriers arise, which need to be resolved by local authorities. Public leadership can make an immediate impact by addressing these barriers.
- *Provide a rationale for the crisis.* A crisis shatters our understanding and expectations of how the world works. In such circumstances, citizens tend to look to their leaders for reassurance and guidance. Leaders are thus in a unique position to explain what is going on, how it came about, and where it is leading society. Leaders can provide a "frame" that anchors the thinking and actions of people on the ground, who are literally lost in the crisis. The narrative does not have to be "true"; it should be convincing and effective in providing a sense of hope.
- *Initiate long-term reconstruction.* While public leaders cannot do much to provide immediate relief on the ground after a catastrophe strikes, they can do much more when it comes to the long-term recovery and reconstruction of the stricken region. This process of recovery will have to begin initially after the immediate phase ends (typically within weeks). The challenge is to connect restoration with prevention of future disasters. In the immediate aftermath of a disaster, public leaders can exploit the shared sense of disbelief and indignation to push for preventive measures that in normal times would be considered politically infeasible or unnecessary.

Resilience as the First Line of Defense

This brief assessment of crisis-leadership challenges and capacities should temper any expectations that public executives and their organizations will bail out victims of a catastrophe immediately after a disaster hits. In the short term, there really is not much that public leaders can do to alleviate suffering imposed by a catastrophe. Effective leaders make their mark in the long run.

The quality of the first response will therefore critically depend on the *resilience* of a society. As the chapters in this book point out, societal resilience depends on the flexibility, improvisation, generosity, and stamina of the stricken population and the first responders (the distinction between these groups is rather superficial in those first hours and days after a catastrophe). During the first hours and days, people have only each other. The first organized assistance will be of local origin, but it will be improvised and less than perfect. It will take time before outside help arrives. The societal fabric of a population thus is a crucial variable.

The critical importance of resilience does not absolve political leaders of their responsibilities. In fact, it just adds an often overlooked task: *to nurture resilience before a crisis occurs*. In the next section, we further explore resilience as the subject of leadership attention and institutional design (cf. Goodin 1996; Weick and Sutcliffe 2001).

Engineering Resilience

In this chapter, resilience is defined in bare terms as the ability to "bounce back" after suffering a damaging blow (cf. Wildavsky 1988). A resilient system or society manages to rapidly recombine available tools and resources in a flexible and often creative way, which enables the system to recover and reconstruct in the wake of a severe, life-threatening type of disturbance. A textbook case is found in the story of *Apollo 13* (immortalized in the blockbuster movie): after a near-fatal explosion in space deprived the ship of crucial life-sustaining functions, the crew managed to use its remaining parts to make up for the lost functions, which allowed for a safe return to earth.

Some organizations and societies appear more resilient than others. So-called high-reliability organizations (HROs), for instance, are defined by their capacity to respond rapidly and flexibly to impending threats (LaPorte 1996; Roe and Schulman 2008). At the societal level, the 2005 bombings in London prompted a remarkable degree of resilience on the part of the city's population (see David Alexander's chapter in this volume). The level of resilience of the New Orleans population and government, in contrast, seemed remarkably low. These are merely impressions, of course, as a precise measure of resilience is not available.

Resilience may be a fairly normal characteristic of self-sustained units of social organization. Not so long ago, for instance, small communities were more or less resilient by necessity.[3] A small community could only survive environmental hardships and deal with periodic setbacks if it exploited the tight social bonds between its members. This example suggests that modernization tends to undercut resilience: when interstates connected small communities across the United States in the 1950s, the need for self-sufficiency disappeared. The financial-economic crisis of 2008–9 revealed how individual countries that had risen on the waves of globalization found themselves with a very limited arsenal of means to "bounce back" quickly.

In a more general sense, tight coupling leads to functional division, which in turn undermines societal resilience. Modernization replaces old-fashioned resilience with the promise of rapid, "just in time" support in times of need. While this modern way of dealing with adversity promises to be more efficient, the proof is in the practice.

We thus arrive at two key (if exploratory) propositions. First, public leaders are responsible for creating the conditions under which resilience is likely to emerge. Second, resilience may be best viewed as an "emerging property" of a "healthy" system (Longstaff 2005). When viewed in conjunction, these propositions sketch a rather imposing task definition for leaders. A primary precondition for resilience is a well-filled societal reservoir of trust in institutions (such as political parties, local government, the president, the media, the judiciary, etc.). In times of adversity, trust facilitates communication, self-organization, mutual coordination, and altruistic behavior. This would mean that in order to build resilient systems, leaders have to build societal institutions that nurture mutual trust. While few will disagree with this ambition, it begs the question of what can be reasonably expected from public leaders.

Fortunately, public leaders have a few strategies at their disposal that are a bit more concrete and feasible. Leaders who seek to improve the level of societal resilience that will help people face the effects of a catastrophe can try to make sure that:

- *Basic response mechanisms are in place.* These mechanisms should work in more or less autonomous fashion: warning, mobilization, registration, evacuation, sheltering, emergency medical care and aftercare, search and rescue, protection of property, information dissemination. These functions are amenable to planning, training, and proper resourcing. They thus fall within the domain of achievable tasks.
- *Potential responders are trained to act independently.* First responders must feel capable to operate "in the dark" and perform the task for which they have trained and seize the initiative. Leaders should instill them (and the organizations to which they belong) with a set of core values and related priorities, which can guide them in their decisions and actions.
- *All potential crisis actors exercise on a regular basis.* Joint exercises build mutual trust and understanding and create awareness with regard to

each other's capacities. During a crisis, responders must know whom they can call and with whom they should try to work. Exercises nurture personal relations that will be a great resource for improvisation and collaboration during a disaster. Leaders should participate in a visible and energizing way.

- *Planning is a continuous and joint activity that is valued for the process (not the outcome).* Joint planning is an intellectual effort to toy with potential problems and possible solutions. In an ever-changing world, there should be no closure to such activities. That's why planning should be continuous; it should not be "closed" by producing a plan (that nobody will use).
- *Mobile information-gathering units are in place.* We know that leaders always find it hard to get an accurate picture of the situation during a crisis. They can preempt this crucial pathology by creating mobile units that are trained to gather information, will produce situation reports, and are equipped to communicate this information. Much can be learned from the media and from such organizations as the U.S. Marine Corps and the U.S. Coast Guard.
- *Administrative capacity exists to organize long-term reconstruction efforts.* Crisis management and reconstruction management are distinctly different activities (as became evident during the years after Hurricane Katrina). A catastrophe will by definition require a long-term reconstruction effort. It is worthwhile to contemplate beforehand which part of the administration should be prepared to coordinate such an effort.

All this is not meant to suggest that public leaders—once resilience is organized—can sit back and leave the work to first responders. They should, of course, prepare for their own role in catastrophe response. They should particularly work on the proven weaknesses of leadership under pressure (Boin et al. 2005):

- *Situational assessment.* Establishing what is left and what still works, understanding what is impossible and what can be done to recombine available capacities.
- *Working with the media.* Leaders must learn to understand how the media works, what it needs, and what leaders should and should not do. They must learn to monitor media without getting absorbed by it.
- *Creating and nurturing expert networks.* Every catastrophe will require some sort of expertise to inform critical decision making. If leaders wait until a crisis materializes, they depend on the availability of

experts. At that time, it is impossible to scrutinize the background and qualities of experts. All this can and should be done beforehand.

- *Identifying capable partners.* The management of catastrophes requires improvisation and flexibility, not only with regard to activities but also with regard to actors. As key organizations may be paralyzed, replacements may become necessary. Leaders should scan the public and private domains for potential partners, mapping capacities, locations, contact persons, and so on.

Circumventing Constraints in the Quest toward Resilience

The approach toward preparation for catastrophic events as laid out above may seem fairly straightforward, but in practice most societies appear woefully and perhaps irresponsibly unprepared to restore critical infrastructures after a breakdown. Public leaders who seek to remedy this situation will encounter four ubiquitous constraints:

- *A top-down orientation.* Most response systems are not designed—and have not evolved the ability—to shift decision-making authority rapidly and flexibly. There are formal procedures, but these are typically designed to shift authority *upward.* A rapid redivision of labor in accordance with situational imperatives tends to create political tensions and administrative paralysis. The design of a resilient system will require a rethinking of traditional response patterns.
- *A persistent need for top-down leadership.* During crises, leaders are expected to lead. This ancient principle still dominates crisis-management preparations in both Europe and the United States. Preparations are not complete without a plan that guarantees the working of a command-and-control model. Reassuring as they may be, such preparations are effectively useless. To invest in resilience—with its emphasis on self-reliance and improvisation—is a hard sell for politicians. The design of a resilient system will require a cultural shift.
- *The institutional vulnerability of modern cities.* The modern mega-city houses the most vulnerable populations: the poor, the homeless, criminals, the mentally ill, addicts, the sick, immigrants—in short, the people who have the least resilience. The city is fractured, anonymous, and hard to manage in normal time. This makes the city environment attractive to many, but it makes it hard to hold together in times of adversity. The design of a resilient system will require a tailor-made approach for big cities.

- *The politics of crisis management.* The immediate aftermath of modern crises has become home to intense politicization that is fueled by the destructive interaction among politicians, media representatives, victims, and citizens (Boin et al. 2005). Perhaps it is impossible to avoid, but recent crises have shown the perverse effects of these dynamics on the effectiveness of the response operation. The design of a resilient system will require public leaders to think through the political vulnerabilities that accompany a heavy emphasis on resilience.

Creating a resilient system may be one of the most daunting executive tasks for public leadership. The biggest hurdle encountered by leaders is the absence of political and societal support to perform this task well. Arguing for a resilient system can be easily misconstrued as a call for a frugal and noncaring society where citizens are encouraged to take care of themselves in the face of a catastrophe. It is therefore important to explain that resilience is not a luxury or a political hobbyhorse. It is a necessity for a society that seeks to prepare itself for transboundary crises and large-scale disasters. Arguing the case for resilience may well be the most pressing leadership challenge.

8 RAPID ADAPTATION TO THREAT

THE LONDON BOMBINGS OF JULY 7, 2005

David Alexander

On a damp and unseasonably cool Thursday in July 2005, bombs set off by suicide terrorists exploded at four locations in the center of London. Exactly two weeks later, technical faults in bomb-making were the only factor that stopped a second wave of outrages from convulsing the city. If the bombs destined to be exploded on July 21 had gone off, London's emergency services would have been stretched beyond their limits by exhaustion after fourteen days of coping with crisis. London is a well-prepared city, but neither its intelligence service nor its civil-protection system is infallible. The metropolis is too large, too diverse, and too cosmopolitan to be immune to premeditated and carefully planned outrages.

The purpose of this chapter is to review the events of July 7, and their aftermath, in terms of the lessons that need to be learned in order to increase the resilience to disaster of metropolitan areas. In this context, "resilience" can be viewed as the ability to deflect, absorb, or abate the impact of a disaster or major incident by preparedness, prudence, and the ability to react in a flexible and efficient manner to an event as it occurs. This means being able rapidly to overcome a significant number of problems and thus to "bounce back," which requires concerted action on the part of all emergency services. It highlights the fact that the key to crisis management is to ensure that all agencies work effectively together during the crisis.

If resilience requires the ability to mount *collective* action in an effective manner, the response of the London emergency services to the bombings was rather mixed. Now it may be that resilience cannot fully be *in-*

vented—that is, it cannot entirely be dreamed up by planners—but it must be *acquired* through experience and testing. Although the local reaction to the events of September 11, 2001, was slow to develop, by 2005 the authorities in London had worked hard to develop business continuity, emergency plans, and sound alliances designed to respond to major incidents. They had behind them the experience of thirty years as a focus of Northern Irish terrorism. Yet the bombs created more disruption than any such events over the previous sixty years. Hence, through lack of adequate experience, mistakes were made, and inadequacies did reveal themselves, as this account will show.

London and Its Emergency Services

In London three hundred languages are regularly spoken. Its center, the cities of London and Westminster (finance and commerce versus government and entertainment), lies at the heart of a metropolis of 7.4 million people—about 25 million if all the towns and counties that each day depend on London to a greater or lesser extent are included.

London proper has thirty-three municipalities, or boroughs, and only recently has it gained an assembly presided over by an elected mayor. Before that, the role of the lord mayor of London was largely symbolic. Moreover, for at least the last thousand years, the relationship between the city's leadership and the national government that the city hosts has been an uneasy one. Organizations that deal with the administration of the whole city have periodically been set up and abolished, reflecting central government's unease about letting London run its own affairs (Ackroyd 2000).

When disasters occur in Britain, the police are usually the lead agency. They direct emergency operations on behalf of the other services and participants. This arrangement stems from a belief that emergencies are primarily matters of public order, an attitude that for better or worse is strongly rooted in British administrative culture (D. Parker and Handmer 1996). Emergency *planners* do exist in Britain—in fact, the UK Emergency Planning Society has more than twenty-seven hundred members—but emergency *managers* are dominated by the so-called blue-light services—police, fire, and ambulance (Hills 1994).[1]

In London the largest police force—though not the only one—is the Metropolitan Police, which has thirty-three thousand officers. The City of London Police Force is a separate, smaller organization that has jurisdiction over the city financial area, and the British Transport Police patrols the railways, underground train system, and buses.

The London Fire Brigade has a long and honorable tradition of service to the capital city. The need for such a force was amply demonstrated in 1666 when a bakery caught fire in the aptly named Pudding Lane (now Monument Lane, site of a tall monument to the Great Fire) and much of the central city was laid waste by the flames. The London Fire Brigade's finest moments came during the Nazi bombing of the city in 1940 and 1941 (the "Blitz," as it is still known). As the city burned under the onslaught of incendiary bombs, firefighters engaged in many acts of heroism. In modern Britain, the "Blitz spirit" is still a vital element of psychological resilience in the face of disasters. For example, it was much in evidence and discussed during the flooding that affected large swaths of central and southern England during July 2007.

The London Ambulance Service comes under the jurisdiction of the National Health Service, which has an active emergency planning branch. It is supplemented by a voluntary organization, the St. John's Ambulance Brigade, which on July 7, 2005, mobilized thirty-seven ambulances, twenty treatment centers, and more than one hundred members of its personnel.

Until the end of the 1990s, it could fairly be stated that emergency response in London was fragmented. This had few negative effects when an event was limited in size and seriousness, as in the case, for example, of the Ladbroke Grove train crash in West London in October 1999. Although thirty-one people died, the event was geographically circumscribed enough not to overtax the organizational and coordination skills of the forces at work. However, shortly afterward the British government decided to set up regions to oversee the county structure, and one of these was established for the London metropolitan area, constituting an equivalent to the prefecture system found in Continental European countries. As a British response to the events of September 11, 2001, in America, the London Resilience organization was born, and the emergency response to potential large events in the future was reorganized by representatives of all the main participants under the banner of the London Emergency Services Liaison Panel (LESLP). London Resilience has a staff of about fifty emergency planners, four fifths of whom are on temporary secondment from the emergency services and other agencies.[2] For emergency planning purposes it has divided London into six regions of differing sizes. The smallest is the central area, whose six boroughs include the city financial district and the strategic installations of government. One of the largest is the western district, which includes, in the London borough of Hillingdon, Heathrow, the world's busiest airport (London Resilience 2005b).

The choice of name for London Resilience is indicative of the British government's desire to shift the emphasis from merely responding to emergencies to preparing for them and managing risks in such a way as to reduce the impact of future crises by foreseeing them and making appropriate preparations. The organization has a role that is dominated by planning, coordinating, and managing information flows.

Vulnerable Transportation Systems

Transportation systems are inherently vulnerable to attack, as the Madrid bombings of March 2004 demonstrate (Bolling et al. 2007). They have long been a favorite target for terrorists in London. In a city of such size and with such a high density of population, they have also been persistently difficult to organize efficiently, let alone protect against attack. The London Underground system (LU, known colloquially as "the Tube") has twelve lines with 275 stations and 408 kilometers of track. It has a staff of twelve thousand people and carries three million passengers a day. Despite high ticket prices, underinvestment has been its hallmark for decades.

For many years, London Underground has suffered maintenance problems. Its record of managing risks is somewhat patchy, and over the years some significant disasters have occurred (Wolmar 2002). During World War II, deep-level stations were used as bomb shelters. In March 1943 a mass panic occurred at Bethnal Green station, and 173 people were crushed to death. Forty-three were killed in the Moorgate station crash of February 1975 and 31 in a fire that occurred at Kings Cross station in November 1987. More recently, near disasters have been caused by the derailment of a train at Chancery Lane and the immobilization of another crowded train in hot, suffocating conditions for six hours. Neither of these emergencies was particularly well managed. Paradoxically, LU's geotechnical risk management is excellent, but its management of other risks to passengers suggests that greater investment is needed in planning, training, and preparation (Scanlon 1996).

As one would expect with the world's oldest underground railway system (it was opened in 1868), the Tube is not very "user-friendly." Train tunnels are narrow, air-conditioning is absent, and passenger access to station platforms is through small, cramped tunnels with many turns and flights of steps. The Underground's emergency signage is very poor. This is odd, given that LU has been involved for seventy-five years in promoting great art (e.g., Sir Eduardo Paolozzi's mosaics at Oxford Circus station and Jacob Epstein's statuary at St James's Park). Moreover, its route map, designed in 1933 by Harry Beck and inspired by an electrical wiring diagram, is a world-famous model of clarity. However, stations such as Waterloo, where four lines interconnect with an overground railway terminus, are confusing to navigate under normal conditions, let alone during an emergency. Evacuation maps have been posted on station platforms for a few years now, but they are neither easy to interpret nor widely consulted. One is left with the impression that managers at LU fear that giving prominence to emergency signage would frighten passengers rather than reassuring them, which is a somewhat retrograde attitude. The net impression is of an underfunded, aging infrastructure that lacks resilience as much as it lacks modernization.

The Underground Train Bombings

Major explosions or collisions in the Tube give rise to conditions that are hot, smoky, cramped, and protracted. At worst, they would be similar to those encountered in the Monte Bianco and Frejus tunnel fires in the Alps (Modic 2003), except that smoke from fires in the London Underground's deep tunnels, which are up to 40 meters below the surface, would have nowhere to go except into the stations. The deep tunnels are 3.5 meters in diameter, which gives a clearance of only 15 centimeters around the trains. Side doors are designed not to be opened manually by passengers, as in the tunnels there is insufficient clearance to exit from them. As this fact is not particularly evident, after the bombs exploded, passengers were injured trying unsuccessfully to force the doors open (London Assembly 2006, 1: 61).

On July 7, 2005, two of the bombings, at Aldgate-Liverpool Street (0851 hrs) and Kings Cross-Russell Square (0856), occurred in deep tunnel lines, and one, at Edgware Road (0917), in the more spacious partially open-air lines of the original London Underground Railway, which was constructed in the nineteenth century. The Edgware Road bomb caused trains to crash into each other, adding a further complication.

Apparently, the bombs were simple hydrogen peroxide–based concoctions. They were detonated in the first carriage of the Kings Cross train, the second carriage of the Edgware Road train, and the third carriage of the Liverpool Street train (most LU trains have six carriages). In all three cases, the explosions gained added force by being detonated in a confined space, which reflected back the blasts and hence greatly increased their power. On two of the trains, fireballs occurred. In all three cases, passengers nearest to the explosions apparently suffered spontaneous limb amputations (from which survival is rare: Leibovici et al. 1996); deep tissue damage that exposed internal organs; and "compartment injuries" in which the force of the blast damages organs, such as the lungs, from within. People were severely burned by flashbacks associated with the blasts, and some were badly affected by inhalation of smoke and dust. On the Edgware Road train, the blast flung a passenger through a window into the path of an oncoming train.

On average the seriousness of blast injuries usually declines markedly with distance from the point of detonation (Wightman and Gladish 2003). However, passengers who were not in the immediate line of the explosions suffered shrapnel injuries, burst eardrums, smoke intoxication, and eye injuries.

After the blasts, there followed a period of darkness in which the air was full of smoke, dust, and oily particulates. Fortunately, the fire did not spread. Although the blasts blew inspection covers out of the floors of carriages and knocked over passengers, they did not blow out all the windows. Where these did break or were knocked out by passengers, cleaner air entered the carriages and dispersed the suffocating smoke.

Panic, hysteria, and screaming occurred in the trains, probably as a result of fear of the consequences of entrapment if fire were to spread through the carriages. However, many people remained lucid. By and large, women tended to display the most practical attitudes. As the published sociological research on disasters would predict, panic was a transient phenomenon of short duration (Quarantelli 2001). It was by no means universal and was restricted to the most stressful moments after the attacks. For the rest of the time, personal resilience was borne out in the many stories of individual resourcefulness among LU employees and passengers (London Assembly 2006, vols. 2–3).

Evacuation Underground

As noted above, with a very small lateral clearance, the deep-tunnel trains could not be evacuated by their side doors. Passengers therefore had to leave by the end doors and walk in the darkness to the nearest stations. They could only do this when they were assured that the 600-volt electrical current had been switched off to the two live rails. In the deep tunnels, periods of twenty to thirty minutes elapsed before people were led to safety by transport police and London Underground staff. In the meantime, some passengers were given no information, possibly because the trains' public address systems had been put out of action, and some were told that an electrical surge appeared to have occurred, an observation that had no basis in fact. As there were up to seven hundred people on each train, it then took up to half an hour to walk to safety, but the evacuees did not show signs of further panic. Throughout the central city area, two hundred thousand people were evacuated from trains and platforms within one hour, which underlines the high level of usage of the London Underground system, as well as a relatively efficient process of clearance, despite the poor signage. In fact, the general evacuation was warmly commended in the London Resilience multiagency debriefing after the disaster (London Resilience 2006, 80).

The fact that passengers emerged, visibly shocked and injured, from stations on either side of the trains in the deep tunnels initially caused the authorities to suppose that there had been twice as many bombs as had actually gone off. Indeed, ambulances were dispatched to seven locations, not all of which were involved in the emergency (London Assembly 2006, 1: 13). Paradoxically, but much as one would expect with anomalous events underground, LU Control did not immediately appreciate the nature and gravity of the situation and hence instituted a level-two (amber) alert rather than declaring a full-scale emergency right from the start. This poses a difficult and somewhat intractable question of how to estimate the seriousness of an underground emergency in its early stages. Rescue was apparently delayed by the need to analyze air samples from the tunnels in order to be sure that the bombs were not contaminated with radionuclides or other toxic substances, which would have required rescuers to put on airtight suits (of which fifteen hundred are stockpiled in London) and use special measures to protect the health of evacuees.

London Underground distinguished among managing the incident, managing its consequences, and managing the recovery. Although this was the most serious incident for sixty years, on July 8 four fifths of the service was back in operation. Deficiencies and deterioration did occur in the response to the incident and in the consequences, but the recovery was well managed. The deficiencies were largely related to the difficulties of recognizing the nature and gravity of the incidents, and communicating and working deep underground, problems that have generated considerable thought and investment since July 2005.

The Bus Explosion

The number 30 bus that exploded in upper Woburn Square (at 0947) was crowded (not least because people had been displaced from the Underground by the blasts there), and hence there were many injuries and thirteen fatalities. Clearly, the blast was directed upward and outward. It was fortuitous that the bus, which had been rerouted due to the cordoning off of Kings Cross station after the explosion there, was passing the headquarters of the British Medical Association when it exploded, and hence doctors, including traumatic injury specialists, were immediately on hand. Early estimation of the death toll was hampered by the fact that people had been blown to pieces. It is surprising that there were not more casualties, given that the bus passed through crowded streets and that the Kings Cross bomb had displaced people from the underground to street-level transportation.

The Emergency Response

London did not have to mobilize its full emergency resources to cope with the bombings. For example, the seven thousand members of the Civil Contingencies Reaction Force were not needed, and the thirteen designated emergency response hospitals in London coped well with the influx of patients. However, the antiterrorist force Special Operations-13 was deployed in full.

As is always the case, rescue operations involved some degree of improvisation (Webb 2004). The underground tunnel between Kings Cross and Russell Square was made structurally unsafe by the explosion (in fact, part of the roof collapsed), but London Underground has a special mobile unit that will shore up tunnels in such cases (unfortunately, it did not have "blue light" status and thus experienced some difficulties in getting quickly to the appropriate sites). Asbestos hazards were probably exaggerated, in that LU has long had a program of removing asbestos and cleaning tunnels by night when they are not in use (although some trains still contain asbestos insulation). Conditions underground were cramped and up to 15 degrees Celsius warmer than on the surface. Hence, for engineers, rescue workers, and forensic investigators, the deep tunnels were difficult to work in for long periods of time.

Of the 700 people who were injured, 350 were treated at the scene in advance medical posts and a similar number were taken to hospital, about 100 of whom became in-patients. Fewer than 25 of them were on the critical list, but several of these would later die of their injuries, bringing the eventual death toll to 56, including the four suicide bombers. Half a dozen hospitals received significant numbers of casualties, and one, the Royal London Hospital, received 183 patients, many of whom were brought there in three double-decker buses.

The blasts caused a range of medical problems that involved all bodily systems: respiratory, cardio-circulatory, muscular, skeletal, nervous, and digestive. As in explosions elsewhere, blast pressure effects, impact injuries, crush syndrome, burns, smoke intoxication, and shrapnel injuries occurred (DePalma et al. 2005).

Communicating in the Emergency

Telephone companies anticipated the surge in demand by increasing call capacity to maximum levels where possible. However, in a small area of central London, the UK Government's "Access Overload Control" system (ACCOLC) was activated on the initiative of the City of London Police, which blocked public use of the telephone networks and gave priority access to the emergency services (London Assembly 2006, 1: 44). Unfortunately, not all emergency services had the ability to use ACCOLC, and there was some dissension as to whether it should have been activated. As mobile telephones were used to detonate the bombs used by terrorists in Madrid in March 2004, it could have been necessary instantaneously to shut down cellular access in case other bombs were ready to be set off. However, it appears that this measure was not taken. Such was the saturation of the cellular network that health service managers found that pagers worked better, even though they had formally been retired from use some years previously. As a result of this and much other experience, cellular telephone networks are not generally considered to be resilient in disasters, although their reliability is gradually improving.

Further communications problems were experienced at the underground sites, both during the initial stages of evacuating the trains and during subsequent remedial work. Radios did not work deep beneath the surface, and existing systems were completely disrupted by the damage caused by the bombs. In the end, the London Fire Service had to resort to runners to convey messages between the trains and the surface command modules. Subsequent investment in new technology is expected to cure this problem, but at considerable cost.

The principal providers of news on the Internet (such as news.bbc.co.uk) received up to one million visitors an hour. Unfortunately, within a very short space of time, the Muslim Council of Britain's Web site received thirty thousand threatening and abusive electronic mail messages. Hence, in both positive and negative senses, members of the public seek information and involvement using the Internet, which needs to respond effectively to the demands made on it in crisis situations.

Terrorism and Security

The perpetrators of the terrorist bombing of London were of course British citizens. It is of note that 10 to 15 percent of UK Muslims are estimated to be sympathetic to the idea of a violent response to world political events. Muslims are a very large minority in British society (perhaps two million people), but the vast majority of them are peaceful, law-abiding citizens who are strongly opposed to violence and whose presence is judged to enrich British society (Werbner 2000).

In the United Kingdom, spending on security has almost doubled since 2000 (H. W. Richardson, Gordon, and Moore 2006). About seventy-five million euros have been spent on chemical, biological, radiological, and nuclear (CBRN) decontamination alone. Moreover, surveillance of public places is at an all-time high: the average Londoner is filmed by close-circuit television cameras 250 times a day (Scanlon 2005). In addition, huge investments are being made in hiring security personnel. On the other hand, of seven hundred people arrested under the UK Prevention of Terrorism Act, only a handful have been tried and convicted, and only some of these had links to the strand of terrorism that led to the London bombings. This underlines the fact that terrorism is notoriously difficult to combat.

When in February 2003 tanks and armored personnel carriers were deployed to Heathrow Airport, it was more likely to have been because of their secure, mobile communication systems than because they were the best means of foiling a potential rocket attack on an aircraft as it landed or took off. There was also a strong element of "being seen to be resilient" in the public eye.

In Britain, all financial institutions are required by law to have business-continuity plans for use in the event of a disaster (London First 2005). Such organizations form part of what is termed the "national critical infrastructure," which includes the various branches of government and the energy supply companies (Boin and McConnell 2007). Moreover, the new basic civil protection law of November 17, 2004, requires all the privatized providers of basic services (transportation, utilities, waste removal, etc.) to participate in the emergency planning process as "second-level responders," whose duties are vital but less central than those of government and the emergency services, which are designated as "first-level responders" (HM Government 2004). Despite the new arrangements, a recent academic study suggests that British emergency services are underfunded, the private sector is underprepared, and the regions outside London are less prepared than the capital (O'Brien and Read 2005). At present there is some doubt whether Operation Sassoon, the plan for large-scale evacuation of central London to the surrounding regions, could be accomplished satisfactorily (London Resilience 2007). Nevertheless, London has three decades of experience with Provisional IRA terrorism. Its emergency services have accumulated much useful experience, and its population is accustomed to carrying on with normal activities despite the risks.

On a theoretical level, direct services to the public, which I shall term civil *protection,* are only part of the full civil *defense* mechanism of counterterrorism preparedness and response. How well the two parts of the system work together—that is, their resilience under the threat of crisis—depends on the strength, continuity, and sensitivity of the linkages (Alexander 2002).

Lessons for Civil Protection

The London bombings are unique events, but they offer at least nine useful lessons for civil protection, emergency medical response, and counterterrorism in any large city.

1. Injuries caused by bomb blasts can be severe and complex, with large numbers of patients involved. In terms of planning, there are few parallels with other kinds of disaster: some would say that coping with bomb-blast injuries is like dealing with many coincident serious vehicle crashes, but only up to a point. Hospitals must prepare for a wide range of different injuries involving many forms of trauma, complex triage, and prolonged surgery (Kluger et al. 2004). The only real parallel is battlefield surgery (Ryan et al. 1991).

2. The seriousness of bomb injuries, and thus the probability of fatalities, increases greatly with proximity to the point of detonation (though it is complicated by containment of the blast or its reflection off solid surfaces). Bombs that explode in crowded, confined spaces will inevitably cause many serious casualties (Leibovici et al. 1996).

3. In a confined space such as an underground tunnel, rescue efforts may be slowed down by the need to use chemical analysis to check for contamination of the air or site of the explosion. It may not be immediately apparent whether the incident involves CBRN contamination or not. In all situations in which a bomb has exploded, rescuers should not be sent in until the incident commander has ascertained that other bombs are not about to explode in the area. This poses a severe dilemma when it is imperative to save lives quickly. There has been no major test of resilience in the face of a CBRN incident since the Aum Shinrikyo attack on the Tokyo subway in 1995.

4. With regard to the risk of underground bomb blasts, attention needs to be given to the problems of ascertaining quickly what has happened and designing robust systems to inform the people involved what to do. Scenario modeling and other procedures should be used

to help speed up the identification of situations that are serious enough to demand a major "red-alert" response. In planning terms, new approaches are needed.

5. Very severe, life-threatening injuries caused by bomb attacks may require substantial work to stabilize a patient's condition before he or she can be moved. This needs equipment, such as specialized tents and portable surgical equipment, that can very rapidly be deployed at the site. There may not even be time to set up an advance medical post.

6. Blast and crush victims need fluids quickly. So do the walking wounded. In the London case, blood supplies were adequate, but saline solutions and other rehydrating fluids were in short supply.

7. Emergency response teams should disturb the site of a bombing as little as possible without, of course, compromising their life-saving objectives. The site is a "scene of crime" and will later be subjected to an intensive forensic investigation.

8. In London, even in the exceptionally difficult situation caused by bombs exploding in deep underground tunnels, outbreaks of panic were limited to conditions in which people believed they were trapped. The incidence of panic should not be overestimated. It is a much misunderstood phenomenon that is transient, short-lived, and surprisingly rare (Quarantelli 2001).

9. The occurrence of repeat attacks in London two weeks after the events of July 7, 2005, underlined the need for continued vigilance and for good lines of communication among intelligence services, the forces of law and order, and those of civil protection. Even if they could not be predicted, all the attacks in London were expected: such was the nature of intelligence on terrorist activity. However, the shooting of the innocent Brazilian Jean Charles de Menezes at the Stockwell underground station on July 22, 2005, illustrates the dangers of poor intelligence, lack of operational communication, and overreaction.

The London Assembly Report

Most of the debate in the UK about the events of July 7, 2005, has revolved around the question of whether British Intelligence could have predicted and prevented the bombings (see HM Government 2006a, 2006b, 2006c). That question is not within the purview of the present article. However, a committee of London Assembly members conducted a painstaking investigation into the response of the emergency services, resulting in a long report and two volumes of verbatim evidence totaling more than seven hundred pages (London Assembly 2006).

The London Assembly report is in places incisively critical of the emergency response to the bombings, in contrast to the London Resilience response, which consisted of a report on the multiagency debriefing held at London's Guildhall on October 5, 2005.[3] Surprisingly, the Assembly's team contained no experts on emergency management: presumably, the team felt that copious expert testimony would compensate for this omission, but that ignores the ways in which evidence is interpreted. Hence, in places the report demonstrates a lack of understanding of the inevitable constraints and limitations of emergency management. For example, recommendation number 7 (London Assembly 2006, 1: 34)—to deploy response services automatically to the nearest two stations when an underground emergency has been identified—falls foul of common logic: until it is established exactly where the event has taken place, it cannot be determined exactly which two stations are involved, especially on the complex of intersecting lines in the central area.

Nevertheless, despite falling frequently into the common trap of applying hindsight logic to matters that could not at the time be foreseen, the London Assembly report does offer useful advice. Some of this is well-known from other events, such as Hurricane Katrina (Bier 2006; Roberts's chapter in this volume). As in Louisiana, so in the London case, interagency communication could have been better. In London this was especially true regarding the common recognition and declaration of a major incident, an act that sets into motion a series of procedures and protocols. There were also imbalances in the allocation of resources that could probably have been avoided by improved design of information flow. Some aspects of this were technological, as in the case of communications in the tunnels and at the stations of the Tube, while others were organizational and interorganizational.

Appropriately, the Assembly team praised the arrangements for temporary mortuary facilities in the wake of the bombings. The London Mass Fatality Plan (London Resilience 2005a) evolved from the somewhat fragmentary response to the repatriation of the bodies of UK victims after the Indian Ocean tsunami of December 2004. It involves costly arrangements with full-scale, self-contained temporary facilities to be set up at any of eleven sites around the capital if the need arises. The political salience of dealing with the dead made this an issue for the living (relatives, in particular) as much as for the deceased.

The most prominent conclusion of the London Assembly report is that emergency planners and managers need to reorient themselves from concentration on their own organizational needs to focus more on the victims and beneficiaries of their work—that is, the stakeholders among the general public (London Assembly 2006, 1: 9 et seq.). There is much good sense in this, and it has already formed the basis of discussion in the emergency management professional literature (Devitt and Burroughs 2007).

One aspect focused on beneficiaries is the need to register the details of people involved in incidents such as the London bombings and provide them with follow-up care, perhaps also to keep better records of incidents and disasters in general (Carley, Mackway-Jones, and Donnan 1998). The Assembly documented various cases of failure to give people medical, social, or epidemiological care and monitoring to an adequate standard as a result of failure to collect, share, or maintain records of their names, addresses, contact numbers, and other data. The consequences of this could be profound and long-lasting. The widespread popularity of incident command systems is a testament to the value of having a well-established administrative mechanism in disaster (Buck, Trainor, and Aguirre 2006), but the emphasis needs to be shifted from the emergency services to managing victims, survivors, and the public. In short, in seeking better integration of civil defense, under the banner of counterterrorism activities, with civil protection, in the interests of direct public service, a balance needs to be struck between all the ingredients of disaster management.

London Resilient?

Metropolitan disaster response is characterized by a certain "embarrassment of riches" in terms of the availability of resources (e.g., 192 New York hospitals could have responded if the collapse of the World Trade Center had caused very many injuries). Hence, it is not usually appropriate to judge a wealthy city on the basis of the aid it can make available; rather, this should be considered in terms of how effectively resources are used. In London on July 7, 2005, there was a certain lack of coordination, particularly in terms of standardized information flow and the synchronization of formal actions among emergency services. This was both a lateral (interorganizational) and vertical (hierarchical) problem. Its roots lie in the emphasis on command and control, when in reality information technology has flattened the chain of command and rendered many notions of authoritarian command obsolete (Stanovich 2006).

British administrative and political culture has become well versed in information management. Yet even here there were mistakes. An interview clip was repeatedly broadcast on television and radio in which the chief constable of the Metropolitan Police, Sir Ian Blair, gave advice to the public that rapidly became out of date. The government's Civil Contingencies Secretariat made great use of its slogan "go in, stay in, tune in," but in the end this proved to be the wrong advice, especially when the mass media should have been encouraging commuters to return home rather than wait for further instructions. The slogan came from a pamphlet on emergency preparedness that was printed in 2004 and delivered to every address in the country. It could be viewed as a means of encouraging passivism in the general population, rather than an active approach to self-protection. On a more positive note, London Resilience has worked hard to provide a good, practical Web site that citizens can access in times of need.[4]

Several aspects of the aftermath of the London bombings confirm the theory of disaster as a betrayal of public trust by the authorities (Horlick-Jones 1995; Roberts's chapter in this volume). First, on the day of the disaster, there was a gigantic surge in public communications and a smaller but still overwhelming surge in communications among the emergency responders. At all levels, government needs to demonstrate mastery and leadership of the "infosphere," both to involve the public responsibly and to present a picture of the emergency response as a professional and well-managed activity. The record of July 2005 in London was decidedly mixed (Scanlon 2005), which underscores the difficulty of improvising what has not been planned or rehearsed. Second, the fact that injured victims and other people who became involved in the incidents were not given adequate aftercare elicited much public indignation and uncovered a significant deficiency in national resilience (London Assembly 2006, 1: 102–16). In the end, the principal lesson for resilience is likely to be the need to refocus emergency management on the beneficiaries and stakeholders among the general public. There are signs that the message is beginning to permeate the British emergency management community (Devitt and Burroughs 2007). Well it might, as resilience will only be achieved if the response to emergency situations takes place in partnership between the professionals and the public.

9   THE PRICE OF RESILIENCE
CONTRASTING THE THEORETICAL IDEAL-TYPE
WITH ORGANIZATIONAL REALITY

Michel van Eeten, Arjen Boin, and Mark de Bruijne

When asked how he had maintained performance in the face of overwhelming adversity, a control room shift manager of the California electricity grid answered: "I have six words: By. The. Seat. Of. Our. Pants." According to most definitions, the shift manager's organization had demonstrated remarkable resilience. Yet his experience of resilience differed dramatically from the theoretical descriptions of the resilience process found in this book.

When surveying the literature on resilient organizations, one cannot help but notice strong overtones of admiration and praise. Weick and Sutcliffe (2001, 14) claim that resilient organizations have "capabilities to detect, contain, and bounce back from those inevitable errors that are part of an indeterminate world." According to Kendra and Wachtendorf (2003, 42), resilience means "redundancy, the capacity for resourcefulness, effective communication and the capacity for self-organization in the face of extreme demands." Sutcliffe and Vogus (2003, 97) define resilience as "the capacity to rebound from adversity strengthened and more resourceful."

References to possible drawbacks of resilience are few and far between. Hill (2000) argues that the view of resilience as a desirable property of institutions is biased toward the Western corporate and public sectors. In a repressive regime, institutional resilience may prevent change when change is desirable. Vickers and Kouzmin (2001) point out that the concept of resilience is used for less than noble purposes. Managers assume and emphasize the resilience of their organization and its members to rationalize their interventions and defend themselves against the "trauma" they have caused in the workplace in the name of efficiency, downsizing, and outsourcing. What managers like to see as "warehouses of resilience" are often, Vickers and Kouzmin argue, "crucibles of pain."

All in all, these observed drawbacks do not seriously undermine the overwhelmingly positive image of resilience. It has consistently been portrayed—in this book too—as the hallmark of organizational success when operating under challenging conditions. In short, we have created a normative ideal.

This begs the question of whether our understanding of resilience is grounded in the experiences of organizational members who have effectively dealt with acute adversity. In the remainder of this chapter, we are interested to see how the theoretical ideal-type of the resilient organization stacks up against recorded practices in such organizations. We pursue this aim in the context of three large-scale sociotechnical systems that are routinely confronted with setbacks and adversity. These case studies remind us of the intricate interplay between operators and technical systems, which is essential to keeping the lights on and preserving delicate ecosystems. They also enrich our understanding of what resilience entails in such sociotechnical systems and what is needed to facilitate the design of resilient systems.

The Organizational Messiness of Resilience

In theory, resilience comprises the ability to cope with unexpected adversity outside normal operating conditions; maintain a functioning system in the face of this adversity; and, in the process of coping, develop new skills that increase the probability of successful coping in the future. The question we address here is: what does resilience look like in practice?

To answer this question, we revisit three case studies on organizations that demonstrated resilience in the face of unprecedented challenges.[1] Each faced adversity beyond what it was supposed to handle and somehow managed to cope with this adversity, maintaining a functioning system and developing new skills and options in the process. Each case also involved interaction between technical and organizational systems, in which the organizations adapted to sudden, unexpected impacts on technical systems and were able to avoid imminent danger. In short, these organizations displayed resilience.

The first case study focuses on three U.S. water-management systems (the San Francisco Bay Delta, the Columbia River Basin, and the Everglades). The organizations managing such systems must seek to reconcile reliability requirements for water supply and quality (e.g., to cities and agriculture) and hydropower generation with new reliability requirements for ecosystem protection and restoration (e.g., saving water-related endangered species or threatened habitat). Their reconciliation forces these organizations to work outside existing organizational structures, procedures, and knowledge. The original study asked how the system managers preserve, restore, and otherwise rehabilitate ecosystems reliably yet at the same time ensure the consistent provision of services (including goods and commodities) from these ecosystems.

The second case concentrates on the California Independent System Operator (CAISO, or ISO for short). This is the focal organization (and control room) for deregulated electricity transmission in California. The original research question: how does the ISO maintain reliable provision of electricity, where those owning the generation and distribution of electricity (privatized generators and restructured "public" utilities) have conflicting goals and interests and where there is an absence of ongoing command and control to ensure reliable energy services? Most informants were from the ISO, and the majority of interviews were undertaken between April and December 2001—which covered the height of the California electricity crisis. The electricity crisis posed major and unanticipated adversity for the ISO, as much of the institutional design broke down—including the means with which to secure the reliable provision of electricity. Notwithstanding the popular view of rolling blackouts, in aggregate terms—both in hours and megawatts (MW)—blackouts were in effect minimal.

The third case centers on the telecommunications sector, which was also trying to cope with rapidly changing conditions. It builds on interviews and control room observations at KPN Mobile, the largest mobile operator in the Netherlands. KPN Mobile has struggled to maintain service reliability under conditions over which it has less and less control and that are in many ways antithetical to how it operated before.

Around 130 key informants were interviewed for these case studies in order to understand how reliable performance was maintained during unprecedented challenges and disturbances. Most of the interviews lasted over an hour, using a standard questionnaire that allowed open-ended probing. All interviews were confidential, and each interviewee was able to amend his or her quoted statements.

Large-Scale Water System Operators

The San Francisco Bay Delta, the Columbia River Basin in the Pacific Northwest, and the Florida Everglades all have large-scale waterworks that are at the heart of multi-billion-dollar restoration efforts for internationally re-nowned ecosystems. The systems are operated by different organizations. The Bonneville Power Administration (BPA), the California Department of Water Resources (DWR), and the South Florida Water Management District (SFWMD) have control rooms that process real-time information on water supply, water quality, flood control, and ecological indicators, including the presence of listed species. BPA and DWR also operate massive hydropower systems.

Rehabilitating ecosystems and simultaneously ensuring the reliability of water, power, and other ecosystem-based services is challenging and costly. The Comprehensive Everglades Restoration Plan was approved for federal and state funding totaling $10.9 billion. In the San Francisco Bay Delta, the CALFED Program (recently renamed Delta Vision) has spent several billion dollars over the past decade and has proposed to commit around ten billion dollars over the next decades. And in the Columbia River Basin, BPA alone has provided over four hundred million dollars per year for fish and wildlife measures (van Eeten and Roe 2002).

The ecosystem-management initiatives in the three regions added new standards for reliable service provision that have highlighted and increased the tight and complex relations between large-scale technical systems for water supply and the ecosystems from which they draw their water. This creates intricate dilemmas: opening a water gate and flooding endangered birds in one area or closing the gate and parching the habitat of the same species someplace else; retaining water in a reservoir to save the fish, sac-rificing fish downstream; controlled burning in order to save the forest, which in turn not only harms air quality but also bleeds pollution into adja-cent aquatic ecosystems. Newly restored floodplains may inadvertently pro-mote the further invasion of exotic species, thereby weakening the popula-tion of threatened native species, thus invoking even more stringent limits on water-supply operations: "The deliberate manipulation or management of ecosystems, therefore, will almost certainly involve some untoward sur-prises," conclude Callicott, Crowder, and Mumford (1999, 28).

Reliability-driven water-system operators had long forcefully resisted trial-and-error learning. Now they could no longer avoid experimentation—sometimes with dramatic consequences. Take the 1999 delta smelt crisis in California. A handful of delta smelt in a sample was enough to close a cross-channel gate, which in turn reduced water quality near pumping stations, thereby breaching urban water standards—triggering the worst urban water-quality crisis in Los Angeles in decades—and lowering wa-ter exports to agriculture by half. Another crisis: releasing dam water for salmon passage meant less electricity for the Bonneville Power Administration's grid. Combined with hot weather, sagging power lines, and a broken backup generator, this led to wholly unexpected grid instability and rapid shutdown of the intertie with the California grid, causing massive blackouts there.

Resilience

How successfully have water-system operators coped with such surprises and disturbances? When it comes to managing ecosystems, "success" is a notoriously thorny concept. The ecosystem is always complex and changing. Thus, any experiment will set in motion a series of events and impacts that entail unknown and possibly massive effects later on. Errors resulting from an experiment or intervention may be irreversible in a system that cannot be controlled and in which decision makers learn only years afterward that what took place was indeed a mistake.

While it may be too soon to draw final conclusions, it seems fair to say that water-system operators displayed remarkable resilience in response to the radically new conditions under which they were forced to operate. By and large, these organizations managed to meet their reliability requirements for water supply, water quality, flood control, and hydropower generation, as well as those for endangered-species protection and other ecological mandates. Each region launched massive multistakeholder multi-billion-dollar planning efforts to reconcile competing reliability requirements, but most of the innovation and resilience were found in the operational processes, not in planning. Setting and managing parameters for operational processes meant, specifically, attempts to reconcile conflicting operations: providing drinking water to the metropolis, selling hydropower on the spot market, protecting water quality from salt-water intrusion, and enabling passage of endangered fishes—all and more need to be done at the same time and without decreasing the reliability of water supply to any of the end users.

In and around control rooms, the high-reliability features identified in the 1990s high-reliability organization (HRO) research dominated: technical competence, high performance at peak levels, search for improvements, teamwork, flexible patterns of organization, high pressures for safety, multiple sources of information and cross-checks, and a veritable culture of reliability—all working through technologies and systems that build in sophisticated redundancies to buffer against potential failure and catastrophe (see, e.g., Rochlin 1993). But there was more.

Interagency management of control rooms. Planning and management of large-scale power and water operations are increasingly interagency processes. Control rooms are the heart of the water and power system, where an array of workstations and screens represents the system in real time and where mandated operations are scheduled and executed together. Each control room is managed by a "team" consisting not only of the service provider operating the control room, such as California's Department of Water Resources and the Army Corps of Engineers, but also of representatives of state and federal fish and wildlife agencies and other environmental units.

The most intense agency interaction takes place over short-term decisions. Short-term planning staff in the BPA work weekly or biweekly with other agencies through their technical management team. CALFED has a similar institution in its "Operations Management Team," as has the SF-WMD for the design of its regulation schedules. Unresolved issues around reconciling reliability mandates are typically pushed to a higher interagency coordination team as a dispute-resolution mechanism.

Yet even when interagency management teams reach agreement, line operators in control rooms may need help. A BPA biologist working as an "interpreter" between the management team and the control room said, "Real-time people would get a planning document they literally couldn't read, so I help make the connections about where the fish are and what they need."

Ecologists in control rooms. This biologist-interpreter supports the control room and is not part of the management overseeing it. His translation is twofold: he puts planning instructions into operational terms and helps relate ecological information to real-time decisions on water and power generation. We found a similar example in Florida, where the senior manager in the SFWMD operations office had hired an environmental scientist to work in the control room. In the manager's words, the scientist would operate constructed wetlands for storm-water treatment and serve as a "translator" between the line operators and the districts' planning staff, where ecologists are now located. Ultimately, the manager hoped to capitalize on "windows where we can enhance both reliability of water supply and ecosystem functions."

Ecologists and line operators frequently describe their respective systems as more than the sum of their parts, displaying nondeterministic behavior, with complexity that can never be fully captured, and therefore making management extremely challenging. Both groups are reluctant to intervene in these systems, because this potentially creates more problems than it solves. Since the reliability mandates of the water and power system have been extended to cover protected species and endangered ecosystems, the congruence and need for cooperation between line operators and ecologists have been reinforced.

Gaming exercises toward comprehensive modeling. Ecosystem management initiatives for the Everglades, the Columbia River Basin, and the San Francisco Bay Delta have used a patchwork of hydrological and ecological models to explore the complex interactions within and between natural and technical systems. These models, while impressive, pose considerable problems, according to their users. In a phrase, the models are patchy, loosely connected—if connected at all, and do not reflect the complexity of the systems they are meant to model.

Difficulties in developing models that directly connect high-reliability operations to the maintenance and/or rehabilitation of ecosystems have increased pressure to find innovative ways to learn about the "whole system." One particularly successful example is a "power-modeling" exercise undergone by teams assigned to generate and evaluate different alternatives for the Comprehensive Everglades Plan. As described by the senior Everglades planner, "The power modeling (initially called tweak week) built up trust, but wasn't a giant love-in.... The [team] evaluated not just ecosystem restoration scenarios, but they also had people evaluating flood and water supply performance of these scenarios. Sometimes you would have water supply [people] saying they were happy, but ecological people saying they weren't. The process was one of constant reformulation, and they were always multipurpose, so in the end different concerns were integrated."

This does not mean that competing reliability mandates are always reconciled in such meetings: "The give and take was lively, sometimes heated, almost always highly professional, but it was unusual (although not without precedent) when the environment was given greater weight than water supply." However, he added, "Admittedly, it is a lot better than before, when operational decisions were made in isolation, based strictly on engineering practices."

Features of the Everglades power-modeling were also found in CALFED gaming exercises. Games typically took place over several days and involved agency officials and stakeholders, including those responsible for water supplies and listed species. Using hydrological and ecological models, they tested various scenarios to allocate water month by month over a timeline. The goal was to identify, capture, and allocate water by finding flexibility in the water-supply system to meet both baseline needs (e.g., legal mandates to meet species needs) and other water-supply needs above and beyond the baseline.

New accounting options. An Environmental Water Account (EWA), CAL-

FED officials have argued, would provide flexibility that achieves ecosystem benefits more efficiently than a regulatory approach and at the same time improves water reliability. There are variants of the EWA, but the general idea is to give regulatory agencies (the U.S. Fish and Wildlife Service, the U.S. National Marine Fisheries Service, and the California Department of Fish and Game) operational control over an account filled with water or assets that are fungible with water. The account would be used to respond to real-time ecological events. Instead of trying to capture all contingencies through standards, which wastes resources ("overshooting") and hampers the flexibility of line operators, regulation would now be limited to providing a baseline level of ecosystem protection. With that baseline met, the EWA would be used to respond to natural variability more efficiently. For example, when real-time monitoring indicates that fish are unlikely to be affected, the "export/inflow ratio" (mandating a maximum ratio of water exported from the delta to the south, compared to water entering the delta from the north) could be "flexed" to provide water for the EWA and to improve water-supply reliability. That water could then provide additional security in more sensitive times.

In effect, the EWA brings ecosystem processes and their reliability mandates into the control room as parameters that can be managed in the real-time optimization process, instead of being static constraints on optimization that undermine reliability. Fisheries agencies enter into direct comanagement over the water-supply system and into a new relationship with line operators. The water account would force fisheries agencies to make tradeoffs among competing ecological objectives—for example, resident fish in the dam versus fish downriver, a burden that line operators feel is now on their shoulders alone. By converting competing objectives of water supply, water quality, power generation, and ecosystem rehabilitation into one currency—in this case water, in BPA's case money—these accounts would structure conflict and compel choice by articulating tradeoffs and forcing priorities. For instance, water or funds used at the beginning of the year would not be available later on for unexpected contingences. In this way, the EWA serves as an operating budget that tightly couples highly interrelated allocation decisions.

The Organizational Experience of Resilience

While the behavior of these respondents fit theoretical notions of resilience, they described their experience in rather different terms. Their responses didn't carry the undertones of confidence, extraordinary capabilities, and success so typical of academic descriptions of resilience. They articulated feeling uncomfortable, insecure, and frustrated about their performance—and understandably so. The conditions that allowed them to feel confident about the reliability of their performance are no longer present. According to an ecologist familiar with the Everglades, "If you don't know how to save [the species] or if what you are doing isn't working, then you have to try new things like experiments. On the other hand, you are not allowed to fail under the current interpretation of the ESA. We can't do anything until we know it won't cause harm....This is butt-stupid." Some respondents question outright whether ensuring reliability is still a valid expectation. One CALFED scientist said, "Biologists don't believe in reliability," to which a line operator responsible for ensuring the reliability of California's State Water Project responded, "We can't believe in anything else." We are not sure which of the two responses sounds more desperate.

This is not to say that these respondents didn't feel they were doing all they could under difficult circumstances. The circumstances, however, left it unclear what it means to "keep the system functioning." A BPA engineer-planner described the system as "overly constrained." There is no solution that allows workers to meet the competing objectives. "So someone has to give, has to relax the constraints, but they won't," he concluded.

By focusing on the most stringent reliability requirements, respondents did manage to perform remarkably well—but not without a price. Part of that price is a constant, nearly obsessive focus on the short term. The short term becomes telescoped into what one interviewee called the "short-short term," where, in the words of another interviewee, "species under threat are treated as emergency room casualties." The long run is foreshortened as well. When the short-short term is daily or even hourly, it is not surprising that people think of the long term as a year or more out, as we found in BPA's power scheduling and planning. Consequently, managing the complex interrelations of water systems and ecosystems becomes all the more urgent at the same time as it becomes riskier to undertake.

So while these organizations have been able to meet the requirements of resilience as outlined in the literature—for example, "keeping errors small and...improvising workarounds that keep the system functioning"—they experience this resilience as fragile, exhausting, confusing, frustrating, and generally untenable. Not exactly a description of organizational effectiveness or success. They have "absorbed" the shock, but they have not "bounced back," at least not to where they came from—an experience their colleagues in the California electricity sector, the crisis still fresh in their minds, would recognize.

An Electricity System Operator

In 1996, California adopted a major restructuring of its system of electricity generation, transmission, and distribution. The state moved from a set of large integrated utilities that owned and operated the generation facilities, the transmission lines, and the distribution and billing systems, and set retail prices under a cost-based regulatory system, to a market-based system consisting of independent generators who sell their power on wholesale markets to distributors, who then sell it to retail customers. The key utilities were forced to sell off most of their generating capacity (except for nuclear and hydropower sources) and to place their transmission lines under the control of a new organization, the California Independent System Operator (ISO), which assumed responsibility for managing a new statewide high-voltage electrical grid. This grid had been primarily formed by the merger of two separate grids formerly owned and managed by the two utilities Pacific Gas and Electric (PG&E) and Southern California Edison (SCE).

The restructuring legislation created a new set of institutions and dynamic relationships. Operators in the ISO control room are closely connected to the outside through multiple communications and feedback systems. Everyone, all the time, uses the telephone; pagers are ubiquitous; internal computers inside the control rooms "talk to" external computers outside; the AGC (Automatic Generation Control) system connects the ISO generation dispatcher directly to privately held generators; the ADS (Automatic Dispatch System) connects the dispatcher directly to the bidder of electricity; dynamic scheduling systems in the ISO connect to out-of-state generators; all kinds of telemetry measurements come back to the control room in real time; Web pages used by the ISO, PG&E, and private generators carry real-time prices and information; and on and on.

The key control room operator in the ISO is the generation (or "gen") dispatcher, whose chief task is to ensure that generation and load are always balanced. "Load" is the demand for electricity, and "generation" is the electricity to meet that load, both of which must be balanced (i.e., made equal to each other) within mandated periods of time; otherwise, service delivery is interrupted as the grid physically fails or collapses. The need to balance load and generation, along with meeting other regulatory parameters, is the reliability requirement of ISO control room operators.

The new system worked fairly well for the first few years. Then disturbances began to emerge, and the system entered a period that is now known as the California electricity crisis (Roe et al. 2003; Roe and Schulman 2008). The crisis was only partly about shortages in electricity generation and the price gouging of private generators. On many fronts, the ISO was faced with volatility and unanticipated incidents. The scheduling of electricity transmission, for example, got pushed into real-time operations. Most of the scheduling is supposed to take place weeks, days, or at least hours in advance, so that there is time to coordinate the complicated schedules and cope with congestion in the network. Real-time imbalance markets were designed to take care of the last percentage or so of total load. Reality looked quite different, according to an ISO operator: "We had days where the load [was] forecasted to be 42,000MW, but our scheduled resources in the morning were 32,000MW, leaving us 10,000MW short that day. How do we deal with this? Ninety-nine percent of the planning has to be done prior to real time. Real time is only to react to what you missed. Real time is not 'I'm short 10,000MW in the day ahead and I'm not doing anything.' Most of the time things did come together, but at a very high price."

At one point, the markets stopped functioning altogether. "I was here, working as a new gen dispatcher, when I saw the market collapse. From one day to the other there were no more bids coming [into the real-time imbalance market]," said a member of the California Energy Resources Scheduling purchasing team. The financial crisis that hastened the fall of the markets took care of the rest. Mensah-Bonsu and Oren (2001, 2) characterize the situation as follows: "The destruction of the utilities' creditworthiness and the resulting responses by suppliers shattered all vestiges of a normal market."

Resilience

In the midst of all this, as the institutional design for the provision of electricity was falling apart, the ISO somehow managed to keep the lights on. Notwithstanding the popular view of rolling blackouts sweeping across California during its electricity crisis, in aggregate terms—in both hours and megawatts (MW)—blackouts were minimal and comparable to previous years (Roe et al. 2003; de Bruijne 2006). The ISO operated closer to the edge of failure than ever before—where failure means uncontrolled blackouts or, worse, grid collapse. In thirty-eight instances, ISO operated with 1.5 percent or less of its operating reserves (table 9.1). The regulatory standard is to have at least 7 percent.

The ISO was able to balance load and generation in real time (i.e., within the current hour or for the hour ahead) by developing and maintaining a repertoire of responses and options in the face of unpredictable or uncontrollable system instability. The options that the ISO control room, as the

Table 9.1 Comparison of California's Stage 1, 2, and 3 Emergencies

Year	Stage 1 (<7 percent OR)	Stage 2 (<5 percent OR)	Stage 3 (<1.5 percent OR)
1998[a][b]	7	5	0
1999[a][b]	4	1	0
2000[a][b]	55	36	1
2001[a][b]	70	65	38
2002[b]	2	1	0
2003[b]	1	0	0
2004[b]	1	0	0

Notes: OR=operating reserves

a. Based on ISO 2001, 9.

b. Based on ISO Web site, Cumulative Totals of Restricted Maintenance Operations, Alert, Warning, Emergency and Power Watch Notices Issues from 1998 to Present, http://www.caiso.com/docs/09003a6080/08/8a/09003a6080088aa7.pdf, August 23, 2005.

focal organization, deploys are network-based—for example, outage coordination is the responsibility of the ISO but involves the other partners in the network. In other words, ISO control management can be categorized in terms of the variety of network-based options available to the ISO (high or low) and the instability of the California electricity system (high or low), as in table 9.2.

"Instability" is the extent to which the focal control room in the ISO faces rapid, uncontrollable changes or unpredictable conditions that threaten the grid and service reliability of electricity supply—that is, conditions that jeopardize the task of balancing load and generation. Some days are characterized by low instability, in the past fondly called "normal days." A clear example of high instability are the days for which a large part of the forecasted loads have not been scheduled through the day-ahead market, which means that for the ISO, actual flows are unpredictable, and congestion will have to be dealt with at the last minute.

"Option variety" is the amount of resources, including strategies, available to the ISO control room to respond to events in the system in order to keep power load and power generation balanced at any given point in time. It includes available operating reserves, other generation capacity, available transmission capacity, and the degree of congestion. High option variety

Editor: Should footnote in Table 9.1 be a instead of b?

Table 9.2   Performance Conditions for California Independent System Operator (CAISO)

		System Volatility	
		High	Low
Network option variety	High	Just-in-time performance	Just-in-case performance
	Low	Just-for-now performance	Just-this-way performance

means, for instance, that a range of resources is available to the ISO, allowing it to operate well within the required regulatory conditions. Low option variety means the resources are below requirements and, ultimately, that very few resources are left and the ISO must operate close to, or even in violation of, some regulatory margins.

These demand different performance modes for achieving reliability (i.e., balancing load and generation) that we term "just-in-case," "just-in-time," "just-for-now," and "just-this-way." Each performance mode represents a dramatically different way of balancing load and generation (Roe et al. 2005; Roe and Schulman 2008).

For the purpose of our discussion, the *just-for-now* performance mode is the most interesting one. When option variety is low but instability is high, just-for-now performance is dominant. Options to maintain power loads and generation have become visibly fewer and increasingly insufficient to meet requirements in order to balance load and generation. This state can result from various factors. Unexpected outages can occur, and loads may increase to the physical limits of transmission capacity; furthermore, the use of some options can preclude or exhaust other options—for example, using stored hydro capacity now rather than later. Just-for-now performance is a state best summed up as one of maximum potential for "deviance amplification": even a small deviation in the market, technology, or another factor in the system can ramify widely throughout the system.

From the standpoint of reliability, this state is untenable over time. Operators are under no illusion that they are in control; they understand how vulnerable the grid is, how limited the options are, and how precarious the balance; they keep communication lines open to monitor the state of the network, and they are busily engaged in developing options and strategies to move out of this state. They do not panic, and indeed, they still retain the crucial option of reconfiguring the electricity system itself by declaring a "stage 3" power emergency—which means controlled blackouts.

"Just-for-now" performance is very fast-paced and best summed up as "firefighting." When options become few and room for maneuverability is tight (e.g., when loads continue to rise while new power generation becomes much less assured and predictable), control operators become even more focused on the major threats to balancing load and generation. As options become depleted, support-staff members in the control room have less and less to add. There is less need for lateral, informal relations. Operators even walk away from their consoles and join others in looking up at the big board on the side wall. "I'm all tapped out," said the generation dispatcher on the day when the ISO had just avoided issuing a stage 3 declaration. In this state, operators and support staff wait for new, vital information, because they are out of options for controlling the Area Control Error (ACE) themselves.

The Experience of Resilience

While ISO demonstrated remarkable resilience, control room operators had a distinctly less heroic perception of their harrowing experiences. Again, the shift manager in the ISO control room, quoted at the beginning of this chapter, described their performance as "By. The. Seat. Of. Our. Pants." Another evening in the control room, the coordinator of the hour-ahead market desk faced a series of problems: reliability standards violations, computer failures, software disasters, path problems and violations, data problems, late submissions by security coordinators, not enough bids in the beep stack for increasing or decreasing, ignoring dispatch orders, shedding load...the list of problems kept expanding to the point that one observer typed into the interview transcript: "How the hell does this add up to reliability?!"

From the perspective of these professionals, what we could describe as being resilient was uncomfortably similar to being lucky. From the control room operator's perspective, good luck is the nonoccurrence of failure in the absence of exercising failure-avoidance options, while bad luck is the occurrence of failure in the presence of exercising failure-avoidance options. Restructuring increases not only the number of different ways to fail but also ambiguity over what options are really available for failure avoidance. Thus, the operator now faces a performance condition where good and bad luck are more important than ever before.

In one sense, luck—whether good or bad—is really just another way to experiment in the face of real-time pressures. What operators call luck, in other words, is real-time improvisation. In another sense, luck is the other face of real-time confusion and incomprehension when messes like those faced by the operator go well when they could have gone bad. In recounting one bad day that turned out well, a shift manager in ISO's control room described how "just by sheer stroke of luck I had made a voltage change at that time and caught what happened." Luck here is a way out for operators when they are at the edge of failure.

In other words, it isn't incorrect to interpret what the respondents term "luck" as flexibility or improvisation—as the literature on resilience tends to do. But this interpretation again overemphasizes confidence, extraordinary abilities, and the reassurance of a successful end result. What is being lost is that luck could as easily be described by the opposites of those values—which would probably get us closer to the experience of operators. This is not the kind of organization that treats luck as part of standard operating procedures. Another shift manager described the close calls and the effect of changing performance conditions on reliability as follows: "How do you get out of that mess? How do you solve the unpredictability? We don't."

The explanation for why this experience in many ways feels like failure lies outside the control room. A senior state government official phrased it like this: "So we deregulated and everybody was happy for three years, and then the missing pieces made the thing blow up. . . . What went wrong in the California deregulation is that different parts of the responsibilities were not located anywhere, such as the responsibility to maintain adequacy and safety." He points to a conclusion that cannot be escaped in hindsight: restructuring left California with an underdesigned system. "All of this happened because the network left a bunch of things unassigned," he pressed. California is not the only system to face this, argues one of the interviewees familiar with out-of-state utility deregulation: "There is a lot that needs to be smoothed out. Now it's the Wild Wild West. We have got a totally new regime, and we don't know where the holes are yet."

One thing is clear: the holes were plugged—temporarily and with luck— and the lights stayed on at enormous cost, both financial and otherwise. A senior ISO engineer phrased his alarm at the far-reaching consequences of the financial destabilization this way: "We, the ISO, the whole system, are on the brink. . . . We've [already] hit the iceberg; we're taking on water fast. And we're not getting the lifeboats in the water on time." At some point, when conditions have made success unattainable, resilience means focusing on the proper way to fail. In fact, for a major Dutch mobile telecom operator, being resilient meant learning to accept failure.

A Mobile Telecommunication Operator

Since the liberalization of the mobile telecommunications market in the 1990s, the Dutch mobile market has evolved into one of the most competitive in Europe. In this market, KPN Mobile is the largest mobile telephony provider. The introduction of the GSM mobile telephony standard and competition transformed the mobile telephony industry dramatically. From 1995 to 2002, the customer base of mobile operator KPN Mobile increased almost sevenfold (Verbist 2002a, 43). Cutthroat competition forced rapid technological innovation. Operators had to introduce new services rapidly to capture customers. The number of services provided by the GSM network increased from five in the early 1990s to more than thirty in 2003.

Many of these, so-called value-added services, required the installation of new technological platforms and architectures on top of the existing platforms. This process began by adding functionalities to existing services, such as text messaging (SMS)—an unexpected and massive success. Billions of messages per year became the major source of revenue for most European operators. With the emergence of GPRS-based data services and mobile Internet, it was no longer a matter of adding functionality to the existing network. Rather, new architectures were introduced, and the mobile telecommunications system became more and more a "network of networks." At the same time, third-party service providers gained access to the network, creating new types of interdependencies in managing the system. While the complexity of the network was increasing, major cost-cutting efforts outsourced key parts of the system, as well as reduced the means to ensure the reliability of its services.

The sum of these developments pushed a system that used to be run as a stable utility service—making as few systems changes as possible to ensure reliability—to cope with a situation whose mode was "change first, ask questions later." Much of the innovation was driven by the introduction of information technology (IT), which, compared to telecommunications technology, is much less reliability oriented and has a reputation for a trial-and-error approach to service development. Almost 50 percent of the major disturbances reported in 2002 were caused by IT-related incidents (Verbist 2002a, 2002b).

A transmission manager explained how network growth has had a dual effect. On the one hand, it has created a more stable system because of more redundancy and intelligence built into the components. "Systems don't go down that easy anymore," he said. However, he added, "We are experiencing more nontransparent problems" in the transmission network as the interactions between the different elements of the mobile network become less predictable and harder to understand.

As a result of this reduced transparency, more incidents were classified as "cause unknown"—accounting for over 15 percent of all critical disturbances in 2002 (Verbist 2002a, 52). The time needed for resolving critical failures also steadily rose since 1998, as failure became less predictable—that is, as the standard deviation of the time it took to solve a problem increased. The company's own maintenance activities were the second-largest cause of service disruptions, right after equipment failure. The fact that planned maintenance, even after extensive assessment and approval procedures, managed to cause disruptions qualifies as a prime example of surprise arising out of complexity.

The system became increasingly complex at the same time new services were brought online at breakneck speed. This combination caused the connection between network and services to become volatile. During earlier phases, when GSM voice telephony was the main and almost only service, failures in network elements had fairly predictable effects on services. This was now no longer the case. While network elements could be monitored fairly closely, it was no longer clear how specific disturbances would affect the mishmash of services. One control room operator said, "We see everything in the network, but our services are like a black hole." It didn't help that new services were brought online before protocols had been developed to manage them reliably. Sometimes the operators didn't even get monitoring tools for the new services that they were now supposed to maintain reliably.

After reading our account of what respondents had told researchers, one employee at KPN asked, half jokingly, "How on earth was it possible that we were able to make phone calls?"

Resilience

Assessing the effects of these challenges on reliability has proven anything but straightforward. Information about issues of network quality and reliability is considered market sensitive, and mobile operators were highly reluctant to allow researchers to analyze their reliability, let alone publish reliability data. Consequently, there is no public long-term record of the reliability performance in the Dutch mobile telephony industry in general or KPN in particular. Nevertheless, there are some indicators that allow us to assess the resilience KPN has demonstrated while coping with the increasingly surprising disturbances in its system.

One indication that KPN was indeed resilient can be found in the number of "calamities"—that is, large-scale failures that affected services to large numbers of KPN customers—over the years (Verbist 2002a, table 4.2, p. 59):

Year	Number of Calamities
1996	59
1997	54
1998	65
1999	91
2000	90
2001	71

Key indicators such as the Call Set-up Success Rate (CSSR) and the Call Completion Rate (CCR), which in the telecommunications industry are considered important proxies for the reliability of service provision, displayed a continuously rising trend during this period. CCR started in 1997 around 96 percent, rapidly climbing in weeks 13–19 in 1997 and subsequently steadily climbing toward 99 percent in January 2000 and holding. Similarly, CSSR steadily climbed from 90 to 98 percent.

The steadily improving key performance indicators testify to the extent to which KPN Mobile was able to cope with the turbulent environment in which it found itself from the late 1990s onward. We found many similarities between the efforts of mobile telephony operators to cope with unexpected events and those of water and electricity system operators.

Their control center was originally set up to act as a clearinghouse for information on failures among different organizational units, external suppliers, and customers. Its role was to monitor the process of handling failures and incidents, not to diagnose or intervene in any way. Those tasks were closely guarded by the specialist units that were in charge of specific parts of the network. Over time, as incidents became more complex and surprising, this compartmentalized approach lost its effectiveness. A transmission manager at KPN Mobile explained: "You need to monitor these things in a different way. Once you see a failure now, you may have a seriously threatened system, instead of a localized failure of a single small line." After a period of turf battles, the control center acquired more responsibilities and the authority to intervene when needed. It grew in staff and budget and renegotiated its links to other units.

During the process of a growing control center, management tried to professionalize its operators by hiring new people with higher levels of education. This turned out to be counterproductive. The new operators had less experience and tended to rely heavily on their formal training. The kinds of incidents where their diagnostic capabilities were most needed were exactly those that defied their training. They received incident information that "couldn't be correct," according to the formal specifications of the system, although it was. They had little tolerance for the ambiguity of information around unanticipated disturbances. After a while, KPN went back to its practice of recruiting people who had operational experience in different parts of the system, even though they may not have had the formal qualifications. Their experience had given them more respect for the complexity of the system and the kind of surprises that it generated, as well as a more varied set of past events to draw from when diagnosing a disturbance.

In sum, we witnessed a shift from planning to real-time operations, from design to improvisation, from analysis to experience, and from risk avoidance to reliability seeking.

The Organizational Experience of Resilience

When KPN operations managers learned of these research findings, one of them asked, "Are you trying to say that our failure to build according to plan, to design a system that is stable, and to operate according to procedure is actually a good thing?" For him the message was clear: the organization had gotten off course, and if it was to become reliable again, it needed to get back on course in a hurry. And he was not alone. Many respondents articulated a feeling of discomfort with the ways in which they were trying to maintain reliability. Control room operators frequently complained that they were forced to conduct operations under conditions that were previously considered unsafe, unprofessional, or unreliable.

One control room operator summarized the feelings of most about the influx of new services: "The network itself generates fewer interruptions than two to three years ago. However, because of all the new services that have been introduced, we have problems controlling the system." Few of these services were rigorously tested, and if they were, it was in an environment that no longer realistically simulated the actual system. A senior network manager remarked: "We used to be able to test everything at least once. Now, that is no longer possible. Testers now say: 'Let's try this.' ... The mobile network still assumes that you are reliable, but you are not in reality. That is impossible."

Testing was replaced by trial and error in real-time operations. Operators even brought in their own mobile phones to help them figure out whether a service was malfunctioning. One KPN employee explained that this was the very situation he had learned to dread: "One of our nightmares is that something is already live on the network, up and running and generating traffic while we still have to learn how these things actually work. And that happens increasingly often." Another manager said: "We have to [introduce these services without proper testing], although I am personally against these practices.... Whatever we implement in our mobile network has to be functioning." When confronted with the apparent successful operation of the mobile network despite these shortcomings in testing, the manager responded, "Yes it is manageable, but only barely."

Even maintenance became a major source of incidents—the second largest, to be precise. One respondent confided: "The pressure to constantly improve the services we provide is the greatest threat to the reliability of the network. You are the victim of your own success.... A lot of interruptions are simply the cause of your own work on the network. If you stay away there is no problem whatsoever.... This time we add a new service. Another time, we introduce a new software version.... You just know that you can expect failures." Referring to one paradoxical result of the industry's financial woes, one respondent added, "Because of the reduction in investments, we have less money to change things, and you see a drop in the number of interruptions and calamities."

A crucial part of KPN Mobile's resilience consisted of operators and managers learning to live outside their comfort zone and accepting certain types of failure. Referring to a particular network element that caused failures, an operator explained: "We still do not know exactly what the cause of these failures was. So now, we just do 'click-click' [and reboot the system]." Many of them improvised the means with which to maintain reliability—which created its own share of problems. A change manager in the network operating center said: "These developments make you very dependent on people. I wouldn't choose this dependence. It's seems like we are going back into the pioneering phase again. I'm not happy with that. But as these chances come up, I take them, even though I feel uncomfortable using these tricks."

Confronting Resilience in Theory and in Practice

Following current thinking on organizational resilience, we would have to conclude that these three case studies present remarkable success stories. The organizations we describe encountered disturbances that were not only surprising but often outside the realm of what their personnel had believed to be possible. The most dramatic example is perhaps the California ISO. Its managers may have thought about coping with market failures, but no one had ever considered that this could include the overnight disappearance of the markets altogether or the sudden loss of creditworthiness of the utilities and the ISO itself. To maintain a functioning system under such conditions truly marks resilience.

Resilience is generally understood to be a desirable characteristic of an organization, but that is not how the operators in our case studies experienced it. They looked back on these episodes as harrowing near misses and saw their escape as the result of luck rather than competence—all in order to serve impossible goals imposed upon their organization by an unforgiving environment. There appears to be a real price attached to being a resilient organization.

In addition, our findings highlight a drawback of resilience that so far has hardly been recognized: reliance on real-time operations has caused these organizations to become preoccupied with what one of our respondents called "the short-short term." Resources, time, and attention were sucked away from planning and preparing for the longer term. These organizations had trouble looking ahead one year, let alone thinking about future threats and priorities. Paradoxically, this also undermines their future resilience, as resources that are consumed now will not be available in the future.

Why does resilience sound so much more reassuring in theory than it looks in practice? We suspect that part of this stems from hindsight. When researchers study resilience, they know the outcome. All empirical cases in the literature that we are aware of connect resilience to success stories—and, conversely, tie failures to a breakdown of resilience (e.g., Weick 1993). Researchers then focus on explaining that success—which, understandably, drives out signals that point to failure.

The situation is the mirror image of that of accident researchers who always find someone who warned well in advance that the accident would happen. Of course, that person is also there issuing dire warnings when the predicted event does not happen—which statistically one would expect to be more often the case. Likewise, the impressive display of resilience we observed in DWR, ISO, KPN, and others could be negated the next day, should any be hit by a major disaster. Does that mean that these organizations weren't really resilient? This seems to be a problem of measurement: we don't measure resilience independent of outcome. In other words, our understanding of resilience is the product of hindsight bias.

The hindsight bias is reinforced by what one could call a bias of incidentalism. The empirical base underlying research on resilience is dominated by cases focusing on incidents. The concept of resilience has been developed from case studies that deal with one-off, short-lived disturbances with a clear beginning and end—often in the field of crisis management or incident analysis. The organization was deemed resilient and successful if it had "bounced back" to the original situation. Because we know the outcome, there is never any need to study resilience separately from it. Indeed, because of the short time frames involved, often there isn't even a possibility of studying the events without knowing the outcome beforehand.

Resilience felt a lot less reassuring for the organizations we studied than the literature suggests. These organizations weren't dealing with a one-off incident, and they did not "bounce back." We saw a system that kept functioning but that didn't return to its original position. The organizations we studied operated in messy institutional environments that remained turbulent. This turbulence may have decreased in comparison to some climactic moment, but it still fluctuates around an average that is substantially higher than before. For the organization, that implies anxiety over whether it can continue to cope—even over whether coping is a reasonable expectation.

All this has consequences for the study of organizational resilience. First, we should begin to define resilience both in terms of *outcome* (bouncing back, emerging stronger) and *process* (grasping crisis dynamics, learning, creating a culture of awareness). Second, we should study whether and how process characteristics are related to outcomes. In our cases, the outcome (resilience) could not be related to expected process characteristics—we may well wonder whether the reverse is true as well. If assumed process characteristics have little or nothing to do with the desired outcome, this will have serious consequences for the prescriptions of resilience that have become so popular.

It would refocus our attention on the plight of operators. In pursuit of that elusive goal of resilience, they engage in activities that come closer to definitions of organizational deviance than the heroic conceptions that dominate the literature on resilient organizations. As the chapters in this book make clear, resilience will become increasingly important in the face of new threats. The operators—the reliability experts who must "deliver" resilience—need better guidance if they are to meet our expectations.

10 PLANNING FOR CATASTROPHE

HOW FRANCE IS PREPARING FOR THE AVIAN FLU
AND WHAT IT MEANS FOR RESILIENCE

Claude Gilbert

We are witnessing the emergence of new threats with fairly specific characteristics. The scale on which they unfold is wide and increasingly global. Their effects can be ascribed to specific agents or events as much as to vulnerabilities peculiar to today's societies. Health threats top the list of these future threats. Epidemics and pandemics are once again provoking concern, especially the possibility of an avian flu–related pandemic on a global scale. This is not simply a matter of a revival of old threat agents; it is the emergence of a new type of threat whose characteristics demand new forms of crisis management.

Most countries have taken and still take this threat very seriously, despite its highly hypothetical nature. This is especially the case in France. The alerts of the World Health Organization (WHO) prompted the French government to devise a response plan that has since been updated annually (Plan "Pandémie Grippale" 2004, 2005, 2006, 2007). Concrete actions were swiftly initiated in addition to the creation of a regularly updated plan, including the appointment of an interministerial delegate specifically in charge of combating a flu pandemic (August 2005). Working groups were set up in various ministries; an interministerial dialogue was initiated, first limited to the ministries that seemed to be most immediately concerned (agriculture, health, interior) and then slowly expanded. Substantial funds were earmarked to support these actions. In parallel, programs were launched in the public research sector to promote the development of specific studies in this field (essentially in the life sciences).

Yet despite this seemingly full-scale mobilization, an important question needs to be considered, concerning France and probably other countries as well: to what extent have the authorities and experts who confront the threat of a pandemic really taken note of the characteristics of this type of situation? In this chapter, I address this question and argue that the idea of resilience (i.e., the capacity for collective action in the face of unexpected extreme events that shatter infrastructure and disrupt normal operating conditions) needs to be given more attention.

A Threat That Poses Unusual Problems

The link between crisis and uncertainty (as a defining characteristic) is well established (Quarantelli and Dynes 1977; Rosenthal, Charles, and t'Hart 1989). In the case of a pandemic, there likely will be an especially high level of diverse uncertainties. Likewise, the possibility of a really long period of crisis on a global scale raises questions with regard to the conditions required to sustain collective life. The pressing question is how collective life, in its most ordinary dimensions, can be sustained in the long term in the face of seriously deteriorated conditions.

Facing Deep Uncertainties

The work of scientific experts in virology and epidemiology, both in France and abroad, indicates that a flu epidemic should be considered inevitable. This conclusion is based on statistics and the history of diseases. The mutation or hybridization of the H5N1 virus seems to be a possible if not probable future cause of such a pandemic. The risk of a pandemic also seems to be closely linked to globalization and the internationalization of human activities. The massive growth of all kinds of trade is considered to be the main factor in rapid, large-scale dissemination of the disease. The risk is therefore associated as much with the actual nature of a future virus as with the prevailing system of international trade and the circulation of humans, animals, and goods, along with the resulting vulnerabilities. These are elements of relative "certainty" that mask many uncertainties.

No one can foresee the severity and precise characteristics of the disease: different modes of propagation (other than by air), incubation time, symptoms and specific ailments, and possibilities of immunization may all differ. Any hypotheses are fragile at best, which seems to limit efforts at anticipation prior to the occurrence of hybridization or mutation of the virus.

Moreover, an H5N1-related pandemic is in itself still hypothetical in so far as a flu pandemic could stem from another virus strain. Likewise, there is no certainty that the pandemic would develop from an epizooty (i.e., a disease that simultaneously affects a large number of animals of the same or different species).

The pandemic could last several weeks, several months, or even a year, with periods of greater or lesser virulence. The main reference in this respect—the Spanish flu of 1918–20—suggests the possibility of a crisis lasting for months, with a progression of (two or three) successive waves of lesser virulence than the first wave. But these data do not seem sufficient to characterize a future pandemic, which in both the WHO and the French plans is presented as being of undetermined duration, virtually impossible to quantify, and corresponding to a single phase. The pandemic is widely conceptualized in linear fashion, starting in one go and ending suddenly. Since 2006, the French plan has begun to differentiate among the conditions for ending a pandemic and to discuss the differences between the phases of escalation and termination.

In many respects, a pandemic is characterized by high levels of uncertainty. These primarily concern the actual course of the pandemic since its propagation could vary widely in terms of both time and space—depending on modes of transmission; the characteristics of the disease; the measures implemented; the level of urbanization; and certain parts of the territory being affected and others not, with different evolutions or time lags. Unlike most so-called civil security crises ensuing from technological accidents, transport accidents, or natural disasters, pandemic crises are not as a rule bound in time and space. The evolving character of crisis, already identified as a major characteristic of the modern crisis (Comfort, Sungu, Johnson, and Dunn 2001; Boin et al. 2003), will be particularly strong in case of a pandemic. Moreover, the diversity of pandemic situations seems to correspond to diverse states of deterioration, once again with highly variable evolutions. Depending on the time and place, the flow of activities and the circulation of goods and people will be disturbed to a greater or lesser degree.

The Necessities of "Ordinary Life" as a Key Priority

Health matters and public order are generally perceived as the main problems of a pandemic. But the management of a pandemic demands rapid prioritization of problems that during other types of crisis can be treated as secondary. In addition to health and public order, it is necessary to identify "maintenance of collective life" as a key challenge of pandemic management.

The need to take into account the constraints of daily life, of ordinary functioning on the scale of the individual and of the society as a whole, is present from the outbreak of a pandemic but intensifies as it develops. This includes the need for families and all basic social groups to carry on meeting the requirements of daily life in one way or another throughout the pandemic (various forms of care, food, evacuation of household refuse, recreation, etc.); the need for "frontline" emergency services (in the fields of health and security and in private practice) to carry on fulfilling the various missions that "normally" fall within their ambit; the need for public- and private-sector hospitals to continue treating various categories of patients (especially with the specific problems posed by the emergency treatment of certain diseases such as heart disease and, even more, so chronic diseases such as cancer, requiring long-term treatment). More generally, the question would rapidly arise of opening up schools, universities, churches, cinemas, and sports clubs, if only partially. Likewise, massive disturbances or lasting interruptions of collective life would quickly raise questions of how people's incomes could be guaranteed (for employees in the private and public sectors or for individuals receiving welfare benefits if the relevant services no longer functioned) and how money would continue to circulate and the means of payment to function.

The maintenance of social life could prove to be particularly problematic in times of pandemic. This would be due above all to the immediate health effects of the pandemic. The functioning of all organizations would be strongly affected by absenteeism, which could amount to 30, 40, or even 50 percent of personnel. More generally, functioning would be affected by the limitation of trade, both nationally and internationally. This would reveal the extent of modern societies' vulnerabilities, resulting from national economies' heavy reliance on other economies, especially when it comes to staple products, electronic components, raw materials, and so on. These strongly interconnected and interdependent networks can lead to a "house of cards" effect between different commercial sectors, especially in respect to the production and distribution of consumer goods, food, and drugs, making it particularly difficult to anticipate the consequences of "infrastructural failure" (Boin and McConnell 2007).

These weaknesses would be rapidly compounded by other types of vulnerability, especially social ones: vulnerabilities due to a large proportion of the population in Western countries being accustomed to comfort after decades of prosperity (with immediate access to a large number of services and goods; food consumption closely linked to mass distribution; the massive use of technologies reliant on electronics, electricity, hydrocarbons, etc.). Further, vulnerabilities relating to marginalization and precarious socioeconomic situations now characterize a significant part of the population, with living conditions that are sometimes critical (e.g., large families living in cramped dwellings, old people living in isolation, squatters, homeless people, migrants without official documents). A lengthy crisis would accentuate this situation and widen the gap between this part of the population and those who are privileged or simply less underprivileged. It would compound certain problems relating to daily subsistence (as witnessed recently in certain crises such as the one following Hurricane Katrina).

Whereas reflection on crisis management tends to diverge from the foundations of usual socioeconomic functioning, in the case of a crisis situation associated with a pandemic it leads us, on the contrary, to take stock of that which is "ordinary" in today's contemporary societies. This is essential if we are to understand the strengths and weaknesses of our societies in a lasting crisis.

A New Problem Treated on the Basis of Past Experience

The threat of a pandemic is characterized by a set of emergent problems that should prompt the authorities to substantially alter their conceptions of crisis management. This would relate as much to the nature of the threat in public health terms as to the structural vulnerabilities peculiar to modern societies. In spite of substantial changes made since 2004 (when the first French pandemic plan appeared), certain features have been constant in the French approach to the threat of a flu pandemic. By examining the various versions of the pandemic plan, the underlying policies, and, more generally, the points of view of different authorities and experts, the main characteristics of the French approach can be identified: recognition of a large-scale threat, monitoring and control of this threat from the health point of view, and management of a pandemic through a framework that is still to a large degree keyed to a state of emergency.

An Anticipated Threat, an Identified Enemy

Rarely has a sanitary threat (with the degree of uncertainty characterizing any threat) been anticipated to such an extent. The Institut de Veille Sanitaire (French Sanitary Watch Institute) has estimated the risk of mortality associated with such a pandemic at 91,000 to 212,000 deaths in France if no specific measures are taken, with a possibility of halving the death rate if the measures provided for in the "flu pandemic" plan (Plan "Pandémie Grippale") are applied. The expected number of potential patients is calculated at 9 to 21 million, for a total population of 59.6 million inhabitants (i.e., a rate of incidence of 15 to 35 percent). It is probable that the disease may affect not only the elderly or people with weak immune systems, but the entire population (with perhaps an even higher risk of incidence and gravity among children, adolescents, and young adults).

The anticipated threat is also treated proactively, yet with a sharper focus on a clearly identified enemy (the H5N1) than on the actual threat of a pandemic. The evolution of the threat has been clearly envisaged, from the arrival of the H5N1 in France to the unfolding of the pandemic, through all intermediate stages. The "flu pandemic" plan is organized in relation to this possible evolution by distinguishing phases: epizooty without human cases, isolated human cases without interhuman transmission, groups of limited and localized human cases, large areas of uncontrolled grouped cases, and so on. Each preidentified phase thus corresponds to a precise characterization of the situation and to a set of measures and a carefully planned mobilization of resources.

The first objective is to organize close surveillance of the H5N1. Its penetration, propagation, and possible mutation or hybridization are the focus of extensive and intensive surveillance. This function has been reinforced considerably in France subsequent to various health-related crises. Measures have been taken in respect to animal health, notably bovine spongiform encephalopathy (BSE) and, more generally, various epidemics and contamination of food: foot-and-mouth disease, salmonellosis, listeriosis, and so on. This positioning is entirely consistent with that of the WHO, which, after the 2003 SARS episodes, is positioning itself increasingly as a body for the international management of alerts.

The second objective of the plan, closely related to the surveillance function, is to prepare a set of actions designed to limit the penetration and spread of the H5N1. These actions consist primarily of police measures: quarantine, limitation of trade, confinement of poultry farms, and so on. Here again, past police actions concerning animal health serve as a reference, backed up by drastic preventive measures (mainly the mass slaughter of poultry), as well as economic measures (compensation and subsidies). The focus on the "animal health" dimension in the prepandemic period helps to illuminate an area of intervention where, in several respects, public authorities can take advantage of a fairly high level of control.

In a sense, the "human health" dimension is monitored less, even if surveillance systems, particularly in isolation in the hospital sector, are provided. Whereas the prepandemic period is divided into several phases, the pandemic period itself corresponds to a single phase. These choices correspond to those the WHO makes at the international level.[1]

These choices also reflect difficulties in addressing problems related to a flu pandemic risk (and, more generally, a pandemic of any emergent disease), due to the inherent level of uncertainty. The focus is therefore rather on prevention of a pandemic and on that which seems immediately manageable and can be forecast in an area relating mainly to animal rather than human health, with a public security component. Without taking this point any further, we simply wish to point out here that, by contrast, there has been no real international policy of risk reduction at the source, especially in Asia, and no real commitment of financial resources to combat the expansion of the virus on poultry farms. Such a policy would certainly have been more effective and less costly.

Preparation for Crisis Management

In regard to the pandemic phase, the authorities are already working at organizing defenses by preparing the mobilization of resources and actors and by planning a set of measures based on classical crisis management concepts. The organization of "defenses" covers both the prepandemic and the pandemic periods. It involves above all the search for a set of means that either act as protections against disease or help to reduce its impact: antivirals, masks, respirators, vaccines, and so on. Mass purchases, the launching of production, regulation of storage problems for masks, and antivirals were all at the heart of the authorities' preoccupations and actions in 2005. Reflection has also been initiated on the distribution of means of defense (mainly masks and antivirals) and on a way of defining and justifying priorities (e.g., giving priority to certain types of staff in charge of health, security, supplies, energy production, etc.). All this reflection and all these actions are developed independent of questions regarding the effectiveness of antivirals, the material conditions of the use of masks, the staff required for using respirators, the time needed to produce vaccines in view of strong production constraints, and so on. In general, the priority given to these types of action and the different kinds of problems that they generate (budgets to define, suppliers to identify, raw materials to find, etc.) leaves little room for doubt or critical questioning.

These actions, relating to a "logic of means," allow for communication designed to reassure and to demonstrate that public authorities are taking preventive action. An early study of twenty-five European countries, published in the April 2006 issue of the *Lancet*, rated France as one of the best prepared, on the basis of precisely this type of criterion (Shortridge 2006). It would be interesting to establish whether the French authorities were more willing than others to engage in this type of action due to previous crises that led to lawsuits, the resignations of cabinet ministers and high-ranking officials, and so on (contaminated blood, a deadly heat wave).

In the mobilization of various actors, the accent is on health workers and, more particularly, on anyone directly or indirectly related to the hospital system. Interesting issues, then, arise concerning the organization of such mobilization, especially to cope with the mass influx of patients, and the part that can and should be played by private medical practice (which ordinarily relies on the public sector to deal with emergencies). The emphasis is also on the mobilization of staff in charge of public security, who have to apply the first emergency measures and manage the anticipated social disorder, especially relating to access to means of protection (mainly antivirals) and medical care (especially via hospitals). Tricky questions remain with regard to the management of large numbers of corpses, absenteeism (of 30, 40, or 50 percent?) due to contamination of front-line workers or of their family members or the breakdown of public transport, and destabilization caused by the deaths of workers or deaths within their families.

The search for means of defense and the mobilization of actors in the areas of health and public security are explained in relation to the main kinds of action envisaged as necessary in case of a proven risk of pandemic: the sudden suspension of most collective life in order to limit contact among people as far as possible. General consensus on this type of action exists among the authorities. It is widely accepted that the government should rapidly take strong measures. For technical and symbolic reasons, these measures have to be few and simple: closing schools and places of public gathering; confining populations or sections of the population to their homes; limiting public transport but allowing the people in charge of emergency care to carry on working. Here again, important questions tend to be overlooked. For instance, for how long can such measures, which establish a sort of "state of emergency," be applied? How can the disorganization of collective life triggered by these measures be dealt with? How can special dispensations, concerning so-called priority staff and activities, be defined and managed?

The management of the first moments of the crisis via the implementation of drastic measures serves as a frame of reference for the management of the entire pandemic, once it has settled in. Measures for treating patients (five hundred thousand plus one million hospitalized, according to the most recent version of the plan) are always envisaged in the framework of a "state of emergency." It seems that health problems are expected to overlap rapidly with problems of public order (related to massive admissions to hospitals, challenges to the priorities established for the distribution of medication, problems of food supplies, etc.). Even though the plan mentions little on this subject, the assumption of extensive social and political disorganization, social and traffic disruptions, and violence is regularly made.

The organization of the continuity of the state completes the apparatus envisaged to cope with an exceptional crisis. This continuity seems to be guaranteed by maintenance of the functioning of state administrations (especially the central ones); public services; and, more broadly, all the entities on which the welfare state is based (primarily by maintaining essential chains of command within the state and between the state and the rest of society). It would be up to the state to supervise and activate all actions during a pandemic, whether they concern health, the provision of essential goods and services, or the maintenance of public order (an aspect always considered essential). This reinforces the somewhat authoritarian nature of pandemic management by the state.

This way of conceiving the management of a pandemic in France is determined above all by lessons from past experience. Anticipation, surveillance, and immediate action appear to be the main features of the adopted policy. All the measures provided rely essentially on the public authorities. Finally, management of the pandemic also seems to depend on what the public authorities can effectively do. The pandemic is approached from three angles—animal health, human health, and public security—that serve as "reference frameworks" for public action strongly marked by "policing," whether it concerns health or public order. Each of these reference frameworks (Goffman 1974) corresponds to actors and organizations that for the most part belong to public agencies (hospitals, emergency medical aid services, fire brigades, police forces, etc.) accustomed to the types of intervention envisaged, to possible requisitioning, and to functioning in emergency mode.

Other modalities of organization enabling collective life to be maintained —primarily on the initiative of local authorities, firms, and NGOs—receive less attention (especially in the first versions of the "flu pandemic" plan). Initially, they were simply taken for granted, since the authorities mobilized the plan. Only in the 2006 and 2007 versions of the plan have measures for supporting the maintenance of collective social and economic functioning by local authorities, firms, NGOs, and individuals received real attention or at least official mention. Yet these actors are some of the key players that have to be taken into account—via modalities still to be defined—if the country is really to prepare itself to face an unusual crisis such as a pandemic.

Resilience as a New Approach to Crisis Management

The choices made in the French plan (especially in its first versions) still reflect a classical approach to crisis management. This approach prioritizes anticipation of problems and solutions in the framework of planning, with strong emphasis on modes of action, usually the war model. The main objective is to avoid the outbreak of a pandemic; to delay its development; and, as far as possible, to limit its effects. This explains the main focus on the pre-pandemic period and the early days of the crisis. The result of this framing is that problems peculiar to a pandemic, such as the long-term management of daily needs or the many uncertainties related to this type of threat, are not addressed head-on. Without being overlooked, they seem to be managed only when there is no alternative. The qualities of improvisation are considered as having to offset the inherent limits in planning. But other approaches could be adopted more willingly than was the case in the middle of the 2000s.[2]

Capacities for Resilience

Taking into account the need to maintain collective life in the long term and in a deteriorated or severely deteriorated context requires recognizing the essential role of actors who are not necessarily part of the government administration and public sphere and who are not given priority in the government plan. Economic actors (especially in communication, energy, transport, refuse removal, distribution of consumer goods, circulation of liquidities, etc.), local authorities, organizations in charge of social action, and so on, are all important in crisis management. This is not necessarily taken for granted in the French political context. It took a long time before partnership with these actors was established.

Only in the most recent versions of the national plan is the importance of the link with local authorities and the business world emphasized. To some extent, they are still considered as state auxiliaries, so that their own logics, specific constraints, and degree of autonomy are not really taken into account. A number of firms, especially in the mass-distribution sector, banking, catering, transport, communications, and the media, have launched initiatives, devised plans, and taken steps to raise awareness. Since communication on these initiatives is limited, it is difficult to know whether the measures envisaged are set in a classical crisis management perspective or to take the specific characteristics of a pandemic into account. The question of the capacity to sustain preparation and/or mobilization should the pandemic not occur (considering the costs that it would entail) is seldom asked. In this respect, the absence of information on preparation for the 2000 bug—and on the impact of that preparation on the fact that there never was a bug—warrants reflection.

More broadly speaking, maintaining collective life in a continually disrupted situation entails recognition of the capacity of various sectors of civil society (nonprofit associations, community organizations, trade unions, etc.) to participate in the endeavor and to seriously consider their essential role in that respect. Likewise, in terms of preparation upstream, it is possible to consider that the population is prepared to hear the truth; to distinguish between that which is important and that which is not; to face up to critical situations once the initial anxiety, shock, and discouragement have passed; and to take charge of some of the necessary actions in situations of crisis, such as precautions and stockpiling (food, masks, medicines, etc., as provided for in the U.S. plan, e.g., with checklists). It seems that actions to raise awareness, directed at charitable organizations or communities, are more developed in English-speaking countries, as are reflection and actions concerning insurance, conditions of recruitment, and the minimum training of voluntary workers who may be called on to help in sanitary matters.

In March 2007, a law was enacted to structure a sanitary reserve of voluntary workers who would be remunerated and insured for liability. It concerns only doctors and advanced medical or paramedical students. At the level of the *communes,* civil security reserves, instituted by the August 2004 law, are still largely unstructured, and there have been few calls for mobilization. The "population" tends to be considered essentially as a potentially threatening entity that is quick to panic, protest, and so on, and that therefore needs to be controlled, above all. Or else, without further explanation, it is simply assumed that what the plan refers to as "neighbourhood solidarity" would spontaneously be organized, ad hoc.

In reality, it is precisely these social and socioeconomic actors who are instrumental for collective adaptation in crises, at various levels—from the family cell to the large corporation, through businesses, schools, and NGOs (Comfort 2002; Comfort et al. 2004). In a crisis it is important not simply to "maintain" collective functions and the continuity of the state but also to achieve collective adaptation. The challenge is not to force changes in modes of organization, as proposed by measures taken in a spirit of emergency, where society comes to a standstill; rather, it is to ensure that the structures and modes of economic and socioeconomic systems continue to function as long as possible, even partially or in very low gear. As many recent studies of individuals and collectives in high-risk activities have shown (e.g., Rasmussen 1997; Amalberti 1996, 2002, 2006), such systems "normally" tend to be characterized by downgraded functioning, dysfunctions, tolerance of failures, and breakdowns.

The ability to maintain the functioning of the most essential systems and networks, if only in a restricted mode or despite major disturbances or failures, can be based on usual management methods and existing networks and cognitive frames. It is then necessary to anticipate the effects produced by the main national measures recommended (concerning, e.g., the closure of schools, restrictions in transport, etc.), to ensure that these exceptional measures are coherent with the maintenance of regular functioning in a downgraded mode. In many respects, accepting and integrating "deteriorations," with a view to enabling a society faced with a pandemic to "last" in the long term, radically changes the perception of crisis management. "Accompanying the crisis" means striving not to depart from the regular ways of doing things (as it is tempting to do in cases of emergency), as well as acknowledging and accepting the deterioration of ordinary modalities in order to adjust to the crisis (without striving to maintain a normal state at all costs). This means adjusting to organizational dysfunctions, to interruptions and even suspensions of networks, to reductions in the supply of goods and services, and so on. It also means adapting to different criteria, norms, and even values. The notion of resilience is used here in the sense of computer technology, where it defines the quality of a system that enables it to function correctly despite the faultiness of one or more of its constituent elements. Reflection on the modalities of preparing for these new types of crisis aims primarily at building up or reinforcing such resilience.

New Modes of Management, New Priorities

By approaching crisis during pandemics from the viewpoint of resilience, new modalities of preparing for or managing crisis can be envisaged. The introduction of the idea of duration, with different possible phases, raises the question of the nature of the problems that would have to be solved and the way in which they would be ranked. Management of the pandemic in an emergency mode, with the application of a set of barrier measures to avoid and above all limit its propagation, can be maintained only for a certain period, probably a few days. The prolonged maintenance of a situation resembling a "state of emergency" or "state of exception" is difficult for two reasons. The first concerns the limits inherent in the mobilization of the agents in charge of activities defined as priorities: limited staff already functioning in an emergency mode, possible contamination of staff, possible exercise of the right to opt out, accumulated fatigue, the need to care for family members, children who no longer attend school, and so on. The second reason is the need to maintain functions essential to collective life, to the basic socio-economic functioning of society, which is incompatible with a "stoppage."

The idea is less to organize continuity through specific measures (e.g., "continuity plans"), in the context of the management of an exceptional situation ("state of emergency"), than to identify that which, in usual modes of functioning, could provide motivation and support for crisis management. Admittedly, there are far more questions on the subject than possible answers and solutions. This is partially due to the very limited feedback on past flu epidemics and especially those that occurred in contemporary societies (1957, 1969) or episodes such as the SARS outbreak in 2003 (probably the most comparable case).

The human and social sciences cannot propose ready-made analyses and recommendations. They can nevertheless open up the field of questions by proposing reflection and cooperation with various actors. For instance, how can our societies, in situations of lasting crisis, function differently and especially in a more restricted way? How can new trade-offs be envisaged between values and economic, social, and moral criteria? How can the articulation between public service logics and market logics be revised— or even new logics be defined at the interface between the two (Comfort 2002)? How can changes in the mode of intervention of actors and organizations be accepted with a degree of "deterioration" of services? How can crisis preparation be linked to preoccupations and problems existing on a daily basis in agencies already functioning in difficult or deteriorated conditions, such as hospitals and many firms? Addressing these questions head-on, thinking about scenarios and debating them in public or other arenas, above all at different levels of society, is an essential challenge.

Another important contribution of the social and human sciences, based on a tradition of crisis research, relates to the fact that one of the essential factors of crisis development is closely linked to the uncertainty and impossibility of characterizing the situation *a minima*. Without milestones in time and space, the various states and stages of a pandemic will be particularly difficult to predict. It can likewise be expected that aspects relating to the virus and the disease itself will be characterized by high levels of uncertainty. Although the plan and measures in France clearly highlight uncertainties, they still largely overlook the measures that could be taken before or during the pandemic (or in the early emergency phase) to reduce these uncertainties and to explain what is happening.

In such circumstances, it is as necessary to maintain the capacity to act, despite a deterioration of systems and networks, so as to create or maintain capacities to account for what is happening. Creating or maintaining such capacities is connected to the "system of meaning" (Fritz 1968); to the process of "sensemaking" (Weick 1993); and to the ability to avoid the real disaster, which would be the incapacity to represent the event (Rosset 1979, 41). Being able to report on a situation regularly (on its health aspects, as well as its economic, social, and political dimensions) and to make forecasts becomes a priority. How, in such circumstances, can measures be designed for closely monitoring the evolution of the disease and for adjusting health care protocols with a view to comparing different medical and hospital practices and different results? How can proactive systems and approaches be established in fields of research and expertise? How can one design procedures and systems that, especially on a territorial basis, make it possible to collect and compare necessarily scant information, to acquire the knowledge required to analyze situations and make forecasts (Comfort, Sungu, Johnson, and Dunn 2001)—knowing that these systems will be faced with the same problems of downgraded functioning as the other structures of society? How, on this basis, can communication be designed that allows for control over the "definition of reality" irrespective of its state of "deterioration"? Moreover, in pandemics, who is responsible for this function, which, in many respects, is of a political nature? The idea would be not only to define the state of "reality" in order to reduce uncertainties but also to draw conclusions on the consequences, at a collective level, of a definition given for this reality. The consequences would be in terms of actions and of ranking the priorities, but also in terms of establishing criteria and norms in a particular situation. In this case, how can questions be treated where political decisions and ethical considerations are closely entangled?

When these various aspects of prolonged and deep uncertainty are taken into account, our perspective on crisis management is shifted even further than when "just" the breakdown of societies is taken into account. The importance of the problem of uncertainty makes it necessary to prioritize the definition of reality, which, in such circumstances, cannot simply be reduced to a question of science and techniques. The issue of resilience forces us to examine a way of "withstanding" uncertainty and adjusting to it and, relatedly, to the exercise of the political function.

Above all, this implies a change of position for the actors concerned, who have to accept the fact that uncertainty will prevail during a pandemic and that they will actively and in various ways have to reduce it. Only in that way might they be able to identify, in complex and shifting realities, the best opportunities for taking action (Jullien 1996). This type of approach corresponds to a fairly radical change in crisis management since it amounts to acknowledging that capacities for defense and anticipation via planning may matter less than the capacity to come to terms with uncertainties and to adjust, with resilience, to largely unpredictable circumstances.

Overcoming Lingering Obstacles

The emergence of new problems and *problematiques* highlighted here is starting to be considered in France. Hence, each new version of the "flu pandemic" plan stresses more emphatically the importance of maintaining collective life after a pandemic has been declared. Yet the specific dimensions of these problems (length of time, deterioration of living conditions, number and type of uncertainties) are not taken completely into consideration. This may simply reflect difficulties of changing modes of management and cognitive frames by considering that in the domain of crisis, as in others, path dependency exists (Pierson 2000). But it could also be seen as the expression of difficulties of another nature, especially political, through the identification of various obstacles opposed to such change.

The first obstacle relates to the traditionally preponderant role attributed to the state in France, in the management of exceptional circumstances. This approach, related to the "state of emergency," still prevails even if various crises, including ones that are moderate in extent, have shown the limits of the state's control over society. As a consequence—in general and irrespective of its nature—the crisis management approach depends on the actors, reference frameworks, and modes of intervention corresponding to what appears to give the authorities a predominant role and the capacity for control. Hence, "civil security crises" are still the main framework of reference when it comes to crisis management. This is especially true since forecasting of crises cannot fit into this frame (like that relating to nuclear accidents) and therefore remains limited, and since notions that could have been useful for crises with more structural effects (such as civil defense) have become obsolete.

Other explanations can also be advanced—for instance, the reluctance that still exists in France to acknowledge the fact that local authorities, the population (not a homogeneous entity but structured by different types of affiliation), economic agents, and so on, can all be actors in their own right in crisis management. This is so despite the obvious role that these actors are called on to play in crisis situations, as observed on multiple occasions, and despite the existence of various laws to encourage the recognition of citizens' active role in this type of situation. Apart from reluctance concerning particular types of actors, the French public authorities are still very much attached—for reasons of legitimacy—to retaining their control over crisis management and its definition, even if this means excluding its new dimensions. This position of the public authorities could be supported to some degree by the attitude of various actors in civil society (especially firms) that, although called on to play a role, do not necessarily want to appear as leading actors (with the problems of liability that this entails). Irrespective of its true capacities, the governmental "centralization reflex" is not really contested, as many still accept that the government has "to make sense of what is going on and to 'do something' to restore order" (Boin and MConnell 2007, 53), as in other crises.

Finally, a last set of obstacles stems from the fact that a pandemic situation of the avian flu kind makes it necessary to assess the extent of the vulnerabilities of modern developed societies. Highly efficient in terms of economic (especially liberal) criteria, these societies are also proving to be extremely fragile (see Boin's chapter in this volume). It is difficult to imagine reverting rapidly to modes of functioning (autarky, autonomous production of essential goods, stockpiling, etc.) typical of economic, social, and political structures whose foundations have largely disappeared. Even if adjustments and changes can be envisaged on the basis of what exists, reflection on this subject is still difficult to initiate in a real public debate. Thus, taking into consideration all the effects that can be induced by a flu pandemic leads us to question the very foundations of our society.

Apart from the fact that the occurrence of a pandemic remains hypothetical and that French decision makers have already experienced "prophesies of disaster" that failed to materialize (especially in the case of BSE), various obstacles still hinder direct analysis of a pandemic situation and the integration of questions in terms of resistance and resilience in crisis management. Because of such obstacles, mainly of a political sort, resilience could stay a "future priority at best" (Boin and McConnell 2007, 57), as is the case for more conventional crises.

Other obstacles exist in the research field: it still seems difficult to connect resilience to the capacity to "make up" for downgraded situations and to start from downgraded functioning in order to find new dynamics and develop new logics. The idea is no longer to consider situations such as pandemics as an intermission, an intervening period between two "normal" states, but really as a situation per se. So the question is: how can these situations be conceptualized without referring to a "normal" state? Here we encounter a disturbing paradox: managing the disruptions induced by the settlement of really unknown and nonconventional situations (Lagadec 2000) probably goes through less brutal changes (particularly in organizational terms) than it would through the anticipated process of turning to downgraded modes of management (Gilbert 2007a). Perhaps this is a better way to define resilience in today's world.

II THE LIMITS OF SELF-RELIANCE
INTERNATIONAL COOPERATION AS A SOURCE
OF RESILIENCE

Mark Rhinard and Bengt Sundelius

In late August 2005, Hurricane Katrina bore down on the Gulf Coast of the United States. Katrina caused severe and catastrophic damage. In addition to ripping homes open and destroying power lines in Mississippi and Louisiana, the storm breached two levees in the city of New Orleans (Seed et al. 2005). Water flooded 80 percent of the city, adding to the destruction and contributing to the deaths of over thirteen hundred residents (Cooper and Block 2006).

Equally troubling was the way U.S. authorities handled the Hurricane Katrina relief effort. A slow and uncoordinated response compounded infrastructure damage and added to the suffering, in turn impairing the ability of New Orleans and other cities along the Gulf Coast to manage a major crisis effectively. Concern was expressed by observers not only within the United States but also from abroad: the international community took part in an unprecedented "role reversal" (Richard 2006a) as foreign governments pledged almost one billion dollars in cash, supplies, equipment, and in-kind services to help save lives and property.

Some of that aid reached its target destination, but much of it did not. Dutch water engineers worked efficiently in repairing broken pumping stations to drain several New Orleans parishes. Canadian Mounties and search-and-rescue teams interacted seamlessly with their U.S. counterparts to provide much-needed assistance. And the Mexican Navy took a large role in clearing out harbors to make way for incoming supply ships. By contrast,

Swedish mobile telecommunications systems, which could have quickly replaced downed emergency call systems, never reached their target, while United Kingdom ready-to-eat meals were stored in deep freezers despite urgent need. French doctors were turned back at Louisiana airports because they lacked U.S. credentials. Austrian disaster-response experts never received flight clearance because of communication errors (Richard 2006a; Reuters 2005).

These latter cases represent a set of cooperation failures and an absence of established United Nations protocol for managing humanitarian assistance. Although clear policy and procedures exist for managing international cooperation among member states of the United Nations under the Organization for Coordination of Humanitarian Assistance, these procedures were not followed, by either the United States or the nations offering assistance. This policy requires the afflicted nation to request assistance from the United Nations, after which the secretary general issues a call to member nations for specific types of assistance (United Nations 1991). Since the United States did not request assistance from the United Nations to meet disaster needs, it did not set in motion any mechanisms for receiving or managing contributions from other nations. The inability of U.S. government agencies to cooperate with foreign governments over the provision of much-needed humanitarian assistance compounded the problems in response operations, exacerbated the suffering of victims, and hampered the ability of stricken areas to bounce back from a major crisis.

In this chapter, we argue that the capacity to cooperate across borders is an important precondition for resilience. Whether we speak of cities, regions, or nations, today's complex crises (of which Hurricane Katrina is an example) can easily outstrip the coping capacities of a single social system. The capacity to draw in necessary resources from outside a particular political-legal jurisdiction, and to incorporate and deploy these, is an essential source of resilience.

To build this argument, we first establish the relationship between international cooperation and resilience, showing how effective cooperation pays dividends in terms of resource distribution, policy coordination, and sensemaking—each an important part of a social system's ability to bounce back from major disturbances. To explain what factors underpin a system's "cooperation capacity," we draw on cooperation studies in three different disciplines—international relations, organizational studies, and social psychology—to outline factors that relate to the interest-based, institution-based, and ideas-based components of successful cooperation.

The large number of cooperation attempts in the Hurricane Katrina response effort, some resulting in success and others in failure, allows us to examine whether the presence of these factors may correlate with outcomes.[1] Future application of this framework could be applied to more familiar examples of international cooperation in disaster relief, such as those related to developing countries accepting aid from abroad. The disasters caused by the 2004 Indian Ocean earthquake in Indonesia, Thailand, Sri Lanka, and India stand out in this respect and have been subjected to considerable scrutiny (Bynander, Newlove, and Ramberg 2005; Strömbäck and Nord 2006; European Commission 2005).

Cooperation as a Source of Resilience

The claim that a "capacity to cooperate" across international borders contributes to societal resilience requires elucidation. Following, we examine what resilience means, what cooperation involves, and how cooperation contributes to resilience.

In this chapter, *resilience* refers to "the capacity of a social system to proactively adapt to and recover from disturbances that are perceived within the system to fall outside the range of normal and expected disturbances" (see Boin, Comfort, and Demchak's chapter in this volume). A social system can refer to a town, city, public airport, industrial firm, or any complex organizational unit. In fact, the exact nature of the system under examination is less important than the factors that contribute to its resilience. Furthermore, resilience implies not just the ability to bounce back from a major crisis, but the capacity to react and adapt before a disturbance escalates into a crisis. We pay special attention in this chapter to how international cooperation can help societies to both fend off and recover from major disturbances.

Cooperation is a slippery concept, even though it is widely invoked in both practice and theory. For practitioners, cooperation between subgovernmental units is often viewed as an ideal situation that, if achieved, can generate government efficiency, effectiveness, and mutually beneficial outcomes. When change is needed, or perceived to be needed, "better cooperation" is usually the clarion call (B. G. Peters 2001).

Academics offer more precision, but their definitions differ according to three distinct research traditions. International relations scholars focus on cooperation among governments; indeed, the topic is a cornerstone of the subdiscipline (for a review, see Milner 1992). Following Keohane, many scholars define cooperation as occurring "when actors adjust their behavior to the actual or anticipated preferences of others, through a process of policy coordination" (1984, 51–52). Cooperation, viewed from this perspective, is an endpoint, something to be achieved over considerable odds. The anarchic state of world affairs throws many obstacles in the way of cooperation, and international relations scholars focus attention on finding useful answers to a key question: what factors might facilitate cooperation?

Management scholars focus on cooperation within and among organizations. They see cooperation as "the process by which individuals, groups, and organizations come together, interact, and form psychological relationships for mutual gain or benefit" (Smith, Carroll, and Ashford 1995, 10). Interaction processes "must generate a willingness of organizations to continue in an enduring relationship" (Ring and Van de Ven 1994). The research focus thus turns toward the social underpinnings of ongoing cooperation. Cooperative relationships must be studied, according to Ring and Van de Ven, as "socially contrived mechanisms for collective action, which are continually shaped and restructured by actions and symbolic interpretations of the parties involved" (1994, 96).

Social psychologists examine cooperation as an exercise between individuals acting as groups; cooperation thus becomes a process of either reconciling identities or adjusting strategies to maximize interests. Scholars interested in the role of identity in generating cooperation focus on social bonds and "in-group" versus "out-group" dynamics (Argyle 1991). Scholars investigating interest maximization focus on the pitfalls and promises of individuals trying to cooperate in mixed-motive games such as the prisoner's dilemma. Behavioral changes, according to this strand of research, depend on incentives, rules, and the number of games played (we explore this more in the next section).

Considering the different types of cooperation explored in each discipline, it is useful to clarify our own *unit of analysis*. We are interested in exploring cooperation across sovereign borders, but not just in terms of executive-level interaction led by heads of government, as the "intergovernmental cooperation" perspective in international relations assumes. We follow the approach of Keohane and Nye (1974), who argue that some of the most intensive cooperation across national borders is taking place among subunits of national governments. This type of "transgovernmental cooperation" involves agencies and organizations that maneuver outside of the strict yoke and attention of central governments (see Keohane and Nye 1974).[2] Risse-Kappen took up this line of analysis in his treatment of U.S.-UK relations during the Cold War (1997; see also Rosenau 1969), while scholars of the European Union over the years have similarly focused on the bureaucratic interpenetration of sovereign governments (Scheinman

1966; Wessels 1997). In short, our focus rests on the assumption that the most prominent actors needing to cooperate internationally before and after major disturbances are governmental organizations composed of individual members. This approach allows us to draw upon the insights of all three literatures above.

Having navigated through definitions, a central question beckons: how can cooperation contribute to resilience? The three literatures, surprisingly, do not directly address the question of cooperation benefits per se. Each *assumes* the benefits of cooperation, making it implicit to the analysis. International relations scholars state that "cooperation provides the actors with gains or rewards" (Milner 1992, 468). Otherwise, that logic suggests, states would not cooperate. For management scholars, cooperation improves "innovation and competitive success" (Beer, Eisenstat, and Spector 1990), generates "strong levels of efficiency and profitability" (Contractor and Lorange 1998), can generate "high-quality decision-making," and is thus "crucial to the success of enterprises" (Smith, Carroll, and Ashford 1995). "If work is accomplished in a fluid, ever-changing pattern of relationships that cut across functional, hierarchical, and national boundaries, high levels of cooperation may allow for an efficient and harmonious combination of the parts leading to high performance" (Smith, Carroll, and Ashford 1995, 11).[3] Social psychologists treat the benefits of cooperation as obvious. Using the example of the prisoner's dilemma, they show how cooperation (which is difficult in the first instance) can lead to mutual benefit. In that game's theoretical example, both prisoners avoid longer jail terms through cooperation.

To find more specific insights on the relationship between cooperation and resilience, we combed the literature further in light of this chapter's basic assumption: that severe disturbances may overwhelm the coping capacity of individual social systems. Coping capacity is never limited to material resources, of course. It also consists of technical expertise, actionable intelligence, emotional support, and other resources that can help a society back onto its feet. The literature reveals three main ways that cooperation can contribute to resilience from this perspective.

Coordination. Although cooperation can have many outcomes, improved coordination is the most celebrated (Smith, Carroll, and Ashford 1995, 11). Coordination is defined generally as the combination of parts to achieve the most effective or harmonious results (Thompson 1967) and is defined by international relations scholars as a situation in which states adapt to each other's policies and protocols so that they work in concert rather than in conflict (Keohane 1974, 52). Once working in coordination, states continue to receive a number of added benefits that are relevant to any discussion about resilience.

The first benefit that can derive from coordination is improved communication. When policies are aligned and different parts of government bureaucracies are working coherently, information flows more freely. Keohane and Nye's (1974) classic study of transnational bureaucratic coordination cites the important role of ongoing communication and face-to-face interaction in setting common expectations and lessening the chance of global conflicts. Keohane and Nye studied U.S.-Canada relations and U.S.-USSR relations and noted how interaction among low-level officials heightened information flows and "affected policy expectations and preferences" (1974, 44). In the context of dealing with severe disturbances, improved communication and clear expectations can go a long way toward accurate threat assessments and a coherent response.

Coordination can lead to converging attitudes and changed behaviors so as to improve decision making across borders under times of stress. Peter Haas's (1992) research agenda on epistemic communities examines exactly this point. As patterns of regularized policy coordination become widespread, transgovernmental elite networks are created that tie officials together based on common interests, shared goals, and shared knowledge (E. B. Haas 1990). Even if government officials do not change their official stance or deviate from formal negotiation positions, the process of coordination can generate collegiality and familiarity. Those traits in turn can facilitate relations in which strict bargaining situations and tit-for-tat behavior give way to flexibility and quicker resolution of problems. Studies of epistemic communities often reference the early work by Keohane and Nye (discussed above), which similarly shows that bureaucratic collegiality across borders helped to ease tensions during stressful negotiations during the Cold War. During some negotiations, Keohane and Nye show, flexible bargaining behavior derived from coordination among low-level officials meant that "concessions need not be requited issue by issue or during each period" (1974, 46).

Finally, effective coordination can improve policy implementation. As Scharpf (1997) showed in examples of the "games real actors play," continuing interaction of network members leads to the coordination of expectations regarding policy goals. Decisions made at one level of the "game," as Pressman and Wildavsky (1973) studied closely, can be more consistently carried out at implementation levels if expectations are aligned from the start of the policy process. When facing a major crisis or disturbance, the ability to ensure that decisions are communicated and acted upon "down the line" can have a major impact on the ability of a social system to bounce back quickly from adversity.

Resource distribution. A resilient system demands the quick distribution of resources, material or otherwise, to resolve a potential disturbance before it happens or to regroup after it strikes. Cooperation can potentially improve the movement and distribution of resources to where they are needed, when they are needed.[4]

One way to think about resource distribution is in terms of logistical supply chains. During major crises, the ability to find, move, and distribute critical supplies is placed at a premium. Supply chains, however, are often among the first set of casualties when a disturbance emerges. Indeed, their breakdown can become part of a "cascading crisis" as initial suffering cannot be abated (Rosenthal, Boin, and Comfort 2001b). For instance, the oft-cited success of Wal-Mart in preserving its supply chains and delivering much-needed potable water during Hurricane Katrina, while official systems broke down, stands as an example of how important such logistical concerns can be. Today's supply chains stretch well beyond local borders and demand service, maintenance, and foresight to keep the entire chain operating during disturbances. Redundancies in such a chain might be achieved only by "sourcing" supplies from outside of the local system. In such situations, cooperation with external and cross-border authorities becomes a major part of ensuring the effective distribution of resources.

Also important is the distribution of "intellectual" resources, meaning information and intelligence that can help a social system make sense of an impending development. Game theorists, to draw upon the literature discussed earlier, examine how full information can assist parties seeking solutions to common problems (Fudenberg and Tirole 1993). For them, international organizations are created as a way to solve the full information problem, which can explain why sovereign states have created organizations ranging from the World Health Organization to the UN Office for the Coordination of Humanitarian Affairs (Jeggle 2001). International relations scholars stress a similar point, making the case that effective cooperation ensures the distribution of information across partners, which can in turn instill confidence in a particular solution to an international problem (Gibbons 1992). They demonstrate that states are more likely to cooperate when information is "full and fair"; usually, a neutral third party can perform this function and thus assist with cooperation (Tallberg 2006; Pollack 2003).

Trust building and social capital. Successful cooperation also helps to build long-term trust between partners. A major part of international relations scholarship in the 1970s examined the cybernetic effects of cross-border transaction. When transactions reached a certain level, trust between nations emerged and foreclosed the option of war between them. This is the definition of a Deutschian "security community," an ideal-type that exemplifies a cooperative relationship built on, and ensuring trust between, different states (Adler and Barnett 1998).

Putnam (1994) refers to the creation of social capital over time, based on notions of generalized reciprocity and social capital generated through repeated interactions. Social psychologists are also quick to emphasize how cooperation can, under certain conditions, lay the ground for mutual trust and a greater appreciation for external points of view.

The "social" benefits of cooperation should not be ignored: government actors, and the general public, see evidence of cooperation as reassuring. The impression that government actors are working together (whether this is accurate or not) can sooth public concern and build confidence in government during a crisis (Rosenthal, t'Hart, and Kouzmin 1991). Smooth social relations and the emergence of trust, in turn, improve the chances of cooperation.

Factors Underlying a "Capacity to Cooperate"

Having discussed the potential benefits that cooperation can bring in relation to resilience, we now turn to examine the crucial preconditions for cooperation to take place by government organizations across borders. The organizations in question here are subgovernmental, sectoral bureaucracies such as agencies and ministries. In an increasingly complex and interdependent world, such organizations must deal with their foreign counterparts directly rather than indirectly through foreign offices or diplomatic mechanisms.[5]

Although subgovernmental relations among states are critical, we do not reject the importance of high-level agreements and executive support as complementary explanations for the capacity to cooperate. Rather, we identify a number of both "high" (executive, diplomatic, formal) and "low" (bureaucratic, organizational, informal) factors that can affect the potential for cooperation during extreme events. This distinction will allow us to gauge the relationship between the two categories at the conclusion of the chapter.

In what follows, we outline a variety of factors that can induce cooperation; put another way, the factors below represent hypothesized prerequisites for cooperation. We group them under the three main headings of interests, institutions, and ideas—often referred to as the "building blocks" of political explanation (Heclo 1993).

Interest Factors

One of the simplest propositions found in the international relations literature is that cooperation takes place only when all partners perceive they can achieve gains. The assumptions underlying this claim are that states are the main actors in international affairs, that they act on the basis of national interests to maximize their own utility, and that the international system is characterized by anarchy. In essence, states jealously guard their own position and cooperate only when they perceive the possibility to increase their own net benefits. This proposition explains why the prisoner's dilemma has proliferated as the key metaphor of international politics: cooperation is desirable, but there are myriad disincentives to working together.

Although we may disagree with this depiction of international politics, the implications of an "interests first" approach is a useful starting point for discussion. First, it suggests that actors are predisposed to cooperation when benefits are clear and calculable (Oye 1985; Axelrod 1984). Without material incentives, it would be difficult to justify to political superiors or domestic publics why actors should cooperate with their foreign counterparts. A strategically acting organization, aiming to increase its net benefit, is thus more likely to display a high capacity to cooperate, however counterintuitive this may appear. Moreover, actors are more likely to cooperate effectively when they perceive a balanced distribution of gains—for example, that others will not benefit dramatically more than they will.

Second, actors are more likely to cooperate if they see cooperation as a long-term endeavor. This lesson stems from the "tit-for-tat" strategy: in an anarchic world, maximizing absolute gains in the prisoner's dilemma is best achieved by following a strategy of reciprocity. Providing assurances that cooperation will continue "in the shadow of the future" is a key prerequisite to cooperation in the short term. As we will see, institution-based factors can encourage states to cooperate over time—hence the value of cooperation frameworks such as the United Nations, NATO, and the European Union.

Both of these interest-oriented considerations rely on the interests and the perception of gains by national agencies and organizations. Yet elite-level, diplomatic declarations can also set a positive framework for cooperation (Pollack 2005; Holsti and Levy 1974; Keohane and Nye 1974). When the United States and Europe hold summits among heads of state, the resulting declarations are often highly symbolic texts promising "greater co-operation" with little or no substance attached. Yet these statements signal to lower-level officials that at high levels there is at least *some* degree of appreciation of the prospect of cooperation. More important, the same statements suggest that cooperation will be a long-term effort and thus serve to encourage repeated cooperation "games." On both counts, such declarations raise the material incentives to work together—and thus build a more general capacity to cooperate among agencies and organizations.

Institutional Factors

At a basic level, all cooperation involves actors pursuing their own interests through collaborative means. But cooperation can, and often does, take place within institutions: sets of rules, procedures, and principles that structure behavior and shape interests (Bulmer 1998; North 1990). These institutions leave their imprint on cooperation efforts and can facilitate or impair the capacity of actors to work together. The literature associated with "new" institutionalism (Hall and Taylor 1996) offers three sets of institutional factors that affect the capacity to cooperate.

First, institutions can facilitate cooperation through the functions they perform. For realist scholars, institutions mitigate the effects of international anarchy and make cooperation possible: they can ensure information about the motivations of others and thus build confidence in agreements and lessen the likelihood of defection. Institutions, sometimes described in this way as international regimes (Jervis 1988; Oye 1986), help to overcome the many transaction costs that may prevent actors, organizations, and states from cooperating in the first instance.

Other scholars emphasize the functional benefits of institutions on cooperation, too, although they are not transfixed on the anarchy assumption. Institutions encourage cooperation, for instance, by serving as neutral third parties (i.e., secretariats) that provide policy-relevant information (e.g., implementation considerations) that may not be available to the various partners. Institutions also include procedures for setting the policy agenda, which keeps cooperation focused and avoids the endless "cycling" problem related to the presence of multiple solutions (Cox and Shepsle 2006). In the EU, for instance, the European Commission has been endowed with unique features that serve the cooperation needs of the EU's member-state governments (Pollack 2003).

Cooperation within institutions is likely to be iterative, which links the discussion of institutions to that of interests, above: when actors repeatedly interact, they are more likely to cooperate. Logically, actors are more likely to cooperate when familiar institutions exist to provide a framework for interaction.

Second, institutions draw actors together and regularize cooperation. International organizations play a major role in cooperation by putting distant officials into direct, regular contact and providing the "physical proximity" and "aura of legitimacy" that enhance the ability to cooperate. Even when interests diverge, regularized interaction leads to a sense of collegiality among participants. This trait can be particularly helpful during times when organizations have to respond quickly (and overcome cooperation obstacles from their own central governments) to work with international partners. Familiar patterns of interaction, communication, and bargaining represent the types of institutions that should facilitate cooperation under duress.

Third, institutions that enhance interaction between international actors nurture the emergence of elite networks and advocacy coalitions, thus facilitating more than generic cooperation: "One of the important but seldom-noted roles of international organizations in world politics is to provide the arena for sub-units of government to turn potential or tacit coalitions into explicit coalitions characterized by direct communication amongst partners" (Keohane and Nye 1974, 51).

Such networks are notable because they go beyond cooperation: they contain actors with aligned interests using their common resources to achieve a particular goal. In other words, they are advocacy coalitions with a mission. Such coalitions were a main driver behind growing transgovernmental relations in the 1970s, such as those that took place between U.S. and USSR agencies outside of the explicit purview of interstate relations (Keohane and Nye 1974). And elite networks continue to drive international policy cooperation, as has been documented in North America (Holsti and Levy 1974; Heclo 1978) and Europe (J. Richardson and Jordan 1979; P. Haas 1990; Rhodes 1990).[6]

Finally, institutions generate and enforce agreements on technical elements of cooperation. As discussed above, high-level political agreements offer broad frameworks stipulating a shared interest in working together. These declarations must be put into operation, however, by organizational personnel with technical expertise. International organizations provide the framework for working together and offer a useful context within which technical agreements can be made to put cooperation into action. Whether or not technical incompatibilities among national systems—food security, for instance—can be ironed out has an important bearing on whether cooperation takes place under times of stress. Institutions, including norms, rules, and standards for technical cooperation, can improve the capacity of cross-border organizations to cooperate. This helps to explain why some disaster scholars have called for global institutional agreements to facilitate interaction at the technical level to prepare for crises (Jeggle 2001).

Ideational Factors

A great number of factors that influence the capacity to cooperate across borders are ideational; that is, they reflect nonmaterial explanations for political outcomes (J. Goldstein and Keohane 1993; Hall and Taylor 1996). As research on crisis management often points out, managing severe disturbances depends on perceptions: first, whether actors perceive a crisis as emerging, and second, how they frame a problem and act upon it (Boin et al. 2005). In this section we examine some similar considerations that affect the capacity of organizations to cooperate internationally.

The first place to look for ideational lubricants to cooperation is in the epistemological bonds that link networks together. These networks often share belief systems that can have a strong effect on cooperation before and after major disturbances. Whereas opposing belief systems may inhibit cooperation, common belief systems have a strong "binding" effect on those who subscribe to them (Sabatier and Jenkins-Smith 1993). Although enlightening, studies of advocacy coalitions can be complemented by an "epistemic communities" approach to better understand cooperation at the international level.

Such a community is a "professional group that believes in the same cause-and-effect relationships, truth-tests to accept them, and shares common values; its members share a common understanding of a problem and its solutions" (E. B. Haas 1990, 40).[7] A community links professionals within particular issue areas. They derive their influence by diffusing new ideas and information generally and by imparting their views to policy makers who need policy advice.

A community facilitates cooperation through the "creation of collective meaning" (Adler and Haas 1992, 368). This amounts to a type of sensemaking, where members diffuse a particular way of viewing policy problems and the ways to address them. Since these networks tend to generate consensus on "cause-and-effect" matters among their own members, cooperation tends to be closely knit and active. When the community imparts its own perspective to decision makers in different states, that perspective "may, in turn, influence the interests and behavior of other states, thereby increasing the likelihood of convergent state behavior and international policy coordination" (P. Haas 1992, 4).

Epistemic communities set the groundwork for cooperation, drawing from their members' own professional backgrounds to present a mainly consensual view of a policy problem's cause-and-effect relationships. The presence of actual epistemic communities stretching across the Atlantic is documented in several cases (Verdun 1999; Drake and Nicolaidis 1992; Ikenberry 1992). U.S. and British economists and policy specialists embraced a set of policy ideas and pushed them in the postwar settlement discussions. During those turbulent times, a community of like-minded economists provided a focus for negotiations and helped policy makers to "make sense" of an uncertain situation (Ikenberry 1992). More recently, a transatlantic community of counterterrorism experts has sought to generate a cooperative policy agenda between the United States and Europe (Mitchell et al. 2007; Sugden 2006). Scholars have also noted that an improvement in international disaster relief requires a more rapid exchange of "professional knowledge and skills" between epistemic-like groups of disaster specialists (Jeggle 2001).

A second set of ideational factors that influence cooperation concerns the presence of trust. This notoriously slippery concept is a central precondition for the presence of "security communities" in the international relations literature. Adler and Barnett (1998), inspired by the earlier writings of Deutsch, argue that states within a security community are much more likely to cooperate and assist one another, rather than wage war upon one another. The determining factor for this state of affairs is the presence of trust generated by increasing transactions: at a certain point, military conflict becomes unthinkable.

For management scholars, a key antecedent for cooperation is also trust. Ring and Van de Ven (1994) define trust as an individual's confidence in the goodwill of the others in a given group and belief that the others will make efforts consistent with the group's goal. A belief that others will faithfully apply their efforts to achieve group goals may result in *informal* cooperation; a belief that a formal hierarchy is in place to reward cooperation may produce *formal* cooperation (Ring and Van de Ven 1994; Argyle 1991).

A summary of the interest-, institution-, and idea-based variables and their corresponding propositions regarding cooperation can be found in table 11.1.

Cooperating after Katrina

To evaluate the plausibility of the propositions outlined above, we now turn to an event that severely tested the capacity of states to cooperate across bor-

Table 11.1 Summary of Cooperation Variables

Category	Propositions
Interest-based variables	Participants must see clear and immediate benefits to cooperation, balanced distribution of gains
	Participants must see cooperation in terms of the "shadow of the future,"—e.g., as ongoing and likely in future situations
	Preexisting political agreements between governments must exist to set the framework for bureaucratic-level cooperation
Institution-based variables	Cooperative organizations must be in place to regularize interaction
	Participants must already be networked by policy communities or other type of interactive network
	Specific rules, technical standards must exist for cooperative activity in question
Idea-based variables	Participants must share professional backgrounds, bound by established community ("epistemic community" thesis)
	Trust, developed over time, must exist among participants

ders. Hurricane Katrina provides us with a fascinating and unique event in U.S. history when the federal government, and its many agencies, had to interact and work with many foreign governments to manage a crisis on its own soil. As such, the disaster presents us with a number of "minicases" of cooperation that allow us to probe the relevance of the theoretical propositions outlined above.

A number of Hurricane Katrina studies offer relevant empirical evidence on the topic of international cooperation (K. R. Klein and Nagel 2007; Cooper and Block 2006; Daniels, Kettl, and Kunreuther 2006; U.S. Senate 2006), as does a host of newspaper articles and online media reports. The richest source of information, however, is Anne Richard's study of the "role reversal" that took place in the aftermath of the storm (2006a). The substantial empirics in Richard's book, verified in other studies and compared against media reports, provide much of the information used in the analysis below.

Methodologically speaking, what follows is less a structured set of case studies than a general "plausibility probe" intended to verify whether our theoretical propositions, outlined above, find any degree of confirmation in empirical reality. If so, we have reason to pursue this line of theoretical argument in future studies and to add additional cases to establish causal-ity (Eckstein 1975). In other words, our methodological ambitions remain modest in simply evaluating the utility of a theoretical framework.

Background

As Hurricane Katrina bore down on the U.S. Gulf Coast, television images of mayhem and destruction beamed across the world. Any notion that the United States, the lone superpower and the world's richest nation, would plan and mount an effective response to Katrina was quickly dashed (Bernstein 2005). A slow response, blame shifting among government leaders, and dramatic pictures of suffering borne by the storm's victims prompted an outpouring of support from people and governments around the world.

Offers of aid and expertise began arriving soon after the hurricane hit the coast on the morning of August 29, 2006. The first offers of help came in from Canada, France, and Honduras. The following day, assistance was pledged from Japan, Russia, Venezuela, and NATO. These were quickly followed by Australia, Belgium, Israel, Italy, Jamaica, Mexico, the Netherlands, and the EU. From British ready-to-eat meals to Jordanian field hospitals, and from Dutch water experts to Canadian search-and-rescue teams, offers of assistance totaled almost one billion dollars in aid. Close and effective cooperation between the United States and foreign governments would determine whether this assistance arrived where it was needed (for a summary, see Richard 2006b).

The United States was not accustomed to receiving aid from other countries, forcing it to respond quickly to a new imperative. It was "a surprise to be a recipient," in the words of one U.S. Foreign Service officer (quoted in Richard 2006a, 6), although the U.S. State Department reassured donors that "no offer that can help alleviate the suffering of the people of the affected area will be refused" (McCormack 2005). Several U.S. agencies struggled with the challenge of working with foreign counterparts, including the State Department, the U.S. Agency for International Development (USAID) Office of Foreign Disaster Assistance (OFDA), the U.S. Department of Homeland Security (DHS), and the Federal Emergency Management Agency (FEMA).

In the final analysis, roughly half of the foreign assistance went unused. Many of the donations were left in foreign airports or remained in storage in U.S. facilities, unable to be processed or distributed. Some foreign governments, which were willing but unable to deliver donations to relieve the suffering along the Gulf Coast, were dismayed by the cooperation problems (J. Brinkley and Smith 2005). Many awkward diplomatic moments occurred both during and after the relief effort, not to mention the difficulties

Table 11.2 Cooperation Attempts between U.S. and Foreign Governments, and Outcomes

Case	Contribution	Propositions Present			Result
		Interest	Institutions	Ideas	
Germany	Rescue pilots, water experts	Yes	Yes	Yes	Success
Canada	Rescue teams, Red Cross teams, navy, coast guard	Yes	Yes	Yes	Success
Netherlands	Water experts, navy	Yes	Yes	Yes	Success
Japan	Warehouse distribution	Yes	Yes	Unclear	Success
Mexico	Supplies, navy cooperation	Yes	Yes	Yes	Success
NATO		Yes	Yes	Unclear	Success
Sweden	Telecommunications equipment	Yes	No	Unclear	Failure
Switzerland	Relief supplies	Yes	Unclear	Unclear	Failure
Austria	Rescue teams, disaster response experts	Yes	No	No	Failure
Hungary	Medical team	Yes	Unclear	No	Failure
UK	Ready-to-eat meals	Yes	No, except for military	Yes	Failure
Venezuela	Fuel, rescue teams	No	No	No	Failure
Cuba	Aid, doctors, rescue teams	No	No	No	Failure

endured by emergency response teams that could not benefit from the aid provided from abroad (Williams 2006, quoted in Richard 2006a, n18).

Yet the case of international contributions to the Hurricane Katrina response effort also reveals examples of effective cooperation. Several countries worked with the United States quickly and seamlessly, deploying aid workers and emergency assistance within hours. That assistance reached victims on the ground and probably served to save lives and forestall additional destruction. The presence of both failed and successful incidents of cooperation in the Hurricane Katrina case affords the opportunity to assess what factors may have conditioned cooperation in both sets of incidents.

Table 11.2 offers an initial overview of the individual cases that will be explored and used in the following analysis. The cases were selected on the basis of variation on the dependent variable—that is, cooperation success or failure. We then delved deeper into each case to examine whether our theoretical propositions may have possibly played a role in explaining those outcomes.

The Pursuit of Interests

As proposed earlier in this chapter, the capacity to cooperate across borders is conditioned first and foremost by compatible interests. We also highlighted insights from game theory that show how cooperation will be smoother if partners know they must cooperate again in the future. Experience allows participants to learn about partners' behavior in the past—that is, to gauge their reliability. The prospect of future cooperation, and the chance that other partners may sanction poor behavior, tends to dampen the likelihood of "shirking" or "defecting" when cooperation looms. Finally, an interest-based approach to understanding cooperation trains our attention toward the presence of high-level political agreements between countries that encourage cooperation.

The impact of interests on international cooperation during Hurricane Katrina was apparent from the outset. The U.S. federal government initially could see no reason to engage with foreign governments. In a television interview, President George W. Bush said: "I'm not expecting much from foreign nations because we haven't asked for it. I do expect a lot of sympathy.... But this country's going to rise up and take care of it" (quoted in Richard 2006a, 6). Without seeing a clear benefit from cooperation, the United States hesitated to engage with international partners even as offers of assistance came pouring in. Two days later, against the backdrop of ongoing suffering and a cascading catastrophe, the U.S. federal government changed its position. The White House mandated FEMA to begin designing procedures for accepting international aid, procedures that did not exist up until that point (see below). FEMA turned to the State Department to assist in the receipt of international aid and to USAID to help with delivery. In both cases, new procedures and protocols had to be put in place (D'Agostino and Williams 2006).

Once U.S. agencies came to recognize the need for, and potential benefits of, aid cooperation with foreign governments, a renewed effort ensued. Low-level agency personnel organized task-specific headquarters in Washington, divided up responsibilities, and began formulating procedures for accepting and delivering assistance. As for foreign governments, the benefits of offering aid were already clear and thus hastened their desire to cooperate. Most donors, including those from Europe, Asia, and North America, shared a basic interest with the United States in assisting citizens and perceived benefits to themselves. The motives behind the donations from abroad included the desire to score political points, the wish to reciprocate previous examples of U.S. generosity, and a sense of duty (Richard 2006a, 34–41). With most donors, generosity and altruism were the main motives for providing assistance, but so were material interest (usually in the form of assuring future reciprocity) and ego gratification (it boosts a country's image in the world to be seen as a donor).

In only two cases do we find unrequited perceptions of mutual interest. The Venezuelan government offered relief workers, humanitarian aid, and subsidized fuel. President Hugo Chavez, a vocal critic of the Bush administration, prompted some commentators to suggest the Venezuelan aid was a ploy intended to score political points at the expense of President Bush (Blum 2005). The U.S. federal government rejected Venezuela's offer of aid. A similar story holds for Cuba, which reportedly prepared to send more than fifteen hundred doctors, together with considerable medicine and supplies. Speaking to a gathering of medical professionals in Havana, the Cuban president, Fidel Castro, announced that the United States had made no response to its offer (Richard 2006a, 40).

There are few examples of formal treaties between the United States and foreign governments regarding disaster relief on American soil. There are, however, many treaties related to collective security and defense, especially between the United States and its North American allies and between the United States and European governments. These treaties contributed to an understanding within the U.S. administration and its agencies that cooperation with partners was to be encouraged, at least once the full extent of the destruction became clear. The German Federal Agency for Technical Relief (THW) and the U.S. government have an agreement in place regarding natural catastrophe assistance, which was often cited by Claus Boettcher, the THW liaison who accompanied a team of eighty-nine flood-fighting specialists and five medical personnel dispatched days after the storm (Richard 2006a, 39). The THW became the main source for pumping New Orleans dry in the downtown area near the Superdome until Hurricane Rita struck in late September (Snapper 2006).

Yet at best, the presence of shared interests should be viewed as a preliminary condition. In some cases, the United States and foreign governments recognized the potential for shared benefits from cooperation. That recognition was required to ensure the start of a cooperation effort, but it was not sufficient to ensure effective outcomes. As we shall see below, other factors played a role in facilitating or inhibiting cooperation. Common interests and the perception of mutual benefits, then, should be viewed as a necessary but not sufficient factor in explaining the capacity to cooperate across borders.

The Presence of Institutions

Institutions facilitate cooperation. The presence of institutions—rules, procedures, and principles—in a cross-border relationship setting provides stable "rules of the game" that encourage regularized interaction and promote communication among partners. Formal cooperation forums, such as NATO and the Transatlantic Business Dialogue, provide such institutions, but so do less formal advocacy networks and cross-border coalitions. We also proposed earlier that technical agreements and operational standards can serve as institutions that improve capacities to cooperate across borders.

The presence—or lack—of institutions structuring the relationship between the United States and foreign governments coming to its aid was a decisive factor in explaining cooperation. NATO was one of the first respondents to the United States' plight and one of the first partners to which the United States reached out. Twelve NATO flights delivered almost 189 tons of relief goods in the aftermath of the storm and subsequent flooding.[8] That endeavor owes much of its success to the well-worn cooperative patterns and military operations standards that had been agreed upon in advance by NATO member states (Richard 2006a, 7).

Regarding direct relations with foreign governments, initial problems on the side of the U.S. federal government can be attributed to the complete lack of procedures for receiving foreign aid. The U.S. National Response Plan for domestic disasters, released by the Department of Homeland Security in 2004, consolidated existing plans and provided a common framework for federal agencies and nonfederal organizations to meet disaster and emergency needs. Under its International Coordination Support Annex, the State Department was to be responsible for international assistance.[9] However, that annex did not clarify how to handle relief supplies arriving in the United States, nor did the State Department have any procedures in place for this task (Richard 2006a, 15). Respective responsibilities were eventually worked out between FEMA and the State Department, but only after four days had passed and several international partners had withdrawn their time-sensitive contributions.

Sweden's Rescue Services Agency, for instance, waited eleven days for approval to transport donations, including mobile communications equipment provided by Ericsson Corporation. By the time of approval, water-purification equipment and thirty thousand blankets had already been off-loaded. The communications equipment, meanwhile, was received too late to be effective in the Hurricane Katrina response, although it was eventually used in the aftermath of Hurricane Rita.

The British contribution to Hurricane Katrina ran into significant obstacles. The British Ministry of Defense sent five hundred thousand ready-to-eat meals to the United States via civilian aircraft on September 5. Each meal contained enough food to last one person twenty-four hours, arriving at Little Rock Air Force Base, where the U.S. Air Force was coordinating military contributions. From there, the meals were transported to fourteen locations in Louisiana. Despite the swift nature of the military-organized reception of the meals, USDA inspectors intervened to stop distribution: the meals did not conform to U.S. standards regarding meat products. Some meals were in parking lots, ready to be distributed to hurricane victims, when they were withdrawn. Eventually, the meals were sent to other countries in the world where they met shared standards (Richard 2006a, 18). Similar examples can be found in cases of aid received from Switzerland, Austria, and several corporate donors.[10]

In contrast, the Canadian contribution to the relief effort was seamless. Richard attributes this success to a "shared history and border, common time zones, and a large number of Canadians living in New Orleans." More specifically, she suggests that "pre-existing relationships between Canadians and American counterparts facilitated Canadian involvement" (2006a, 20–21).

Two dimensions of the Canadian assistance effort should be highlighted. First, military cooperation between the two countries took place without many hitches. Within days, the Canadian armed forces had launched "Operation UNISON," which included more than one thousand personnel, three warships, and one coast guard vessel. Sailing from Nova Scotia on September 6, the group carried several tons of relief supplies and unloaded them in Pensacola, Florida, six days later, before sailing on to Gulfport and Biloxi. There, Canadian Navy personnel worked alongside the U.S. Army Corps of Engineers, while military divers worked with their counterparts to clear essential navigation lanes. Cooperation between Canadian and U.S. armed forces has been a regular occurrence for many years, carried out under a series of agreements regarding joint training and exercise. In addition, Canadian Air Force helicopters took over search-and-rescue operations in the U.S. Northeast, in order to free U.S. Coast Guard personnel for deployment to the Gulf Coast. A similar story holds for NORAD, the North American Aerospace Defense Command, a Cold War–era military operation in which both U.S. and Canadian armed forces take part (Cooper and Block 2006). The two militaries coordinated their response via NORAD, since, with very clear protocols in place, the two militaries could act as one. Richard suggests that under NORAD, "Canadian and American militaries have attained a high level of interoperability—they train together and share common command structures, language, and standards" (2006a, 22).

Second, Canadian mounted police and civilian rescue teams faced almost no obstacles to entering and operating within the United States. Again, this is attributable not only to preexisting relations but also to an integrated security and defense space that served to facilitate cooperation during Katrina.

Another example of successful bilateral cooperation was between the United States and the Netherlands. A preexisting agreement between the U.S. Army Corps of Engineers and the Dutch Public Works and Water Management Agency (Rijkswaterstaat) helped to speed important contributions from the Netherlands. When the hurricane hit, Dutch water-management experts came quickly to New Orleans and brought mobile pumps. Five Dutch experts established mobile pumping stations in Plaquemines Parish, while other Dutch officials worked on fixing damaged pumps. Months after the initial response, Dutch engineers were still at work, while also assisting the U.S. Army Corps of Engineers with a crucial hurricane-protection study in 2006. The Dutch team was awarded military medals by the U.S. Army Corps of Engineers.

Several other examples of effective cooperation involve Germany, Japan, and Mexico. In each case, existing relationships, past experience, and common standards smoothed the path toward cooperation. In the German and Mexican examples, shared military procedures account for much of the success, although preestablished civilian assistance agreements also seem to have had a salutary effect on relations (Richard 2006a, 17, 26, 38–39; German Embassy 2005).

Medical teams from foreign countries did not fare as well. Hungary sent doctors to assist in the effort, but they were told to stand down when they contacted the U.S. Department of Health and Human Services upon their arrival. Foreign doctors cannot practice medicine in the United States without a license. The state of Louisiana waived those rules several days after the storm and agreed not to impose sanctions on foreign doctors operating in good faith (K. R. Klein and Nagel 2007).

In sum, it would appear that institutions, in the shape of formal multilateral organizations, established policy networks, and common procedures, played a factor in most of the successful cases of international cooperation during Hurricane Katrina. NATO and NORAD allowed militaries to facilitate aid delivery. Cross-border networks, such as those between the United States and Canada and between the United States and Mexico, sped the delivery of aid on its way. And pre-agreed-upon procedures for expertise sharing and assistance ensured that engineers from the Netherlands, aid organizations from Canada, and military personnel from Germany were able to cooperate effectively with U.S. officials. The British case suggests that institutional factors assisting cooperation are complex and multifaceted: although the United States and the UK share much in common and enjoy high-level political consensus on security matters, operational and technical standards for working together on matters like Hurricane Katrina differ significantly.

Adherence to Common Ideas

The last condition that influences the "capacity to cooperate" is the presence of shared cognitive and normative frameworks. Common professional backgrounds and cognitive frameworks used to tackle problems can facilitate cooperation and build trust in working together to achieve common outcomes.

Untangling the influence of ideas from factors like shared interests and facilitating institutions can be a challenge (Hall and Taylor 1996; Keohane and Nye 2003). In combing the empirics on Hurricane Katrina, we took note of any evidence of social bonds between the United States and foreign countries, preestablished networks among respective agencies, and communities of professionals working together across borders. In these cases, shared cognitive and normative frameworks may help to explain cooperation.

The relationship between the United States and Canada, for instance, is one that reveals such ideational frameworks (see, e.g., Holsti 1971; Keohane and Nye 1974; Fox 1977). Government officials view one another's territories as neither foreign nor domestic, using a unique term within the Canadian embassy to the US—*intermestic*—to describe relations between the two countries. These relations assume a special character because they are based on not only a shared border but also a common culture and fundamentally compatible ideas about government and society (Sundelius 2005). One analyst describes a "common security space" underpinned by a common approach (E. Gilbert 2007). As Risse-Kappen points out, however, "ideas do not float freely" (1994). Agency must also be accounted for in this analytical perspective, since ideational frameworks are often "carried," promoted, or blocked by strategically placed actors, organizations, and interest groups. The groups that span borders and harbor similar cognitive and normative scripts are most likely to exhibit a capacity to cooperate.

A common perspective on search and rescue was on display when a forty-six-member team of specialists from British Columbia worked with Louisiana counterparts to assemble within hours and deploy to New Orleans. The team, which included trained first responders from the fire department, police, ambulance service, and public works, was in the city by September 1. Its members integrated quickly into the Louisiana State Police Search and Rescue chain of command and encountered few obstacles to cooperation. The joint team, assigned to a neighborhood of New Orleans, rescued 119 people and administered medical treatment to 172 via a small emergency treatment center (Cooper and Block 2006). By September 6, exhausted and having addressed the immediate rescue needs, the members of the Canadian team turned their places over to teams from California and Tennessee. The common background and similar professional training of these team members have been credited with their quick deployment and swift integration into U.S. search-and-rescue teams (Richard 2006a, 2006b).

Military services, which are well-known for sharing professional norms about service and sacrifice and which tend to operate according to standard operating procedures stemming from shared military history, might be expected to cooperate fairly smoothly during such an extreme event as Hurricane Katrina. The evidence seems to confirm this expectation. Not only the Canadian Navy, which shares long-standing ties and familiar structures with the U.S. Navy, but also the Dutch and Mexican navies provided essential assistance to the Hurricane Katrina response. Dutch frigates positioned themselves to assist the U.S. Navy with medical personnel and evacuation procedures. The Mexican Navy sent a ship that anchored alongside the Dutch frigates and deployed amphibious landing vehicles and helicopters in cooperation with the other navies present. The Singapore Air Force, which has Chinook helicopters permanently stationed in Texas, took part in aid delivery and rescue operations under the leadership of the U.S. Coast Guard (Mateo 2006).

A shared professional background may account for smooth cooperation between Red Cross agencies in Canada and the United States. Organizations in both countries deployed in tandem to Houston, Texas, to receive and distribute aid. The common "Red Cross ethos," Richard argues, "allowed for a smooth reception for the Canadians" (2006a, 22).[11]

One of the major obstacles to international cooperation in Hurricane Katrina was the presence of conflicting mind-sets regarding cooperation. One mind-set, based on diplomacy imperatives, led to a focus on foreign policy considerations when deciding whether and how to accept aid. Another mind-set was based on effective response, which tended to emphasize the time-sensitive nature of aid and the need to save lives. Different agencies in the U.S. federal government, it could be said, subscribed to conflicting mind-sets regarding priorities and led to slow and ineffective response. As Richard puts it, the federal government "failed to balance disaster response needs with foreign policy objectives." Richard quotes one disaster expert who complained that "diplomacy got in the way of effective disaster response" (2006a, 43). The lack of a common cognitive framework regarding aid donations seems to have contributed to this inability to cooperate effectively.

Moving toward Resilience through Cross-Jurisdictional Cooperation

Analyzing international cooperation in the aftermath of Hurricane Katrina reveals a mixture of successes and failures. Cooperation between the United States and some foreign countries worked smoothly, as aid workers integrated with U.S. counterparts and supplies reached suffering victims. In other cases, money, goods, and technical experts never reached their intended targets. Failed cooperation meant that valuable supplies were left sitting in foreign airports, were stranded in U.S. storage facilities, or were even returned to their source.

Although further analysis is required to untangle the array of causal factors that may have conditioned cooperation, our findings help to answer a central question posed in the introduction to this volume: what does "resilience" look like in practice, and how might social systems work toward it? By showing how cross-jurisdictional cooperation contributes to resilience, unraveling some key factors that explain cooperation capacity, and testing those factors in the case of the Hurricane Katrina response, we shed light on the multifaceted concept of resilience.

As modern crises and disasters become ever more complex, and as our societies become ever more interdependent, the capacity to reach across borders and draw in essential resources becomes increasingly important to ensuring the survival of interdependent social systems. In this chapter, we focused primarily on the conditions that enable such capacity among national governments and their agencies, using crisis *response* as our empirical frame of reference. In an age of complex, transboundary crises (Boin and Rhinard 2008), crisis *prevention* will become increasingly challenging as well. Harnessing multiple resources across sovereign boundaries and fragmented professional communities will require mechanisms for forging a "global approach" (Jeggle 2001). Subsequent chapters in this book study that challenge and widen our understanding of the full range of resources required to effectively manage crises through international cooperation. As crises grow more complex and the world draws closer together, the ability to cooperate effectively to identify, mobilize, and deploy those resources across borders will be a key source of societal resilience.

12 INTERNATIONAL DISASTER RESILIENCE
PREPARING FOR TRANSNATIONAL DISASTER

Thomas W. Haase

On Monday, April 6, 2009, at approximately 3:30 in the morning, the Abruzzo mountain region of Central Italy was shaken by an earthquake that measured 6.3 on the Richter scale (U.S. Geological Survey 2009). Nestled within a lush valley, and surrounded by the Apennine Mountains, is L'Aquila, the capital city of the Abruzzo region and home to more than seventy thousand Italian citizens. Officially established in the thirteenth century, L'Aquila has a historical lineage that can be traced back to early Roman times. The movement along the highly active Celano-L'Aquila fault system not only flattened large sections of residential and commercial structures but also destroyed numerous cultural and architectural treasures located in the region. The earthquake destroyed or rendered uninhabitable more than eleven thousand buildings (International Federation of Red Cross and Red Crescent Societies 2009c).

Equally tragic was the human impact. Statistics released a week after the event revealed that 298 lives had been lost, 1,000 others suffered various forms of injury, and 17,000 needed temporary housing (International Federation of Red Cross and Red Crescent Societies 2009b). Although the damage caused by the L'Aquila earthquake did not cross national boundaries per se, the events that began to unfold after the shaking stopped indicated that the international community would play a critical role in the response and recovery efforts. Indeed, by the Monday after the earthquake, dozens of organizational actors from around the world had mobilized personnel and initiated operations that would provide assistance to the affected population.

In the hours after the earthquake, the Italian government activated its domestic disaster response system and indicated that it would not require international assistance (Swissinfo 2009). Although the surge of concern that follows a major disaster event generates substantial offers of assistance from international actors, many national governments have rejected, or at least initially resisted, offers of international assistance. For instance, after the Sumatran earthquake and tsunami of 2004, the Indonesian government hesitated before allowing international organizations access to the province of Aceh, which had until that time experienced thirty years of civil conflict. The United States, following the devastation of New Orleans by Hurricane Katrina and the breakdown of its disaster management system, rejected outright dozens of offers of assistance from the international community (CREW 2007). Even Myanmar, one of the least developed countries in the world, followed this pattern of resistance after Cyclone Nargis came ashore on May 2, 2008 (Denby 2008). The reluctance to accept international assistance often wanes after national governments recognize the impact of the disaster upon their affected communities.

When a national government does accept external assistance, the challenge for decision makers is to coordinate activities among response organizations to ensure the effective distribution of domestic, as well as international, assistance. The ever-increasing connectedness and interdependence of today's international community place significant pressure on the decision makers responsible for disaster management operations. Disaster events, historically confined to a single community or region, now have the potential to affect the social, economic, and political systems of countries around the world (Wachtendorf 2000). If a national response system fails to manage a localized disaster effectively, the effects can expand outward and could threaten domestic security or even regional and international security. The question is how to improve the framework of policy and practice to enable the international community to assist national governments to mitigate and respond more effectively to disaster events.

This chapter seeks to contribute to the discussion of international disaster resilience by highlighting gaps in current international disaster management policy and analyzing how these gaps contributed to the communication and collaboration difficulties that occurred during the international response to the 2004 Sumatran earthquake and tsunami. The findings presented by this exploratory analysis indicate that while international disaster management has evolved substantially over the last forty years, much of the progress has been achieved at the national and subnational levels. While this is an important step, significantly less success has been achieved at the international level. Consequently, the mechanisms needed for international resilience have yet to be developed or implemented. Building upon the theoretical framework discussed by Mark Rhinard and Bengt Sundelius (see chapter 11 in this volume), this chapter argues that international resilience requires the development of sociotechnical systems that not only help to facilitate disaster response but also improve the ability of disaster managers to facilitate recovery, mitigation, and prevention activities in at-risk communities.

The Evolution of International Disaster Management Policy

The genesis for modern disaster management policy occurred in 1755 when Lisbon, the capital city of Portugal and the fourth-largest European city, was all but destroyed by an earthquake and tsunami of unprecedented scale (Dynes 2005). Since that time, the responsibility for disaster management activities has largely fallen on the modern nation-state. During the 220 years that followed the devastation of this powerful European city, the response of national governments to the risks of natural and man-made disasters has been neither adequate nor consistent. To fill many of the voids, nongovernmental organizations such as the International Committee of the Red Cross began to conduct disaster response activities at the international level during the middle of the eighteenth century. When nation-states did make progress, they focused their attention on the national and subnational levels. Only during the last forty years has a cohesive interest in the development of functional disaster management institutions and mechanisms at the international level emerged. There are two parallel trends in the evolution of disaster management policy at the international level. The first trend relates to the emergence of the foundations for a cohesive international disaster management policy. The second relates to the development of bilateral and regional policies between nation-states to deal with issues of disaster management.

International Policy Developments

A significant development in international disaster management policy occurred on December 22, 1989, when the General Assembly of the United Nations declared the 1990s the International Decade for Natural Disaster Reduction. In Resolution 42/236, the United Nations recognized the need for the international community to "reduce through concerted action, especially in developing countries, the loss of life, property damage and social and economic disruption caused by natural disasters" (United Nations

1989). Emphasizing the critical role of technology and science in reducing disaster risk, the resolution called upon national governments to formulate national disaster prevention and mitigation programs, increase public awareness of disasters, and improve the availability of emergency response supplies in disaster-prone areas. At the time, the international community was primarily concerned with developing scientific and technical means to mitigate the consequences of natural disasters.

Yet many members of the disaster management community recognized that, although science and technology were necessary components of an effective disaster management system, they were not sufficient. In May 1994, the international community met in Yokohama, Japan, and agreed that the economic and social consequences of disaster had risen and that successful disaster management would require more than response activities. Acknowledging this problem, the international community adopted the Yokohama Strategy and Plan of Action for a Safer World. Considered a major policy shift, the Yokohama Strategy recognized that to reduce the consequences of disaster and the need for disaster relief, policy makers would have to focus on all four elements of the disaster cycle: prevention, mitigation, preparedness, and response and relief.

The plan of action outlined in the Yokohama Strategy identified specific tasks that would need to be implemented at the local, national, regional, and international levels (United Nations 1994). At local and national levels, governments would express their commitment to vulnerability reduction, improve risk assessment and warnings, develop cooperative relationships with nongovernmental organizations, stimulate community participation, and adopt national disaster management legislation and policies. At the regional level, organizations would identify common vulnerabilities, improve communications regarding natural disasters, establish early warning mechanisms, and develop mutual assistance agreements. At the international level, nation-states would, through bilateral agreements and multilateral cooperation, improve the exchange of information on disaster reduction policies and technologies; ensure cooperation in the areas of research, science, and technology; and recognize the need for adequate coordination in international disaster management. As a policy document, the Yokohama Strategy represented a concerted international effort to get the full range of stakeholders, across the various levels of jurisdiction and fields of expertise, involved in helping communities reduce their disaster vulnerability.

As the International Decade for Natural Disaster Reduction drew to a close, the United Nations recognized that disaster management remained a critical policy issue for the international community. The United Nations also recognized that future progress in the field of disaster management would require an unprecedented amount of cooperation from the international community. On December 22, 1999, the General Assembly adopted Resolution 54/219 and called upon governments to continue to:

> cooperate and coordinate their efforts with the Secretary-General and the Under-Secretary-General for Humanitarian Affairs, the United Nations system, nongovernmental organizations and other partners, as appropriate, to implement and to develop further a comprehensive strategy to maximize international cooperation in the field of natural disasters, based upon an effective division of labour, from prevention to early warning, response, mitigation, rehabilitation and reconstruction, including through capacity-building at all levels, and the development and strengthening of global and regional approaches that take into account regional, subregional, national and local circumstances and needs, as well as the need to strengthen coordination of national emergency response agencies in natural disasters. (United Nations 1999)

This resolution established the foundation for the creation of the International Strategy for Disaster Reduction (ISDR), which is an international framework composed of a partnership of actors from the governmental, nongovernmental, academic, and scientific communities that seek to reduce disaster risk around the world. This community of actors would be managed by an interagency secretariat and the Interagency Task Force for Disaster Reduction. The interagency secretariat is responsible for coordinating natural disaster strategies and programs and for bridging the gaps between those working in the disaster management and in the humanitarian assistance fields. Chaired by the undersecretary general for humanitarian affairs at the United Nations, the Interagency Task Force for Disaster Reduction is mandated to identify gaps in disaster reduction policies and generate recommendations for remedial actions.

The second major policy development occurred in January 2005, when the United Nations ISDR held the World Conference on Disaster Reduction in Kobe, Japan. The conference was well attended and included representatives from more than 150 governments, twenty-one international nongovernmental organizations, and dozens of United Nations bodies and programs (United Nations 2005b). Attendance by the general public was also substantial, and the public forum received more than forty thousand visitors (United Nations 2005b). Acting in unison, the participants declared that communities must continue to be strengthened against the risk of disaster and that this could be accomplished by fostering a culture of disaster prevention and resilience. To achieve their goal of reducing disaster losses, both in terms of "lives lost and in the social, economic and environmental assets of communities and countries," the participants adopted a new policy declaration, the Hyogo Framework for Action 2005–2015: Building the Resilience of Nations and Communities to Disasters. The participants hoped that this policy declaration would serve as the official blueprint for the reduction of vulnerability in at-risk communities around the world.

The Hyogo Framework for Action identifies three strategic goals for the global improvement of disaster management. The first goal is "to increase the effective integration of disaster risk considerations into sustainable development policies, planning and programming at all levels, with a special emphasis on disaster prevention, mitigation, preparedness and vulnerability reduction" (United Nations 2005a, 3). The second goal is to develop and strengthen "institutions, mechanisms and capacities at all levels, in particular at the community level, that can systematically contribute to building resilience to hazards" (United Nations 2005a, 4). The final goal is to systematically "incorporate risk reduction approaches into the design and implementation of emergency preparedness, response and recovery programs in the reconstruction of affected communities" (United Nations 2005a, 4). The priorities for those who signed onto the Hyogo Framework for Action were to ensure that risk reduction is both a national and a local priority, to improve the disaster monitoring and warning systems, to build a culture of safety and resilience, to reduce risk factors, and to strengthen preparedness at all jurisdictional levels.

As with the International Decade for Natural Disaster Reduction, there would be different tasks for the stakeholders operating at the various levels of jurisdiction. In 2005, the tasks were more prescriptive. At the national level, states would assist the progress of their risk-reduction activities, develop procedures for reviewing progress against the framework for action, and adopt the domestic and international legal instruments necessary to reduce disaster risk. At the regional level, organizations would promote programs for technical cooperation and standards for the sharing of information and the mobilization of resources. These organizations would also explore the development of regional capacities for risk detection and early warning systems for disasters. Finally, at the international level, organizations would work with the United Nations to assist developing countries in improving their disaster resilience. Further, international organizations would work together to support the collection of data for the development of early warning systems for natural hazards. With these new policy developments, there was hope that the world would significantly reduce disaster losses by 2015.

Bilateral and Regional Policy Developments

In parallel with progress at the international policy level, nation-states have also been engaged in activities to resolve disaster management issues among themselves. While the specific details of such policies are beyond the scope of this chapter, the overwhelming majority of the national-level agreements take the form of bilateral or mutual aid agreements between national governments (Fisher 2007). The bilateral arrangements cover a range of issues and address matters such as the provision of technical assistance, customs and visas, the identification of information-sharing requirements, and the distribution of response costs, as well as the specific processes for the initiation and cessation of disaster assistance. National governments also sign mutual aid agreements, typically in the form of memoranda of understanding that are developed on a case-by-case basis with nongovernmental organizations. For example, the International Federation of Red Cross and Red Crescent Societies has entered into agreements with sixty-nine separate national governments, and these mutual aid agreements identify the parameters within which disaster response operations may take place (Fisher 2007, 5).

Closely related to the mélange of national agreements has been the emergence of regional agreements, entered into simultaneously by multiple national governments, which deal with disaster management issues. Many of these regional agreements follow geographical boundaries, for example, the Organization of American States, the European Union, and the Association of South-East Asian Nations (ASEAN). As members of regional organizations have become increasingly concerned about disaster risk, they have moved to standardize policy and practice with respect to issues such as access to the disaster location, development of collaboration mechanisms, logistics, the role of military units, the training of personnel, identification of the deceased, and control of disaster relief contributions. An example of where such a regional agreement has gained traction occurred after the Sumatran earthquake and tsunami of 2004, when several member states of ASEAN advanced a treaty called the Agreement on Disaster Management and Emergency Response. Although not yet fully adopted as law, Article III of the treaty details six core disaster management policy principles for the region: (1) respect for sovereignty and territorial integrity; (2) acknowledgment that the state that requests assistance shall direct relief and recovery operations; (3) the need to prevent disasters though prevention and mitigation efforts; (4) the need to strengthen collaboration and cooperation in prevention, mitigation, response, and recovery; (5) the need to mainstream disaster risk reduction into national and subnational policies and practice;

and (6) the need for a community-based approach to addressing disaster risks (ASEAN 2005). By taking a more comprehensive approach, such regional disaster management agreements are designed to fill the voids left by both international policy and bilateral and mutual aid agreements between national governments.

The Patchwork of International Policy

Clearly, policy developments at the international level reflect the manner in which nations and local communities think about disaster. The first major shift was the movement away from the narrow emphasis on disaster relief to a more holistic conception of disaster. Today, there are few who would dispute that disaster risk reduction, and in turn the social and economic consequences of disaster, require policy makers to consider the role of prevention, mitigation, preparedness, and relief—as well as recovery—in their national and local disaster management plans. The second major shift in policy thinking was the realization that linkages exist between disaster management and sustainable development. Rather than waiting to rebuild a community after a disaster strikes, urban and economic planners in developing counties could sow the seeds for resilience in at-risk communities long before the occurrence of a natural disaster. The third major shift has been the recognition that the consequences of disaster can have a significant effect on the international community and that a cooperative framework must be developed to ensure the efficient transfer of goods and services across jurisdictional boundaries during a time of crisis.

Notwithstanding these developments, it is clear that the international legal and policy framework for disaster management is insufficient to handle not only contemporary disaster threats but also the problems caused by the megadisasters that will inevitably strike densely populated urban areas. First, the framework for disaster management at the international level remains, at best, a patchwork system of legal structures and policy declarations that not only results in divergent gaps in policy between nations but also creates the potential for legal disputes and confusion during emergency situations. Second, disaster management policy at the international level remains overwhelmingly focused on improving national and local capacity, especially in developing countries. While this is a critical step in the march toward disaster-resilient communities, attention can also be directed toward developing standardized policies and mechanisms to facilitate effective action at the supranational level. Third, although there has been a movement toward the development of regional early warning systems, policy discussions at the international level have failed to address the need for the design, implementation, and interoperability of technical systems that are necessary for the management of disaster response and recovery operations. Failing to resolve the policy issues that exist at the international level today will only increase the risk of damage imposed upon at-risk communities. In a strange twist of irony, the consequences of future disasters may no longer be simply the result of the disaster event itself, but of the ineffective response to that event.

The Expansion of International Disaster Management Actors

Corresponding to the evolving international disaster management policy context, the international community has seen a significant rise in the number of organizational actors that participate in disaster management activities. Following a disaster event, hundreds of organizations descend on the disaster scene and begin to conduct operations. When there are disruptions in communications, or ineffective information flows among decision makers, this web of organizations adds to the uncertainty found in disaster environments. Further, many of these organizations operate outside the disaster management plans implemented in the affected community.

To improve coordination, decision makers will often group response organizations according to their primary response function. This is logical, given that these organizations specialize in a diversity of functions, for instance, logistics, financial support, communication, coordination, search and rescue, health care, infrastructure repair, transportation, and temporary shelters. While a functional classification helps to organize activities, it is does not enable policy makers to capture the full potential of organizations that operate in a given disaster management and response system. Given this recent surge in the number of organizations interested in disaster management, the issue for policy makers has become how to manage effectively this dynamic community of organizations.

The organizations involved in a given disaster management system can also be categorized vertically by their level of jurisdiction and horizontally by their source of funding. In terms of their level of jurisdiction, the overwhelming majority of organizations operate primarily at the local, provincial, and national levels. Other organizations are established to operate in the international arena, their primary mission to coordinate and support the activities of national and subnational organizations. In terms of their funding source, disaster management organizations generally fall into one of three distinct categories. Public organizations perform governmental functions and are usually responsible for the design, implementation, and execution of official disaster management policies and procedures. Other public organizations, such as the United Nations, are funded by taxpayers through government contributions and work in close collaboration with national and subnational organizations. Equally important is the proliferation of nonprofit disaster management organizations. These organizations usually have expertise around a specific disaster management function or deliver assistance to a specific assemblage of beneficiaries. They range in size from the vast network of chapters that make up the International Federation of Red Cross and Red Crescent Societies, to small locally focused organizations such as the Ibrahim Nain Foundation in Indonesia, which only operate in specific target communities. Rounding out this classification schema are private organizations. This category includes organizations such as airline and shipping companies, utility companies, telecommunications companies, and transportation companies, which have all begun to play critical roles in disaster management activities and consequently have begun to integrate their disaster management plans and activities more closely with those of public and nonprofit organizations.

When categorized vertically and horizontally, these organizations do not just constitute a set of actors organized around specific disaster functions, but rather represent a scalable set of actors that, if properly integrated, could serve as the foundation upon which international disaster resilience could be developed. Only when the vertical and horizontal classification framework is fused with the functional classification framework, however, is the true nature of the disaster management system revealed. Very little work has been done at the international level to map the full range of actors that are involved in disaster management activities. The mapping that has been done occurs primarily through the United Nations, but even then, as was the case in Indonesia following the Sumatran earthquake and tsunami, these mapping activities have been initiated only after response activities are recorded. An exploratory analysis of the organizational activities that occurred in Indonesia after the tsunami revealed a bifurcation in the response system. There existed an official system, which consisted of organizations that operated within the framework designed by the Indonesian government and the United Nations, and an unofficial system, which consisted of organizations that did not. The problem of bifurcation could be resolved with a census of international organizational actors that are certified to participate in disaster management activities.

Impediments to International Disaster Management

The evolution of policy and the expansion of organizational actors have been a mixed blessing for those involved in international disaster management. These developments have reflected the emergence of a global consensus among policy makers and organizations that the consequences of disasters, as well as the mode of response actions, possess a transnational character and will often require the movement of goods and services across jurisdictional boundaries. Yet the lack of a cohesive policy and technical framework, necessary to ensure that organizations responding to disaster events can collaborate and cooperate effectively, has created a number of impediments that constrain the effectiveness of international disaster management activities. The critical challenge for policy makers is not just to assess the extent of the damage in the disaster-affected area but also to identify and integrate the various capabilities of the responding organizations, many of which are arriving to conduct operations in an unfamiliar environment.

The failure to identify and integrate the various capacities of the heterogeneous collection of organizations that respond to disaster events can have a devastating effect on response operations. In part, the problem relates to the inability to provide policy makers with actionable information (Comfort 1999). To make effective decisions in uncertain disaster environments, policy makers must have two general types of information. They need access to information that allows them to comprehend the extent of the physical and social damage in the affected area, as well as information that allows them to comprehend the nature of the organizations present in the response system and their respective levels of resources, personnel, and capacities. Information deficiencies can undermine the development of collaboration and coordination, creating mismatches between the needs of those affected by the disaster and the activities being conducted, as well as the resources being delivered, by response organizations. For example, in Indonesia, some response organizations were so awash in relief funding that they attempted to declare "ownership" of entire villages and worked to exclude other response organizations from conducting response and reconstruction operations in the area. The transnational character of disaster consequences, as well as the growing involvement of international actors in disaster management, indicates the need for international disaster resilience.

The Development of International Disaster Resilience

In the Hyogo Framework for Action, the United Nations affirmed the principle that developing resilient communities provides the most effective means to manage disaster (United Nations 2005a). Resilience is defined as "the capacity of a system, community or society potentially exposed to hazards to adapt, by resisting or changing in order to reach and maintain an acceptable level of functioning and structure. This is determined by the degree to which the social system is capable of organizing itself to increase this capacity for learning from past disasters for better future protection and to improve risk reduction measures" (United Nations 2005a, 4). Yet designing strategies for achieving resilience remains a continuing policy issue.

Policy makers have long emphasized structural and nonstructural mitigation, the reformation of disaster response organizations, and the implementation of detailed operational plans and procedures to reduce disaster risk. While these approaches have improved decision making in localized events, they have done little to help manage the complexities of large, multijurisdictional disasters. The challenge is to understand how these components contribute to disaster resilience at the international level. The goal is to engage the organizational actors involved in disaster management at the international level to operate as members of a single epistemic community (E. B. Haas 1990). In this international community, decision makers would use information technology to collect and analyze information related to a disaster event. The information would be disseminated "in real time" across the system's full spectrum of disaster management actors. Given their increased situational awareness about existing opportunities and constraints, decision makers would be able to rapidly identify and implement appropriate warning and response strategies.

Once selected, these strategies would be simultaneously transmitted throughout the disaster management network, which would be designed to cover issues of disaster warning, response, and recovery. Supported by an integrated collection of feedback loops that provide continuous information updates, the decision makers would be able to quickly detect and disseminate information related to the constraints and opportunities that arise. This process ensures that the organizations in the response system, without centralized coordination, could learn to "mutually adjust" and "fit" their response capacities and capabilities to the demands of the operational environment (Comfort 1999). Analogous to the "edge of chaos" principle found within complex adaptive systems theory, the continual process of learning ensures that, as circumstances in the operational environment change, the response strategies and activities of decision makers and organizations also change (Holland 1995; Gell-Mann 1994).

While the notion of an international disaster-resilient community presents a challenge to the conventional wisdom that administrative centralization is critical for the effective management of disasters, an important step must be taken before resilient systems can be built and implemented. Specifically, there exists the need to understand the development and evolution of disaster management and public administrative networks (Goldsmith and Eggers 2004; O'Toole and Meier 2004; Agranoff 2006, 2007). Yet there is little empirical research available for examination (Provan, Fish, and Sydow 2007), and many questions about international resilience remain unanswered. Examining how an international response system evolves in an actual disaster event can provide insight into this policy problem. First, which organizations are able to gain access to, and operate within, international disaster response systems? Second, what are the primary characteristics of organizations that operate in such systems; what are their sources of funding, whether public, private, or nonprofit; and what are their levels of jurisdictional authority? Third, how rapidly, and on what dates, do the organizations enter the international disaster response systems? Finally, and perhaps most important, to what extent do interactions among response organizations drive the structural evolution of the international response system? Addressing these questions will not only identify the organizational composition of the disaster response system but also identify the organizational gaps that often undermine the communication and coordination necessary for developing international resilience.

Indonesia and the Great Sumatran Earthquake and Tsunami of 2004

No event illustrates the need to improve international disaster resilience better than the Indonesian response to the Sumatran earthquake and tsunami of December 26, 2004. The organizations that conducted response activities in Indonesia after the tsunami were exposed to significant constraints, which undermined their ability to trace decisions related to threat detection, damage assessment, information collection and dissemination, and collaboration. While these organizations ultimately formulated response strategies to cope with the constraints, the record of disaster operations revealed gaps between Indonesia's disaster response plan and the capacity of its response system to conduct operations in a large, multijurisdictional environment (Tsunami Evaluation Coalition 2006; Comfort 2007a). The Indonesian tsunami response system provides a case study that can be used to explore the factors that support and inhibit the resilience of large, multijurisdictional response systems.

The Indonesian case illustrates the dynamics that evolve in a country that was not prepared for a major disaster event.[1] While an informal response system emerged after the tsunami, it had to develop—often on an ad hoc basis—the capacity to respond to the needs of those affected by the disaster. The laws and regulations related to disaster management that had been adopted by the Indonesian government prior to 2004 were often vague and piecemeal. This legal uncertainty contributed to a number of difficulties. First, although there were many laws and regulations that referred to "emergencies" or "disasters," they often did not define with any precision the types of events that fell into these categories. Second, there were instances when, even though the Indonesian government recognized the need to take action, it often did not identify the specific agencies that would fulfill this responsibility. Equally problematic was that BAKORNAS PBP, the organization responsible for the coordination of disaster management activities in Indonesia, was an ad hoc governmental coordination board, which lacked the legal and budgetary authority to direct and implement disaster management policy throughout Indonesia.

The existence of a patchwork system of laws, regulations, and institutions does not mean that the Indonesian government was unaware of the threats posed by natural disasters. The laws and regulations implemented throughout Indonesia indicate that the government acknowledged that disasters would have detrimental political, social, and economic effects on the country. Rather, the political and economic transformations that had occurred throughout the country prior to 2004 precluded the Indonesian government from making disaster management a priority (National Coordinating Board 2004). At the time of the tsunami, the Indonesian government had not overcome this political impasse and did not have an institutional framework in place to prepare for, and respond to, events such as the tsunami. This fact was made painfully clear on the morning of December 26, 2004, when the tsunami struck Sumatra. The wave not only washed away entire communities but also destroyed the limited institutional frameworks upon which response to the event would have been developed. The international disaster response community was equally unprepared for such a situation.

Preliminary findings from an exploratory analysis of the Indonesian response to the 2004 Sumatran earthquake and tsunami (Comfort 2007a; Comfort and Haase 2007) offer insight into the dynamics of the response system. Three specific questions were addressed by this research. First, what was the organizational composition of Indonesia's tsunami response system? Second, to what extent did the activities of these organizations drive the development of Indonesia's tsunami response system? Third, to what extent did organizational interactions drive the structural evolution of

Table 12.1   Organizations Identified in the Interacting Response System

| | Source of Funding | | | | | | | | | |
| | Public | | Private | | Nonprofit | | Special Interest | | Totals | |
	N	%	N	%	N	%	N	%	N	%
Level of Jurisdiction										
International	99	28.3	23	6.6	26	7.4	2	0.6	150	42.9
National	57	16.3	28	8.0	19	5.4	2	0.6	106	30.3
Provincial	10	2.9	1	0.3	3	0.9	1	0.3	15	4.3
Local	50	14.3	15	4.3	14	4.0	0	0.0	79	22.6
Totals	216	61.7	67	19.1	62	17.7	5	1.4	350	100

Indonesia's tsunami response system? The emphasis on these questions is driven by two complementary factors: the need to address the gap in the literature on administrative networks and the need to understand fully the development and evolution of disaster response systems.[2]

System Composition

The findings for the composition of the tsunami response system indicate that the system itself was extremely large. Indeed, in its entirety, the system consisted of 554 distinct organizational actors, representing a diverse spectrum of response organizations. Continuing with the analysis, the dataset was limited to include only the organizations that were engaged in interactions with other organizations (e.g., that conducted joint operations; exchanged information, resources, and/or personnel; or collaborated). This network was labeled the interacting Indonesian tsunami response network. The results presented in table 12.1 indicate that there were 350 organizational actors in Indonesia's interacting response system. This system was extremely diverse, in terms of both size and resource levels and missions and goals. The striking thing about this network of actors was how quickly it developed. For instance, prior to the tsunami, there were only five foreigners working in Aceh province. During the month after the tsunami, approximately forty-five hundred foreigners, along with tens of thousands of Indonesian volunteers, flooded into Aceh province.

The organizational composition data reveal two interesting characteristics of the interacting response system. First, the system was asymmetric in terms of the type of organizations that were present. A review of the figures indicates that 216, or 61.7 percent, of the organizations were public. Equally interesting is that, of the identified organizations, 150, or 42.9 percent, were international. This reflects the willingness of the Indonesian government to accept external assistance after realizing that the disaster could not be managed without the support of the international community. Second, the system was scalable, meaning that a local actor could search horizontally (across public/private/nonprofit organizations) or vertically (across local/provincial/national/international organizations) to acquire the information and resources needed to complete response actions. These figures suggest that composition of the informal response system was sufficiently diverse to enable it to adapt to the constraints and opportunities present in the post-tsunami disaster environment.

System Growth

The findings for the growth of the response system show the evolving nature of the response system. By January 8, 2005, approximately 266, or 78.5 percent, of all interacting organizations identified in the response system had begun to conduct operations.[3] Equally striking is the rate of system growth. For instance, between December 26, 2004, and December 29, 2004, the number of organizations that entered the system grew rapidly and reached approximately 35 percent. Then, from December 29, 2004, until January 1, 2005, there was a period of extremely slow growth. After January 1, 2005, the system again began to expand in size. The plateau in system growth, which can be clearly seen in figure 12.1, may have been the result of two factors. First, given the lack of communication with the areas affected by the tsunami, governmental and nongovernmental actors were uninformed as to the scope and scale of the disaster. Indeed, it was not until Vice-President Jusuf Kalla returned to Jakarta after an information-gathering trip to Aceh province that perceptions began to change. Second, there was hesitation on the part of the Indonesian government to "internationalize" Aceh province, which had experienced thirty years of conflict between government forces and the Free Aceh Movement (GAM). Then, after January 1, 2005, new organizations were again detected in the response system. This increase in growth may be attributed to three events that occurred on January 1, 2005: (1) the arrival of the U.S. Navy, specifically the USS *Abraham Lincoln* taskforce; (2) the Indonesian Ministry of Finance's reduction of import duties on relief goods to zero; and (3) the World Health Organization's initial coordination meeting, which led it to start scaling up its operations.

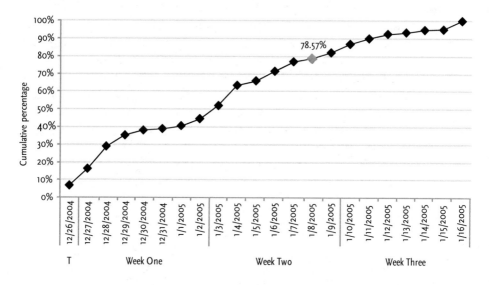

Fig. 12.1. Change in cumulative percentage of organizations detected in the interacting tsunami response system

System Evolution

Social networks analysis can be used to document how structural relations influence social and political outcomes with respect to a given policy issue. Traditional network studies examine the network, or the perceived network, at a single point in time. Rather than focusing on these dates in isolation, or combining the data into a single metanetwork, this exploratory research sought to understand the nature of the structural changes that occurred during this transition.

One of the most fundamental ways to investigate change within Indonesia's tsunami response system is to examine the number of organizations engaged in interactions on specific dates, as well as the types of response activities that occurred on those specific dates. As shown in figure 12.2, the number of organizations engaged in interactions was not stable throughout the period under analysis. Rather, the number and types of interactions engaged in by organizations changed significantly during the three weeks after the tsunami. While there were clear periods of elevated activity, the response organizations shifted the focus of their activities. Through visual observation of the results, Indonesia's interacting tsunami response system can be separated into three distinct periods of activity.

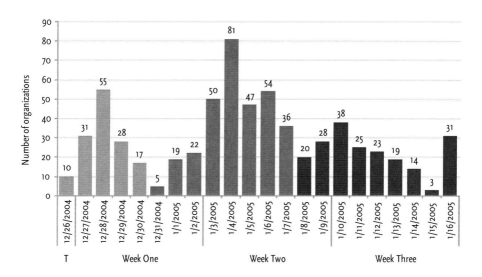

Fig. 12.2. Number of organizations engaged in interactions by date

The first period lasted from December 26, 2004, to December 30, 2004, peaking on December 28, when fifty-five organizations were identified interacting with other organizations within the response system. The majority of activities that occurred during this period of time were related to the damage and loss assessments and initial response. The second period lasted from December 31, 2004, to January 7, 2005, peaking on January 4, when eighty-one organizations were engaged in interactions. During this period, the focus of activities shifted to tasks that were related to health, logistics, and coordination issues. The final period lasted from January 8, 2005, to January 16, 2005, peaking on January 10, when thirty-eight organizations were interacting with other organizations. Again, the focus of the activities shifted during this period to addressing issues of security, the sheltering of displaced persons, and recovery of the affected regions.

Two additional factors may have shaped the context of disaster operations in Indonesia. First, although limited, this empirical record indicates that, even though policy makers expressed concern about the security of disaster response personnel in the days after the tsunami, the majority of security activities did not occur until the third week of the response. Second, it took more than five days before the organizations in the response

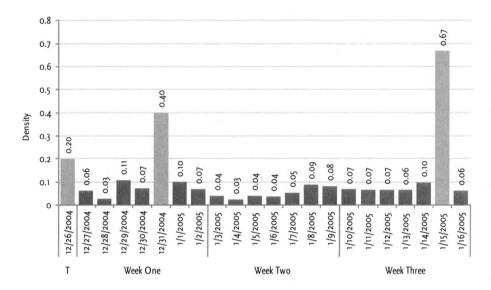

Fig. 12.3. Density of organizational interactions by date

system were able to get the necessary logistics in place, mostly from international actors, to start the effective movement of goods and personnel to the victims. While such findings may or may not be surprising, they do present an empirical record of the lack of disaster resilience at the international level.

The structure of the interacting response system is revealed by a review of the density of interactions among organizations at a given time.[4] As figure 12.3 shows, the daily density of the interactions among response organization in the Indonesian response system was extremely low. More important, the relatively low density rates present in the response system did not change over time. This finding indicates that the organizations in the system were not interacting with each other to provide coordinated assistance. Indeed, later action reports revealed that organizations missed numerous opportunities for collaboration and cooperation (Tsunami Evaluation Coalition 2006). In some instances, the lack of information prevented organizations from realizing that they had an opportunity to collaborate on an issue area or in a particular location. In other instances, some organizations realized they could have interacted but chose not to do so, focusing instead on the performance of separate operations.

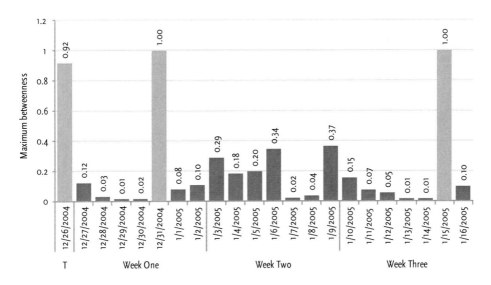

Fig. 12.4. Maximum betweenness of organizations in the interacting tsunami response system

A second way to evaluate the structure of the response network is to examine the average betweenness centrality of the actors in the network.[5] In other words, are there actors in the response network that control the flow of information and resources? Although not reported here, the average betweenness scores for organizations in the informal response network were extremely low, which could indicate that no single organization acted as the "gatekeeper." The data in figure 12.4 represent the maximum betweenness scores for the organizations identified in the interacting response network. Again, while the overall scores are low, the data indicate that some organizations had relatively high betweenness scores. More important, with the exception of January 7–8, 2005, a set of highly central actors emerged within the tsunami response system. For example, with maximum betweenness scores of .2874 and .2109 respectively, the Association of South East Asian Nations and the Office of the President of Indonesia were the two most central actors in the response network for January 3, 2005. Likewise, with a maximum betweenness score of .3651, the Indonesian Chamber of Commerce was the most central actor in the network for January 9, 2005.

These findings indicate that certain organizations possessed more centralized control over the flow of information and resources in the response

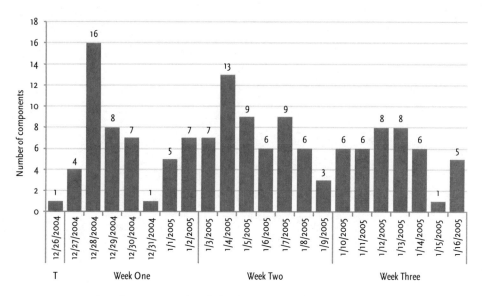

Fig. 12.5. Number of components identified in the interacting tsunami response system by date

system than others. Yet actors such as the Indonesian Chamber of Commerce may have had a high betweenness score simply because they had a large number of interactions with many organizations on one specific date, as opposed to consistent activity in the response system. When the non-critical actors are excluded, other organizations, for example, the Indonesian Ministry of Health and the World Food Program, are identified as the most central actors in the response network, in terms of their betweenness scores. These findings do not fully explain why difficulties occurred in the response system, especially with the lack of coordination. To be resilient, a system must have the capacity to adapt—that is, organizational decision makers must have the ability to move information and resources throughout the response system.

The extent to which such movement is possible can be examined by analyzing the number of components present in the Indonesian tsunami response system.[6] The number of components in the Indonesian response system, on a day-by-day basis, is presented in figure 12.5. These results indicate that the response system was actually composed of multiple disconnected groups. For example, on December 28, 2004, sixteen separate groups of organizations were conducting response operations. On January 4, 2005, thirteen groups of organizations were identified. On average, there were just over 6.5 components in operation on each of the days within the twenty-two-day period under analysis. While many of these groups were indeed conducting response activities, for example, collecting information or delivering supplies such as medicine or tents, they were doing so in isolation, without the assistance of organizations operating in other components. The tsunami response unfolded not as a result of actions taken by organizations within a single unified system, but rather as a result of the actions taken by organizations in a collection of distinct and independent response systems. As a result, the information and resources available to the organizations operating in one component were not available to the organizations operating in another component, and vice versa. These empirical data support the general consensus that, although the Indonesian response system displayed remarkable capacity to respond to an unprecedented disaster event, the disconnections that existed within the system created asymmetries of information, resources, and personnel throughout the system (Tsunami Evaluation Coalition 2006).

A Sociotechnical Framework for International Disaster Resilience

There is an emerging consensus on the need for more effective international disaster management policy. Significant progress has been made, especially in the years since the United Nations designated the 1990s the International Decade for Natural Disaster Reduction. At the local level, citizens have become aware of threats in their communities and have started to take action, often on their own, to mitigate the potential consequences of disaster. At the national level, governments have passed legislation calling for the creation of national and subnational policies and institutions to address disaster management issues. The international community has also made critical progress. By not only agreeing to come together to discuss disaster management issues but also recognizing the transnational character of disaster, nations acknowledge that the reduction of disaster risk will require cooperation and collaboration across jurisdictional boundaries. Yet the lack of a cohesive policy and technical framework at the international level has impeded the development of international disaster resilience. Indeed, the secretary general of the United Nations, in his "Report on the Implementation of the International Strategy for Disaster Management," indicated that, at its current rate of change, the international community will be unable to meet its goal of reducing disaster losses by 2015 (United Nations 2007).

The lack of resilience at the international level was clearly evident in the response to the 2004 Sumatran earthquake and tsunami. After the collapse of the formal Indonesian response system, hundreds of organizations rushed into Banda Aceh, the overwhelming majority of which had little experience with either disaster response or the affected region. Although these organizations came together to form the basis of a scalable and heterogeneous response system, failures in communication prevented decision makers from fully leveraging the capacity of the response system. Rather, these response organizations broke off into separate components that were structurally isolated from each other. As a result, the decision makers in the system struggled not only to identify the needs of the affected population but also to match the needs of these groups with the resources available in the system. This led to the development of additional problems, for example, organizational competition and the unequal distribution of relief supplies.

While the Indonesian response system ultimately managed the uncertainties present in the post-tsunami environment, many of the problems that arose during the recovery period can be directly traced to mistakes that were made during the response period. To reduce disaster risk, it is imperative that the international community establish the foundation for international resilience, which would support national governments engaged in disaster management activities.

The development of international disaster resilience will require a sociotechnical approach, which can facilitate system learning and adaptation through the examination of "the relationships and interrelationships between the social and technical parts of [a] system" and of how these relationships enhance organizational knowledge and effectiveness (Coakes, Willis, and Clark 2002, 5). On the social side, the international community can support national governments in their efforts to pass and enforce disaster management legislation within their jurisdictions. It could do so by developing a single disaster management treaty that would strengthen the Hyogo Framework for Action and replace the current patchwork of bilateral, regional, and multilateral agreements. Finally, the international community can develop standardized disaster management policies and procedures, perhaps through some form of international certification, which will help policy makers to better manage the nongovernmental organizations that populate the international disaster management arena.

On the technical side, governments can design and implement international systems that facilitate the transfer of information and resources, not only during the response period but also during the mitigation, preparation, and recovery phases of the disaster cycle. Disaster management systems, regardless of the phase of the disaster cycle, must maintain high levels of interoperability between their technical and social components. A properly designed technical system would ensure that information flows and feedback loops function among the organizations in the system (Comfort et al. 2001; Comfort 2005). Only then can information be transformed into the knowledge policy makers need to take effective action. Given the rising threats posed by transnational disasters, and the need to coordinate disaster management activities across international boundaries, the international community can continue to help develop political and technical systems at national and subnational levels, while also bridging the gaps among these systems to encourage the development of international resilience.

13 DESIGNING RESILIENT SYSTEMS

INTEGRATING SCIENCE, TECHNOLOGY, AND POLICY
IN INTERNATIONAL RISK REDUCTION

Hui Ling, Taieb Znati, and Louise Comfort

When a massive earthquake, measuring 9.3 moment magnitude on the Richter scale of earthquake intensity, occurred on December 26, 2004, at 7:58 a.m. (local time) off the western coast of Sumatra, Indonesia, it triggered not only a devastating tsunami wave that struck coastal communities in twelve nations around the Indian Ocean basin but also a wave of concern, interest, and commitment in the global scientific community, focused on discovering new methods of detecting tsunamis and protecting coastal communities from their catastrophic consequences. Geophysicists have long considered earthquakes nearly impossible to predict (Field, Milner, et al. 2007), but tsunamis offer a modest possibility for early detection, depending upon the location of the triggering undersea landslide and its distance from shore. Further, new developments in sensor technologies for monitoring seismic movements and integrating this information with changes in the water column and speed of the advancing wave have enabled scientists to explore new methods for early tsunami detection in order to transmit these data to land-based organizations that could mobilize rapid evacuations for communities at risk.

This chapter presents a design for integrating critical technologies with human organizational systems in order to increase resilience in risk-prone communities. Technologies enable human resilience in uncertain physical environments by systematically monitoring risk conditions and transmitting that information to practicing managers. Understanding the role of the instruments and the methods of collecting data in challenging physical environments requires a review of the data-collection instruments and how they contribute to the improved performance of organizational systems (Hutchins 1995). This chapter presents a design for the physical instrumentation of sensors in a network for early detection of near-shore tsunamis.

The threat of tsunamis is inherently an international policy problem, one that requires collaboration among nations that border the same ocean basins. It is also a difficult, interdisciplinary problem that has long challenged disaster managers and scientists alike. Significant progress has been made with the development of deep ocean buoys that can detect seismic movement accurately and transmit this information via the Global Seismographic Network to coastal nations in advance of the oncoming wave (Leith, Gee, and Hutt 2009). A more difficult problem is the threat of near-shore tsunamis in which the undersea landslide occurs within fifty miles of shore and the warning time for the advancing wave to coastal communities is less than fifteen minutes (Bernard et al. 2006).

A key question for scientists and disaster managers is whether appropriate technologies could be integrated to design a method that would allow both early tsunami detection for near-shore tsunamis and quick and accurate communication of that information to on-shore emergency service organizations in time to protect their communities. This is a problem of risk assessment that was previously considered beyond human intervention, one that can only be addressed by designing appropriate technologies to support detection and informed action for land-based emergency response organizations.

Importantly, the difficulty of this problem has attracted the interest and engagement of an interdisciplinary group of geophysicists, engineers, computer scientists, policy analysts, and disaster managers from many nations. It has also won the interest and financial support of research organizations from the United States, the European Union, Japan, and of course nations with coastal communities exposed to near-shore tsunami risk. In its best form, an emerging "epistemic community" is clearly focused on this research problem. Scientific organizations supported by funds from their respective governments have joined this collaborative effort to explore constructive methods to mitigate the global risks of near-shore tsunamis, which disproportionately affect island nations. For example, the National Oceanic and Atmospheric Administration (NOAA) of the United States supports a Tsunami Research Program, as do the meteorological agencies of Japan, Australia, Germany, Indonesia, and other nations (U.S. Congress

2006). The Intergovernmental Oceanographic Commission (IOC), established by the United Nations in 1960, focused specifically on the problem of tsunami detection and warning after the 2004 Sumatran earthquake and tsunami (IOC 2005).

Global efforts to address this problem do not diminish the scientific and technical difficulties of solving it. This chapter introduces one aspect of an international, interdisciplinary research effort to devise a method of early detection of tsunamis using underwater sensor networks (UWSNs) to detect the generation of a tsunami wave and to communicate that information to land-based emergency services organizations.[1] This research focuses on the threat of near-shore tsunamis off the coast of western Sumatra, and represents a collaborative effort among Indonesian and U.S. scientists and researchers to address a difficult sociotechnical problem. Importantly, the project has received the full support of U.S. and Indonesian scientific and governmental organizations in terms of data collection, access to facilities, expert advice, and counsel. While the research is ongoing, this chapter considers the challenging problem of how and where to locate underwater sensors so they will communicate data reliably via a network to inform decision making by practicing managers regarding tsunami risk.

This research explores feasible methods of mitigating tsunami risk by monitoring the challenging underwater environment. To the U.S. National Science Foundation, it represents the type of "high-risk, high-pay-off" research that requires investment of time, resources, and experimentation over the long term to achieve measurable results. Such efforts, relatively new, are inherently interdisciplinary, interorganizational, and international.

Design of a Data Collection Model for Early Tsunami Detection

This chapter examines the interdependence of social and technical systems, exploring advances in the design of underwater sensor networks as a model for developing resilient technical systems that are able to renew their performance after damaging dislocation to support key organizational functions for communities exposed to recurring risk. Although underwater sensor networks are important for many applications—for example, offshore drilling for oil or monitoring the health of coral reefs—their application in this study focuses on the design of a low-cost, effective means for early detection of near-shore tsunami waves in order to inform on-shore emergency service organizations of a threat to coastal communities. To carry out this study, we selected a field study region off the western coast of Sumatra, adjacent to the city of Padang. Padang is the capital of the province of West Sumatra, a metropolitan region of approximately 900,000 inhabitants. The city has historically been subject to both earthquakes and tsunamis and has been identified by the government of Indonesia as a priority region for disaster-risk reduction.

We are fortunate to have the support of researchers at Bandung Institute of Technology, Bandung, and the State Ministry of Research and Technology, Jakarta, Indonesia, and their willing collaboration in the design, implementation, and evaluation of the proposed model in this Indonesian community that is exposed to recurring seismic and tsunami risk. The larger research project will assess the processes of search, exchange, recognition, interpretation, communication, and action in reference to risk at three levels of aggregation of information—individual, organizational, and system-wide—but these processes depend upon developing the technical capacity to detect and transmit tsunami risk at its earliest indication.

The benefit of this sociotechnical approach is the potential for insight into the cognitive processes involved in moving from individual perception of risk, to group formation, to collective action to mitigate risk and facilitate response to danger. The objective is to determine at what points, and to what extent, human capacity to process information regarding risk can be enhanced by appropriately designed information technology. While the full study will include four phases of decision making in an evolving disaster,[2] this chapter will focus only on early-stage detection of tsunami risk and the design of a technical network of sensors for detection and communication of data regarding tsunami risk from the ocean environment to on-shore emergency services organizations.

Early-Stage Detection of Risk

This stage will use a network of technical sensors to present data on a series of initially vague changes in indicators of seismic and tsunami risk. These sensors will include ocean-bottom detection of seismic movement, pressure-sensor reports of rising water columns, and sensor reports of wave speed as the wave moves past a series of sensors. From the perspective of each organization (e.g., firefighters or members of the police department), these reports will be transmitted to a central information-processing system for integration and analysis to create a cumulative profile of risk for the whole community. The information-processing system, specified as a virtual server for each organizational unit, will be designed in a bowtie architecture to allow each organization to receive information relevant to its mission.

In typical scenarios, the single centralized server analyzes the data from multiple sensors to detect any type of risk to the whole community and then transmits the resulting information to individual decision makers with different levels of authority and responsibility for emergency response. We will expedite the transmission and analysis by filtering such data within the sensor network; a layer above the sensors will provide the views of specific areas of risk and provide to each organizational unit separate views for its particular set of responsibilities. In addition, a repository of raw data will be provided to satisfy the need for more detailed information about an event, if needed.

Three sets of indicators will be used to illustrate low, medium, and high degrees of risk. For example, an initial report from a network of ocean-bottom sensors may indicate low-level seismic activity in a specific region of the ocean floor. A second report from bottom-pressure sensors in the same region may indicate a rising water column in the ocean volume. A third report may indicate a rapid increase in the speed of waves in the same geographic area. Any single report may not be cause for alarm, but the set of reports together may indicate a major threat of tsunami. Tsunami emergency managers would register to receive such information, and only such information would be delivered to their consoles, during normal operating scenarios. The question in this phase is to determine at what point in the presentation of cumulative information regarding risk individual decision makers would recognize the potential threat as one that requires action.

The first step in the design of this network is the location of the sensors on the ocean floor in order to maximize their capacity to communicate with one another, as well as to minimize the cost in terms of the number of sensors to be deployed. It is essential to understand both the capacity of sensors in designing these networks and the limitations of their operations in an ocean environment. A critical function of the sensors is to estimate the location of other sensors in the network to enable communication among them. This is not easy in an ocean environment, subject to shifting currents and passing ships.

Underwater sensors can collect many different types of data, varying from the temperature, density, pressure, salinity, acidity, hydrogen, and turbidity of the water being monitored, to the seismic activity of the ocean floor. Underwater sensors, equipped with acoustic modems, can communicate with each other directly or through multiple hops, using acoustic channels. The data at each sensor are then transmitted back to surface stations for further processing. Underwater sensor networks are envisioned as a key technology for implementing a large variety of applications, such as environmental monitoring, disaster prevention, seismic monitoring, and tactical surveillance.

To implement these applications, the geographical location of each sensor node is required. It is obtained through an integrated device such as a

GPS receiver or inferred by exchanging messages among sensor nodes. For instance, the storm surges produced by Hurricane Katrina resulted in numerous breaches and the consequent flooding of approximately 75 percent of the metropolitan areas of New Orleans. If an underwater sensor network had been deployed to monitor the condition of the levees of New Orleans, potential warnings about when and where the breaches might occur could have been reported to local authorities before the levees started to fail. This critical information, if provided, could have reduced the loss of property and lives in New Orleans, if not avoided such losses completely.

The problem of locating each sensor node, referred as "location discovery," has been extensively investigated for terrestrial sensor networks, and many schemes have been proposed to address it. Most proposed schemes require the location of some nodes in the network to be known in advance. These nodes are termed anchor nodes or reference nodes. The unresolved nodes then estimate their location after sufficient information is gained through the exchange of messages with reference nodes. Once an unresolved node successfully gains knowledge of its location, it becomes a new reference node and starts to provide its location information to other unresolved nodes in the network. The process continues, hop by hop, until all nodes resolve their position or no unresolved node can resolve its location.

A simple example of location estimation is described in figure 13.1. Given the location of three reference nodes and the distance from an unresolved node to these three nodes respectively, the unresolved node can determine its own location by trilateration, a method of determining the relative positions of three or more points by treating these points as vertices of a triangle of which the angles and sides can be measured. An unresolved node may also be able to determine its own location using collaborative multilateration (ML) (Savvides, Han, and Strivastava 2001). Other information such as direction of reference nodes may also be used to estimate the location of unresolved nodes (Malhotra et al. 2005).

During the location-discovery process, each unknown sensor node must gain sufficient information, such as the locations of and distances to three or more reference nodes, in order to determine its own position. To enable the discovery of the locations of all unknown sensor nodes, a sufficient number of reference nodes and degree of network connectivity must exist in the network. The location-estimation process requires an unresolved node to gain sufficient information from neighboring resolved nodes through communication in order to discover its location. This means that a sufficient number of neighbors of the unresolved node must have resolved their locations in order to provide reference points for the unresolved node. In the ter-

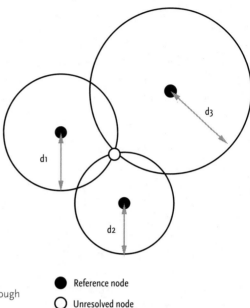

Fig. 13.1. Location estimation through trilateration

● Reference node

○ Unresolved node

restrial sensor network, this requirement can easily be achieved by increasing the number of reference nodes or the degree of network connectivity. In UWSNs, however, it is common for an unresolved sensor node to not have three or more resolved neighboring nodes. This is due to the fundamental differences between terrestrial sensor networks and UWSNs. Radio communications, the technology of choice for the physical layer in terrestrial networks, can only be used at extra-low frequencies to achieve long-distance propagation through conductive seawater. Unfortunately, extra-low frequencies require large antennas and consume excessive amounts of power (Akyildiz, Pompili, and Melodia 2005). To overcome this shortcoming, acoustic waves are mainly used for communication underwater. In addition to large propagation delays caused by the slow propagation speed of sound waves (around 1500 m/s), the complex underwater environment severely impairs the acoustic communication channel due to multipath and fading effects.

The unique characteristics of underwater sensor networks, in turn, pose a set of new challenges for location discovery, as summarized below:

• *The initial placements of reference nodes are limited.* Reference nodes usually discover their location through external devices such as GPS. As mentioned previously, radio frequency (RF) waves are heavily attenuated underwater, which limits the use of GPS to above or near sea surface. Such a restriction forces reference nodes to be placed at or close to sea surface. The remaining nodes of the UWSN must rely on location information propagation to resolve their own locations.

- *The number of reference nodes is limited.* Terrestrial sensors are cheap and typically densely deployed within the field. Underwater sensors, in contrast, are still expensive and sparsely deployed (Heidemann et al. 2006). A limited number of nodes results in low network connectivity, which in turn reduces the number of resolved neighbors for a given node.

- As a result, many nodes cannot discover their locations using the multilateration scheme. Consequently, a new scheme must be in place to enable the continuation of location discovery through the whole network. We propose to utilize the "out-of-range" information at both reference nodes and unresolved nodes to refine or determine the location sensor nodes in UWSNs, when sufficient information is not available. In the proposed scheme, an unresolved node with only two neighboring resolved nodes can determine its location under some conditions. Further, an unresolved node with only one neighboring resolved node may also be able to refine its location estimation using "out-of-range" information. As a result, the proposed scheme can significantly increase the number of resolved nodes after location discovery when the degree of network connectivity is low. The proposed scheme is also resilient to the failure of reference nodes. As long as the network is sufficiently connected and a certain number of reference nodes exist in the network, the out-of-range information can be utilized to help sensor nodes find their locations through information exchange.

Related Research

Localization schemes that use reference nodes can be classified into two main categories: range-based schemes and range-free schemes. Range-based schemes mainly consist of two basic phases: distance (or angle) estimation and distance (or angle) combination. Distance estimation explains how the distance or angle between two nodes is estimated. In the distance-combination phase, these types of information are combined to derive the location of the unresolved nodes.

The most popular methods used in distance estimation include received signal strength indicator (RSSI); time-based methods—time of arrival

(ToA) and time difference of arrival (TDoA)—and angle-of-arrival (AoA) techniques (J. Gibson 1999). RSSI measures the power of the sensor's signal at the receiver and derives the distance between the sender and receiver, based on the known transmission power and propagation model. Time-based methods record the time of arrival (ToA) or time difference of arrival (TDoA) and translate it directly into the distance based on the known signal propagation speed. ToA and TDoA are used at GPS (Hofmann-Wellenhof, Lichtenegger, and Collins 1997) and Cricket (Priyantha, Chakraborty, and Balakrishnan 2000) for distance estimation. The AoA system estimates the angle from which signals are received and derives node positions using geometric relationships (Malhotra et al. 2005).

In underwater sensor networks, surface buoys typically serve as reference nodes, because they can determine their location using GPS. Other nodes may also be used as reference nodes, provided that a priori knowledge of the deployed area is available. These reference nodes form an infrastructure of location service, and other nodes in the network directly derive their location based on the reference nodes. For example, seaweb technology, a system developed by the U.S. Navy to track autonomous underwater vehicles (AUV), relies on these additional anchor nodes deployed on the seabed at predetermined locations (Rice 2005). Prospector, a commercial system developed by Sonardyne, also deploys acoustic transponders on the seabed at known locations (Sonardyne 2009). Both systems can locate nodes in the network within a margin of error of several meters. These approaches, however, cannot be generally applied to UWSNs, because they require prior knowledge of the locations of the deployed area and a large number of reference nodes in the network. In many cases, it is very difficult to gain the location knowledge of the deployed area in advance.

Instead of relying on prefixed anchor nodes, distributed positioning algorithms assume anchor nodes to be randomly distributed throughout the network. Nodes only communicate with their one-hop neighbors and compute the distances to their one-hop neighbors. Multilateration techniques, such as atomic, collaborative, and iterative multilateration, are then used to estimate the location of sensor nodes (Savvides, Han, and Strivastava 2001). The n-hop multilateration scheme (Savvides, Han, and Strivastava 2002) examines the conditions under which one-hop, two-hop, and n-hop multilateration can uniquely determine the nodes' location. The ad-hoc positioning system (APS) (Niculescu and Nath 2001) uses four different distance metrics, ranging from minimum hop count and sum of hop lengths, to local geometric constructions, to location nodes in the network. A variant of APS utilizes angle-of-arrival of signals received from anchor nodes for location estimation (Niculescu and Nath 2003a). These schemes rely on a high level of network connectivity so that each node can gain sufficient information for location estimation. Further, a high percentage of anchor nodes must exist to achieve a small value of location error at each sensor node. The sparse network topology, caused by the high cost of individual acoustic sensors in UWSNs, significantly reduces the effectiveness of these distributed positioning schemes. To overcome this problem, our scheme uses additional out-of-range information, available in the network, for location discovery when the number of available anchor nodes is small and network connectivity is low in the underwater sensor network.

The schemes presented by Sichitiu and Ramadurai (2004) and Priyantha et al. (2005) use mobile beacons whose locations are always known to aid location discovery in terrestrial sensor networks. The mobile beacon nodes traverse the sensor network and disseminate their locations to other nodes in the network. While a mobile beacon in terrestrial networks can easily gain its location through external devices such as GPS, it is still a challenge to locate the mobile beacon nodes in UWSNs.

Range-free localization schemes (Niculescu and Nath 2003b; Wong et al. 2005; Chandrasekhar and Seah 2006; He et al. 2003) do not use range or bearing information for location-estimation purposes. As a result, these schemes are generally simpler than range-based schemes. However, these schemes provide only a coarse estimation of a sensor node's location.

DV-hop (Niculescu and Nath 2003b) employs a classical distance vector exchange protocol to maintain a node's distance, in terms of hops to all anchor nodes. The hop distance is translated into physical distance after an average distance per hop is estimated based on the hop distance and geographical distance among anchor nodes. The estimated distance to anchor nodes is then used to perform triangulation at each node for location estimation. The DV-hop algorithm performs well only in networks that have uniform and dense node distribution.

A variant of DV-hop, density-aware hop-count localization (DHL) (Wong et al. 2005) is proposed to improve the accuracy of location estimation when the node distribution is not uniform. DHL incorporates the density of a node's neighborhood into the average hop distance estimation. Consequently, it can estimate more accurately the location of sensor nodes than DV-hop in real deployment scenarios of sensor networks.

The area localization scheme (ALS) (Chandrasekhar and Seah 2006) locates sensor nodes into a certain area, instead of an exact coordinate. Each anchor node sends out beacon signals at a set of predefined power levels. The sensors measure the lowest power level that they can receive from each anchor node. The information is then synthesized into an n-dimensional coordinate, where the ith coordinate represents the lowest power level from the ith anchor node. The granularity of the scheme depends on the interval of power levels at which each anchor node is configured to broadcast its beacon signals.

Approximate point in triangle (APIT) (He et al. 2003) uses RSSI of beacon signals received from anchor nodes to determine if a sensor node is inside a given triangle. The APIT tests are carried out with all different combinations of audible anchor nodes. The test results are then aggregated, and the location is estimated as the center of gravity of the intersections of all these triangles. The scheme requires a large level of node density to achieve a good level of accuracy of location estimation.

Several other schemes are also proposed to ensure robust location estimation against range-estimation errors (Kwon et al. 2005; Moore et al. 2004), to reduce the number of beacon signals used for location discovery (Fang, Du, and Ning 2005), or to reduce location-measurement-error accumulations (Ji and Zha 2004). Despite all the existing schemes for location discovery in sensor networks, the problem of location estimation in underwater sensor networks, where many sensor nodes do not have sufficient information to use multilateration for location estimation due to the limited number of anchor nodes and the low level of connectivity, is still challenging. We propose to explore "out-of-range" information to refine or determine sensor nodes' location in underwater sensor networks, when sufficient information is not available for multilateration. The analysis and simulation results show that the proposed scheme is very effective in locating sensor nodes in underwater sensor networks.

Location Discovery Using Out-of-Range Information

In the typical UWSN environment considered in this study, there are two types of nodes in the network, namely reference nodes and unresolved sensor nodes. Since the reference nodes obtain their position through external devices such as GPS, they can only be placed at the sea-surface level because the external devices only work in the air. Figure 13.2 describes an example network for illustration purposes.[3]

The reference nodes disseminate their positions to neighboring unresolved sensor nodes by broadcasting a message to them. An unresolved sensor node, in contrast, measures its distance to each of the neighboring reference nodes. If more than three neighbor nodes are reference nodes, an unresolved node then estimates its own location using trilateration. In ad-

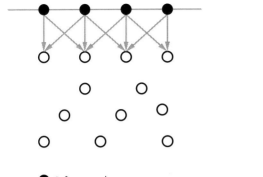

● Reference node

○ Unresolved sensor node

Fig. 13.2. An illustration example of underwater sensor network

dition, the least squares method is used to refine a sensor node's location in an overdetermined system. Otherwise, each unresolved sensor node sends a query message to nonneighboring nodes to check whether they can help to resolve its location using out-of-range information. Once its location is resolved, an unresolved node becomes a resolved node and disseminates its own position in the same way as reference nodes do.

Out-of-Range Information

Out-of-range information is based on the following observation: if two sensor nodes, N1 and N2, cannot hear signals from each other, then the distance between them must be larger than r1, the transmission range of N1, and r2, the transmission range of N2. In reality, the transmission range of a sensor may be irregular (Zhou et al. 2004). Therefore, the transmission range from a sensor node depends on where the destination is. However, the observation is still valid if r1 and r2 are replaced with the minimum range over all directions that N1 and N2's signal propagates. The observation is formally defined as following:

$$N1, N2 \text{ are not neighboring nodes} \Rightarrow$$
$$dist\ (N1, N2) > max(min(r1\alpha), min(r2\alpha)) \quad (1)$$

For simplicity, let r be max(min(r1α), min(r2α)) in the rest of the chapter.

In range-based location-discovery schemes, an unresolved node can estimate its own location if three or more than three neighboring reference nodes are available. Otherwise, the unresolved node is not able to resolve its

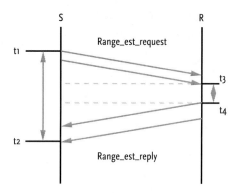

Fig. 13.3. Range estimation

own location. A detailed explanation of how the out-of-range information is utilized to resolve an unresolved node's position in several scenarios is presented in the chapter's appendix.

Range Measurement

There are many alternative methods to measure the distance between two nodes in UWSN. Received signal strength indicator (RSSI)–based approaches estimate the distance between two nodes, according to the received signal strength at the receiver node, the transmission power at the sender node, and the signal propagation model. Due to the complicated underwater environment, acoustic signal propagation is subject to surface reflection, bottom reflection, and backscattering. It also suffers from attenuation loss and losses due to air bubbles and external sources of noise such as fish noise. As a result, RSSI-based distance estimation is subject to wide variance.

In contrast, ToA- or TDoA-based approaches calculate the distance from the signal propagation speed and the propagation time between sending and receiving nodes. Unlike the RSSI-based approach for distance estimation, ToA-based ranging technique is not severely affected by the acoustic signal-propagation environment. It requires time synchronization between the transmitting node and the receiving node in varying degrees. ToA-based ranging techniques are mostly preferred in underwater sensor networks because they provide more accurate distance estimation in general.

In the following, we present a ToA-based technique for range estimation in underwater sensor networks. The proposed scheme requires only loose clock-frequency synchronization between sender and receiver.

Node S starts the range estimation by sending a "range est request" message, m, to R. S also records the time when m is actually sent out through an acoustic signal. Upon receiving m from S, node R replies to S with a "range est reply" message. The time difference between when m is received and when the "range est reply" message is actually sent out through acoustic signal is carried in the "range est reply" message. Let TD denote the transmission time of a packet; S then computes the propagation delay after the "range est reply" message from R is received. The distance is then estimated as the product of the acoustic signal-propagation speed and the propagation delay.

$$\frac{(t2-t1)-(t4-t3)-TD(Request)+TD(Reply)}{2}$$

The proposed scheme does not require strict clock synchronization between S and R. It only requires that S and R run at the same clock frequency. Therefore, even if the clock values at S and R are different, the distance can still be accurately estimated as long as S's clock and R's clock run at the same frequency. Further, since $(t4-t3)$ is typically small, an insignificant difference between the clock frequency of S and R does not incur a big variance of the estimated distance.

Localization Scheme

Given a range-estimation technique, we now describe our localization scheme. Initially, the reference nodes broadcast their location information to their neighboring nodes. Upon receiving the location of a reference node, an unresolved node measures its distance to the reference node using the technique described above. If three or more neighboring nodes have resolved their positions, the unresolved node can discover its location using trilateration. Otherwise, the unresolved node seeks help from nonneighboring nodes for determining or refining its own position.

Figure 13.4 presents the major steps of the localization process executed at a reference node, R. The reference node starts the localization process by announcing its location to neighboring nodes. It then keeps waiting for messages from other nodes. Based on the type of the message received, the reference node, R, responds as follows:

- Upon receiving a "range est request" message from an unresolved node U, R replies with a "range est reply."
- If a "location help" message for U is received, R simply discards this message if it has already processed the help request from U. Other-

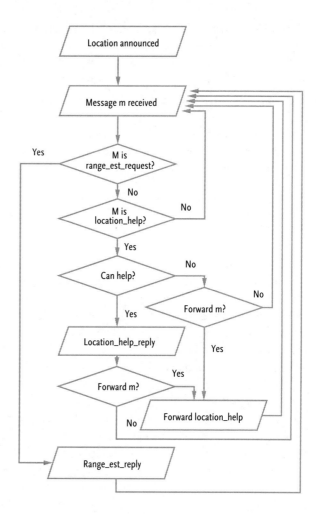

Fig. 13.4. Localization algorithm at reference nodes

wise, R checks conditions 1 and 2 and sends a "location help reply" to U if it can determine or refine U's location using "out-of-range" information. If R cannot utilize its "out-of-range" information to uniquely locate U's position, R decreases the "time to live" (TTL) of the "location help" message by one and forwards the "location help" message to its neighbors when the time to live is bigger than zero.

The main steps of the localization scheme at an unresolved node are described in figure 13.5. Each unresolved node, U, basically waits for messages from other nodes and acts corresponding to the type of the message, as shown in the following diagram:

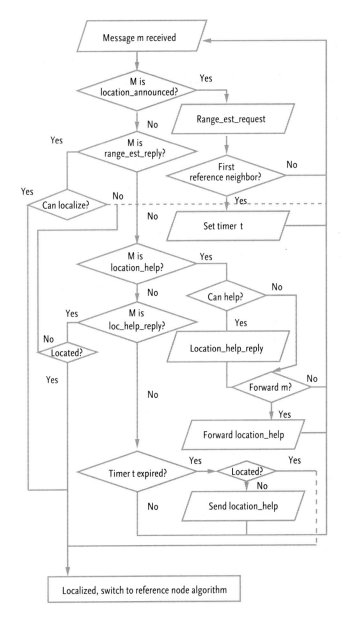

Fig. 13.5. Localization algorithm at unresolved nodes

- After receiving a "location announcement" message from R, U puts R's ID and location information in its resolved node table. It then sends a "range est request" message to R. U also starts a timer, t, if the "location announcement" is the first announcement message it receives.
- After a "range est reply" is received from R, U computes the distance between R and itself. If three or more resolved nodes have replied, U can estimate its location and become a resolved node and then execute the localization algorithm for reference nodes.
- If timer, t, expires and U still cannot resolve its location, U initializes the TTL of the "location help" message to be h and sends it out to its neighboring nodes.
- Upon receiving a "location help" message for another unresolved node U_1, node U simply discards this message if it has already processed the message. Otherwise it extracts the reference node information in the message and determines if its location information can help to determine or refine U_1's position. The conditions of case 3 to case 6 (see the chapter's appendix) are checked based on the role of U and U_1. If U's information can be utilized to determine or refine U_1's location, U replies to U_1 with a "location help reply" message. Otherwise, U decreases the TTL of "location help" by 1 and forwards the "location help" to its neighbors if the TTL is greater than 0. U also forwards the "location help" message if U_1's location cannot be uniquely determined by U. After receiving a "location help reply," U extracts the reply information and resolves or refines its location. If U's location is resolved, U becomes a resolved node and executes the localization algorithm for reference nodes.

After the reference nodes in UWSN gain their positions using external devices, they start the location scheme by sending out a "location announcement" message. Unresolved nodes then start to exchange messages with the reference nodes. Once its position is resolved, an unresolved node becomes a resolved node and starts to follow the resolved node's rules. The message exchange continues until no node can gain any additional information about its location.

Performance Evaluation

Methodology

The simulation is developed using a computational simulation program, Glomosim 2.03 (UCLA 2009). A set of different scenarios is simulated to evaluate the effectiveness of location discovery using out-of-range information. In the simulated network, the nodes at the top of the network are configured as reference nodes to simulate the constraint that the reference nodes must be close to sea surface at UWSN.

The simulated network extends over an area of 1000m x 1000m. The acoustic signal-propagation speed varies from hundreds of meters to thousands of meters. In the simulation, a transmission range of 250m is considered. For simplicity, it is assumed that every sensor has the same value of minimum transmission range, r. The proposed location-discovery scheme is simulated at the application layer. The initially configured reference nodes start to broadcast location information at the beginning of the simulation. All the messages are delivered using user datagram protocol (UDP) and retransmitted three times if not received. Each node maintains a neighbor table so that it knows if it is out of the range of another node. Given the same number of reference nodes and the same topology, the number of resolved nodes in the network is used to assess the effectiveness of the proposed scheme after the location discovery is complete. In addition, the number of unresolved nodes whose position can be refined using out-of-range information is also presented. In order to show the effectiveness of using out-of-range information for location discovery, the proposed scheme is compared to the basic multilateration localization scheme.

Effect of the Number of Hops (h) to Ask for Help for Location Estimation

Generally, any node out of the transmission range of an unresolved node might be able to refine or determine the unresolved node's location. Therefore, an unresolved node might want to set h as the network diameter and send its "location help" message to all nodes in the network in order to maximize the probability that its location can be determined or refined. However, a large value for h leads to a high number of "location help" messages transmitted in the network. Hence, the value of h is critical to the performance of the proposed scheme, and care must be taken to configure the value of h.

Figure 13.6 presents the number of resolved nodes after the location discovery in a network of twenty-four nodes and thirty-two nodes. In both scenarios, four nodes are initially configured as reference nodes. The value of h varies from 2 to 5. As the results suggest, only a slight increase is ob-

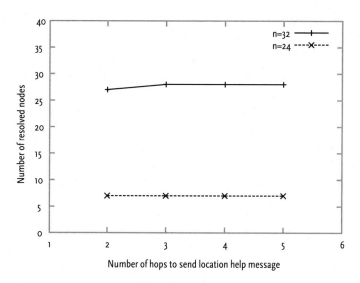

Fig. 13.6. The effect of h in networks with four reference nodes

served in the network of thirty-two nodes when h increases from 2 to 3. The number of resolved nodes remains the same in the scenario of the network with twenty-four nodes. The reason is that nodes that are multihops away may be geographically too far from the unresolved node U, so that they are out of the range of any possible location at which U might reside. Therefore, a practical setting for h is 2 or 3.

Effect of Average Node Degree

The effectiveness of using out-of-range information to locate sensor nodes depends on network connectivity and topology. Figure 13.7 presents the number of resolved nodes after location discovery with out-of-range and without out-of-range information in a set of scenarios. The number of nodes in the network increases from sixteen to fifty, while the number of reference nodes remains at four. The average node degree in each scenario is listed in table 13.1. The average node degree does not always increase as the number of nodes in the network increases. Although this seems to be wrong, a further look at the topology shows that it could actually occur. This observation stems from the fact that nodes are uniformly placed over the entire area. In uniform placement, the area is divided into a number of cells, and a node is

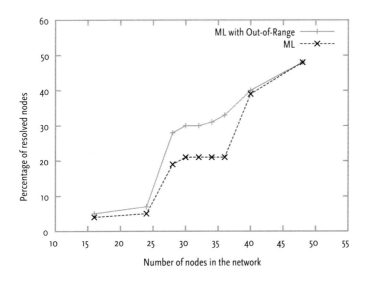

Fig. 13.7. The effect of node degree in location discovery

Table 13.1   Average Node Degree g in a Network of n Nodes

n	16	24	28	30	32	34	36	40	48
g	1.80	3.10	4.90	5.00	4.80	4.82	4.83	6.90	7.30

randomly placed within each cell. A slight increase in the number of nodes can create an additional cell that has only a few nodes placed.

When the network has a total of sixteen nodes, both multilateration and our scheme cannot locate any other node's location since the network is partitioned. No out-of-range information is useful in this scenario due to the lack of connectivity. Our scheme resolves more nodes' location than the basic multilateration scheme as the connectivity increases. As the network becomes highly connected, almost all nodes can resolve their location using the basic multilateration scheme. As a result, no out-of-range information is needed in these cases. In UWSN, sensors are typically connected with a small value of average node degree. Therefore, the proposed scheme can be very effective in resolving other sensor nodes' location.

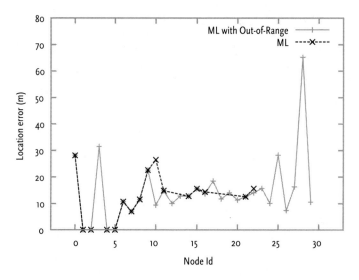

Fig. 13.8. Location estimation error with 5 percent ranging measure error

Location Estimation Error

Although very accurate distances can be measured between nodes using acoustic signals (Savvides, Han, and Strivastava 2001), the complex underwater environment causes errors in the ranging technique. In this section, we investigate how the ranging errors affect the location of sensor nodes estimated after the location discovery phase.

Figure 13.8 presents the location errors at each resolved node after location discovery using "out-of-range" information and the multilateration approach. In both approaches, the measured distances between nodes are used to derive the location of unresolved nodes. Consequently, varying degrees of location errors are expected at the estimated locations of the resolved nodes. The location error at a resolved node depends on the accuracy of locations of its neighboring resolved nodes and the ranging errors. Most nodes, resolved both in the multilateration approach and in the proposed scheme, show an estimation error between 10m and 20m. The proposed scheme can discover some extra nodes' position using "out-of-range" information. In contrast, the error accumulation during the location-discovery process results in a relatively large location error in some nodes.

In multilateration-based localization schemes for sensor networks, each unresolved node must gain sufficient information, such as three reference nodes, in order to discover its location. In underwater sensor networks, however, it is common for an unresolved sensor node not to have three or more resolved neighboring nodes, due to the sparse network topology and limited availability of reference nodes. As a result, many nodes cannot discover their locations using the multilateration scheme.

We proposed utilizing the "out-of-range" information at both reference nodes and unresolved nodes to refine or even determine the location of sensor nodes in UWSNs when sufficient information is not available to use multilateration. The analysis, documented in the chapter's appendix, has shown that an unresolved node with only two neighboring resolved nodes can determine its location under some conditions. Further, an unresolved node with only one neighboring resolved node may also be able to refine its location estimation using "out-of-range" information. The simulation results show that the proposed scheme can significantly increase the number of resolved sensor nodes after location discovery, when the network connectivity is low. The increase can be as great as 50 percent in some scenarios.

The techniques presented here offer a solution to the critical problem of location discovery, which is essential for designing sensor networks that offer a promising means for early detection of near-shore tsunamis. It represents an advance in technical systems that would support the timely monitoring of key indicators of tsunami risk and the transmission of information to emergency services organizations to enable them to take action to reduce risk for their communities. As such, it constitutes a sociotechnical approach to the early detection of tsunami risk that could not be addressed by emergency services organizations alone.

The capacity to achieve distributed cognition in practice depends upon the processes of communication and the organizational infrastructure that are already in place, including the technology itself. This chapter provides an example of using technology as a central actor with human actors in a resilience system. In designing means to support cognition in resilient communities, no matter what the surprise, the tools and instruments of data collection for decision making are as important as the operators of the system. The research reported here focuses on the design of instruments to contribute to a resilient sociotechnical information infrastructure for the early detection of tsunami risk.

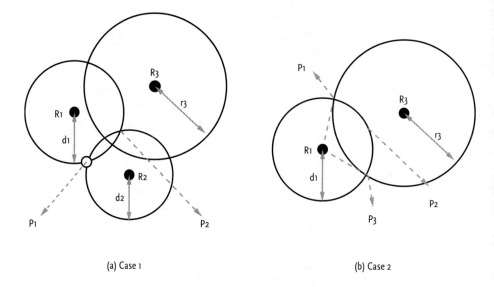

(a) Case 1   (b) Case 2

Fig. 13.9. Reference node uses out-of-range information to resolve/refine an unresolved node's position

Appendix: Detailed Documentation of Out-of-Range Location Estimation for Sensor Networks

Cases 1 and 2 show how a nonneighboring resolved node refines other unresolved nodes' position. In addition, an unresolved node can also explore its "out-of-range" information to refine other nonneighboring unresolved nodes' locations under certain conditions in cases 3, 4, 5, and 6. Whether a node N is out of the transmission range of U can be determined by sending messages between neighboring nodes. If N learns of U's existence through multiple hop messages and U is not in N's neighbor list, N can infer that U is out of its transmission range. In all of the following cases, it is assumed that node N does not hear a signal from U.

Case 1: N is a resolved node, and U has two neighboring resolved nodes

In the scenario presented in figure 13.9(a), the unresolved node has two neighboring reference nodes, R1 and R2. The distance measured from the unresolved node to R1 and R2 is d1 and d2, respectively. Obviously, there are two possible positions that the unresolved node might be, P1 and P2, given this knowledge. Let us assume that another reference node, R3, exists in the network and that the unresolved node cannot hear a signal from R3. Furthermore, P2 is in R3's transmission range, while P1 is not. Therefore, it can be inferred that the unresolved node can only reside in P1 because it would hear a signal from R3 if it were at P2.

Let (xR,yR) be the coordinate of the reference node R; let (x_1,y_1) and (x_1',y') be the two possible positions of the unresolved node U, and let r be the minimum transmission range of R. R can resolve U's location if it can hear a signal from one of these two possible positions, but not both. The condition is expressed as follows:

$$(\sqrt{(x_R-x_1)^2+(y_R-y_1)^2} > r \ \&\& \ \sqrt{(x_R-x_1')^2+(y_R-y_1')^2} \leq r)$$

$$|| \ (\sqrt{(x_R-x_1)^2+(y_R-y_1)^2} \leq r \ \&\& \ \sqrt{(x_R-x_1')^2+(y_R-y_1')^2} > r) \qquad (2)$$

Case 2: N is a resolved node, and U has one neighboring resolved node

In this case, the "out-of-range" information at the reference node is not able to determine a unique position for the unresolved node. Nonetheless, it can reduce the potential set of locations where the unresolved node may reside in the network. In the example scenario described in figure 13.9(b), the reference node, R3, is not a neighbor of the unresolved node. Further, the unresolved node is d1 away from reference node R1. Apparently, the unresolved node cannot reside in the arc P1P2P3. Therefore, the potential area in which the unresolved node resides is reduced to a smaller arc.

Let (xR1,yR1) be the position of the reference node, R1, of an unresolved node U, and let d1 be the distance from U to R1. A reference node, R2 located at (xR2,yR2), can refine U's location if it can hear a signal from any possible location of U. The condition can be expressed as follows:

$$(\sqrt{(x_{R2}-x_{R1})^2+(y_{R2}-y_{R1})^2} \leq r+d1) \qquad (3)$$

As a result, the unresolved node, U, cannot reside in the following area, where otherwise U would hear a signal from R1.

$$\{(x,\ y)\ |\ (\sqrt{(x-x_{R1})^2+(y-y_{R1})^2} = d1 \ \&\&$$

$$(\sqrt{(x-x_{R2})^2+(y-y_{R2})^2} \leq r\}$$

Case 3: N is an unresolved node with two neighboring resolved nodes, and U has two neighboring resolved nodes

In the scenario described in figure 13.10(a), an unresolved node, N, has two neighboring resolved nodes, R3 and R4. Given its distance to R3 and R4, d3 and d4, N can calculate its two potential locations: P3 and P4. Similarly, the unresolved node, U, has two neighboring resolved nodes, R1 and R2, and computes its own possible positions: P1 and P2. Further, the distance between P3 and P1 and the distance between P4 and P1 are smaller than U's minimum transmission range, r. Based on the fact that N is not a neighbor of U, U can determine that it must be located at P2.

In general, an unresolved node, N, located at either (x1,y1) or (x₁′,y′), can determine the location of another unresolved node, U, located at either (x,y) or (x′,y′), if both of its possible locations are within the transmission range, r, from one

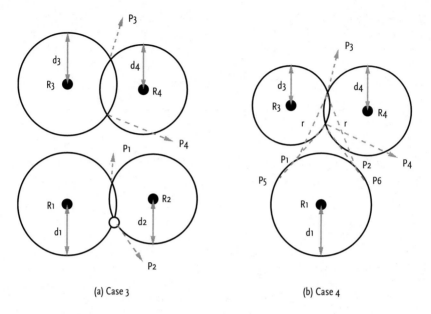

(a) Case 3　　　　　　　　　　　　　(b) Case 4

Fig. 13.10. Unresolved node uses out-of-range information to resolve/refine another unresolved node's position

potential location of U. Combined with the fact that N must be more than r away from N, one of the two potential locations of U can be eliminated. As a result, the location of U can be determined. The condition is expressed as follows:

$$(\sqrt{(x-x_1)^2+(y-y_1)^2}\leq r \;\&\&\; \sqrt{(x-x_1^i)^2+(y-y_1^i)^2}\leq r)$$

$$\|\,(\sqrt{(x'-x_1)^2+(y'-y_1)^2}\leq r \;\&\&\; \sqrt{(x'-x_1^i)^2+(y'-y_1^i)^2}\leq r) \qquad (4)$$

Case 4: N is an unresolved node with two neighboring resolved nodes, and U has one neighboring resolved node

The scenario presented in figure 13.10(b) demonstrates how an unresolved node, N, helps to reduce the area in which another unresolved node, U, may reside. Similar to case 3, node N has two neighboring resolved nodes, R3 and R4. The potential location for N is either P3 or P4. The distance between the unresolved node, U, and its neighboring resolved node, R1, is d1. Further, both the distances between P3 and R1, and between P4 and R1, are smaller than r + d1. Based on the fact that N cannot hear a signal from U, the unresolved node, U, cannot reside in arc P1P2 if N is at P3. Similarly, U cannot reside in arc P5P6 if N is at P4. In this example scenario, arc P1P2 is covered by arc P5P6. Therefore, the unresolved node, U, cannot reside in arc P1P2 no matter where N is located.

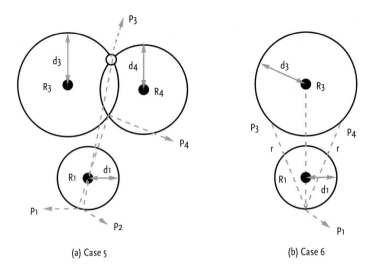

| (a) Case 5 | (b) Case 6 |

Fig. 13.11. Unresolved node uses out-of-range information to resolve/refine another unresolved node's position

In general, consider an unresolved node, U, which is d away from its neighboring resolved node R1, located at (x_{R1}, y_{R1}). An unresolved N, located at either (x_1, y_1) or (x_1', y'), can refine U's position, if both of its possible locations can hear a signal from U. The condition is expressed as follows:

$$(\sqrt{(x_1-x_{R1})^2 + (y_1-y_{R1})^2} \leq r+d \;\&\&\; \sqrt{(x_1'-x_{R1})^2 + (y_1'-y_{R1})^2} \leq r+d) \qquad (5)$$

As a result, the unresolved node, U, cannot reside in the following area:

$$\{(x, y) \mid \sqrt{(x-x_{R1})^2 + (y-y_{R1})^2} = d \;\&\&\;$$
$$\sqrt{(x-x_1)^2 + (y-y_1)^2} \leq r \quad \&\&\;$$
$$\sqrt{(x-x_1')^2 + (y-y_1')^2} \leq r\}$$

Case 5: N is an unresolved node with one neighboring resolved node, and U has two neighboring resolved nodes

Similar to case 3, the scenario presented in figure 13.11(a) also describes how an unresolved node, N, helps to determine the location of another unresolved node, U. This case differs from case 3 in that the unresolved node, N, has only one neighboring resolved node. In figure 13.11(a), U is located at either P3 or P4. N is located at d1 away from the resolved node R1. P1 is the farthest point from P4 among all the possible locations where N might be. If P4P1 is smaller than r, it can be easily concluded that U must reside at P3, because otherwise U would be a neighboring node of N.

Generally, consider an unresolved node, U, located at either (x,y) or (x´y´). An unresolved node, N, which is d away from its neighboring resolved node, R1, can determine U's position if N would hear a signal from one possible location of U, no matter where it can be. Therefore U cannot be at that location but must be at the other possible location, since U would hear a signal from N otherwise. The condition is expressed as follows:

$$(\sqrt{(x-x_0)^2+(y-y_0)^2}\le r, \ \forall(x_0,\ y_0), \ \sqrt{(x_0-x_{R1})^2+(y_0-y_{R1})^2}=d$$

$$\| \ (\sqrt{(x'-x_0)^2+(y'-y_0)^2}\le r, \ \forall(x_0,\ y_0), \ \sqrt{(x_0-x_{R1})^2+(y_0-y_{R1})^2}=d \qquad (6)$$

Condition 6 can be simplified into the following equivalent condition after a short derivation:

$$\sqrt{(x-x_{R1})^2+(y-y_{R1})^2}\le r-d1 \ \| \ \sqrt{(x'-x_{R1})^2+(y'-y_{R1})^2}\le r-d1 \qquad (7)$$

Case 6: N is an unresolved node with one neighboring resolved node, and U has one neighboring resolved node

In the illustration scenario described in figure 13.11(b), both unresolved nodes N and U have only one neighboring resolved node. Further, let P3 and P4 be these two positions where U might be located, and the maximum distance from P3 and P4 to N are both smaller than r. As a result, it is easy to conclude that the unresolved node, U, cannot reside in the arc P3P4.

In general, consider an unresolved node, U, which is d away from its neighboring resolved node located at (xR1,yR1). The unresolved node, N, which is d´ away from its neighboring resolved node located at (xR2,yR2), can refine U's location if N can hear a signal from some of the possible locations of U no matter where it might be. The condition is expressed as follows:

$$\sqrt{(x_{R1}-x_{R2})^2+(y_{R1}-y_{R2})^2}\le r+d-d \qquad (8)$$

As a result, the unresolved node, U, cannot reside in the following area:

$$\{(x,\ y) \ | \ \sqrt{(x-x_{R1})^2+(y-y_{R1})^2}=d \ \&\&$$

$$\sqrt{(x-x')^2+(y-y')^2}\le r, \ \forall(x',\ y')$$

$$\sqrt{(x'-x_{R2})^2+(y'-y_{R2})^2}\le d'\}$$

In summary, the location of an unresolved node, U, with two neighboring resolved nodes can be determined using "out-of-range" information if all of the possible positions of the helping node, N, fall in the shadow area described in

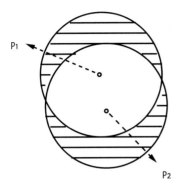

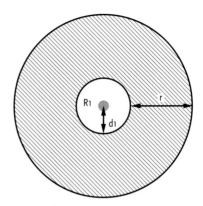

(a) Resolving area for an unresolved node
with two potential locations

(b) Refining area for an unresolved node
with one resolved neighboring node

Fig. 13.12. Location discovery using out-of-range information

figure 13.12(a). Any reference node located in the area, or any unresolved node whose possible locations are within the area, can locate U, once the "location help" message for U is received. Similarly, the location of an unresolved node U, with only one neighboring resolved node, can be refined if all possible locations of the helping node are within the shadow area in figure 13.12(b).

14 RESILIENCE REVISITED

AN ACTION AGENDA FOR MANAGING EXTREME EVENTS

Louise K. Comfort, Arjen Boin, and Chris C. Demchak

Defining Resilience (Revisited)

In the early spring of 2009, the city of Fargo, North Dakota, came under threat of the rapidly rising Red River. Flood threats occur periodically as the snow melts up north and spring rains are heavier than usual. The citizens of Fargo thus know what a flooding Red River can do. As the river rose higher than ever before, the people of Fargo sprang into action. In a remarkable display of perseverance, determination, and collective action, they prepared for the worst. In driving sleet and icy cold, young and old filled sandbags and worked to strengthen the levees. Watching around-the-clock television coverage of Fargo's plight, one could not help but be impressed with the shared will to withstand this impending disaster.

New Orleans in the wake of Hurricane Katrina did not prompt similar feelings of admiration (as observed more than once in this book). Whereas Fargo is associated with a shared desire among its citizens to withstand and overcome this threat, New Orleans in 2005 will forever evoke images of desperation and defeat. Four years after the disaster, the Crescent City is still facing a steep road toward full recovery.

Some cities do better in the face of disaster than others (Vale and Campanella 2005). It is tempting to describe apparent success in terms of resilience and apparent failure in terms of a shopping list of explanatory variables (e.g., political culture, the weak designs of protective structures, incompetent leadership). Resilience then becomes a synonym for survival and the prescribed antidote for administrative shortcomings. This is too simple, as we argued in the introductory chapter of this book. We strongly believe that resilience is crucial in the face of changing threats, but we are also acutely aware that resilience is not easily defined, measured, or engineered. The chapters in this book aim to help us further down this road toward understanding resilience.

One lesson we have learned is that a shared definition of resilience is unlikely to materialize any time soon. In the first chapter, we defined resilience rather broadly as the capacity "to proactively adapt to and recover from disturbances that are perceived within the system to fall outside the range of normal and expected disturbances." This definition was intended as a baseline against which others could be assessed and compared. Quite a few authors displayed a tendency—implicitly or explicitly—toward a broader definition that includes efforts of prevention, mitigation, risk management, and crisis management. Others stuck with a narrower interpretation, focusing solely on quick recovery after a disaster. While agreement on exact wording remains elusive, all authors seem to agree that the term *resilience* refers to an important if not critical feature of a society or organization.

A fundamental lesson of this book is that resilience is the outcome of a long-term process. It is the outcome of an institutionalized approach that accepts surprise as an inevitable event whose magnitude and rippling consequences can be anticipated through knowledge, emerging tools, consensual social collaboration, and preparations to be flexibly innovative. Far from a fix-it-and-forget-it approach, enduring resilience is a balancing act between risk and resources, between vulnerabilities and escalating or unmanagable catastrophe.

This volume helps tease out some of the key design principles and inherent constraints that must be negotiated in an effort to further societal resilience. Taken together, these insights constitute what we call a sociotechnical approach toward resilience. This approach is a way of seeing—it helps to identify vulnerabilities and devise adaptive responses. It is not a *how-to-do-it* approach; the world, after all, is too complex for simple answers. Yet it is much more than an easy sweep of loosely joined chapters. In fact, we argue that this way of seeing represents a sea change—a paradigm change, if you will—that gives rise to an effective response to an ever more dangerous world.

Resilience as a Web of Practice

What have we learned from this global tour of organizational policy and practice in managing extreme events? The scholars whose work is included in this book have examined the management of extreme events from multiple perspectives and in different settings. Our initial inquiry framed the problem of resilience as one confronting current managers responsible for disaster-risk reduction in communities exposed to changing risk. The authors in chapter 2 examined the concept of resilience from a theoretical perspective, reviewing how other theorists defined and characterized differences in the capacity of communities to anticipate, respond to, and recover from adverse events. Chapters 3 through 13 explored the practices of governments, organizations, and communities as they struggled to cope with adverse events and the extent to which there was a recognizable set of characteristics that identifies a "resilient community."

Running through the chapters of this book is a set of seven themes that, taken collectively, characterize the phenomenon of resilience. These characteristics emerge more from direct observation of practice in disaster environments than from any abstract conceptualization of administrative performance. Yet this set of themes reveals a logical interdependence that distinguishes communities that engage in these practices from communities that do not. These seven themes fall into two subsets, one that describes the structure within which organizations take action to reduce risk and a second that describes the interorganizational processes that constitute resilient performance.

Structuring Conditions

Three conditions structure the action arena that supports, or inhibits, the emergence of resilience in practice. Each of these conditions represents a sliding scale that increases or decreases the intensity and impact of a given hazard upon a community exposed to disaster risk.

First, *societies are complex systems* that adapt to changing conditions at varying rates and with varying degrees of success, depending upon the initial conditions of economic, engineered, social, scientific, and information infrastructure that are in operation when extreme events occur. These conditions do not necessarily support disaster-risk reduction in societies exposed to recurring risk. Separate actions taken by different organizations to meet particular goals may create barriers to mobilizing timely, informed action to reduce risk for the entire community. For example, the requirement of state licenses for physicians to practice medicine, while considered a protective policy against medical malpractice, may inhibit the ability of physicians to offer medical assistance across state lines in a catastrophic disaster.

Second, *disaster risk is a global phenomenon,* affecting developed and developing nations alike. Yet the same disaster event may have highly variable consequences in different locations, depending upon the initial conditions and the community's capacity to act. The consequences of failure in one location may ripple across borders, creating a cascade of failure in other locations. The spread of SARS and Avian flu, and the 2008–9 subprime mortgage crisis, illustrate the interconnected, interdependent web of social, economic, technical, and policy interactions that often precipitate or escalate crises.

Third, *any given risk* may have multiple triggers and multiple components and consequently *represents an interdisciplinary phenomenon* that requires knowledge and expertise from a range of sources. No single discipline, agency, or jurisdiction will have all of the knowledge required to devise an informed strategy of action for a threat that will affect different groups in the population differently. Yet each threat is likely to have key characteristics, each location key constraints that can be identified and monitored before a threat occurs. Consequently, the organization of action and the search for and exchange of information and resources essential to support action require access to a broad range of knowledge sources, experience, and technical infrastructure that will allow managers to focus attention on frequent threats but also to identify the unexpected surprise event at an early stage.

Processes of Resilient Performance

In addition to the three structural conditions outlined above, four processes characterize resilient performance in the face of disaster risk. As emphasized by nearly every author in this volume, *resilience is a dynamic process* that balances risk against resources, time against severity of loss, cost against uncertainty, learning against error. These tensions run throughout the decision-making process that each manager confronts, and the multiplicative results of decisions taken separately contribute greatly to the complexity of any instance of disaster operations. It is the continuing task of determining in different instances and at different times for the same event not only the appropriate balance in actions for a single organization but the impact of that decision on other organizations that makes decision making in disaster environments an ever-changing process subject to review and revision.

Related to this dynamic process, resilience reflects a *differential rate of change over time.* In a complex society, many organizations, communities, and jurisdictions are taking actions to reduce disaster risk simultaneously. Each organization is changing in a dynamic society, but most are operating at different rates of change in different areas of performance. The challenge is to synchronize these simultaneous actions to move approximately in the same direction and to avoid organizational collision and dysfunction (Strogatz 2003).

The third process is the *scalable development of capacity* to manage risk. Given the dynamic process by which risk escalates and deescalates across organizational and jurisdictional boundaries, different organizations and jurisdictions have different rates of exposure to risk, as well as different levels of authority to command resources, personnel, and access to information in managing risk. Again, this process represents a sliding scale for managers, and their ability to move up and down a jurisdictional hierarchy or across different organizational boundaries affects the degree of resilience their community is able to muster.

A final process that is integral to the development of resilience is the adoption of smart technologies to support organizational performance in risk-prone environments. This task offers both promise and risk: promise in that technologies will enable researchers and policy makers to explore the conditions of risk more systematically than previously possible, but also risk in recognition that these technologies are subject not only to misinterpretation by their human managers but also to faulty design and technical failure, even as they seek to minimize risk to human communities.

Chapters 3, 4, and 13 in this volume present models of the design and application of technologies to support decision processes for disaster managers. Each model extends the data-collection and reasoning processes of human managers in complex risk environments. None can function without human management and interpretation, and all can fail without watchful monitoring, but included in a sociotechnical approach to risk reduction, each offers promise of addressing policy problems that could not be solved before.

This set of structural conditions and action processes outlines the arenas within which resilience can be initiated, cultivated, and demonstrated. Resilience is the outcome of a learning process, which relies on the capacity of managers and researchers to build communities of knowledge to support innovation, discovery, integration of new information, and rapid correction of error. Resilience in this form evolves from practice and represents a web of human and organizational interactions that support collective learning to achieve long-term goals.

Resilience Reframed

Given the characterization of resilience as a set of structural conditions within which dynamic processes operate to enable communities to reduce disaster risk, the next task becomes reframing resilience as an operational term that can be incorporated into the design of action strategies that communities, at different levels of development and in different risk environments, can adopt as a common global framework.

The challenge, then, is to frame the vision of resilient communities in such a way that it can be achieved by policy makers at different levels of responsibility, authority, and exposure to risk. Four concepts, framed in action terms, would give fresh meaning and substance to the term *resilient communities*. The adoption of these concepts represents a significant change in the design and implementation of public policy, one in which citizens, emergency managers, and policy makers are all engaged in the daily process of building capacity for resilient and sustainable risk management. Adoption of these key concepts by governments at the local, state, national, and international levels into their policies and practices would create and sustain stronger performance in disaster-risk reduction.

Distributed Cognition

The concept of distributed cognition (Hutchins 1995) captures the process of creating knowledge for action in changing environments. To Hutchins, knowledge in any action situation is distributed—that is, no one person or organization holds all of the information and knowledge necessary to complete a task. Further, if the task is being conducted in real time, the process is an interactive one, with multiple participants contributing their specific knowledge that is relevant to the shared objective. The purpose of such a group is not only to share specific information that others may not have or know but also to identify and correct error as it appears in order to keep the common task focused and accurate.

In this process, the tools and instruments of data collection for decision making are as important as the operators of the system. Distributed cognition is the result of a systems approach, in which anyone can distort or correct the system, and all participants have a responsibility for maintaining and operating the system. This approach builds directly on the construct of "epistemic communities" (E. B. Haas 1990), or groups of knowledgeable people who are committed to a common goal. In common parlance among emergency managers, it means building a "common operating picture" that allows actors with different responsibilities at different locations to coordinate their actions to achieve a shared goal of disaster-risk reduction.

The capacity to achieve distributed cognition in practice depends upon the processes of communication and the organizational infrastructure that are already in place. In small groups, the communication is face-to-face, but in large-scale regional operations, the interactive communication and feedback among participating organizations and groups require a technical infrastructure to support organizational search and exchange of information. Decision support systems such as the bowtie architecture and the Atrium (as described in this volume) are examples of applications that provide timely, valid information to practicing decision makers.

Measurement and Monitoring of Changing Conditions and Performance

In order to implement a strategy for creating distributed cognition, it is essential to determine the key parameters that indicate increasing risk and, equally important, the key parameters that measure declining risk. This information, aggregated, analyzed, and disseminated in a timely process, could inform managers of current operating conditions and enable them to make the consequent adjustments in performance for the organizational systems that they manage. Such skills, and the equipment and trained personnel needed to perform them, are a central component of building a capacity for resilience in communities exposed to risk.

The Human Capacity to Learn

The basis for resilience is the human capacity to learn, both from prior experience, including error, and from examples of innovative or effective performance. Essential to resilience is the capacity to identify and correct error, setting the example for prompt acknowledgment of mistakes and updating of inaccurate information. In a changing society, this function is central to maintaining and sustaining resilient performance. Again, this capacity requires a set of skills for accessing, storing, searching, and analyzing information, as well as the ability to draw inferences from current experience and to apply such insights to operational performance.

Building a Sociotechnical Infrastructure

Implicit throughout the chapters of this volume is the importance of a sociotechnical infrastructure. The critical functions of cognition, communication, coordination, and control all depend upon the reliable operation of a technical information infrastructure to support the search for and the exchange and validation of information from the risk environment to inform practice in real time (Comfort 2007b). Technologies have improved remarkably to enable low-cost, real-time detection of risk and timely transmission of this information to responsible policy makers. The difficulty, more often, lies in the organizational constraints imposed by the lack of informed policies or of leaders who are able to articulate clearly the steps required for collaborative action.

In summary, this set of cognitive skills—distributed cognition, measurement and monitoring, and the capacity to detect and correct error—supported by a sociotechnical infrastructure to facilitate these processes in organizational and jurisdictional settings provides the foundation for building resilience. Importantly, the building blocks of this process will be essentially the same at each jurisdictional level and in every country of the world.

Toward a Sociotechnical Approach

Not so long ago, well-run societies prepared for safety threats and systemic disturbances in a fairly straightforward manner. After the threats were identified, defined, and ranked in terms of likelihood and potential impact, a specific plan was formulated to prevent each threat and deal with it should it emerge anyway. After a new threat or disaster had surprised society, the cycle would start anew. This is what Aaron Wildavsky (1988) refers to as a strategy of anticipation.

The prevalence of this strategy came on display in the years following the 9/11 attacks on the United States (Flynn 2005). Policy makers tried to root out terrorism at home and abroad. They defined a whole range of responses to a wide variety of possible terrorist attacks. They did all this in the face of clear evidence that their strategy was not working: the Anthrax attacks, the renditions, the secret prisons, and the deadly occupation of Iraq all signaled a response to adversity that somehow appeared lagging and ineffective at best. If we view Hurricane Katrina and 9/11 together, we must conclude that this paradigm no longer works.

Wildavsky forwarded a strategy of resilience as the workable alternative to anticipation (see also Flynn 2007; Ramo 2009). This strategy requires a near-revolutionary change in thinking. Accepting that inevitable and "rude" surprises will occur sooner or later (LaPorte 2007), it forces policy makers to prepare for the unknown. For policy makers steeped in a rational paradigm of goal-means thinking, this is quite a switch indeed. Rather than planning toward a well-defined situation (a specific disaster such as a flood or hurricane), they must prepare for unstructured events that are characterized by surprise, uncertainty, and undefined causal relationships.

A sociotechnical perspective, as forwarded in this volume, allows policy makers to prepare for the unknown. Taken together, these principles guide policy makers toward embracing surprise, facilitating self-organizing reflexes in society, exploiting modern technology, and engaging in international arenas to plot a way out of disaster.

Building a resilient community is one of the most daring challenges that modern societies face. Not only is it hard, as we lack complete "design knowledge," but the principles of a sociotechnical approach outlined above typically encounter deeply entrenched political-administrative constraints. We mention several here, but this list is far from exhaustive.

It is, for instance, hard to maintain political and societal momentum for long-term policy efforts such as these. After a disaster, the calls for "lessons learned" are widely heard. Yet the challenge of transforming the bitter experience gained from one devastating event into improved performance in response to the next threat is not easy (Stern 1997). Over time, interest and action in disaster preparedness wane. Changes in resources, personnel, technologies, and organizational priorities shift the focus of the stricken community away from risk reduction, and the community lapses into patterns of inaction and inattention that leave it again vulnerable to known threats.

Cognitive blinders built into policies and politics make resilience a "hard sell," something akin to an impossible job (cf. Hargrove and Glidewell 1990). It is hard to sell policy makers and politicians on the need for sophisticated causal analysis that foregoes the simple linear causal chains that characterize most contemporary policies. To state that crises and disasters are not preventable (because the causal chains delivering them are simply too complex to understand) is to invite derision. A leader gets further by promising to "smoke them out of their holes" than by admitting that the causes of terrorism remain largely unknown. A call for the increased use of technologies typically runs aground on internal resistance (policy makers generally are averse to change in their daily routines). A call for an increased role of international institutions is close to suicidal, at least for U.S. politicians. Budgetary constraints compound the problem.

The deepest problem may well be the ingrained belief that leaders should lead in times of crisis (Boin et al. 2005). When the response appears to proceed well, leaders eagerly claim credit (Rudy Giuliani serves as an instructive example). When things fall apart, leaders are in trouble (consider the political damage suffered by President George W. Bush in the wake of Hurricane Katrina). Building a resilient system thus carries few potential rewards: if all goes well, leaders can no longer take the credit; when things go badly, they are sure to take the flak.

An Agenda for Future Research

While we believe that the sociotechnical approach is a paradigmatic change that needs to be pursued vigorously, we realize that the available knowledge is still too limited to guide institutional design efforts. In this section, we identify the most pressing research challenges that require sustained attention from the academic community. These themes return frequently throughout the chapters of this volume, underlining their relevance for practitioners and whetting our research appetites.

Identifying precepts for leadership. The chapters make clear that the necessary change can only be achieved under the tutelage of a solid cohort of resilience-oriented leaders. It is equally clear, however, that we do not have a convincing model for leadership that involves "selling the unsellable" (cf. Hargrove and Glidewell 1990). Rather than succumbing to a flight into abstractions, we propose to study critical cases of effectively designed resilience to unearth the role that leadership played. For instance, we can comparatively study cities that bounced back quickly after a disaster and those that did not (Vale and Campanella 2005). We can do the same for organizations, studying whether and how leadership makes a difference in so-called high-reliability organizations (Schulman 1996). It is only after thorough study that we can make detailed suggestions to leaders (the issue is too important to get it wrong).

Getting multilevel governance to work. A resilient society requires multilevel governance: higher levels of governance must support lower levels when the latter's capacities are overburdened by the disaster. Simple as it sounds, multilevel governance often fails during a crisis or disaster. Higher levels tend to pair micromanagement with low levels of situational awareness, an approach that rarely works in times of disaster. The idea of resilience compensates for some of these weaknesses, as first responders and citizens improvise and cope (at least for a while). In a resilient system, higher levels of governance must *facilitate* rather than manage. How this can be done effectively and in a timely fashion must be further researched.

Involving the public. The first line of defense in a resilient system consists of prepared citizens. One of the greatest challenges to state and local disaster managers is preparing citizens or somehow coaxing them to prepare themselves. Even in disaster-prone areas (such as the U.S. Gulf states), people appear to have short memories: they downplay risks and expect too much of their government. Academic research has offered surprisingly little in this regard. We need to understand how practitioners can alter the risk perception of people in a cost-effective way. In addition, we need a better understanding of the role of the private sector in creating and maintaining risk awareness. This will require a multidisciplinary effort involving risk and crisis researchers, as well as public administration, communication, and marketing scholars.

Improving human-technology interfaces. A sociotechnical approach advocates the use of modern technology to facilitate rapid learning and enhance situational awareness. The development of useful technology is proceeding at an astounding pace (Baer et al. 2005). Public administrators work in an environment that is not conducive to the smooth adoption of new technologies. At least part of that has to do with a long legacy of technological promises that were never delivered. Engineers love to develop new technologies, but they do not always understand the needs of practitioners or the constraints they encounter in their work. We know of examples where the integration of technology *has* worked, but these are easily outnumbered by examples of failures. We know why technologies fail to catch on; we need research that explains why some technologies are adopted. These intertwined critical infrastructures also make up a "global socio-technical infrastructure" (GSTI)[1] that may be accessed through international cooperation and may enhance resilience before a disaster strikes.

Improving cognition and situational awareness. Resilience would be greatly improved if first responders could quickly gain a clear and accurate picture of the evolving situation. Getting such a picture remains one the biggest challenges of crisis management. The right technology and the effective operation of multilevel governance (see above) would undoubtedly help. Recent research in the field of natural decision making (Schraagen et al. 2008) and organizational culture (Weick and Sutcliffe 2001) has taught us much about the way people try to make sense of rapidly evolving situations. Yet we still lack workable knowledge that will help crisis managers understand what is going on and help them communicate. One way to gain this knowledge would be to study how media regularly seem to accomplish this difficult task.

Improving international cooperation. A broadening, deepening, and tightening of the international dimension in sociotechnical resilience is not only necessary but inevitable. The 2008–9 financial crisis is but a warning of how a paucity of foreknowledge, a lack of flexibility in recombining resources effectively when surprised, and a lack of collaborative sensemaking can disrupt the global community. Yet international institutions are ill equipped and poorly financed and lack the legitimacy to play an effective role at this point in time. Even the most developed supranational association—the European Union—is far removed from fulfilling a full-fledged role in enhancing societal resilience in its member states (Boin and

Rhinard 2008). More research is needed to explore how international institutions can lend a hand before and during a disaster.

Determining the price of resilience. The chapters in this book largely confirm the idea that resilience has somewhat of a "feel-good" aspect: everybody seems to want organizations and societies to become resilient. Yet we should question who benefits from resilience. We may hypothesize that societal elites generally would favor resilience in the wake of a disaster (as they have the most to gain from their society "bouncing back" to predisaster levels).[2] Others may want to see a different society emerge, as several of the authors in this volume imply. Moreover, we have not considered the price of designing resilience: it may well be that the opportunity costs are higher than the benefits. All this suggests that we need a better normative foundation for the resilience concept.

A Global Action Plan

The difficult task is to translate a sociotechnical approach to resilience into action, at a sufficient scale and scope that change in performance does occur. Changing behavior at local, state/provincial, national, and international levels only occurs when the underlying values of the actors shift, based on valid information and free choice (Argyris and Schön 1995). The task is to devise a program of action that engages key actors at different levels of operation in disaster-risk reduction. The full range of incentives, analytical techniques, leadership strategies' information search, exchange, and feedback processes, and well-crafted public policies will need to be organized and implemented for a long-term effort to achieve this goal.

We close this chapter, and this volume, with a set of tasks that would reinforce existing efforts to build resilience at the community level and extend this effort to communities exposed to disaster risk in states, provinces, and nations across the world. These tasks offer an opportunity for engaging the groups that can directly bring about change in the process of disaster-risk reduction. The cost is long-term commitment by responsible leaders and active researchers to build the basis for change in policy and practice (Sabatier and Smith 1993). Such a long-term effort consists of:

- Developing systematic knowledge bases of physical, engineered, and social characteristics of communities exposed to risk
- Conducting hazard assessments of risk and vulnerable populations for a given region
- Assessing a community's capacity to manage the identified risk
- Developing a strategy for mitigating the identified risk
- Developing a broad program of active engagement for citizens—for

example, volunteer activities in firefighting, first aid, and hazards and threat assessments

- Reviewing progress, reflecting on actions taken, and redesigning them to ensure continuing progress

The vision of resilient communities is clear. Newly deepening, long-linked global pathways for disease, climate disruptions, and human conflict will produce "rude surprises" with truly awful consequences (LaPorte 2007). It is only a matter of time before we experience deadly cascades that will test the resilience of modern society. It is time to position societal resilience at the center of policy making and technology development. This should happen with an eye toward helping nations that cannot survive alone.

This volume offers a way of looking and thinking—the sociotechnical approach to resilience—that nurtures flexible, knowledge-driven preparedness across all communities at risk. The approach cannot be but a first step toward necessary change. It is now up to practitioners and academics to work across traditional divides to further probe the feasibility and desirability of the paradigmatic change advocated in the pages of this volume. There is little time to lose.

NOTES

Chapter 1: Introduction

1. For an intriguing counterperspective, see Wildavsky 1988.

2. A voluminous literature exists on patterns and pitfalls of crisis management. For an overview, see Comfort 1988; Rosenthal, Charles, and t'Hart 1989; Boin 2004; Rodriguez, Quarantelli, and Dynes 2006.

3. We have made a choice to introduce a subjective dimension in order to take account of the perceptions of those within the system. If people do not perceive a disturbance as extraordinary, it does not make sense to speak of resilience. Here we follow the academic discourse on definitions of crisis (see Boin et al. 2005).

Chapter 2: Resilience

1. For an alternative view, see Brand and Jax 2007; Folke 2006; Gallopin 2006; Kaplan 2005.

2. Arguably, the following quote best captures this fascination with hardship: "A five-year-old child watched helplessly as his younger brother drowned. In the same year, glaucoma began to darken his world. His family was too poor to provide the medical help that might have saved his sight. His parents died during his teens. Eventually he found himself in a state institution for the blind. As an African American he was not permitted to access many activities within the institution, including music. Given the obstacles he faced, one would not have easily predicted that he would someday become a world renowned musician. This man's name was Ray Charles" (S. Goldstein and Brooks 2005, xiii). For criticism in psychology regarding this "Americanized" theme, see, e.g., Pendall, Foster, and Cowell 2007.

3. For a research database on the resilience concept in ecology, see Janssen 2007; Janssen et al. 2006.

4. This means that the measurement of "ecology resilience" is much more difficult if not impossible, because the only sure way to detect thresholds is to cross them (Allen, Gunderson, and Johnson 2005; Bennett, Cumming, and Peterson 2005; Carpenter, Westley, and Turner 2005).

5. This stands in sharp contrast with product optimization and stable resource production, which become increasingly vulnerable to surprise. "Ecological resilience" is therefore considered antithetical to optimization.

6. Rochlin (1991, 103) describes the vital difference: "If one has perfect knowledge, correct information, and a verified knowledge-based model that encompasses all possible variations, then one can indeed exercise 'control' over outcomes.... Management, on the other hand, involves decision-making under the acceptance of irreducible uncertainty, using heuristic models that are corrected on the fly, as necessary, as part of on-line trial and error learning."

7. This does not mean that resilience at the individual level necessarily translates into resilience at the organizational level (Riolli and Savicki 2003, 228).

8. Similarly, McDonald (2006, 173) argues that "the concept of resilience would seem to require both the capacity to anticipate and manage risks before they become serious threats to the operation, as well as being able to survive situations in which the operation is compromised."

9. See CIP 2007 for a response from the critical infrastructure protection community that considers protection and emergency management to include anticipation as well as resilience, with a focus on protection and prevention as well as mitigation and response.

10. It should be stated here that these findings closely resemble the theoretical model that Perrow (1984) drew with regard to the management of large-scale sociotechnical systems.

11. Personal communication with Todd LaPorte.

Chapter 3: Designing Adaptive Systems for Disaster Mitigation and Response

An earlier version of this paper was presented at the American Political Science Association meeting in Chicago in September 2007. This version includes additional analyses of the status data from the situation reports and a beginning analysis of the networks and subnets involved in disaster response. We warmly thank the professional staff at the Louisiana Office of Homeland Security and Emergency Preparedness for making the situation reports available to us for analysis. We also thank Thomas W. Haase for his critical review and formatting of the paper and Clayton Wukich for his thoughtful comments. This work was supported in part by National Science Foundation grant #0729456, "Decision, Risk, Uncertainty: Designing Resilience for Communities at Risk: Decision Support for Collective Action under Stress."

1. Knabb, Rhome, and Brown 2005.

2. There are no situation reports available for August 31, 2005, the second day after the storm.

Chapter 4: Lessons from the Military

1. Note that militaries themselves vary on the extent of their concern with surprise; often their surprise-reducing efforts have become opaque to themselves as tradition or as "just the way things are done." The more consciously engaged militaries are found among professionalized and/or generally experienced or expeditionary armies, generally in Westernized nations.

2. Keegan's (2003) book on intelligence in war is particularly enlightening on the topic of forecasting knowledge. As a side note, the United States did not fare much better. A colleague with a fascination for isolated islands tells a story of working during the Falklands period and voluntarily bringing his own hobby copy of a USGS topological map of the Falklands into the agency for analysis because none was otherwise available in time.

3. For more details on these failures and more in-depth analysis, see Cohen and Gooch 1990.

4. The literature on complexity is incomplete. Examples of conceptual difficulties with complexity and surprise exist even in some of the better works. For example, redundancy is either a cure for or a cause of complexity, depending on the author chosen (Landau 1969; Lanir, Fischhoff, and Johnson 1988, 100). Even Perrow (1984, 280), in an otherwise excellent book, seems to muddle the concept of complexity by linking it to loose coupling and, indirectly, to both greater and lesser redundancy. For an excellent work specifically on the development of a science of complexity, see Waldrop 1992.

5. Despite Donald Rumsfeld's assertions, there is no analytical value in the term *unknown unknowns*. His staff appears to have misinformed him, or he just got the term wrong in his statements as U.S. secretary of defense.

6. *Rogue* stands for "Rochlin's Observation of Generally Unpleasant Events," in acknowledgment of the contributions to the study of high-reliability organizations and similar military systems by Gene Rochlin, an extraordinary scholar and mentor. The term *rogue* emerged from a back-of-the-napkin conversation in Berkeley in 1985, when I sought a convenient term for these particularly negative surprises.

7. This concept was originally an adaptation of the groundbreaking empirical work of scholars Nonaka and Takeuchi (1997). These two Japanese scholars studied the use of enterprise networks in successful Japanese corporations in the early 1990s. This adaptation was made with the realization that the success of the Japanese corporations was heavily influenced by Japanese corporate culture and its presumption of consensus. Since this cultural assumption cannot be made for cultures without this deeply held value, the Atrium model is socially constructed as a colleague and integrated into the organization in ways intended to build consensus, as well as the usual provision of knowledge associated with any enterprisewide system.

8. Precise definitions of the essential elements of virtuality are difficult to find. Gibson and Gibbs (2006, 245) provide the clearest summary definition that is both cognitively researchable and intuitively appropriate: virtuality is "a multifaceted higher order construct comprising four independent defining characteristics identified in previous literature: geographic dispersion, electronic dependence, dynamic structural arrangements, and national diversity. Although they each contribute to the virtuality of the team, they are likely to have unique effects and should be considered independently."

9. These include organizations that are tightly linked, as in a single institution, and those that are loosely allied save for episodic intense joint operations, as in an emergency community.

10. Gasson (2005) suggests four stages of sense-making. These are, roughly, shared goal definition; the recognition and clarification of all participants' organizational practices and tacit assumptions; the identification of external influences; and, finally, the explicit creation of mutually useful knowledge.

11. For example, today's "avatar" (a computerized representation of a physical body) does not yet provide as much implicit body information as individuals collect instinctively in face-to-face encounters, although that fidelity is improving rapidly (Moore, Ducheneaut, and Nickell 2007).

12. Paraphrased from, and with apologies to, James Surowiecki, author of *The Wisdom of Crowds*, a book by a business economics journalist examining how large num-

bers of people independently making quantifiable choices may outperform experts in predicting ground truths (Surowiecki 2005). My rewording acknowledges Surowiecki's point that collective wisdom is out there to be collated. However, this work also incorporates the more skeptical view of both Surowiecki's expertise and his prediction methods, presented in a book review by the prominent quantum physicist M. P. Silverman (Surowiecki and Silverman 2007).

Chapter 5: Building Resilience

1. Similarly, Thomas Birkland (1997, 14) observes that without news coverage, "there is no way for a broader public to learn of an event and perhaps mobilize in response to it."

2. For example, the *Malone Farmer,* the newspaper serving the farm community of Malone, New York, reported on the earthquake one week later, on April 25, 1906.

3. For example, a 1997 study observes that policy makers' most important sources of information are usually the *New York Times* and the *Washington Post* (Birkland 1997, 33)—perhaps true at the time, but obviously not today.

4. Data provided by Alexa.com.

5. Data provided by Technorati.com.

6. See http://www.google.com/trends.

7. A Pew Research Center poll conducted on September 6–7, 2005, found that 67 percent of respondents believed President Bush could have done more in relief efforts. The federal government's performance was rated more harshly than that of state and local governments. In an Associated Press/Ipsos poll conducted on September 16–18, 2005, 70 percent of Americans said that the federal government should have been better prepared for Katrina. A Fox News/Opinion Dynamics poll conducted on September 13–14, 2005, found that 48 percent of registered voters thought that the federal government had sole or shared responsibility for post-Katrina problems. A Gallup poll conducted on September 5–6, 2005, found that 31 percent of respondents thought that President Bush and federal agencies were most responsible for post-Katrina problems; 25 percent held state and local officials most responsible.

8. Consider the technologies not yet established in 2000: Google, blogs, wiki sites, YouTube and other video-sharing Web sites, and low-cost digital photography and videography. In addition, there is the continued decline of traditional media and the rise of cable- and Web-based news.

9. Indeed, many conservative policy makers continued to doubt the wisdom of a strong federal role in emergency response even after Katrina. The Florida governor Jeb Bush, brother of the president, told Congress that "federalizing emergency response to catastrophic response would be a disaster as bad as Hurricane Katrina" (Waugh 2006, 38).

10. Consider, for example, the elaboration of internal rules and procedures on human resources or financial management or procurement, or the elaboration of information technologies, or simply the elaboration of organizational structures. Organizations that have gone through this process of development over several decades are more likely to be challenged by the task of coordination than they might have been ab initio.

11. Results of the Office of Personnel Management's 2006 Federal Human Capital Survey were released in January 2007. Of thirty-six agencies included in the survey,

DHS ranked thirty-sixth in job satisfaction, thirty-sixth in leadership, thirty-sixth in results-oriented culture, and thirty-third in talent management.

12. Reserve forces are organized within state national guards, but these may be called into service by the president without the consent of state governments.

13. While trust in the civilian component of federal government has generally declined over the last three decades, trust in the military has risen substantially (A. Roberts 2008, 114).

14. For a criticism of reliance on the language of war in the U.S. case, and a discussion of the treatment of counterterrorism efforts by the British government, see Howard 2002.

15. See Section 1076 of the National Defense Authorization Act of 2007, signed by the president in October 2006. Many governors protested about this amendment to the Insurrection Act, and Congress reversed itself the following year. The repeal was included in the 2008 Defense Authorization Act, which was signed into law on January 28, 2008.

Chapter 6: Federal Disaster Policy

1. North Carolina Disaster Recovery Task Force, available at http://www.dem.dcc .state.nc.us/taskforce/execsum.htm.

Chapter 7: Designing Resilience

I thank David Alexander for his detailed comments on this chapter.

1. In the words of Gerald Rosenthal, "no defense is inviolate" (cited in Wildavsky 1988, 11).

2. The first step in increased global crisis awareness was the looming millennium problem, which, of course, never materialized. In response to this transnational threat, Western societies combined prevention with preparatory measures. We can only guess whether the absence of the millennium problem may have nurtured a false belief in the power of prevention.

3. I am indebted to Nat Howell for this example.

Chapter 8: Rapid Adaptation to Threat

1. See http://www.the-eps.org.

2. See http://www.londonprepared.gov.uk.

3. I was present at that meeting, which was carefully stage-managed. Though it was very informative about the logistics involved in the emergency response, the atmosphere was too political and controlled for any serious discussion of the shortcomings. Moreover, the mass media were completely excluded from the debriefing. Hence the resulting document (London Resilience 2006) is rather bland. However, on pp. 17–22 it does contain a detailed rebuttal of some of the criticisms made in the London Assembly report.

4. See http://www.londonprepared.gov.uk.

Chapter 9: The Price of Resilience

1. The descriptions of the three case studies draw from previously published studies that two of the three authors of this chapter undertook with our U.S. colleagues Emery Roe and Paul Schulman (see van Eeten and Roe 2002; Schulman et al. 2004; Roe et al. 2005; de Bruijne 2006; and van Eeten et al. 2006).

Chapter 10: Planning for Catastrophe

This text was written in mid-2007, so it didn't take into account the last updates of the French government's plans.

1. The new nomenclature, which appeared in the WHO's 2005 plan, contains more details on the prepandemic phase, whereas in 1999 the division into several phases primarily concerned the pandemic itself.

2. Since 2007, a set of evolutions occurred in the French plan, but also in its numerous technical information sheets and with the actions of the interministerial delegation on avian flu. The questions addressed below are taken into greater account or at least more directly formulated, but they are still relevant, and many problems are long-lasting.

Chapter 11: The Limits of Self-Reliance

The authors would like to thank Åsa Fritzon and Cecilia Mobach, both of the Swedish Institute of International Affairs, for valuable research assistance with this chapter. We are also grateful for comments received from Arjen Boin, Chris Demchak, two anonymous reviewers, and the participants in a workshop on the resilience concept held at Leiden University, Netherlands, on June 8–9, 2007.

1. In addition, the multilevel, federal character of the U.S. government reveals the essential jurisdictional questions and highlights one central question: Who in the U.S. government acts on behalf of the country in disaster situations? What is the role of the federal level versus the constituent states? This same question is being asked in other regions of the world where disaster cooperation is on the rise, including the European Union, which faces these questions as the issue of "solidarity" during extreme events presents itself. The findings of this study can thus also help us to improve our understanding of international cooperation on disaster management questions in other parts of the world.

2. Winham (1979) took a similar tack, arguing that the classical distinction in bureaucratic theory between policy formulation (by low organizational levels) and policy negotiation and execution (by executive elites) could not be applied when analyzing empirical cases of U.S.-USSR subgovernmental relations. He wrote (1979, 129) that we are now in an era where "the essential task of foreign policy is being defined as reducing uncertainty in the international system, and where the responsibility for managing the increasing complexity of external relations seems to have fallen to the working level of government" (see also Nelkin 1979).

3. It should be said that cooperation does not always have beneficial effects. Cooperation does not mean the absence of discord, as international relations scholars are keen to point out. On the contrary, cooperation is part of the management of discord in the international environment. If actors' intentions were harmonious, there would be no need for cooperation. Management scholars and transaction-cost economists have found that cooperation can be used in adverse ways, encouraging bullying, conformity, and collusion against others. With those caveats in mind, we nevertheless focus on the pursuit of a common goal by different states and cooperation as an advantageous way to reach this goal.

4. In such cases, cooperation with entities outside the social system will be necessary. Transatlantic cooperation during the Cold War is illustrative of the point: European societies lacked many of the capacities that might be required to adapt and

recover from a Soviet attack. In anticipation, elaborate cooperation procedures were put in place to bolster European capacities before, during, and after an attack. Hurricane Katrina offers another example, in reverse. European governments aimed to assist the United States at a time when it seemingly lacked its own capacities to recover from the effects of the storm. In both cases, government agencies tried to reach across borders in order to build capacity in each others' systems. Effective cooperation thus became a key part of resilience.

5. Keohane and Nye (1974, 43) encouraged scholars to study "transgovermental relations" as a new field in international relations, defined as "sets of interactions among sub-units of different governments that are not controlled or closely guided by the policies of the cabinets or chief executives of those governments." Reflecting a more general turn away from interstate relations (controlled by national executives), the authors spawned a great deal of research focused on the bureaucratic contacts taking place below the apex of organizational hierarchy (see also Karvonen and Sundelius 1990).

6. This has been evident in relationships among close allies, such as the United States and Canada, or among the countries in the British Commonwealth (Holsti 1971). Even in states that are politically distant, regular patterns of interaction can lead to policy coordination among bureaucracies. A good example here is the relationship between U.S. and Soviet space officials, who were engaged in technical talks on cooperation in the 1970s that went well beyond what high-ranking security officials on both sides had authorized. When crises in the space programs broke out, these relationships helped to cool tensions (Keohane and Nye 1974).

7. A wide variety of studies have identified epistemic communities at work in the international policy environment. For an overview, see P. Haas 1997.

8. See the NATO situation reports compiled at http://www.nato.int/eadrcc/2005/katrina/.

9. See the December 2004 National Response Plan (NRP) at http://www.iir.com/GLOBAL/FusionCenter/NRP/baseplan.pdf for more information. The "International Coordination Support Annex" of that document provides a brief, and rather vague, set of protocols for dealing with foreign governments. The NRP was updated in May 2006 to revise those protocols in light of lessons learned from Katrina.

10. For more information on private donations pledged during Hurricane Katrina, see Richard 2006a.

11. For more information on the participation of the International Red Cross in the Hurricane Katrina response, see "International Red Cross Deploys More Than 80 Experts to Hurricane Katrina Response," press release, September 3, 2005, at http://www.ifrc.org/docs/News/pr05/50005.asp?05/05EA015.pdf.

Chapter 12: International Disaster Resilience

I would like to thank Louise K. Comfort, of the Graduate School of Public and International Affairs, University of Pittsburgh, for her support and guidance during earlier drafts of this chapter. Furthermore, without her patience and persistence, I would never have been introduced to the field of public administration and international disaster management. I also thank Gunes Ertan, Leonard Huggins, Namkyung Oh, and Clayton Wukich, my colleagues at the Center for Disaster Management, the Graduate School of Public and International Affairs, University of Pittsburgh, for their support. This research was supported in part by National Science Foundation grant #0729456, "Decision, Risk, and Uncertainty Program: Designing Resilience for Communities at Risk: Decision Support for Collective Action under Stress."

1. Given the size and scope of the event, it is unreasonable to assume that any country could ever have been adequately prepared.

2. The three questions were investigated using a mixed-method research design. The *unit of analysis* is the organizations that participated in the "Indonesian tsunami response system," and the *unit of observation* is the "interorganizational interactions" exchanged among response organizations. Data were collected and analyzed through the content analysis and coding of *Jakarta Post* articles from December 26, 2004, through January 17, 2005. To identify and evaluate the network structure of the Indonesian response system, the articles were parsed to identify organizations involved in the tsunami response, as well as relevant activities and interactions. Organizations were coded by name, date, and order of entry; level of jurisdiction (international, national, provincial, or municipal); and source of funding (public, private, or nonprofit). Interorganizational interactions were coded according to the organization that initiated the interaction, the organization(s) that received the interaction, and the nature of the transaction. These data were then converted into a series of relational matrices, which represent the series of interactions detected between response organizations during the period under analysis. The network analysis software Ora was then used to analyze the size, number of interactions, density, betweenness centrality, and number of distinct components that were present in the system over time (Carley 2009).

3. It should be noted that two other exploratory datasets, one for Thailand in 2004 and one for Katrina in 2005, had similar patterns; the response systems reached 80 percent capacity within the first two weeks.

4. A social network's density is the number of edges in a graph, expressed as a proportion of the maximum possible number of organizations (Scott 2001, 71).

5. Betweenness measures the extent to which a node lies between other connected nodes in a network (Freeman 1979).

6. A component is defined as a set of nodes that are linked to one another through continuous changes of connections (Scott 2005, 102).

Chapter 13: Designing Resilient Systems

1. This research is funded by the U.S. National Science Foundation, grant #0729456, "Decision, Risk, and Uncertainty Program: Designing Resilience for Communities at Risk: Improving Decision Making to Support Collective Action under Stress," National Science Foundation, September 1, 2007–August 31, 2010. L. K. Comfort, Principal Investigator, T. Znati and D. Mosse, Co-Principal Investigators. H. Ling, T. W. Haase, and A. Zagorecki, Graduate Student Researchers, University of Pittsburgh, Pittsburgh, PA.

2. These stages include: *early stage detection of risk, emerging risk, rapid onset and response,* and *rescue and recovery.*

3. In reality, UWSN is mostly deployed in three-dimensional spaces. However, for simplicity, the proposed approach is presented in two-dimensional space. The proposed scheme can be easily extended from two-dimensional space to three-dimensional space with a straightforward modification.

Chapter 14: Resilience Revisited

1. Current work by Demchak and Gaycken explores the 2008 financial crisis and the rippling effects of hackers and cyberwar, studying these examples of nasty surprises moving across borders, through a world densely and structurally interwoven through an increasingly coupled underlying infrastructure, the GSTI.

2. We thank Todd R. LaPorte for this insight.

REFERENCES

Ackroyd, P. 2000. *London: The biography*. London: Vintage.

Adler, E., and M. N. Barnett, eds. 1998. *Security communities*. Cambridge: Cambridge University Press.

Adler, E., and P. M. Haas. 1992. Conclusion: Epistemic communities, world order, and the creation of a reflective research program. *International Organization* 46: 367–90.

Agranoff, R. 2006. Inside collaborative networks: Ten lessons for public managers. *Public Administration Review* 66: 56–65.

———. 2007. *Managing within networks: Adding value to public organizations*. Washington, DC: Georgetown University Press.

Aguirre, B. E. 2006. *On the concept of resilience*. Newark: Disaster Research Center, University of Delaware.

Akyildiz, I. F., D. Pompili, and T. Melodia. 2005. Underwater acoustic sensor networks: Research challenges. *Ad Hoc Networks* 3: 257–79. Available at http://www.ece.rutgers.edu/~pompili/paper/Akyildiz_AdHoc05.pdf.

Alesch, D. J., and W. J. Petak. 1986. *The politics and economics of earthquake hazard mitigation*. Boulder: Institute of Behavioral Sciences, University of Colorado.

Alexander, D. 2002. From civil defence to civil protection—and back again. *Disaster Prevention and Management* 11 (3): 209–13.

———. 2006. Globalization of disaster: Trends, problems and dilemmas. (Capstone essay). *Journal of International Affairs* 59 (2): 1 (22).

Allbaugh, J. M. 2001. Testimony before the Veterans Affairs, Housing and Urban Development and Independent Agencies Subcommittee of the Senate Appropriations Committee. May 16.

Allen, C., L. Gunderson, and A. R. Johnson. 2005. The use of discontinuities and functional groups to assess relative resilience in complex systems. *Ecosystems* 8 (8): 958–66.

Alterman, E. 1998. *Who speaks for America? Why democracy matters in foreign policy*. Ithaca: Cornell University Press.

Amalberti, R. 1996. *La conduite des systèmes à risques*. Paris: PUF.

———. 2002. Revisiting safety and human factors paradigms to meet the safety challenges of ultra complex and safe systems. In *System safety: Challenges and pitfalls of interventions*, ed. B. Willpert and B. Falhbruch. Amsterdam: Elsevier. 265–76.

———. 2006. Optimum system safety and optimum system resilience: Agonist or antagonist concepts? In Hollnagel, Woods, and Leveson 2006, 253–74.

Argyle, M. 1991. *Cooperation: The basis of sociability.* London: Routledge.

Argyris, C., and D. A. Schön. 1996. *Organizational learning II: A theory of action perspective.* Reading, MA: Addison-Wesley.

Arsenault, D., and A. Sood. 2007. Resilience: A systems design imperative. Available at http://cs.gmu/edu/~asood/scit/CIPP%20Resilience%20Series%20Sood%20Arsenault.pdf.

ASEAN (Association of Southeast Asian Nations). 2005. Agreement on disaster management and emergency response. Available at http://www.aseansec.org/17579.htm.

Axelrod, R. 1984. *The evolution of cooperation.* New York: Basic Books.

Axelrod, R., and M. D. Cohen. 1999. Harnessing complexity: Organizational implications of a scientific frontier. New York: Free Press.

Babington, D., and A. Cinelli. 2009. Italy seeks survivors, prepares to bury quake dead. April 8. Reuters Foundation. Available at http://www.reliefweb.int/rw/rwb.nsf/ db900sid/SNAA-7QW4PV?OpenDocument&rc=4&cc=ita.

Baer, M., K. Heron, O. Morton, and E. Ratliff. 2005. *Safe: The race to protect ourselves in a newly dangerous world.* New York: HarperCollins.

Baker, C. 2001. Lack of commercials cost television networks about $500 million. *Washington Times,* September 19.

Baker, E. J. 1993. Coastal development invites hurricane damage. *USA Today Magazine* 121 (2576): 68–70.

Barry, J. 2005. The prologue, and maybe the coda. *New York Times,* September 4.

Baton Rouge Advocate. 2005. Frustration boils; Mayor Nagin, Blanco irate about delays. *Baton Rouge Advocate,* September 2.

Baumgartner, F. R., and B. D. Jones. 1993. *Agendas and instability in American politics.* Chicago: University of Chicago Press.

Beer, M., R. Eisenstat, and B. A. Spector. 1990. *The critical path to corporate renewal.* Cambridge, MA: Harvard Business School Press.

Bennett, E. M., G. S. Cumming, and G. D. Peterson. 2005. A systems model approach to determining resilience surrogates for case studies. *Ecosystems* 8 (8): 945–57.

Berkes, F. 2007. Understanding uncertainty and reducing vulnerability: Lessons from resilience thinking. *Natural Hazards* 41 (2): 283–95.

Berkes, F., J. Colding, and C. Folke. 2003a. Introduction. In Berkes, Colding, and Folke 2003b, 1–30.

———, eds. 2003b. *Navigating social-ecological systems: Building resilience for complexity and change.* Cambridge: Cambridge University Press.

Bernard, E. N., H. O. Mofjeld, V. V. Titov, C. E. Synolakis, and F. I. González. 2006. *Tsunami: Scientific frontiers, mitigation, forecasting, and policy implications.* Philosophical transactions of the Royal Society. Series A., Mathematical, physical, and engineering sciences. 364(1845), doi: 10.1098/rsta.2006.1809, 1989–2007.

Bernstein, R. 2005. Europe's response: An odd mixture. *International Herald Tribune,* September 14.

Bier, V. 2006. Hurricane Katrina as a bureaucratic nightmare. In Daniels, Kettl, and Kunreuther 2006, 243–54.

Birkland, T. A. 1997. *After disaster: Agenda setting, public policy, and focusing events.* Washington, DC: Georgetown University Press.

———. 2006. *Lessons of disaster: Policy change after catastrophic events.* Washington, DC: Georgetown University Press.

Birkland, T. A., R. J. Burby, D. Conrad, H. Cortner, and W. K. Michener. 2003. River ecology and flood hazard mitigation. *Natural Hazards Review* 4 (1): 46–54.

Block, R. 2005. U.S. had plan for crisis like Katrina. *Wall Street Journal,* September 19.

Blum, J. 2005. Chavez pushes petro-diplomacy. *Washington Post,* November 22.

Boin, A. 2004. Lessons from crisis research. *International Studies Review* 6 (1): 165–74.

———. 2005. From crisis to disaster: Toward an integrative perspective. In Quarantelli and Perry 2005, 153–72.

Boin, A., M. Ekengren, and M. Rhinard. 2006. *Functional security and crisis management capacity in the European Union: Setting the research agenda.* Report commissioned by the Swedish Emergency Management Agency. Stockholm: Swedish National Defence College.

Boin A., P. Lagadec, E. Michel-Kerjan, and W. Overdijk. 2003. Critical infrastructures under threat: Learning from the anthrax scare. *Journal of Contingencies and Crisis Management* 11: 99–104(6).

Boin, A., and A. McConnell. 2007. Preparing for critical infrastructure breakdowns: The limits of crisis management and the need for resilience. *Journal of Contingencies and Crisis Management* 15: 50–59.

Boin, A., and M. Rhinard. 2008. Managing transboundary crises: What role for the European Union? *International Studies Review* 10 (1): 1–26.

Boin, A., and D. Smith. 2006. Terrorism and critical infrastructures: Implications for public-private crisis management. *Public Money and Management* 26 (5): 295–304.

Boin, A., E. Stern, P. t'Hart, and B. Sundelius. 2005. *The politics of crisis management: Public leadership under pressure.* Cambridge: Cambridge University Press.

Boin, A., A. McConnell, and P. t'Hart, eds. 2008. *Governing after crisis: The politics of investigation, accountability and policy change.* Cambridge: Cambridge University Press.

Boin, A., and M. J. G. van Eeten. 2007. Veerkracht: Nieuw wondermiddel voor het openbaar bestuur? [Resilience: New magic potion for public administration?] *Bestuurskunde* 16 (2): 73–81.

Bolling, R., Y. Ehrlin, R. Forsberg, A. Rüter, V. Soest, T. Vikström, P. Örtenwall, and H. Brändström, eds. 2007. KAMEDO Report 90: Terrorist attacks in Madrid, Spain, 2004. *Prehospital and Disaster Medicine* 22 (3): 252–56.

Bonanno, G. A. 2004. Loss, trauma, and human resilience. *American Psychologist* 59 (1): 20–28.

Bosher, L., P. Carrillo, A. Dainty, J. Glass, and A. Price. 2007. Realizing a resilient and sustainable built environment: Towards a strategic agenda for the United Kingdom. *Disasters* 31 (3): 236–55.

Bowman, A., and G. Krause. 2003. Measuring policy centralization in U.S. intergovernmental relations. *American Politics Research* 31 (3): 301–25.

Bowman, K. 2006. Public opinion on taxes. April 12. Washington, DC: American Enterprise Institute.

Brand, F. S., and K. Jax. 2007. Focusing the meaning(s) of resilience: Resilience as a descriptive concept and a boundary object. *Ecology and Society* 12 (1): 23–38.

Brecher, M. 1979. *Studies in crisis behavior.* New Brunswick: Transaction Publishers.

Brinkley, A. 2003. A familiar story: Lessons from past assaults on freedoms. In *The war on our freedoms,* ed. R. C. Leone. New York: Public Affairs. 23–46.

Brinkley, D. 2006. *The great deluge.* New York: William Morrow.

Brinkley, J., and C. S. Smith. 2005. U.S. unprepared to receive foreign aid. *International Herald Tribune,* September 9.

Brookings Institution. 2005. *New Orleans after the storm: Lessons from the past, a plan for the future.* Special analysis. October. Washington, DC: Brookings Institution.

Bruneau, M., and K. Tierney. 2006. Resilience: Defining and measuring what matters. Paper presented at the Multidisciplinary Center for Earthquake Engineering Research Annual Meeting, June 28, Arlington, VA.

Buck, D. A., J. E. Trainor, and B. E. Aguirre. 2006. A critical evaluation of the Incident Command System and NIMS. *Journal of Homeland Security and Emergency Management* 3 (3).

Buckle, P. 2006. Assessing social resilience. In Paton and Johnston 2006, 201–404.

Bulmer, Simon J. 1998. New institutionalism and the governance of the single European market. *Journal of European Public Policy* 5 (3): 365–86.

Bunderson, J. S., and K. M. Sutcliffe. 2002. Comparing alternative conceptualizations of functional diversity in management teams: Process and performance effects. *Academy of Management Journal* 45 (5): 875–93.

Burby, R. J. 1994. Floodplain planning and management: Research needed for the twenty-first century. *Water Resources Update* 97: 44–47.

———. 2005. Have state comprehensive planning mandates reduced insured losses from natural disasters? *Natural Hazards Review* 6 (2): 67–81.

———. 2006. Hurricane Katrina and the paradoxes of government disaster policy: Bringing about wise governmental decisions for hazardous areas. *ANNALS of the American Academy of Political and Social Science* 604: 171–91.

Burby, R. J., T. Beatley, P. R. Berke, R. E. Deyle, S. P. French, D. Godschalk, E. J. Kaiser, J. D. Kartez, P. J. May, R. Olshansky, R. G. Paterson, and R. H. Platt. 1999. Unleashing the power of planning to create disaster-resistant communities. *Journal of the American Planning Association* 65 (3): 247–58.

Burby, R. J., and L. C. Dalton. 1994. Plans can matter! The role of land use plans and state planning mandates in limiting the development of hazardous areas. *Public Administration Review* 54: 229–38.

Burby, R. J., S. P. French, and A. C. Nelson. 1998. Plans, code enforcement, and damage reduction: Evidence from the Northridge earthquake. *Earthquake Spectra* 14 (1): 59–74.

Burby, R. J., and P. J. May. 1996. *Making governments plan: State experiments in managing land use.* With P. Berke, L. Dalton, S. French, and E. Kaiser. Baltimore: Johns Hopkins University Press.

———. 1998. Intergovernmental environmental planning: Addressing the commitment conundrum. *Journal of Environmental Planning and Management* 41 (1): 95–111.

Burke, R. J. 2005. Effects of 9/11 on individuals and organizations: Down but not out! *Disaster Prevention and Management* 14 (5): 629–38.

Burt, R. 1992. *Structural holes: The social structure of competition.* Cambridge, MA: Harvard University Press.

Busenberg, G. J. 2001. Learning in organizations and public policy. *Journal of Public Policy* 21 (2): 173–89.

Bynander, F., L. Newlove, and B. Ramberg. 2005. *Sida and the tsunami of 2004: A study of organizational crisis response.* Stockholm: Crismart.

Callicott, J. B., L. Crowder, and K. Mumford. 1999. Current normative concepts in conservation. *Conservation Biology* 13 (1): 22–35.

Carley, K. M. 2002. Computational organizational science and organizational engineering. *Simulation Modeling Practice and Theory* 10 (5–7): 253–69.

———. 2009. Ora: Organizational Risk Analyzer. Version 1.8.6. Copyright © 2001–2009. Center for Computational Analysis of Social and Organizational Systems (CASOS), Carnegie Mellon University. Available at http://www.casos.cs.cmu.edu.

Carley, S., K. Mackway-Jones, and S. Donnan. 1998. Major incidents in Britain over the past twenty-eight years: The case for the centralised reporting of major incidents. *Journal of Epidemiology and Community Health* 52: 392–98.

Carpenter, S., B. Walker, J. M. Anderies, and N. Abel. 2001. From metaphor to measurement: Resilience of what to what? *Ecosystems* 4 (8): 765–81.

Carpenter, S., F. Westley, and M. Turner. 2005. Surrogates for resilience of social-ecological systems. *Ecosystem* 8 (8): 941–44.

Carrington, P. J., J. Scott, and S. Wasserman. 2005. *Models and methods in social network analysis.* New York: Cambridge University Press.

Carroll, J. S. 1998. Organizational learning activities in high-hazard industries: The logics underlying self-analysis. *Journal of Management Studies* 35 (6): 699–717.

Casti, J. L. 1994. *Complexification: Explaining a paradoxical world through the science of surprise.* New York: Abacus.

CDC (Centers for Disease Control and Prevention). 2006. CDC fy 2006 and fy 2007 budget fact sheet. March 31. Atlanta: Centers for Disease Control and Prevention.

Chandrasekhar, V., and W. K. G. Seah. 2006. Localization scheme for underwater sensor networks—survey and challenges. In *Proceedings of the IEEE OCEANS Asia Pacific Conference,* May, Singapore. Available at http://wuwnet.engr.uconn.edu/papers/p033-chandrasekhar.pdf.

Chang, K., D. Lewis, and N. McCarty. 2001. *The tenure of political appointees.* Madison: University of Wisconsin.

Chateauraynaud, F., and D. Torny. 1999. *Les sombres précurseurs. Une sociologie pragmatique de l'alerte et du risque.* Paris: Editions de l'EHESS.

Cho, S., L. Mathiassen, and D. Robey. 2006. Dialectics of resilience: A multi-level analysis of a telehealth innovation. *Journal of Information Technology* 22 (1): 24–35.

CIP (Critical Infrastructure Protection Program). 2007. *Critical thinking: Moving from infrastructure protection to infrastructure resilience.* Arlington: George Mason University.

Clarke, L. 1999. *Mission improbable: Using fantasy documents to tame disaster.* Chicago: University of Chicago Press.

———. 2006. *Worst cases: Terror and catastrophe in the popular imagination.* Chicago: University of Chicago Press.

CNN.com. 2005a. Lt. Gen. Honore a "John Wayne dude." September 3. Available at http://www.cnn.com/2005/US/09/02/honore.profile/.

———. 2005b. Transcript: Anderson Cooper 360 Degrees. September 1. Available at http://transcripts.cnn.com/TRANSCRIPTS/0509/01/acd.01.html.

―――. 2005c. Transcript: CNN Live Saturday. September 10. Available at http://transcripts.cnn.com/TRANSCRIPTS/0509/10/cst.11.html.

Coakes, E., D. Willis, and S. Clark, eds. 2002. *Knowledge management in the sociotechnical world: The graffiti continues.* London: Springer-Verlag.

Coakes, E., D. Willis, and R. Lloyd-Jones. 2000. *The new socio-tech: Graffiti on the long wall.* London: Springer-Verlag.

Cohen, D. 1998. Amateur government. *Journal of Public Administration Research and Theory* 8 (4): 450–97.

Cohen, E. A., and J. Gooch. 1990. *Military misfortunes: The anatomy of failure in war.* New York: Free Press.

Comfort, L. K., ed. 1988. *Managing disaster: Strategies and policy perspectives.* Durham: Duke University Press.

―――. 1994a. Risk and resilience: Inter-organizational learning following the Northridge earthquake of 17 January 1994. *Journal of Contingencies and Crisis Management* 2: 157–70.

―――. 1994b. Self organization in complex systems. *Journal of Public Administration Research and Theory* 4 (3): 393–410.

―――. 1999. *Shared risk: Complex systems in seismic response.* New York: Pergamon.

―――. 2002. Rethinking security: Organizational fragility in extreme events. *Public Administration Review* 62: 98–107.

―――. 2005. Risk, security and disaster management. *Annual Review of Political Science* 8: 335–56.

―――. 2006a. Cities at risk: Hurricane Katrina and the drowning of New Orleans. *Urban Affairs Review* 41 (4): 501–16.

―――. 2006b. Communication, coherence, and collective action: The impact of Hurricane Katrina on communications infrastructure. *Public Works Management and Policy* 11 (1): 1–16.

―――. 2007a. Asymmetric information processes in extreme events: The December 26, 2004 Sumatran earthquake and tsunami. In *Communicable crises: Prevention, response, and recovery in the global arena,* ed. D. E. Gibbons. Charlotte, NC: Information Age Publishing, Inc. 135–65

―――. 2007b. Crisis management in hindsight: Cognition, communication, coordination, and control. *Public Administration Review,* special issue, *Administrative Failure in the Wake of Katrina:* S188–96.

Comfort, L. K., M. Dunn, D. Johnson, R. Skertich, and A. Zagorecki. 2004. Coordination in complex systems: Increasing efficiency in disaster mitigation and response. *International Journal of Emergency Management* 2 (1–2): 62–80.

Comfort, L. K., and T. W. Haase. 2007. The role of cognition in disaster response. Paper presented at the Academy of Management Conference: Symposium on Complex Organizational Decision-Making and Large-Scale Crisis Management under Risk, August 6–8, Philadelphia.

Comfort, L. K., D. Mosse, and T. Znati. 2009. Managing risk in real time: Integrating information technology into disaster risk reduction and response. *Commonwealth: A Journal of Political Science* 15: 27–46.

Comfort, L. K., Y. Sungu, D. Johnson, and M. Dunn. 2001. Complex systems in crisis: Anticipation and resilience in dynamic environments. *Journal of Contingencies and Crisis Management* 9: 144–58.

Commoner, B. 1979. *The politics of energy.* New York: Knopf.

Congressional Budget Office. 2005. *The long-term budget outlook.* December. Washington, DC: Congressional Budget Office.

Contractor, F. J., and P. Lorange. 1988. *Cooperative strategies in international business.* Lexington: Heath.

Cook, R. I., and D. D. Woods. 1994. Operating at the sharp end: The complexity of human error. In *Human error in medicine,* ed. M. S. Bogner. Hillsdale: Lawrence Erlbaum. 255–310.

Cooke, A. 2006. *American home front, 1941–1942.* New York: Grove/Atlantic.

Cooper, C., and R. Block. 2006. *Disaster: Hurricane Katrina and the failure of homeland security.* New York: Henry Holt.

Coovert, M. D., and L. F. Thompson. 2001. *Computer supported cooperative work: Issues and implications for workers, organizations and human resource management.* Thousand Oaks, CA: Sage Publications.

Coutu, D. L. 2002. How resilience works. In *Harvard Business Review on building personal and organizational resilience.* Boston: Harvard Business School Press. 1–18.

Cox, G. W., and K. A. Shepsle. 2007. Majority cycling and agenda manipulation: Richard McKelvey's contributions and legacy. In *A positive change in political science: The legacy of Richard McKelvey's most influential writings,* ed. J. A. Aldrich, J. E. Alt, and A. Lupia. Ann Arbor: University of Michigan Press. 19–40.

CREW (Citizens for Responsibility and Ethics in Washington). 2007. CREW's Hurricane Katrina international offers of assistance matrix. July 27. Available at http://www.citizensforethics.org/files/Katrina%20Matrix.pdf.

Crossan, M., M. P. E. Cunha, D. Vera, and J. Cunha. 2005. Time and organizational improvisation. *Academy of Management Review* 30: 129–45.

Crupi, A. 2005. Cable News Nets, Weather Channel earn stunning ratings for Katrina coverage. *MediaWeek,* August 31.

Csete, M., and J. Doyle. 2004. Bow ties, metabolism and disease. *Trends in Biotechnology* 22 (9): 446–50.

Curtis, W. J., and D. Cicchetti. 2003. Moving research on resilience into the twenty-first century: Theoretical and methodological considerations in examining the biological contributors to resilience. *Development and Psychopathology* 15 (3): 773–810.

Cutter, S. L., and C. T. Emrich. 2006. Moral hazard, social catastrophe: The changing face of vulnerability along the hurricane coasts. *ANNALS of the American Academy of Political and Social Science* 604: 102–12.

D'Agostino, D. M., and M. Williams. 2006. Policies and procedures are needed to ensure appropriate use of and accountability for international assistance. Testimony before the Committee on Governance Reform, U.S. House of Representatives. U.S. Government Accountability Office (GAO) Report, GAO-06-600T. Available at http://www.gao.gov/cgi-bin/getrpt?GAO-06-600T.

Daniels, R. J., D. F. Kettl, and H. Kunreuther, eds. 2006. *On risk and disaster: Lessons from Hurricane Katrina.* Philadelphia: University of Pennsylvania Press.

Davidson-Hunt, I. J., and F. Berkes. 2003. Nature and society through the lens of resilience: Toward a human-in-ecosystem perspective. In Berkes, Colding, and Folke 2003b, 53–82.

Dean, C. 1996. Is it worth it to rebuild a beach? Panel's answer is a tentative yes. *New York Times,* April 2.

de Bruijne, M. 2006. *Networked reliability, institutional fragmentation and the reliability of service provision in critical infrastructures.* Delft: Delft University of Technology.

———. 2007. Networked reliability: From monitoring to incident management. In *Proceedings of the Fourth International Conference on Information Systems for Crisis Response and Management,* ed. B. v. d. Walle, P. Burghardt, and K. Nieuwenhuis. Brussels: VUB Press.

de Bruijne, M., and M. J. G. van Eeten. 2007. Systems that should have failed: Critical infrastructure protection in an institutionally fragmented environment. *Journal of Contingencies and Crisis Management* 15: 18–29.

de Bruijne, M. L. C., M. J. G. van Eeten, E. M. Roe, and P. Schulman. 2006. Assuring high reliability of service provision in critical infrastructures. *Journal of Critical Infrastructures* 2 (2–3): 231–46.

Demchak, C. C. 1991. *Military organizations, complex machines: Modernization in the U.S. armed services.* Ithaca: Cornell University Press.

———. 2006a. Embracing surprise in resilient complex critical infrastructures: Rapid crisis response lessons from military organizations and the Atrium model. Paper presented at SEMA/ECMA Conference on "Future Challenges for Crisis Management in Europe," Stockholm, Sweden, May 4–5, 2006.

———. 2006b. Noticing unknowns in self-surprising systems. Paper presented at Managing Extreme Events: Transatlantic Perspectives, March 2–4, 2006, Pittsburgh.

Demchak, C. C., and E. Werner. 2007. Exploring the knowledge nexus. *Security Studies Quarterly* 1 (2): 58–97.

Denby, K. 2008. Burma cyclone: Up to 50,000 dead and millions homeless, but still no call for aid. *Times Online,* May 7. Available at http://www.timesonline.co.uk/tol/news/world/asia/article3883123.ece.

DePalma, R. G., D. G. Burris, H. R. Champion, and M. J. Hodgson. 2005. Blast injuries. *New England Journal of Medicine* 352 (13): 1335–42.

Devitt, K., and P. Burroughs. 2007. Planning to help…helping to heal. *Blueprint (UK Emergency Planning Society Magazine)* 48: 22–23.

DeYoung, K. 2006. A fight against terrorism—and disorganization. *Washington Post,* August 9.

DHS (Department of Homeland Security). 2004a. National response plan. December. Washington, DC: Department of Homeland Security.

———. 2004b. Review of the status of Department of Homeland Security efforts to address its major management challenges. March. Washington, DC: Office of the Inspector General.

———. 2005a. Major management challenges facing the Department of Homeland Security. December. Washington, DC: Office of the Inspector General.

———. 2005b. Transcript of press conference with acting secretary of homeland security Admiral James Loy on the fy 2006 budget. February 7. Washington, DC: Department of Homeland Security.

Dinmore, G. 2007. U.S. spy chief quits post to join Rice. *Financial Times,* January 5.

Dirckinck-Holmfeld, L., and K. E. Sorensen. 1999. Distributed computer supported collaborative learning through shared practice and social participation. In Hoadley and Roschelle 1999, article 15.

Dizard, W. P. 2005. Who's at home for DHS. April 18. Available at http://www.gcn.com/print/24_8/35527-1.html.

Drabek, T. E. 1985. Managing the emergency response. *Public Administration Review* 45: 85–92.

Drake, W. J., and K. Nicolaidis. 1992. Ideas, interests, and institutionalization: Trade in services and the Uruguay round. *International Organization* 46: 37–100.

Draper, T. 1991. *A very thin line: The Iran-Contra affairs.* New York: Hill and Wang.

Dunkelberger, L. 2005. Building code sparks debate; Hurricane-prone counties may need higher standards for wind protection; panhandle exemption. *Ledger,* August 8.

Dynes, R. R. 2005. The Lisbon earthquake of 1755: The first modern disaster. In *The Lisbon earthquake of 1755: Representation and reactions,* ed. T. E. D. Braun and J. B. Radner. Oxford: Voltaire Foundation. 34–50.

Eckstein, H. 1975. Case study and theory in political science. In *Handbook of political science,* ed. F. Greenstein and N. W. Polsby. Reading, MA: Addison-Wesley. 79–137.

———. 1992. *Regarding politics: Essays on political theory, stability, and change.* Berkeley: University of California Press.

Edmondson, A. C. 2003. Speaking up in the operating room: How team leaders promote learning in interdisciplinary action teams. *Journal of Management Studies* 40 (6): 1419–52.

Edmonson, R. G. 2005. DHS releases national response plan. *Journal of Commerce Online,* January 6.

Ervin, C. K. 2006. *Open target: Where America is vulnerable to attack.* New York: Palgrave Macmillan.

European Commission. 2005. Progress report on the European Commission's response to the Indian Ocean tsunami of 26 December 2004 and reinforcing EU disaster and crisis response in third world countries. November 18. 1P/05/1444. Brussels: EU Commission Progress Report.

Executive Office of the President. 2001. Statement by the president in his address to the nation. September 11. Washington, DC: Office of the Press Secretary.

———. 2005a. President discusses hurricane relief in address to the nation. September 15. Washington, DC: Executive Office of the President.

———. 2005b. President's remarks during hurricane briefing in Texas. September 25. Washington, DC: Executive Office of the President.

Fang L., W. Du, and P. Ning. 2005. A beacon-less location discovery scheme for wireless sensor networks. In *Proceedings of IEEE INFOCOM,* March, Miami. Available at: http://www.cis.syr.edu/~wedu/Research/paper/beaconless_infocom05.pdf.

Farber, D. A., R. G. Bea, K. Roberts, E. Wenk, and K. Inkabi. 2007. Reinventing flood control. *Tulane Law Review* 81 (4): 1085–1127.

FEMA (Federal Emergency Management Agency). 2004. National response plan. Washington, DC: Federal Emergency Management Agency.

———. 2005a. Help after a disaster: Applicant's guide to the Individuals and Households Program. Washington, DC: Federal Emergency Management Agency.

———. 2005b. National incident management system. Washington, DC: Federal Emergency Management Agency.

Field, E. H., K. R. Milner, and the 2007 Working Group on California Earthquake Probabilities. 2007. Forecasting California's earthquakes—what can we expect in

the next thirty years? United States Geological Survey. Available at http://pubs
.usgs.gov/fs/2008/3027/fs2008-3027.pdf.

Fiksel, J. 2003. Designing resilient, sustainable systems. *Environmental Science and
Technology* 37 (23): 5330–39.

Fisher, D. 2007. Law and legal issues in international disaster response: A desk study.
International Federation of Red Cross and Red Crescent Societies.

Fleischer, A. 2005. *Taking heat: The president, the press, and my years in the White
House.* New York: William Morrow.

Flin, R. 2006. Erosion of managerial resilience: From Vasa to NASA. In Hollnagel,
Woods, and Leveson 2006, 223–34.

Florida Department of Community Affairs. 1995. Summary of state and local emergency management capabilities. Tallahassee: Florida Department of Community
Affairs.

Floridi, L. 2007. A look into the future impact of ICT on our lives. *Information Society*
23 (1): 59–64.

Flynn, S. 2005. *America the vulnerable.* New York: Harper Perennial.

———. 2007. *The edge of disaster: Rebuilding a resilient nation.* New York: Random
House.

Foer, F. 2005. The mole: The case against Anderson Cooper. *New Republic,* September 26, 9.

Folke, C. 2006. Resilience: The emergence of a perspective for social-ecological systems analyses. *Global Environmental Change* 16 (3): 253–67.

Folke, C., J. Colding, and F. Berkes. 2003. Synthesis: Building resilience and adaptive capacity in social-ecological systems. In Berkes, Colding, and Folke 2003b,
352–86.

Fox, A. B. 1977. *The politics of attraction: Four middle powers and the United Sates.* New
York: Colombia University Press.

Freeman, L. C. 1979. Centrality in social networks: Conceptual clarification. *Social
Networks* 1: 215–39.

Freitag, R. 2001. The impact of project impact on the Nisqually earthquake. *Natural Hazards Observer* 25 (5). Available at http://www.colorado.edu/hazards/o/ar-
chives/2001/may01/may01a.html #nisqually.

Friedkin, N. E. 1981. The development of structure in random networks: An analysis
of the effects of increasing network density on five measures of structure. *Social
Networks* 3: 41–52.

Friedman, T. L. 2005. *The world is flat.* New York: Farrar, Straus, and Giroux.

Fritz, C. E. 1968. Disasters. In *International encyclopedie of the social sciences,* ed.
P. L. Sills. New York: Collier-MacMillan. 3: 202–7.

Fudenberg, D., and J. Tirole. 1993. *Game theory.* Cambridge, MA: MIT Press.

Gabriel, R. A. 1985. *Military incompetence: Why the American military doesn't win.* New
York: Hill and Wang.

Galbraith, J. R. 1977. *Organization design.* Reading, MA: Addison-Wesley.

Gallopin, G. C. 2006. Linkages between vulnerability, resilience, and adaptive capacity. *Global Environmental Change* 16 (3): 293–303.

GAO (General Accounting Office). 1996. Disaster assistance: Improvements needed
in determining eligibility for public assistance. April 30. Washington, DC: General Accounting Office.

————. 1998. Disaster assistance: Information on federal costs and approaches for reducing them. March 26. Washington, DC: General Accounting Office.

————. 2004. Aviation security: Challenges exist in stabilizing and enhancing passenger and baggage screening operations. February 12. Washington, DC: General Accounting Office.

————. 2006a. Aviation security: Enhancements made in passenger and checked baggage screening. April 4. Washington, DC: Government Accountability Office.

————. 2006b. Hurricane Katrina, report to the congressional committees. Washington, DC: Government Accountability Office.

————. 2006c. Hurricane Katrina: Preliminary observations regarding preparedness, response and recovery. March 8. Washington, DC: Government Accountability Office.

Garrett, T., and R. Sobel. 2003. The political economy of FEMA disaster payments. *Economic Inquiry* 41 (3): 496–509.

Gasson, S. 2005. The dynamics of sensemaking, knowledge, and expertise in collaborative, boundary-spanning design. *Journal of Computer-Mediated Communication* 10 (4).

Gell-Mann, M. 1994. *The quark and the jaguar: Adventures in the simple and the complex.* New York: W. H. Freeman and Company.

Gerber, B. J. 2007. Disaster management in the United States: Examining key political and policy challenges. *Policy Studies Journal* 35 (2): 227–38.

German Embassy. 2005. Fact sheet—Germany responds quickly with assistance to U.S. in aftermath of Hurricane Katrina. Washington, DC: German Embassy to the United States of America. Available at http://www.germany.info.

Gertz, B. 2006. Intelligence intransigence. *Washington Times,* February 6.

Geschwind, C. H. 2001. *California earthquakes: Science, risk, and the politics of hazard mitigation.* Baltimore: Johns Hopkins University Press.

Gibbons, R. 1992. *A primer in game theory.* Hemel Hempstead: Harvester-Wheatsheaf.

Gibson, C. B., and J. L. Gibbs. 2006. Unpacking the concept of virtuality: The effects of geographic dispersion, electronic dependence. *Administrative Science Quarterly* 51: 451–95.

Gibson, J., ed. 1999. *The mobile communications handbook.* New York: IEEE Press.

Gilbert, C. 2002. From one crisis to the other: The shift of research interests in France. *Journal of Contingencies and Crisis Management* 10: 192–202.

————. 2007a. *Les crises sanitaires de grande ampleur: Un nouveau défi?* Paris: La Documentation Française, INHES.

————. 2007b. Crisis analysis: Between normalization and avoidance. *Journal of Risk Research* 10 (7): 925–40.

Gilbert, C., and E. Henry. 2006. Divergences or complementarity within the research into crises in France? *International Journal of Emergency Management* 3 (1): 5–11.

Gilbert, E. 2007. Leaky borders and solid citizens: Governing security, prosperity and quality of life in a North American partnership. *Antipode* 39 (1): 77–98.

Gittell, J. H., K. Cameron, and S. G. P. Lim. 2005. Relationships, layoffs, and organizational resilience: Airline industry responses to September 11. *Journal of Applied Behavioral Science* 42 (3): 300–329.

Glantz, M. D., and J. L. Johnson, eds. 1999. *Resilience and development: Positive life adaptations.* New York: Kluwer Academic/Plenum Publishers.

Glantz, M. D., and Z. Sloboda. 1999. Analysis and reconceptualization of resilience. In Glantz and Johnson 1999, 109–26.

Gleick, J. 1987. *Chaos: Making a new science.* New York: Penguin Books.

Godschalk, D. R. 2003. Urban hazard mitigation: Creating resilient cities. *Natural Hazards Review* 4 (3): 136–43.

Goffman, E. 1974. *Frame analysis: An essay on the organization of experience.* New York: Harper and Row.

Goggin, M. L., A. M. Bowman, J. P. Lester, and L. J. O'Toole. 1990. *Implementation theory and practice: Toward a third generation.* Glenview, IL: Scott Foresman/Little Brown.

Goldsmith, S., and W. D. Eggers. 2004. *Governing by network: The new shape of the public sector.* Washington, DC: Brookings Institution.

Goldstein, J., and R. O. Keohane, eds. 1993. *Ideas and foreign policy: Beliefs, institutions, and political change.* Ithaca: Cornell University Press.

Goldstein, S., and R. B. Brooks, eds. 2005. *Handbook of resilience in children.* New York: Springer.

Goodin, R. E., ed. 1996. *The theory of institutional design.* Cambridge: Cambridge University Press.

Goodman, P. S., L. S. Sproull, and Associates. 1990. *Technology and organizations.* San Francisco: Jossey-Bass Publishers.

Gordon, M. R., and B. E. Trainor. 2006. *Cobra II: The inside story of the invasion and occupation of Iraq.* New York: Pantheon Books.

Gosselin, P., and J. Hook. 2005. A comeback for big government. *Los Angeles Times,* September 10.

Governor's Disaster Planning and Response Review Committee. 1993. Report of the Governor's Disaster Planning and Response Review Committee. Tallahassee: Governor's Disaster Planning and Response Review Committee, State of Florida.

Grabowski, M. R., and K. H. Roberts. 1999. Risk mitigation in virtual organizations. *Organization Science* 10 (6): 704–21.

Greenley, G. E., and M. Oktemgil. 1998. A comparison of slack resources in high and low performing British companies. *Journal of Management Studies* 35 (3): 377–98.

Gunderson, L. H. 2003. Adaptive dancing: Interactions between social resilience and ecological crises. In Berkes, Colding, and Folke 2003b, 33–52.

Gunderson, L. H., and C. S. Holling, eds. 2002. *Panarchy: Understanding transformations in human and natural systems.* Washington, DC: Island Press.

Gunderson, L. H., C. S. Holling, L. Pritchard, and G. D. Peterson. 2002. Resilience. In *Encyclopedia of global environmental change,* ed. T. Munn. New York: Wiley. 530–31.

Haas, E. B. 1990. *When knowledge is power: Three models of change in international organizations.* Studies in International Political Economy 22. Berkeley: University of California Press.

Haas, P. 1990. *Saving the Mediterranean.* New York: Columbia University Press.

———. 1992. Introduction: Epistemic communities and international policy coordination. *International Organization* 46: 1–35.

———, ed. 1997. *Knowledge, power and international policy co-ordination.* Columbia: University of South Carolina Press.

Hale, A., and T. Heijer. 2006. Defining resilience. In Hollnagel, Woods, and Leveson 2006, 35–40.

Hall, P. A., and R. C. R. Taylor. 1996. Political science and the three new institutionalisms. *Political Studies* 44 (5): 936–57.

Hamel, G., and L. Välikangas. 2003. The quest for resilience. *Harvard Business Review,* September, 1–13.

Hamilton, L. 2003. Testimony before the Select Committee on Homeland Security. September 9. Washington, DC: Wilson International Center for Scholars.

Handmer, J., and S. R. Dovers. 1996. A typology of resilience: Rethinking institutions for sustainable development. *Organization Environment* 9 (4): 482–511.

Hargrove, E. C., and J. C. Glidewell, eds. 1990. *Impossible jobs in public management.* Lawrence: Kansas University Press.

Haythornthwaite, C. 2005. Introduction: Computer-mediated collaborative practices. *Journal of Computer-Mediated Communication* 10 (4).

He, T., C. Huang, B. M. Blum, J. A. Stankovic, and T. Abdelzaher. 2003. Range-free localization schemes for large scale sensor networks. In *MobiCom '03: Proceedings of the ninth annual International Conference on Mobile Computing and Networking.* New York: ACM Press. Available at http://www.cs.virginia.edu/~th7c/paper/APIT_CS-2003-06.pdf.

Heclo, H. 1977. *A government of strangers: Executive politics in Washington.* Washington, DC: Brookings Institution Press.

———. 1978. Issue networks and the executive establishment. In *The new American political system,* ed. A. King. Washington, DC: American Enterprise Institute. 232–51.

———. 1993. Ideas, interests, and institutions. In *The dynamics of American politics: Approaches and interpretations,* ed. L. C. Dodd and C. Jillson. Boulder: Westview Press. 366–94.

Heidemann J., W. Ye, J. Wills, A. Syed, and Y. Li. 2006. Research challenges and applications for underwater sensor networking. In *Proceedings of the IEEE Wireless Communications and Networking Conference,* April, Las Vegas. Available at http://www.isi.edu/~johnh/PAPERS/Heidemann06a.pdf.

Henry, E. 2007. *Amiante: Un scandale improbable. Archéologie d'un problème public.* Rennes: PUR.

Hermann, E., J. Call, M. V. Hernández-Lloreda, B. Hare, and M. Tomasello. 2007. Humans have evolved specialized skills of social cognition: The cultural intelligence hypothesis. *Science* 317: 1360–66.

Hermitte, M. A. 1996. *Le sang et le droit: Essai sur la transfusion sanguine.* Paris: Seuil.

Hill, A. 2000. Revisiting institutional resilience as a tool in crisis management. *Journal of Crisis and Contingencies Management* 8 (2): 109–18.

Hills, A. E. 1994. Co-ordination and disaster response in the United Kingdom. *Disaster Prevention and Management* 3 (1): 66–71.

HM Government. 2004. Civil Contingencies Act 2004, chapter 36. London: Stationery Office.

———. 2006a. Government response to the Intelligence and Security Committee's report into the London terrorist attacks on 7 July 2005. London: Stationery Office.

———. 2006b. Intelligence and Security Committee report into the London terrorist attacks on 7 July 2005 (Cm 6785). London: Stationery Office.

———. 2006c. Report of the official account of the bombings in London on 7th July 2005 (HC 1087). London: Stationery Office.

Hoadley, C. M., and J. Roschelle, eds. 1999. *Proceedings of the 1999 Conference on Computer Support for Collaborative Learning*. Palo Alto, CA: Stanford University.

Hofmann-Wellenhof, B., H. Lichtenegger, and J. Collins. 1997. *Global positioning system: Theory and practice*. 4th ed. New York: Springer-Verlag.

Hofstadter, D. R. 1999. *Godel, Escher, Bach: An eternal braid*. 1980. New York: Basic Books.

Holland, J. H. 1995. *Hidden order: How adaptation builds complexity*. Reading, MA: Addison-Wesley.

Holling, C. S. 1973. Resilience and stability of ecological systems. *Annual Review of Ecology and Systematics* 4 (1): 1–23.

———. 1996. Engineering resilience vs. ecological resilience. In *Engineering within ecological constraints*, ed. P. C. Schulze. Washington, DC: National Academy Press.

Hollnagel, E., D. D. Woods, and N. Leveson, eds. 2006. *Resilience engineering: Concepts and precepts*. Aldershot: Ashgate Publishing Limited.

Holsti, K. J. 1971. *The United States and Canada: In conflict in world politics*. Ed. S. Spiegel and K. Waltz. Cambridge, MA: Winthrop.

Holsti, K. J., and T. A. Levy. 1974. Bilateral institutions and transgovernmental relations between Canada and the United States. *International Organization* 28: 875–901.

Homeland Security Advisory Council. 2003. Summary of inaugural meeting. June 30. Washington, DC: Department of Homeland Security.

———. 2007. Report of the Culture Task Force. January. Washington, DC: Homeland Security Advisory Council.

Homer-Dixon, T. 2001. *The ingenuity gap*. London: Vintage.

Horlick-Jones, T. 1995. Modern disasters as outrage and betrayal. *International Journal of Mass Emergencies and Disasters* 13 (3): 305–15.

Hoschka, P. 1996. *Computers as assistants: A new generation of support systems*. Mahwah, NJ: Lawrence Erlbaum Associates.

Howard, M. 2002. What's in a name? How to fight terrorism. *Foreign Affairs* 81 (1): 8.

Hsu, S. 2005. Leaders lacking disaster experience; "Brain drain" at agency cited. *Washington Post*, September 9.

Hutchins, E. 1995. *Cognition in the wild*. Cambridge, MA: MIT Press.

Ikenberry, G. J. 1992. A world economy restored: Expert consensus and the Anglo-American postwar settlement. *International Organization* 46: 289–321.

International Federation of Red Cross and Red Crescent Societies. 2009a. Italy: Earthquake DREF operation no. MDRIT001 update no. 1. April 15. Available at http://www.reliefweb.int/rw/rwb.nsf/db900sid/PSLG-7QXG8K?OpenDocument.

———. 2009b. Italy: Sheltering the homeless of Abruzzo an urgent challenge. April 7. Available at http://www.reliefweb.int/rw/rwb.nsf/db900sid/EDIS-7QVKCX?OpenDocument.

———. 2009c. Italy's worst quake in nearly thirty years strikes city of L'Aquila. April 6. Available at http://www.reliefweb.int/rw/rwb.nsf/db900sid/PSLG7QUH8X?OpenDocument.

IMF (International Monetary Fund). 2006. Public information notice: IMF concludes 2006 Article IV consultation with the United States. July 28. Washington, DC: International Monetary Fund.

IOC (Intergovernmental Oceanographic Commission). 2005. Intergovernmental Coordination Group for the Indian Ocean tsunami warning and mitigation system. Resolution IOC-XXIII-12. IOC Assembly, 23rd Session, June 21–30.

ISO. 2001. Second annual report on market issues and performance, April 1999–December 2000. Folsom, CA.

ISO Properties. 2005. What? Why? When? And what do I do? Available at http://www.isomitigation.com/bcegs/0000/bcegs0002.html.

Jacelon, C. S. 1997. The trait and process of resilience. *Journal of Advanced Nursing* 25 (1): 123–29.

Jacobs, N. 2002. Co-term network analysis as a means of describing the information landscapes of knowledge communities across sectors. *Journal of Documentation* 58 (5): 548–62.

Janis, I. L. 1989. Crucial decisions: Leadership in policymaking and crisis management. New York: Free Press.

Janssen, M. A. 2007. An update on the scholarly networks on resilience, vulnerability, and adaptation within the human dimensions of global environmental change. *Ecology and Society* 12 (2): 9–26.

Janssen, M. A., M. L. Schoon, W. Ke, and K. Borner. 2006. Scholarly networks on resilience, vulnerability and adaptation within the human dimensions of global environmental change. *Global Environmental Change* 16 (3): 240–52.

Jay, C., M. Glencross, and R. Hubbold. 2007. Modeling the effects of delayed haptic and visual feedback in a collaborative virtual environment. *ACM Transactions on Computer-Human Interaction* 14 (2).

Jeggle, T. 2001. The evolution of disaster reduction as an international strategy: Policy implications for the future. In Rosenthal, Boin, and Comfort 2001b, 316–41.

Jervis, R. 1988. Realism, game theory, and cooperation. *World Politics* 40: 317–49.

———. 1997. System effects: Complexity in social and political life. Princeton: Princeton University Press.

Ji, X., and H. Zha. 2004. Sensor positioning in wireless ad-hoc sensor networks using multidimensional scaling. In *Proceedings of INFOCOM 2004*, March. Available at http://www.ieee-infocom.org/2004/Papers/55_2.PDF.

Johnson, D. E. 2002. *Preparing potential senior army leaders for the future.* Santa Monica: Rand Corporation.

Johnson, D. L. 2006. Service assessment. Hurricane Katrina, August 23–31, 2005. June. Silver Spring, MD: Department of Commerce, National Oceanic and Atmospheric Administration, National Weather Service.

Johnson, J. 1998. Citizens inspire flood program participation. *American City and County* 113 (13): 24.

Jones, D. K. C. 2001. Anticipating the risks posed by natural perils. In *Accident and design: Contemporary debates in risk management,* ed. C. Hood and D. K. C. Jones. London: Routledge, 2001. 14–30.

Jullien, F. 1996. *Traité de l'efficacité.* Paris: Grasset.

Kam, E. 1988. *Surprise attack: The victim's perspective.* Cambridge, MA: Harvard University Press.

Kaplan, H. 2005. Understanding the concept of resilience. In Goldstein and Brooks 2005, 39–47.

Kastens, G. *Building a beehive: Observations on the transition to network-centric operations.* Newport, RI: Strategic Research Department, Naval War College, U.S. Navy.

Kaufman, W., and O. H. Pilkey. 1983a. *The beaches are moving: The drowning of America's shoreline*. Durham, NC: Duke University Press.

———. 1983b. *The beaches are moving: The drowning of America's shoreline: With a new epilogue, living with the shore*. Durham, NC: Duke University Press.

Keegan, J. 2003. *Intelligence in war: Knowledge of the enemy from Napoleon to Al-Qaeda*. London: Hutchinson.

Kendra, J. M., and T. Wachtendorf. 2003. Elements of resilience after the World Trade Center disaster: Reconstituting New York City's emergency operations centre. *Disasters* 27 (1): 37–53.

———. 2006. Community innovation and disasters. In Rodríguez, Quarantelli, and Dynes 2003, 316–44.

Keohane, R. O. 1984. *After hegemony: Cooperation and discord in the world political economy*. Princeton: Princeton University Press.

Keohane, R. O., and J. S. Nye. 1974. Transgovernmental relations and international organizations. *World Politics* 27: 39–62.

Kettl, D. 2004. System under stress: Homeland security and American politics. Washington, DC: CQ Press.

———. 2006. Is the worst to come? *ANNALS of the American Academy of Political and Social Science* 604: 273–87.

Klein, K. R., and N. E. Nagel. 2007. Mass medical evacuation: Hurricane Katrina and nursing experiences at the New Orleans airport. *Disaster Management and Response* 5 (2): 56–61.

Klein, R., K. Nichols, and F. Thomalla. 2003. Resilience to natural hazards: How useful is this concept? *Environmental Hazards* 5 (1–2): 35–45.

Kluger, Y., K. Peleg, L. Daniel-Aharonson, and A. Mayo. 2004. The special injury pattern in terrorist bombings. *Journal of the American College of Surgeons* 199 (6): 875–87.

Knabb, R., J. Rhome, and D. Brown. 2005. Tropical cyclone report, Hurricane Katrina, August 23–30, 2005. December 20. National Hurricane Center.

Korvonen, L., and B. Sundelius. 1990. Interdependence and foreign policy management in Sweden and Finland. *International Studies Quarterly* 34 (2): 211–27.

Kosar, K. 2005. Disaster response and appointment of a recovery czar: The executive branch's response to the flood of 1927. October 25. Washington, DC: Congressional Research Service.

Kovach, B., and T. Rosenstiel. 1999. *Warp speed: America in the age of mixed media*. New York: Century Foundation Press.

———. 2001. *The elements of journalism: What newspeople should know and the public should expect*. New York: Crown Publishers.

Kreijns, K., P. A. Kirschner, and W. Jochems. 2003. Identifying the pitfalls for social interaction in computer-supported collaborative learning environments: A review of the research. *Computers in Human Behavior* 19 (3): 335–53.

Krieger, J. L. 2005. Shared mindfulness in cockpit crisis situations: An exploratory analysis. *Journal of Business Communication* 42 (2): 135–67.

Kwon, Y. M., K. Mechitov, S. Sundresh, W. Kim, and G. Agha. 2005. Resilient localization or sensor networks in outdoor environments. In *Proceedings of the twenty-fifth IEEE International Conference on Distributed Computing Systems (ICDCS)*, June 6–10, Columbus, OH. Available at http://osl.cs.uiuc.edu/docs/tr2449/tr2449.pdf.

Lagadec, P. 2000. *Ruptures créatrices*. Paris: Editions d'Organisation.

Lagadec, P., and H. Laroche. 2005. *Retour sur les Rapports d'Enquête et d'Expertise Suite à la Canicule de l'été 2003*. Cahiers du GIS Risques Collectifs et Situations de Crise no. 4. CNRS—Maison des Sciences de l'Homme-Alpes, 274 pp.

Landau, M. 1969. Redundancy, rationality, and the problem of duplication and overlap. *Public Administration Review* 29: 346–58.

Lanir, Z., B. Fischhoff, and S. Johnson. 1988. Military risk-taking: C3I and the cognitive functions of boldness in war. *Journal of Strategic Studies* 11 (1): 96–114.

LaPorte, T. M. 1999. Contingencies and communications in cyberspace: The World Wide Web and non-hierarchical co-ordination. *Journal of Contingencies and Crisis Management* 7: 215–24.

LaPorte, T. R., ed. 1975. *Organized social complexity: Challenge to politics and policy*. Princeton: Princeton University Press.

———. 1996. High reliability organizations: Unlikely, demanding, and at risk. *Journal of Contingencies and Crisis Management* 4: 60–71.

———. 2007. Critical infrastructure in the face of a predatory future: Preparing for untoward surprise. *Journal of Contingencies and Crisis Management* 15: 60–64.

LaPorte, T. R., and P. M. Consolini. 1991. Working in practice but not in theory: Theoretical challenges of "high-reliability organizations." *Journal of Public Administration Research and Theory* 1 (1): 19–47.

LaPorte, T. R., and G. I. Rochlin. 1994. A rejoinder to Perrow. *Journal of Contingencies and Crisis Management* 2: 221–27.

Lasswell, H. D. 1958. *Politics: Who gets what, when, how*. New York: Meridian Books.

Leavitt, M. 2005. Releasing the HHS proposed budget for fy 2006. February 7. Washington, DC: Department of Health and Human Services.

Le Guen, J. M., and J-P Door. 2006a. *Le H5N1: Une menace durable pour la santé animale. Rapport fait au nom de la Mission d'Information sur la Grippe Aviaire*. Mesures préventives, tome 2 (no. 2883). Paris: Assemblée Nationale.

———. 2006b. *Menace de pandémie grippale: Préparer les moyens médicaux. Rapport fait au nom de la Mission d'Information sur la Grippe Aviaire*. Mesures préventives, tome 1 (no. 2833). Paris: Assemblée Nationale.

———. 2006c. *Plan pandémie: Une stratégie de gestion de crise. Rapport fait au nom de la Mission d'Information sur la Grippe Aviaire*. Mesures Préventives, tome 3 (no. 2833). Paris: Assemblée Nationale.

Leibovici, D., O. N. Gofrit, N. Stein, S. C. Shapira, Y. Noga, R. J. Heruti, and J. Shemer. 1996. Blast injuries: Bus versus open-air bombings. A comparative study of injuries in survivors of open-air versus confined-space explosions. *Journal of Trauma: Injury Infection and Critical Care* 41 (6): 1030–35.

Leith, W. S., L. S. Gee, and C. R. Hutt. 2009. U.S. Geological Survey Global Seismographic Network—five-year plan 2006–2010. U.S. Geological Survey Open-File report 2009-2013, 27 pp. Available at http://pubs.usgs.gov/of/2009/1013/.

Leonard, H. B., and A. M. Howitt. 2006. Katrina as prelude: Preparing for and responding to Katrina-class disturbances in the United States. *Journal of Homeland Security and Emergency Management* 3 (2): 2–20.

Levinthal, D., and C. Rerup. 2006. Crossing an apparent chasm: Bridging mindful and less-mindful perspectives on organizational learning. *Organization Science* 17 (4): 502–13.

Levy, J. 1994. Learning and foreign policy: Sweeping a conceptual minefield. *International Organization* 48: 279–312.

Liarokapis, F. 2006. An exploration from virtual to augmented reality gaming. *Simulation and Gaming* 37 (4): 507.

Light, P. C. 1995. *Thickening government: Federal hierarchy and the diffusion of accountability.* Washington, DC: Brookings Institution.

Lipton, E. 2006a. Former antiterror officials find industry pays better. *New York Times*, June 18.

———. 2006b. Homeland Security Inc. *New York Times*, June 19.

Lipton, E., C. Drew, S. Shane, and D. Rohde. 2005. Breakdowns marked path from hurricane to anarchy. *New York Times*, September 11.

London Assembly. 2006. *Report of the 7 July Review Committee.* London: Greater London Assembly. Available at http://www.london.gov.uk/assembly/reports/7july/report.pdf.

London First. 2005. *Secure in the knowledge: Building a secure business.* London: National Counter Terrorism Security Office.

London Resilience. 2005a. *London mass fatality plan.* London: Government Office for London.

———. 2005b. *Strategic emergency plan, version 2.1.* London: Government Office for London.

———. 2006. *Looking back, moving forward: The multi-agency debrief: Lessons identified and progress since the terrorist events of 7 July 2005.* London: London Regional Resilience Forum, Government Office for London.

———. 2007. *London strategic emergency plan.* London: London Regional Resilience Forum, Government Office for London.

Longstaff, P. H. 2005. Security, resilience and communication in unpredictable environments such as terrorism, natural disasters and complex technology. Program on Information Resources Policy, Center for Information Policy Research, Harvard University. Available at http://www.pirp.harvard.edu.

Los Angeles Times. 2005. Put to Katrina's test. *Los Angeles Times*, September 11.

Louisiana Office of Homeland Security and Emergency Preparedness. 2005. Situation reports. Baton Rouge: Louisiana Office of Homeland Security and Emergency Preparedness.

Lowenthal, M. 2006. *Intelligence: From secrets to policy.* Washington, DC: CQ Press.

Luthar, S. S., ed. 2007. *Resilience and vulnerability: Adaptation in the context of childhood adversities.* 2nd ed. Cambridge: Cambridge University Press.

Luthar, S. S., and D. Cicchetti. 2000. The construct of resilience: Implications for interventions and social policies. *Development and Psychopathology* 12 (4): 857–85.

Luthar, S. S., D. Cicchetti, and B. Becker. 2000. The construct of resilience: A critical evaluation and guidelines for future work. *Child Development* 71 (3): 543–62.

Luthar, S. S., and G. Cushing. 1999. Measurement issues in the empirical study of resilience. In Glantz and Johnson 1999, 129–60.

Luthar, S. S., J. A. Sawyer, and P. J. Brown. 2006. Conceptual issues in studies of resilience: Past, present, and future research. *Annals of the New York Academy of Sciences* 1094 (1): 105–15.

Maguire, B., and P. Hogan. 2007. Disasters and communities: Understanding social resilience. *Australian Journal of Emergency Management* 22 (2): 16–20.

Malhotra, N., M. Krasniewski, C. Yang, S. Bagchi, and W. Chappell. 2005. Location estimation in ad-hoc networks with directional antennas. In *Proceedings of the twenty-fifth IEEE International Conference on Distributed Computing Systems (ICDCS)*, June 6–10, Columbus, OH. Available at http://cobweb.ecn.purdue.edu/~dcsl/publications/papers/2005/localization_icdcs05_cameraready.pdf.

Malhotra, Y. 2002. Is knowledge management really an oxymoron? Unraveling the role of organizational controls in knowledge management. In *Knowledge mapping and management*, ed. D. White. New York: IDG. 1–13.

Mallak, L. A. 1999. Toward a theory of organizational resilience. Paper presented at the Portland International Conference on Management of Engineering and Technology, 1999 (PICMET '99), Technology and Innovation Management, July 25–29, Portland. 1–25.

Mann, T. E., and N. J. Ornstein. 2006. *The broken branch: How Congress is failing America*. New York: Oxford University Press.

Manyena, S. B. 2006. The concept of resilience revisited. *Disasters* 30 (4): 434–50.

Mason, B. 2006. *Community disaster resilience: A summary of the March 20, 2006, workshop of the Disasters Roundtable*. Washington, DC: National Research Council.

Masten, A. S., and J. Obradovic. 2006. Competence and resilience in development. *Annals of the New York Academy of Sciences* 1094 (1): 13–27.

Masten, A. S., and J. L. Powell. 2007. A resilience framework for research, policy, and practice. In Luthar 2007, 155–80.

Mateo, L. 2006. The calm before the storm: Texas soldiers prepare for hurricane rescues. *U.S. National Guard News*, August 16. Available at http://www.ngb.army.mil/news/archives/2006/08/081606-TX_hurr_prep.aspx.

May, P. J. 1990. Reconsidering policy design: Policies and publics. *Journal of Public Policy* 11 (2): 187–206.

———. 1992. Policy learning and failure. *Journal of Public Policy* 12 (4): 331–54.

———. 1993. Mandate design and implementation: Enhancing implementation efforts and shaping regulatory styles. *Journal of Policy Analysis and Management* 10 (2): 634–63.

———. 1994. Analyzing mandate design: State mandates governing hazard-prone areas. *Publius* 24 (2): 1–16.

———. 1995. Can cooperation be mandated? Implementing intergovernmental environmental management in New South Wales and New Zealand. *Publius* 25 (1): 89–113.

May, P. J., and T. A. Birkland. 1994. Earthquake risk reduction: An examination of local regulatory efforts. *Environmental Management* 18 (6): 923–39.

McConnell, A., and L. Drennan. 2006. Mission impossible? Planning and preparing for crisis. *Journal of Contingencies and Crisis Management* 14: 59–70.

McCormack, S. 2005. Daily press briefings. U.S. Department of State, Washington DC, September 7.

McDonald, N. 2006. Organisational resilience and industrial risk. In Hollnagel, Woods, and Leveson 2006, 155–80.

MCEER. 2006. MCEER's resilience framework. Buffalo: MCEER, University at Buffalo, State University of New York.

McEntire, D. A. 2001. Triggering agents, vulnerabilities and disaster reduction: Towards a holistic paradigm. *Disaster Prevention and Management* 10 (3): 189–96.

McEntire, D. A., C. Fuller, C. W. Johnston, and R. Weber. 2002. A comparison of disaster paradigms: The search for a holistic policy guide. *Public Administration Review* 62: 267–81.

McFadden, R. 2005. Bush pledges more troops as the evacuation grows. *New York Times*, September 4.

McLuhan, M., and Q. Fiore. 1967. *The medium is the message*. New York: Random House.

Mendonça, D., G. E. G. Beroggi, and W. A. Wallace. 2001. Decision support for improvisation during emergency response operations. *International Journal of Emergency Management* 1 (1): 30–38.

Mensah-Bonsu, C., and S. Oren. 2001. *California electricity market crisis: Causes, remedies and prevention*. Folsom: CAISO.

Merton, R. K. 1936. The unanticipated consequences of purposive social action. *American Sociological Review* 1 (6): 894–904.

Miller, C. J., A. J. Higgins, A. A. Archer, C. S. Fletcher, T. Ton, and R. R. J. MacAllister. 2007. Meta-organizational resilience: Emerging thoughts on the resilience of complex agricultural value chains. In *Building and sustaining resilience in complex organizations: Pre-proceedings of the first International Workshop on Complexity and Organizational Resilience*, ed. R. Kay and K. A. Richardson. Mansfield: ISCE. 65–84.

Miller, G. 1967. The magical number seven, plus or minus two: Some limits on our capacity for processing information. In *Psychology of communication*. New York: Basic Books. 14–44.

Milner, H. 1992. International theories of cooperation amongst nations. *World Politics* 44: 466–96.

Ministère de la Santé. 2005. Plan de lutte contre une pandémie grippale. Ministère de la Santé, France.

Mintz, J. 2005. Infighting blamed for reducing effectiveness. *Washington Post*, February 2.

Missiroli, A., ed. 2005. Disasters, diseases, disruptions: A new d-drive for the European Union. Chaillot paper no. 83. Paris: Institute for Security Studies.

———. 2006. Disasters past and present: Challenges for the EU. *Journal of European Integration* 28 (5): 423–36.

Mitchell, N. J., K. G. Herron, H. C. Jenkins-Smith, and G. D. Whitten. 2007. Elite beliefs, epistemic communities and the Atlantic divide: Scientists' nuclear policy preferences in the United States and European Union. *British Journal of Political Science* 37 (4): 753–64.

Mittler, E. 1997. A case study of Florida's emergency management since Hurricane Andrew. Natural Hazards Research Working Paper no. 98. Boulder: Natural Hazard Research and Applications Information Center, University of Colorado.

Modic, J. 2003. Fire simulation in road tunnels. *Tunnelling and Underground Space Technology* 18 (5): 535–30.

Moore, D., J. Leonard, D. Rus, and S. Teller. 2004. Robust distributed network localization with noisy range measurements. In *Proceedings of the second ACM Conference on Embedded Networked Sensor Systems (SenSys '04)*, November, Baltimore. Available at http://rvsn.csail.mit.edu/netloc/sensys04.pdf.

Moore, R. J., N. Ducheneaut, and E. Nickell. 2007. Doing virtually nothing: Awareness and accountability in massively multiplayer online worlds. *Computer Supported Cooperative Work (CSCW)* 16 (3): 265–305.

Mühlenbrock, M., and U. Hoppe. 1999. Computer supported interaction analysis of group problem solving. In Hoadley and Roschelle 1999, article 50.

National Commission on Terrorist Attacks upon the United States. 2004. Final report. New York: Barnes and Noble Books.

National Coordinating Board for Disaster Managment and Internally Displaced People Affairs. 2004. Indonesia: National information. *United Nations: International strategy for disaster reduction* 35.

National Research Council. 2001. *The Internet's coming of age.* Washington, DC: National Academy Press, Computer Science and Telecommunications Board.

Neilson, G. L., and B. A. Pasternack. 2005. *Results: Keep what's good, fix what's wrong, and unlock great performance.* New York: Crown Business.

Nelkin, D. 1979. Scientific knowledge, public policy and democracy. *Knowledge: Creation, Diffusion, Utilization* 1: 106–22.

Nelson, M. 1982. A short, ironic history of American national bureaucracy. *Journal of Politics* 44 (3): 747–78.

Newman, M., A-L. Barabasi, and D. J. Watts. 2006. *The structure and dynamics of networks.* Princeton: Princeton University Press.

News and Observer. 2007. Grants go to clean up water, hog lagoons. *News and Observer,* October 22. Available at http://www.newsobserver.com/news/story/745784.html.

New York Times. 1900a. Anxiety in St. Louis. *New York Times,* September 10.

———. 1900b. Galveston may be wiped out by storm. *New York Times,* September 9.

———. 1906. Congress gives aid to stricken cities. *New York Times,* April 19.

Niculescu, D., and B. Nath 2001. Ad hoc positioning system (APS). In *Proceedings of IEEE Global Communications Conference (GLOBECOM),* November 25–29, San Antonio. Available at http://www.cs.rutgers.edu/dataman/papers/aps-globecomm.pdf.

———. 2003a. Ad hoc positioning system (APS): Using AoA. In *Proceedings of INFOCOM 2003,* San Francisco, April 1–3. Available at: http://www.comsoc.org/confs/ieee-infocom/2003/papers/42_04.PDF.

———. 2003b. DV based positioning in ad hoc networks. *Telecommunication Systems* 22: 267–80.

NOAA (National Oceanic and Atmospheric Administration). 1972. *A study of earthquake losses in the San Francisco Bay area.* Washington, DC: National Oceanic and Atmospheric Administration.

Nonaka, I., and H. Takeuchi. 1997. A new organizational structure (hyper-text organization). In *Knowledge in organizations,* ed. L. Prusak. Boston: Butterworth-Heinemann. 99–134.

North, D. C. 1990. *Institutions, institutional change and economic performance.* Cambridge: Cambridge University Press.

O'Brien, G., P. O'Keefe, J. Rose, and B. Wisner. 2006. Climate change and disaster management. *Disasters* 30 (1): 64–80.

O'Brien, G., and P. Read. 2005. Future UK emergency management: New wine, old skin? *Disaster Prevention and Management* 14 (3): 353–61.

OECD (Organization for Economic Cooperation and Development). 2003. Emerging risks in the twenty-first century: An agenda for action. Paris: Organization for Economic Cooperation and Development.

Olsson, C. A., L. Bond, J. M. Burns, D. A. Vella-Brodrick, and S. M. Sawyer. 2003. Adolescent resilience: A concept analysis. *Journal of Adolescence* 26 (1): 1–11.

Olsson, P., C. Folke, and F. Berkes. 2004. Adaptive comanagement for building resilience in social-ecological systems. *Environmental Management* 34 (1): 75–90.

Ornstein, N., and T. Mann. 2003. Perspectives on House reform of homeland security. May 19. Washington, DC: American Enterprise Institute.

O'Rourke, T. D. 2007. Critical infrastructure, interdependencies, and resilience. *Bridge* 37 (1): 22–30.

O'Toole, L. J., Jr., and K. J. Meier. 2004. Public management in intergovernmental networks: Matching structural networks and managerial networking. *Journal of Public Administration Research Theory* 14 (4): 469–94.

Oye, K. A. 1985. Explaining cooperation under anarchy: Hypotheses and strategies. *World Politics* 38: 1–24.

———, ed. 1986. *Cooperation under anarchy.* Princeton: Princeton University Press.

Pariès, J. 2006. Complexity, emergence, resilience... In Hollnagel, Woods, and Leveson 2006, 43–53.

Parker, C. F., and E. K. Stern. 2005. Bolt from the blue or avoidable failure? Revisiting September 11 and the origins of strategic surprise. *Foreign Policy Analysis* 10 (3): 301–31.

Parker, D., and J. Handmer, eds. 1996. *Hazard management and emergency planning: Perspectives on Britain.* London: James and James.

Paton, D. 2006. Disaster resilience: Building capacity to co-exist with natural hazards and their consequences. In Paton and Johnston 2006, 3–10.

Paton, D., and D. Johnston. 2001. Disasters and communities: Vulnerability, resilience and preparedness. *Disaster Prevention and Management* 10 (4): 270–77.

———, eds. 2006. *Disaster resilience, an integrated approach.* Springfield, IL: Charles C Thomas Publisher.

Paton, D., L. Smith, and J. Violanti. 2000. Disaster response: Risk, vulnerability and resilience. *Disaster Prevention and Management* 9 (3): 173–79.

Pendall, R., K. A. Foster, and M. Cowell. 2007. *Resilience and regions, building understanding of the metaphor.* Berkeley: University of California, Institute of Urban and Regional Development.

Perrow, C. 1984. *Normal accidents: Living with high-risk technologies.* New York: Basic Books.

———. 1986. *Complex organizations: A critical essay.* New York: Random House.

———. 1994. The limits of safety: The enhancements of a theory of accidents. *Journal of Contingencies and Crisis Management* 2: 212.

———. 1999. *Normal accidents: Living with high-risk technologies.* 2nd ed. Princeton: Princeton University Press.

———. 2007. *The next catastrophe: Reducing our vulnerabilities to natural, industrial, and terrorist disasters.* Princeton: Princeton University Press.

Peters, B. G. 2001. *The politics of bureaucracy.* London: Routledge.

Peters, R. D., B. Leadbeater, and R. J. McMahon, eds. 2005. *Resilience in children, families, and communities: Linking context to practice and policy.* Online ed. New York: Kluwer Academic/Plenum Publishers.

Pew Research Center. 2004. Bottom-line pressures now hurting coverage, say journalists. May 23. Washington, DC: Pew Research Center for the People and the Press.

Pfiffner, J. 1987. Political appointees and career executives: The democracy-bureaucracy nexus in the third century. *Public Administration Review* 47: 57–65.

Pickett, S. T. A., M. L. Cadenasso, and J. M. Grove. 2004. Resilient cities: Meaning, models, and metaphor for integrating the ecological, socio-economic, and planning realms. *Landscape and Urban Planning* 69 (4): 369–84.

Pierson, P. 2000. Increasing returns, path dependence, and the study of politics. *American Political Science Review*, June.

Pilkey, O. H. 1998. *The North Carolina shore and its barrier islands: Restless ribbons of sand, living with the shore.* Durham: Duke University Press.

Platt, R. H. 1999. *Disasters and democracy.* Washington, DC: Island Press.

Pollack, M. A. 2003. *The engines of European integration: Delegation, agency, and agenda setting in the EU.* Oxford: Oxford University Press.

———. 2005. The new transatlantic agenda at ten: Reflections on an experiment in international governance. *Journal of Common Market Studies* 43 (5): 899–919.

Posner, R. A. 2005. *Remaking domestic intelligence.* Stanford: Hoover Institution Press.

Postman, N. 1986. *Amusing ourselves to death: Public discourse in the age of show business.* New York: Penguin Books.

Prater, C. S., and M. K. Lindell. 2000. Politics of hazard mitigation. *Natural Hazards Review* 1 (2): 73–82.

Premier Ministre. 2006. Plan gouvernemental de prévention et de lutte "pandémie grippale." Premier Ministre, France.

———. 2007. Plan gouvernemental de prévention et de lutte "pandémie grippale." Premier Ministre, France.

Pressman, J., and A. Wildavsky. 1973. *Implementation: How great expectations in Washington are dashed in Oakland.* Berkeley: University of California Press.

Preston, M., and S. Crabtree. 2002. Turf battles erupt over new department. *Roll Call,* June 10.

Priyantha, N. B., H. Balakrishnan, E. Demaine, and S. Teller. 2005. Mobile-assisted localization in wireless sensor networks. Proceedings of *IEEE INFOCOM,* March 13–17, Miami. Available at http://nms.lcs.mit.edu/papers/assisted-localization.pdf.

Priyantha, N. B., A. Chakraborty, and H. Balakrishnan. 2000. The cricket location-support system. In *Proceedings of the sixth annual International Conference on Mobile Computing and Networking (MOBICOM).* New York: ACM Press. Available at http://www2.parc.com/spl/members/zhao/stanford-cs428/readings/Location/Balakrishnan_cricket_mobicom00.pdf.

Project for Excellence in Journalism. 2007. *The state of the news media 2007.* Washington, DC: Project for Excellence in Journalism.

Provan, K. G., A. Fish, and J. Sydow. 2007. Interorganizational networks at the network level: A review of the empirical literature on whole networks. *Journal of Management* 33 (3): 479–516.

Putnam, R. 1994. *Making democracy work: Civic traditions in modern Italy.* Princeton: Princeton University Press.

Quarantelli, E. L. 1980. *The study of disaster movies: Research problems, findings, and implications.* Newark: Disaster Research Center, University of Delaware.

———. 1988. Disaster crisis management: A summary of research findings. *Journal of Management Studies* 25 (4): 373–85.

————, ed. 1998. *What is a disaster?* London: Routledge.

————. 2001. The sociology of panic. In *International encyclopedia of the social and behavioural sciences,* ed. N. Smelser and P. B. Baltes. New York: Pergamon Press. 102–30.

Quarantelli, E. L., and R. R. Dynes. 1977. Response to social crises and disasters. *Annual Review of Sociology* 3: 23–49.

Quarantelli, E. L., P. Lagadec, and R. A. Boin. 2004. A heuristic approach to future disasters and crises: New, old and in between types. In Rodriguez, Quarantelli, and Dynes 2006, 16–41.

Quarantelli, E. L., and R. Perry, eds. 2005. *What is a disaster? Further perspectives on the question.* Philadelphia: Xlibris Press.

Raab, J., and H. B. Milward. 2003. Dark networks as problems. *Journal of Public Administration Research and Theory* 13 (4): 413–39.

Raban, J. 2005. September 11: The view from the West. *New York Review of Books* 52 (14): 4–8.

Radin, B. A., R. Agranoff, A. O'M. Bowman, C. G. Buntz, J. S. Ott, B. S. Romzek, and R. H. Wilson, eds. 1996. *New governance for rural America: Creating intergovernmental partnership.* Lawrence: University of Kansas Press.

Ramo, J. C. 2009. *The age of the unthinkable.* Boston: Little, Brown and Company.

Rasmussen, J. 1997. Risk management in a dynamic society, a modeling problem. *Safety Science* 27 (2–3): 183–214.

Redman, C. L., and A. P. Kinzig. 2003. Resilience of past landscapes: Resilience theory, society, and the longue dureé. *Ecology and Society* 7 (1).

Reeves, M. M. 1986. Public opinion and federalism. *Publius* 17 (3): 55–65.

Regulatory Intelligence Data. 1999. North Carolina, FEMA announces buyout strategy. *Industry Group* 99 (October 14). Accessed through http://www.elibrary.com, March 11, 2000.

Relyea, H. 2005. Homeland Security: Department organization and management—implementation phase. January 3. Washington, DC: Congressional Research Service.

Rerup, C. 2001. "Houston, we have a problem": Anticipation and improvisation as sources of organizational resilience. *Comportamento Organizacional e Gestao* 7 (1): 27–44.

Reuters. 2005. German plane denied entry into U.S. Reuters News Agency, September 10.

Rhodes, R. A. W. 1990. Policy networks: A British perspective. *Journal of Theoretical Politics* 2 (3): 292–316.

Rice, J. 2005. Seaweb acoustic communication and navigation networks. In *Proceedings of the International Conference of Underwater Acoustic Measurements: Technologies and Results,* June–July, Heraklion, Crete. Available at http://www.dtnrg.org/docs/papers/UAMeasurements2005Rice2.pdf.

Richard, A. C. 2006a. *Role reversal: Offers of help from other countries in response to Hurricane Katrina.* Washington, DC: Center for Transatlantic Relations of Johns Hopkins University.

————. 2006b. When the world wanted to help America. *International Herald Tribune,* August 30.

Richardson, H. W., P. Gordon, and J. E. Moore, eds. 2006. *The economic impact of terrorist attacks.* Cheltenham, UK: Edward Elgar.

Richardson, J., and G. Jordan. 1979. *Governing under pressure: The policy process in a post-parliamentary democracy.* Oxford: Martin Robertson.

Riley, J. R., and A. S. Masten. 2005. Resilience in context. In Peters, Leadbeater, and McMahon 2005, 13–25.

Ring, P. S., and A. H. Van de Ven. 1994. Developmental processes in cooperative interorganizational relationships. *Academy of Management Review* 19: 90–118.

Riolli, L., and V. Savicki. 2003. Information system organizational resilience. *Omega* 31 (3): 227–33.

Risse-Kappen, T. 1994. Ideas do not float freely: Transnational coalitions, domestic structures, and the end of the Cold War. *International Organization* 48: 185–214.

———. 1997. *Cooperation among democracies: The European influence on U.S. foreign policy.* Princeton: Princeton University Press.

Roberts, A. 2008. *The collapse of Fortress Bush: The crisis of authority in American government.* New York: New York University Press.

———. 2009. The path not taken: Leonard White and the macrodynamics of administrative development. *Public Administration Review* 69: 764–75.

Roberts, K. H. 1989. New challenges in organizational research: High reliability organizations. *Industrial Crisis Quarterly* 3 (2): 111–25.

———. 1990a. Managing high reliability organizations. *California Management Review* 32 (4): 101–13.

———. 1990b. Some characteristics of one type of high reliability organization. *Organization Science* 1 (2): 160–75.

———, ed. 1993. *New challenges to understanding organizations.* New York: Macmillan.

Rochlin, G. I. 1991. Iran Air Flight 665 and the USS *Vincennes:* Complex large scale military systems and the failure of control. In *Social responses to large technical systems, control or anticipation,* ed. T. R. LaPorte. Dordrecht: Kluwer Academic Publishers. 99–125.

———. 1993. Defining high reliability organisations in practice. In K. H. Roberts 1993, 11–32.

———. 1999. Safe operation as a social construct. *Ergonomics* 42 (11): 1549–60.

———. 2000. *Trapped in the Net: The unanticipated consequences of computerization.* Princeton: Princeton University Press.

———. 2001. Networks and the subversion of choice: An institutionalist manifesto. *Journal of Urban Technology* 8 (3): 65–96.

Rochlin, G. I., T. R. LaPorte, and K. H. Roberts. 1987. The self-designing high-reliability organization: Aircraft carrier flight operations at sea. *Naval War College Review* 40: 76–90.

Rodriguez, H., E. L. Quarantelli, and R. Dynes, eds. 2006. *Handbook of disaster research.* New York, New York: Springer.

Roe, E. M. 1998. *Taking complexity seriously: Policy analysis, triangulation, and sustainable development.* Boston: Kluwer Academic.

Roe, E. M., and P. Schulman. 2008. *High reliability management: Operating on the edge.* Stanford: Stanford University Press.

Roe, E. M., P. Schulman, M. J. G. van Eeten, and M. L. C. de Bruijne. 2003. Real-time reliability: Provision of electricity under adverse performance conditions arising from California's electricity restructuring and crisis. A report prepared for the California Energy Commission, Lawrence Berkeley National Laboratory, and the Electrical Power Research Institute. San Francisco: Energy Commission.

—————. 2005. High reliability bandwidth management in large technical systems. *Journal of Public Administration Research and Theory* 15 (1): 263–80.

Rolf, J. E., and J. L. Johnson. 1999. Opening doors to resilience intervention for prevention research. In Glantz and Johnson 1999, 229–49.

Rood, J. 2005. FEMA's decline. *Government Executive*, September 28.

Roosa, M. W. 2000. Some thoughts about resilience versus positive development, main effects versus interactions, and the value of resilience. *Child Development* 71 (3): 567–69.

Rose, A. 2004. Defining and measuring resilience to disasters. *Disaster Prevention and Management* 13 (4): 307–14.

Rosenau, J. N. 1969. Towards the study of national-international linkages. In *Linkage politics: Essays on the convergence of national and international systems*, ed. J. N. Rosenau. New York: Free Press.

Rosenthal, U., A. Boin, and L. K. Comfort. 2001a. The changing world of crises and crisis management. In Rosenthal, Boin, and Comfort 2001b, 5–27.

—————, eds. 2001b. *Managing crises: Threats, dilemmas, opportunities*. Springfield, IL: Charles C Thomas.

Rosenthal, U., M. T. Charles, and P. t'Hart, eds. 1989. *Coping with crises: The management of disasters, riots, and terrorism*. Springfield, IL: Charles C Thomas.

Rosenthal, U., P. t'Hart, and A. Kouzmin. 1991. The bureau-politics of crisis management. *Public Administration* 69: 211–33.

Rosset, C. 1979. *L'objet singulier*. Paris: Minuit.

Rossi, P. H., J. D. Wright, and E. Weber-Burdin. 1982. *Natural hazards and public choice: The state and local politics of hazard mitigation*. New York: Academic Press.

Rothkopf, D. J. 2005. *Running the world: The inside story of the National Security Council and the architects of American power*. New York: PublicAffairs.

Ryan, J. M., G. J. Cooper, I. R. Haywood, and S. M. Milner. 1991. Field surgery on a future conventional battlefield: Strategy and wound management. *Annals of the Royal College of Surgeons of England* 73 (1): 13–20.

Sabatier, P. A. 1987. Knowledge, policy-oriented learning, and policy change. *Knowledge: Creation, Diffusion, Utilization* 8: 649–692.

—————. 1991. Toward better theories of the policy process. *PS: Political Science and Politics* 24 (2): 144–56.

Sabatier, P. A., and H. C. Jenkins-Smith. 1993. *Policy change and learning: An advocacy coalition approach, theoretical lenses on public policy*. Boulder: Westview Press.

Salamon, L. M., and M. S. Lund. 1989. The tools approach: Basic analytics. In *Beyond privatization: The tools of government action*, ed. L. M. Salamon. Washington, DC: Urban Institute Press. 23–49

Sarker, S. 2005. Knowledge transfer and collaboration in distributed U.S.-Thai teams. *Journal of Computer-Mediated Communication* 10 (4).

Savvides, A., C. C. Han, and M. B. Srivastava. 2001. Dynamic fine-grained localization in ad-hoc networks of sensors. *Proceedings of the seventh annual International Conference on Mobile Computing and Networking (MOBICOM01)*, July, Rome. Available at http://portal.acm.org/citation.cfm?id=381693.

Savvides, A., H. Park, and M. B. Srivastava. 2002. The bits and flops of the n-hop multi-lateration primitive for node localization problems. In *Proceedings of the first ACM International Workshop on Wireless Sensor Networks and Applications*

(WSNA). New York: ACM Press. Available at http://nesl.ee.ucla.edu/projects/smartkg/docs/wsna_final.pdf.

Scanlon, T. J. 1996. Changing a corporate culture: Managing risk on the London Underground. *International Journal of Mass Emergencies and Disasters* 14 (2): 175–94.

———. 2005. Strange bed partners: Thoughts on the London bombings of July 2005 and the link with the Indian Ocean tsunami of December 26th 2004. *International Journal of Mass Emergencies and Disasters* 23 (2): 149–58.

Scavo, C., R. C. Kearney, and R. J. Kilroy. 2006. Challenges to federalism: Homeland security, disaster response, and the local impact of federal funding formulas and mandates. Paper presented at American Political Science Association, August 31–September 3, 2006, Philadelphia.

Scharpf, F. W. 1997. *Games real actors play: Actor-centered institutionalism in policy research*. Boulder: Westview Press.

Scheinman, L. 1966. Some preliminary notes on bureaucratic relationships in the European economic community. *International Organization* 20: 750–73.

Schmitt, E., and T. Shanker. 2005. Military may propose an active-duty force for relief efforts. *New York Times,* October 11.

Schneider, J. 1985. Social problems theory: The constructionist view. *Annual Review of Sociology* 11: 209–29.

Schoon, I. 2006. *Risk and resilience: Adaptations in changing times*. Cambridge: Cambridge University Press.

Schraagen, J. M., L. G. Militello, T. Ormerod, and R. Lipshitz, eds. 2008. *Naturalistic decision making and macrocognition*. Aldershot: Ashgate.

Schulman, P. 1993. The analysis of high reliability organizations: A comparative framework. In K. H. Roberts 1993, 33–54.

———. 1996. Heroes, organizations and high reliability. *Journal of Contingencies and Crisis Management* 4: 72–82.

Schulman, P., and E. M. Roe. 2007. Designing infrastructures: Dilemmas of design and the reliability of critical infrastructures. *Journal of Contingencies and Crisis Management* 15: 42–49.

Schulman, P., E. M. Roe, M. J. G. van Eeten, and M. L. C. Bruijne. 2004. High reliability and the management of critical infrastructures. *Journal of Contingencies and Crisis Management* 12: 14–28.

Schwartz, P. 2003. *Inevitable surprises: Thinking ahead in a time of turbulence*. New York: Gotham Books.

Scoones, I. 1999. New ecology and the social sciences: What prospects for a fruitful engagement? *Annual Review of Anthropology* 28: 479–507.

Scott, J. 2001. *Social network analysis: A handbook*. London: Sage.

Seed, R. B., P. G. Nicholson, R. A. Dalrymple, J. Battjes, R. G. Bea, G. Boutwell, J. D. Bray, B. D. Collins, L. F. Harder, J. R. Headland, M. Inamine, R. E. Kayen, R. Kuhr, J. M. Pestana, R. Sanders, F. Silva-Tulla, R. Storesund, S. Tanaka, J. Wartman, T. F. Wolff, L. Wooten, and T. Zimmie. 2005. Preliminary report on the performance of the New Orleans levee systems in Hurricane Katrina on August 29, 2005. Report 05/01, November. Berkeley: University of California, CITRIS.

Selznick, P. 1957. *Leadership in administration*. New York: Harper & Row.

Setbon, M. 1993. *Pouvoirs contre SIDA. De la transfusion sanguine au dépistage. Décisions et pratiques en France, Grande Bretagne et Suède*. Paris: Seuil.

Seymour, W. 1988. *Decisive factors in twenty great battles of the world.* London: Sidgwick and Jackson.

Sichitiu, M. L., and V. Ramadurai. 2004. Localization of wireless sensor networks with a mobile beacon. In *Proceedings of IEEE International Conference on Mobile Ad-Hoc and Sensor Systems (MASS),* October, Fort Lauderdale. Available at http://www4.ncsu.edu/~mlsichit/Research/Publications/oneMobileBeaconTR.pdf.

Shafer, J. 2005. The rebellion of the talking heads. *Slate,* September 2.

Shane, S. 2006. Year into revamped spying, troubles and some progress. *New York Times,* February 28: 12.

Sheffi, Y. 2005. *The resilient enterprise: Overcoming vulnerability for competitive advantage.* Cambridge, MA: MIT Press.

——. 2007. Building a resilient organization. *Bridge* 37 (1): 30–38.

Shibutani, T. 1966. *Improvised news: A sociological study of rumor.* New York: Bobbs-Merrill.

Short, J. F., Jr., and L. Clarke. 1992. *Organizations, uncertainties, and risk.* Boulder: Westview Press.

Shortridge, K. 2006. Influenza pandemic preparedness: Gauging from EU Plans. *Lancet* 367 (9520): 1374–75.

Simon, H. A. 1997. *The sciences of the artificial.* 4th ed. Cambridge, MA: MIT Press.

Smith, K. G., S. J. Carroll, and S. J. Ashford. 1995. Intra- and interorganizational cooperation: Toward a research agenda. *Academy of Management Journal* 38 (1): 7–23.

Snapper, Greg. 2006. Hail to the tank. *Precast Solutions Magazine* (Winter). Available at http://www.precast.org/publications/solutions/2006_winter/hailtothetank.htm.

Sonardyne. 2009. USBL, Fusion LBL, Prospector, and Scout USBL. Product overviews available at http://www.sonardyne.com/Products/A-Z/index.html.

Sproull, L. S., and S. B. Kiesler. 1991. *Connections: New ways of working in the networked organization.* Cambridge, MA: MIT Press.

Stallings, R. A. 1995. *Promoting risk: Constructing the earthquake threat.* New York: DeGruyter.

Stanovich, M. 2006. Network-centric emergency response: The challenges of training for a new command and control paradigm. *Journal of Emergency Management* 4 (2): 57–64.

Starr, R., J. Newfrock, and M. Delurey. 2003. Enterprise resilience: Managing risk in the networked economy. *Strategy Business* 30: 1–10.

Steinberg, M., and R. J. Burby. 2002. Growing safe. *Planning* 68 (4): 22–23.

Stern, E. K. 1997. Crisis and learning: A balance sheet. *Journal of Contingencies and Crisis Management* 5: 69–86.

Stiles, K. W. 2006. The power of procedure and the procedures of the powerful: Antiterror law in the United Nations. *Journal of Peace Research* 43 (1): 37.

Strogatz, S. H. 2003. *Sync: The emerging science of spontaneous order.* New York: Hyperion.

Strömbäck, J., and L. Nord. 2006. Mismanagement, mistrust and missed opportunities: A study of the 2004 tsunami and Swedish political communication. *Media, Culture and Society* 28 (5): 789–800.

Sugden, J. 2006. Security sector reform: The role of epistemic communities in the UK. *Journal of Security Sector Management* 4 (4): 1–20.

Summerton, J., and B. Berner. 2003. Constructing risk and safety in technological practice: An introduction. In *Constructing risk and safety in technological practice,* ed. J. Summerton and B. Berner. London: Routledge. 1–23.

Sundelius, B. 2005. Disruptions: Functional security for the EU. In Missiroli 2005, 67–84.

Sunstein, C. R. 2006. Irreversible and catastrophic. *Cornell Law Review* 91 (4): 841–97.

Surowiecki, J. 2005. *The wisdom of crowds: Why the many are smarter than the few and how collective wisdom shapes business economies, societies, and nations.* New York: Anchor Books.

Surowiecki, J., and M. P. Silverman. 2007. The wisdom of crowds. *American Journal of Physics* 75: 190.

Sutcliffe, K. M., and T. J. Vogus. 2003. Organizing for resilience. In *Positive organizational scholarship,* ed. K. S. Cameron, J. E. Dutton, and R. E. Quinn. San Francisco: Berrett-Koehler Publishers. 94–110.

Swissinfo. 2009. Swiss offer help after Italian quake. April 6.

Sylves, R., and W. Cumming. 2004. FEMA's path to homeland security: 1979–2003. *Journal of Homeland Security and Emergency Management* 1 (2).

Taleb, N. N. 2007. *The black swan: The impact of the highly improbable.* New York: Random House.

Tallberg, J. 2006. *Leadership and negotiation in the European Union.* Cambridge: Cambridge University Press.

Tarter, R. E., and M. Vanyukov. 1999. Re-visiting the validity of the construct of resilience. In Glantz and Johnson 1999, 25–100.

t'Hart, P. 1993. Symbols, rituals and power: The lost dimension in crisis management. *Journal of Contingencies and Crisis Management* 1: 36–50.

Thompson, J. D. 1967. *Organizations in action: Social science bases of administrative theory.* New York: McGraw-Hill.

Tierney, K. 2003. *Conceptualizing and measuring organizational and community resilience: Lessons from the emergency response following the September 11, 2001 attack on the World Trade Center.* Newark: Disaster Research Center, University of Delaware.

Tierney, K., C. Bevc, and E. Kuligowskim. 2006. Metaphors matter: Disaster myths, media frames, and their consequences in Hurricane Katrina. *ANNALS of the American Academy of Political and Social Science* 604: 57–81.

Trist, E. L., F. Emery, and H. Murray. 1997. The social engagement of social science: A Tavistock anthology. Vol. 3, Socio-ecological perspective. Philadelphia: University of Pennsylvania Press.

Tsunami Evaluation Coalition. 2006. Joint evaluation of the international response to the Indian Ocean tsunami. July. Available at http://www.tsunami-evaluation.org.

Turner, B. A. 1978. *Man-made disasters.* London: Wykeham.

Tyson, A. S. 2005. Pentagon plans to beef up domestic rapid-response plans. *Washington Post,* October 13.

United Nations. 1989. General Assembly Resolution 42/236: International decade for natural disaster reduction. Available at http://daccess-dds-ny.un.org/doc/RESOLUTION/GEN/NR0/549/95/IMG/NR054995.pdf?OpenElement.

———. 1991. General Assembly Resolution 46/182: Strengthening of the coordination of humanitarian emergency assistance of the United Nations. Available at http://daccess-dds-ny.un.org/doc/RESOLUTION/GEN/NR0/582/70/IMG/NR058270.pdf?OpenElement.

———. 1994. Yokohama strategy and plan of action for a safer world. Adopted at World Conference on Natural Disaster Reduction, Yokohama. Available at http://www.unisdr.org/eng/about_isdr/bd-yokohama-strat-eng.htm.

———. 1999. General Assembly Resolution 54/219: International decade for natural disaster reduction: successor arrangements. Available at http://daccess-dds-ny.un.org/doc/UNDOC/GEN/N00/271/75/PDF/N0027175.pdf?OpenElement.

———. 2005a. Hyogo framework for action: 2005–2014: Building the resilience of nations and communities to disasters. Available at http://www.unisdr.org/eng/hfa/hfa.htm.

———. 2005b. Report of the World Conference on Disaster Reduction. January 18–22, Kobe, Hyogo, Japan. Available at http://www.unisdr.org/wcdr/intergover/official-doc/L-docs/Final-report-conference.pdf.

———. 2007. Implementation of the international strategy for disaster reduction. Report of the Secretary General. Available at http://www.unisdr.org/eng/about_isdr/basic_docs/SG-report/SG-report-61-229-eng.pdf.

UCLA (University of California, Los Angeles). 2009. GloMoSim Manual. Available at http://pcl.cs.ucla.edu/projects/glomosim.

U.S. Commission on National Security/Twenty-First Century. 2001. Road map for national security: Imperative for change. February 15. Washington, DC: U.S. Commission on National Security/Twenty-First Century.

U.S. Congress. 2000. Public Law 106-390: Disaster Mitigation Act to amend the Robert T. Stafford Act of 1988. Enacted October 30, 1988.

———. 2006. Public Law 109-424: Tsunami warning and education act. Enacted December 20, 2006. Available at http://nctr.pmel.noaa.gov/education/science/docs/tsunami_act_public_law.pdf.

U.S. Geological Survey. 2009. Magnitude 6.3—Central Italy. April 6. Available at http://earthquake.usgs.gov/eqcenter/eqinthenews/2009/us2009fcaf/.

U.S. House of Representatives. 2005. A failure of initiative: Final report of the Select Bipartisan Committee to Investigate the Preparation for and Response to Hurricane Katrina. Report no. 109-377. Washington, DC: U.S. Government Printing Office. Available at http://www.gpoaccess.gov/serialset/creports/katrina.html.

———. 2006. House Committee on Government Reform. The growth of political appointees in the Bush administration. May. Washington, DC: House Committee on Government Reform, Minority Staff.

U.S. Senate. 2003. Creating foresight: How resilience engineering can transform NASA's approach to risky decision making. October 29.

———. 2006. Senate Homeland Security and Governmental Affairs Committee. Hurricane Katrina: A nation still unprepared. May. Washington, DC: Government Printing Office.

Vale, L. J., and T. J. Campanella, eds. 2005. *The resilient city: How modern cities recover from disaster*. New York: Oxford University Press.

van Creveld, M. 1977. *Supplying war: Logistics from Wallerstein to Patton*. New York: Cambridge University Press.

———. 1989. *Technology and war: From 2000 BC to the present*. New York: Free Press.

van Eeten, M. J. G., and E. M. Roe. 2002. *Ecology, engineering and management: Reconciling ecological rehabilitation and service reliability*. New York: Oxford University Press.

van Eeten, M. J. G., E. M. Roe, P. Schulman, and M. L. C. de Bruijne. 2006. When failure is not an option: Managing complex technologies under intensifying interdependencies. In *Management of technology: An introduction*, ed. R. Verburg, R. Ortt, and W. M. Dicke. London: Routledge. 306–22.

van Heerden, I., G. P. Kemp, W. Shrum, E. Boyd, and H. Mashriqui. 2005. Initial assessment of the New Orleans' flooding event during the passage of Hurricane Katrina. Baton Rouge: Center for the Study of Public Health Impacts of Hurricanes, Louisiana State University.

Verbist, S. 2002a. Data exploration KPN mobile calamities 1995–2002. The Hague: NMCC KPN Mobile, Confidential.

———. 2002b. Reliability in mobile telecom under rapidly changing conditions. Master's thesis, Faculty of Technology, Policy and Management. Delft: TU Delft.

Verdun, A. 1999. The role of the Delors Committee in the creation of EMU: An epistemic community? *Journal of European Public Policy* 6 (4): 308–28.

Vickers, M. H., and A. Kouzmin. 2001. "Resilience" in organizational actors and rearticulating "voice": Towards a humanistic critique of new public management. *Public Management Review* 3, (1): 95–119.

Vogus, T. J., and T. M. Welbourne. 2003. Structuring for high reliability: HR practices and mindful processes in reliability-seeking organizations. *Journal of Organizational Behavior* 24 (7): 877–903.

Volcker, P. A. 1988. *Public service: The quiet crisis*. Washington, DC: American Enterprise Institute.

Wachtendorf, T. 2000. When disasters defy borders: What we can learn from the Red River flood about transnational disasters. *Australian Journal of Emergency Management* 15 (3): 36–41.

Waldrop, M. M. 1992. *Complexity: The emerging science at the edge of order and chaos*. New York: Simon and Schuster.

Walker, B., L. H. Gunderson, A. Kinzig, C. Folke, S. Carpenter, and L. Schultz. 2006. A handful of heuristics and some propositions for understanding resilience in social-ecological systems. *Ecology and Society* 11 (1).

Walker, B., and D. Salt. 2006. *Resilience thinking: Sustaining ecosystems and people in a changing world*. Washington, DC: Island Press.

Walker, D. M. 2000. Managing in the new millennium: Testimony before the Senate Committee on Governmental Affairs. March 29. Washington, DC: General Accounting Office.

Wallace, H. 2005. An institutional anatomy and five policy modes. In *Policy-making in the European Union*, ed. H. Wallace and M. A. Pollack. New York: Oxford University Press. 49–90.

Warrick, R. 1982. Vulnerability, resilience, and collapse of society, by Peter Timmerman, 1981. Environmental Monograph no. 1, Institute for Environmental Studies, University of Toronto. *Climatic Change* 4 (2): 208–10.

Waugh, W., Jr. 2006. The political costs of failure in the Katrina and Rita disasters. *ANNALS of the American Academy of Political and Social Science* 604: 57–81.

Webb, G. 2004. Role improvising during crisis situations. *International Journal of Emergency Management* 2 (1–2): 47–61.

Weick, K. E. 1979. *The social psychology of organizing*. Reading, MA: Addison-Wesley.

———. 1987. Organizational culture as a source of high reliability. *California Management Review* 29 (2): 112–27.

———. 1993. The collapse of sensemaking in organizations: The Mann Gulch disaster. *Administrative Science Quarterly* 38: 628–52.

———. 1995. *Sensemaking in organizations.* Paperback ed. Thousand Oaks: SAGE Publications.

———. 1998. Improvisation as a mindset for organizational analysis. *Organization Science* 9 (5): 543–55.

———. 2001. *Making sense of the organization.* Malden, MA: Blackwell Publishing.

Weick, K. E., and K. Sutcliffe. 2001. *Managing the unexpected: Assuring high performance in an age of complexity.* San Francisco: Jossey-Bass.

Weick, K. E., K. Sutcliffe, and D. Obstfeld. 1999. Organizing for high reliability: Processes of collective mindfulness. In *Research in organizational behavior,* ed. B. M. Staw and R. Sutton. Greenwich: JAI Press. 21, 81–123.

———. 2002. High reliability: The power of mindfulness. In *On high performance organizations,* ed. F. Hesselbein. and R. Johnston. San Francisco: Jossey-Bass. 7–18.

———. 2005. Organizing and the process of sensemaking. *Organization Science* 16 (4): 409–21.

Werbner, P. 2000. Divided loyalties, empowered citizenship? Muslims in Britain. *Citizenship Studies* 4 (3): 307–24.

Wessels, W. 1997. An ever closer fusion? A dynamic macropolitical view on integration processes. *Journal of Common Market Studies* 35 (2): 267–99.

Westrum, R. 1982. Social intelligence about hidden events: Its significance for scientific research and social policy. *Knowledge: Creation, Diffusion, Utilization* 3: 381–400.

———. 2006. A typology of resilience. In Hollnagel, Woods, and Leveson 2006, 55–66.

Whelton, A. J., P. K. Wisniewski, S. States, S. E. Birkmire, and M. K. Brown. 2006. Lessons learned from drinking water disaster and terrorism exercises. *Journal of the American Water Works Association* 98 (8): 63–73.

White, J. B., M. T. Schmitt, and E. J. Langer. 2006. Horizontal hostility: Multiple minority groups and differentiation from the mainstream. *Group Processes and Intergroup Relations* 9 (3): 339.

Whitlock, C., and B. Williams. 1996. Damage may top $4 billion. *News and Observer,* September 15.

Wightman, J. M., and S. L. Gladish. 2003. Explosions and blast injuries. *Annals of Emergency Medicine* 37 (6): 664–78.

Wildavsky, A. B. 1969. *The presidency.* Boston: Little Brown.

———. 1988. *Searching for safety.* New Brunswick: Transaction.

———. 1995. *But is it true? A citizen's guide to environmental health and safety issues.* Cambridge, MA: Harvard University Press.

Wilensky, H. L. 1967. *Organizational intelligence: Knowledge and policy in government and industry.* New York: Basic Books.

Wilson, J. Q. 1989. *Bureaucracy: What government agencies do and why they do it.* New York: Basic Books.

Wing, S., S. Freedman, and L. Band. 2002. The potential impact of flooding on confined animal feeding operations in eastern North Carolina. *Environmental Health Perspectives* 110 (4): 387–91.

Winham, Gilbert R. 1979. Practitioners' views of international negotiation. *World Politics* 32: 111–35.

Wirtz, J. J. 2006. Responding to surprise. *Annual Review of Political Science* 9: 45–65.

Wise, C. R. 2006. Organizing for homeland security after Katrina: Is adaptive management what's missing? *Public Administration Review* 66: 302–18.

Wolmar, C. 2002. *Down the tube: The battle for London's Underground.* London: Aurum.

Wong, S. Y., J. Lim, R. S. Rao, and W. K. Seah. 2005. Multihop localization with density and path length awareness in non-uniform wireless sensor networks. In *Proceedings of the sixty-first IEEE Vehicular Technology Conference (VTC2005-Spring)*, May–June, Stockholm, 4: 2551–55.

Woods, D. D. 2005. Creating foresight: Lessons for enhancing resilience from Columbia. In *Organization at the limit: Lessons from the Columbia disaster*, ed. W. H. Starbuck and M. Farjoun. Malden, MA: Blackwell Publishing. 289–308.

———. 2006. Essential characteristics of resilience. In Hollnagel, Woods, and Leveson 2006, 21–34.

Woods, D. D., and E. Hollnagel. 2006. Prologue: Resilience engineering concepts. In Hollnagel, Woods, and Leveson 2006, 1–6.

Woodward, B. 2002. *Bush at war.* New York: Simon and Schuster.

Work, P. A., S. M. Rodgers, and R. Osborne. 1999. Flood retrofit of coastal residential structures: Outer Banks, North Carolina. *Journal of Water Resources Planning and Management* 125 (2): 88–93.

Wright, M., and A. Masten. 2005. Resilience processes in development. In Goldstein and Brooks 2005, 17–37.

Zegart, A. B. 1999. *Flawed by design: The evolution of the CIA, JCS, and NSC.* Stanford: Stanford University Press.

———. 2006. American intelligence: Still stupid. *Los Angeles Times,* September 17.

Zhou, G., T. He, S. Krishnamurthy, and J. A. Stankovic. 2004. Impact of radio irregularity on wireless sensor networks. In *Proceedings of the second international Conference on Mobile Systems, Applications, and Services (MobiSys)*, Boston, June 6–9. Available at http://www.cs.virginia.edu/papers/radio_irregularity.pdf.

CONTRIBUTORS

DAVID ALEXANDER is the Contract Professor of Disaster Management at CESPRO, the Center for Risk and Civil Protection Studies, University of Florence, Italy. His books include *Natural Disasters* (1993), *Confronting Catastrophe* (2000), and *Principles of Emergency Planning and Management* (2002). He is the coeditor of the journal *Disasters*. He teaches disaster planning and crisis management in Italy and elsewhere in Europe and is the administrative director of a large project on vulnerability assessment funded by the European Commission. For many years, Alexander taught disaster studies at the University of Massachusetts, Amherst, but in 2002 he returned to Europe to continue his work in this field.

THOMAS A. BIRKLAND is the William T. Kretzer Professor of Public Policy in the School of Public and International Affairs at North Carolina State University and was an associate professor of public administration and the director of the Center for Policy Research at the State University of New York (SUNY), Albany. He is the author of two books and several articles on the political and policy aspects of disasters, including *Lessons of Disaster* (2006) and *After Disaster* (1997). His current research interests are in the policy aspects of long-term recovery and in policy failure and learning following major disasters.

ARJEN BOIN is an associate professor at the Public Administration Institute of Louisiana State University and a professor of public administration at Utrecht University's School of Governance. He is also a founding director of Crisisplan. His recent books are *The Politics of Crisis Management* (2006), *Governing after Crisis* (2008), and *Crisis Management: A Three Volume Set of Essential Readings* (2008). Boin serves on the editorial boards of *Risk Management* and the *Journal of Contingencies and Crisis Management*. He is the American editor for *Public Administration*.

LOUISE K. COMFORT is a professor of public and international affairs and the director of the Center for Disaster Management, University of Pittsburgh. She is a fellow of the National Academy of Public Administration and the author or coauthor of four books, including *Shared Risk: Complex Systems in Seismic Response* (1999). She has published articles on information policy, organizational learning, and sociotechnical systems and is the book review editor of the *Journal of Comparative Policy Analysis*. She has engaged in field studies following seventeen earthquake disasters in thirteen countries, most recently with the Earthquake Engineering Research Institute's reconnaissance team following the September 30, 2009, earthquake in Padang, Indonesia.

MARK DE BRUIJNE is an assistant professor in the School of Technology, Policy and Management, Delft University of Technology, the Netherlands. His research focuses on issues of reliability, critical infrastructure management, and the consequences of institutional fragmentation. He has (co)written articles on this subject, which have appeared in the *Journal of Contingencies and Crisis Management* and the *Journal of Public Administration Research*. His recent work focuses on resilience and explores the consequences of institutional fragmentation on security and the reliability of service provision in critical infrastructures for individuals and organizations that are responsible for the management and operation of these infrastructures.

CHRIS C. DEMCHAK holds a PhD in political science from Berkeley, an MPA in economic development from Princeton, and an MA in energy engineering from Berkeley. She is an associate professor in the Strategic Research Department of the U.S. Naval War College and was previously an associate professor with the School of Governance and Public Policy, University of Arizona. She publishes on large-scale organizations and cybered security strategy ("theory of action," "behavior-based privacy," the cybered military model Atrium). She is the author of *Military Organizations, Complex Machines* (1991) and is completing a manuscript entitled "Wars of Disruption and Resilience." Her current research focuses on comparative cyber commands, national security resilience, and game-based simulations in security analysis.

GUNES ERTAN is a student in public policy and international development at the Graduate School of Public and International Affairs, University of Pittsburgh. Ertan holds an MPA degree from Bowling Green State University and a bachelor's degree in sociology from the Middle East Technical

University in Ankara, Turkey. Her research interests lie in the analysis of collaborative interactions among nonprofit and public organizations and the evolution of networks of organizations in dynamic contexts.

CLAUDE GILBERT is the research director at the Centre National de la Recherche Scientifique (UMR PACTE, IEP de Grenoble). He holds a PhD in political science, and his research interests are in crisis prevention and crisis management, public policies, and organizational vulnerability. In the former decade, he was in charge of several national research programs on collective risk and crisis in the field of social science in France. His more recent works are about pandemic prevention in France.

THOMAS W. HAASE received his doctorate from the Graduate School of Public and International Affairs (GSPIA), University of Pittsburgh. Haase has focused his studies on public administration and international security, and he seeks to identify the factors that facilitate resilience in administrative systems that operate in uncertain and rapidly changing conditions. His dissertation evaluates the resilience of the administrative system that operated in Indonesia after the earthquake and tsunami of December 26, 2004. He has also worked as an adjunct faculty member at the University of Pittsburgh and has taught courses in administrative law, public policy, and global governance.

HUI LING is a PhD graduate of the Department of Computer Science, University of Pittsburgh, in 2010. He received his BS and MS degrees from Nanjing University in 1999 and 2002, respectively. His major research interests include routing and security protocols in mobile ad hoc and wireless sensor networks. He has been working on several projects funded by the National Science Foundation, including Secure CITI: A Secure Critical Information Technology Infrastructure for Disaster Management and DRU: Designing Resilience for Communities at Risk: Decision Support for Collective Action under Stress. He is a member of the Institute for Electrical and Electronics Engineers (IEEE) and is currently a software engineer at ECI Telecom in Pittsburgh.

NAMKYUNG OH received his PhD from the Graduate School of Public and International Affairs at the University of Pittsburgh in April 2010. His research interest is in building collaborative intergovernmental relationships, especially designing resilient disaster management systems using social network analysis and multiagent-based computational simulation. Namkyung holds a MPA degree from Seoul National University, Korea. He has worked for the president of Korea and several research institutes in Korea.

Oh joined the Center for Disaster Management in 2005 and is currently working on comparative analysis of the disaster response networks of major hurricanes, including Katrina and Gustav. In September 2010, he will be an assistant professor of public administration and urban policy at the University of Akron in Ohio.

MARK RHINARD is a senior research fellow and the coordinator of the Europe Research Program at the Swedish Institute of International Affairs. His expertise includes the institutional processes and politics of European Union cooperation, with a special focus on internal, external, and "homeland" security policy making in the EU. He earned his doctorate from Cambridge University and teaches regularly at universities and research institutes across Europe. His latest book, entitled *Framing Europe: Policy Shaping Strategies of the European Commission,* will be published in 2010.

ALASDAIR ROBERTS is the Jerome L. Rappaport Professor of Law and Public Policy at Suffolk University Law School. His books include *The Logic of Discipline: Global Capitalism and the Architecture of Government* (2010), *The Collapse of Fortress Bush: The Crisis of Authority in American Government* (2008), and *Blacked Out: Government Secrecy in the Information Age* (2006). He is a fellow of the U.S. National Academy of Public Administration; an honorary senior research fellow of the School of Public Policy, University College London; and the coeditor of the journal *Governance.*

STEVE SCHEINERT is a PhD candidate in international security and international development. Scheinert earned a master's degree in public policy from the Thomas Jefferson Program in Public Policy in 2006 and a bachelor's degree in international relations in 2004 from the College of William and Mary. He joined the IISIS team in 2007, focusing on data management and research methods. Outside of IISIS, he has focused on the impact of postconflict and transitional justice systems on state reconstruction efforts and now wishes to apply the research methods associated with complex adaptive systems to postconflict reconstruction.

BENGT SUNDELIUS is the head of the Department of Security and Strategy of the Swedish National Defence College and a professor of government, Uppsala University. He was the chief scientist of the Swedish Emergency Management Agency from 2004 through 2008. He serves as the Swedish agreement director for the Science and Technology Agreement between the government of Sweden and the U.S. Department of Homeland Security. He has served as a *rapporteur* on the European Security Research and Innovation Forum and now serves on the EU Commission FP7 Security Advisory

Group for European security research. He was the founding chair of the Nordic International Studies Association, and has served as the vice president of the International Studies Association.

MICHEL J. G. VAN EETEN is a professor of public administration at the Faculty of Technology, Policy and Management, Delft University of Technology, the Netherlands. He also teaches in several programs in executive education at the Netherlands School of Public Administration in the Hague. He received a master's degree in public administration from Leiden University and a PhD in public policy from Delft University of Technology. He has published on environmental policy, large technical systems, ecosystem management, high-reliability theory, land-use planning, flood control and dike improvement, transportation policy, symbolic language in policy, and recasting intractable policy issues. He serves on the editorial board of *Policy Sciences*.

TAIEB ZNATI is a professor in the Department of Computer Science, University of Pittsburgh, with a joint appointment in telecommunications at the Department of Information Science and in computer engineering at the School of Engineering. He currently serves as the director of the Computer and Network Systems Division at the National Science Foundation. Znati also served as a senior program director for networking research at the National Science Foundation. In this capacity, Znati led the Information Technology Research (ITR) Initiative, a National Science Foundation cross-directorate research program, and served as the chair of the ITR Committee.

INDEX

Note: page numbers in italics refer to figures. Those followed by n refer to endnotes, with note number.

Bandung Institute of Technology, 247

Barnett, M. N., 208

basic services: deterioration in flu pandemic, 192–93; maintaining as issue in pandemics, 183–84, 188, 189–90; as second responders, 152

Baton Rouge, Hurricane Gustav's effects on, 132

Belgium, 210

Blair, Ian, 157

blame, danger of initiating, 135–36

Blanco, Kathleen Babineaux, 103

Blitz, London Fire Brigade in, 145

"Blitz spirit," as model of resilience, 145

Boettcher, Claus, 213

Boin, A., 87

Bonneville Power Administration (BPA), 161–63, 166

bottleneck organizations, in disaster management systems, 51–54, 60

bounce back: components of, 197; in definitions of resilience, 30–32, 107–8; good emergency response facilitating, 143; organizations' failure to, 166, 178–79

bowtie architecture: in communication of risk, 37–39, 38; in tsunami early warning system, 247–48

Boxing Day tsunami (2004). See tsunami, Indian Ocean

Britain, 66, 151. See also United Kingdom

British Medical Association, 150

Brown, Michael: criticized for handling of Katrina, 85, 93; as FEMA head, 97, 99–100, 127

building codes: enforcement of, 121–22; on floodplains, 124; in Florida's hurricane policies, 119; funds available for mitigation through, 114–15; mitigation through, 109, 113–15; mitigation through in federal disaster policies, 111–12, 115–18; mitigation through in hurricane policies, 118–23; project- vs. product-oriented mitigation through, 109, 113–14

Burby, R. J., 110–11, 114, 121

bus explosion, in 2005 London bombings, 149–50

Bush, George W., 93; criticized for Katrina response, 85, 288n3; cutting FEMA, 96–97, 107, 127; devolution of federal government and, 95–96; militarizing disaster responses, 102–3; National Response Plan developed under, 98; pressure to cut taxes, 96–97; responses to Katrina, 102, 212

Bush, Jeb, 288n9

buyouts, of hazard-prone land, 113, 124

CALFED Program. See Delta Vision (CALFED Program renamed)

California: earthquake policies in, 114, 124; electrical system of, 162, 167–72

California Independent Operator (CAISO or ISO), resilience in, 160, 167–72, 177

Canada: helping after Katrina, 196, 217–18; offers of help after Katrina, 210, 215; U.S. history of cooperation with, 215–17

capacity of community, in risk detection, 36

capacity to act: collective, 181; in crisis leadership, 134–36, 192–93; failure of risk detection impairing, 42; information technology increasing, 35, 40; as measure of resilience, 39–40; self-organization in resilient communities', 49–50

capacity to cooperate, 217–19

Castro, Fidel, 213

casualties: French projection from avian flu, 184; from Katrina, 196; from L'Aquila earthquake, 220; from 2005 London bombings, 149–50

catastrophes: disaster vs., 131; effects of, 131–32; role of leaders in, 133

"Catastrophic Harm Precautionary Principle" (Sunstein), 64

causes, search for disasters', 10, 280

cellular telephone systems: case study of resilience in, 160; reliability standards in, 174–75; resilience in, 151, 160, 173–77; used to activate bombs, 151

centralization, of crisis management, 27, 107, 194–95; move away from, 231–32

Charles, Ray, 285n2

Chavez, Hugo, 213

City of London Police Force, 144

Civil Contingencies Reaction Force (Britain), 150

civil defense: civil protection vs., 153, 156; FEMA role in, 95

civil protection: civil defense vs., 153, 156; lessons from 2005 bombings for, 153–54

civil security, as focus in crisis management, 194

Clinton, Bill, 93, 97, 110; FEMA and, 95–96

Coastal Area Management Act of 1974 (North Carolina), 123–24

Coast Guard, U.S., 215, 218

cognition: in disaster context, 33–34; distributed, 277–78; sociotechnical infrastructure supporting, 279

Cold War, 201, 291n4

collaboration, 73–74, 140, 230; development of knowledge through, 74–76; resilience from, 81–82; in tsunami response policies, 245, 246. *See also* cooperation; coordination

collective action, 181, 276

collective life, 181; maintaining in pandemics, 182–84, 188–90, 194; maintaining *vs.* suspending, 187, 191

collective wisdom, 73, 288n13

Columbia River Basin water-management system, 159–66

combined arms operations, military, 74; U.S. and Canada military, 215–16

Comfort, L K., 26

command-and-control processes, 107; in communication of risk, 37–39; as obsolete in disasters, 127, 130, 135, 141, 156

common knowledge base, 35–36. *See also* common operating picture

common operating picture, 277–78; creation of, 39, 93; importance of, 42; lacking in Katrina, 59

"common security space," 217

communication: after 2005 London bombings, 151, 155; among underwater sensor networks in tsunami early warning system, 248–65; California Independent Operator depending on, 167–72; cooperation and, 201, 214; danger of waiting for restoration of, 135; in distributed cognition, 277–78; in emergency management policies, 120; facilitation of, 51, 75–77, 214, 279; lack of, 4, 51, 133, 155; lost in disasters, 40, 59, 135, 235; to make common knowledge base, 35–36; military failures in spite of improved, 68; need for improvement in interagency, 100, 155; of risk information, 34, 36–39, 42, 245

communities: capacity to address hazards, 108, 127; different levels of resilience in, 272–73; enhancing resilience of, 84, 115, 125; mitigation processes by, 110, 115; modernization reducing resilience of, 138–39; planning by, 121

communities, resilient, 108; building blocks for, 28, 277–80; capacity to act in, 39–40, 49–50; characteristics of, 138, 142; importance of developing, 230–31

Complex Adaptive System Theory, 26

complexity, 287n4; effects of, 69–70, 129; influence on problem-solving ability, 36–37; knowledge burden and, 62, 71–72; mobile telecommunication networks' increasing: 173–74; organizations' resistance to change and, 84–85

Comprehensive Emergency Management, Florida's, 119

Comprehensive Everglade Restoration Project, 161, 164

computers: as colleagues in Atrium, 74–75, 78, 287n7; fear of millennium problem in, 189–90, 289n2; increased risks and benefits with, 29–30

Congress, U.S.: committee system of, 98–99, 105; content of hearings by, 115–18; expanding Defense Department role in disasters, 101–3; on homeland security, 98–99; investigating FEMA's response to Katrina, 97; political use of disaster declarations and relief by, 113; subsidies by encouraging risky behaviors, 110. *See also* government, U.S. federal

Constitution, U.S., 86

construction standards, on floodplains, 124

continuity of operations: in French plans for avian flu pandemic, 187–88, 190–91; as goal in disaster management, 34–35; as military equivalent of resilience, 63; in organizations stressed by resilience demands, 168–71, 178–79

Cooke, Alastair, 88

Cooper, Anderson, 92–93

cooperation, 134, 290n3; attempts after Katrina, 197–98, *211*; benefits of, 200, 202–3, 213; in bilateral and regional disaster policies, 226–27; capacity for, 217–19; definitions of, 198–99; diplomatic declarations of, 204–5; factors facilitating, 199, 205–8, 214–17, 287n12; factors facilitating and inhibiting, 213; failures after Katrina, 210, 213, 219; formal *vs.* informal, 203–8; influences on, 212, 218–19; motives for, 204, 212–13; of organizations involved in tsunami response, 236–41; successes after Katrina, 211, 213, 215–16, 219; technical, 206–7;

cooperation, *(cont.)*
variables in, *209. See also* collaboration; coordination
cooperation, international: after Katrina, 196–97, 208–19, 211, *211*, 215–16; in disaster management, 223–24; promotion of, 223, 282–83; as resilience source, 197–203; UN coordinating, 197
coordination, 64; as benefit of cooperation, 200–201; in immediate aftermath of disaster, 11, 103; interagency, 122, 162–63; lacking, 97–99, 156, 240–41; leaders' role in, 136–37; obstacles to, 98, 230; of organizations in disaster management, 4, 221, 228–29; promotion of, 136–37, 139–40; in reducing risks, 276
coping capacity, 200
crisis, 182, 285n3; disaster *vs.*, 131; evolution of, 182; leaders giving rationale for, 137, 192–93; uncertainty in, 181. *See also* disasters
crisis and disaster literature, 11
crisis management, 34; classical approach to, 189; consideration of all actors in, 194; constraints on federal government's role in, 93–101, 105; development of international, 221–22; expectations of government in, 103–4, 280, 288n3; failures after Katrina, 129–30, 196, 210; failures causing lost faith in government, 130, 133–34; federal government's, 98, 103–5, 288n9; foci of, 190–94; French state keeping control of, 194–95; government pressured into, 87–88, 93; importance of competent, 129; influences on, 71, 91, 93, 132, 155, 189–90, 282; leadership weaknesses in, 140–41; military, 67; perceptions in, 207; politics of, 142; reducing uncertainty in, 192–93; responsibility for, 86, 144, 288n3; U.S. presidents using military in, 86–87, 101–4. *See also* disaster management
critical infrastructures, 62, 132, 152, 183, 286n9
critical systems, 64, 69
Cuba, offer of aid after Katrina, 213

daily life, maintaining in pandemics, 183–84
Davenport, Iowa, 115
decision-making processes, in disaster management, 41

decontamination, possible need for, 149, 152, 153
Defense, Department of (U.S.), 102–3
Delta Vision (CALFED Program renamed), 161, 163–65
de Menezes, Jean Charles, 154
Department of Community Affairs, Florida, 121
developing countries, efforts to increase resilience of, 222, 225, 227
diplomacy: declarations of cooperation in, 204–05; effects of international aid left unused on, 210–11; foreign policy in response to international aid offers, 218–19
disaster and crisis management field, 26–28, 31–32
disaster cycle, 109, 223, 227, 242, 286n9
disaster declarations, political use of, 113
disaster management: competence of, 133, 228; importance of resilient communities in, 230–31; information needed by policy makers in, 230, 242–43; international cooperation in, 221, 223–24, 230, 235, 242; organizations involved in, 50–58, 228, 230, 232. *See also* crisis management
Disaster Mitigation Act of 2000, 110, 114, 121, 126
disaster planning, 114, 144; for avian flu pandemic, 180–95; importance of process *vs.* product, 134, 140; by London Resilience organization, 145
disaster plans: evolution of pandemic, 188, 194; irrelevance in catastrophes, 11, 130, 133–34, 140; required for UK businesses, 152
disaster policies: bilateral and regional, 226–27; failures in, 112, 233; federal, 126–27; in French preparation for pandemic, 184; international, 222–25, 227–28, 230, 241; as political, 126–27
Disaster Relief Act of 1974 (U.S.), 95
disasters: agreement on existence of, 86–87; as betrayal of public trust, 157; from cascading small errors, 65, 67, 71, 129; crisis *vs.*, 131; definition of, 130–31; information technology changing public responses to, 87–93, 288n2; international effects of, 221, 227, 274–75; made of natural and social aspects, 86; mitigation of, 109–10, 114–15; natural, 95, 106,

108; predicted *vs.* surprise, 2; pre- *vs.* postimpact, 107; reducing losses from, 109–10, 224–25, 228; Stafford Act funds allotted for, not hazards, 114–15, 126–27. *See also* crisis

distributed cognition, 277–78

doctors, 150, 197, 213, 216

Dovers, S. R., 26

Dutch Public Works and Water Management Agency (Rijkswaterstaat), 216

early warning systems: development of technology for, 227–28; Hyogo Framework promoting, 225; Indian Ocean tsunami spurring search for, 244–46; Yokohama Strategy promoting, 223

earthquakes, 117, 244; in California, 88, 114, 124; in China, 2; Congress focusing on relief *vs.* mitigation for, 115–18, *116*; in L'Aquila, Italy, 220–21; in Lisbon, Portugal, 222; mitigation for, 111, 114

E2 Atrium. *See* Atrium model

ecology: competing objectives in, 165; study of resilience in, 16–21, *17*, 21, 285n4

economic measures, in preventing avian flu pandemic, 185–86

economy: interdependence of, 183; need to maintain during pandemics, 183, 188. *See also* financial-economic crises

ecosystem management, 16, 18–20, 162; water-management systems and, 159–66

efficiency, 23, 73, 159, 195

electricity, 132; California Independent Operator managing, 160, 167–72; generation by water-management systems, 159–66; shutdown of California power grid, 162

elites: networks facilitating cooperation, 206; support for resilience, 283

emergencies, in London Underground, 146

emergency management: Florida's policies, 119–20; resilience *vs.*, 35. *See also* crisis management; disaster management

Emergency Management, Preparedness, and Assistance Trust Fund (Florida), 121

emergency operations center, using bowtie architecture in communication of risk, 37–39

emergency planning. *See* disaster planning

emergency response. *See under* response

emergency services: in Britain, 151–52; in London bombings, 143, 154–56; maintaining in pandemics, 183–84; tsunami early warning information going to, 247, 265

employees: effects of resilience demands on, 158, 165–66, 171–72, 176–77, 179; job satisfaction of, 97–98, 289n11; loss of control by, 170–71; need to maintain work life during pandemics, 183

endurance, 11, 138

energy supply companies, disaster planning required by, 152

engineering: enhancing resilience through, 84; for mitigation, 109–11

engineering resilience, 17, 17–19

England, 145. *See also* Britain; London; United Kingdom

environmental damage: from flood-control projects, 110; from hog farm lagoon overflows, 124

Environmental Water Account (EWA), 164–65

environments, physical, built, and social, 3; interactions among in disasters, 27

epistemic communities, 201, 207–8, 231, 245; distributed cognition in, 277–78

Europe, in transatlantic cooperation during Cold War, 291n4

European Commission, facilitating cooperation, 205

European Union, 210, 226, 282–83

evacuation: in Florida's hurricane policies, 119; from London Underground trains, 146–49, 151; Operation Sassoon plan for London's, 152

Everglades water-management system, 159–66

expertise, 64, 202; ecologists in water-system management, 163–64; epistemic communities of, 207–8; international offers after Katrina, 196–97, 210; leaders' role in creating networks of, 140–41

explosions: efforts to preserve crime scenes in, 154; injuries from, 147–48, 150, 153–54; possible toxic contamination from, 153

Falkland Islands, 66

Fargo, North Dakota, 272

FBI, criticized for not preventing 9/11, 85

Federal Emergency Management Agency (FEMA), 37, 95, 97, 100; budget cuts in, 96–97, 107, 127; individual assistance

ing Hyogo Framework for Action, 225; policy formulation *vs.* policy negotiation, 290n2; responsibilities in crisis management, 86, 93, 96

government, local, 113, 194; disaster preparedness by, 114, 121, 126; mitigation plans required of, 114, 123; prevention and mitigation by, 114, 127

government, national (England), 144, 152

government, national (France): keeping control of crisis management, 194–95; planning for in pandemic, 188; willingness to undertake disaster preparedness, 186–87

governments, national: cooperation of subunits of, 199, 203–8, 291n5, 291n6; disaster policies of, 223, 241; disaster response by, 2–3, 5, 222, 242; initially rejecting foreign assistance, 212, 221; mutual aid agreements by, 226–27; in search for early warning system for tsunamis, 245; trust in, 203

governments, regional: England setting up, 145; mutual aid agreements by, 226–27

governments, state, 289n12; disaster preparedness and, 114, 121, 126; learning from disasters, 118–19; mitigation and, 114, 126

Governor's Hurricane Conference (Florida), 119

GPS, and underwater sensor networks, 248–52

Grenada, U.S. invasion of, 67

ground truths: collective sharing and refining, 73; effects of ignorance of, 65–67, 71

Gustav, Hurricane, 132

Haas, Peter, 201

Hamilton, Lee, 98

Handmer, J., 26

Hart/Rudman Commission on National Security, 97

Hazard Mitigation Grant Program (HMGP), 114

hazards: Florida's awareness of hurricane, 119; local, calling for local prevention and mitigation efforts, 127; Stafford Act funds allotted for disaster instead of, 114–15; toxic, feared in London Underground bombings, 149, 150. *See also* risk

health, 185, 237; pandemics and, 182, 186, 188. *See also* medical care

health, animal, 188

Heathrow Airport, security at, 152

high-reliability organizations (HROs), 23–24, 138, 281, 287n6; water systems as, 162, 164

High Reliability Theory (HRT), 23

Hill, A., 158

hog farms, on floodplains, 124

Holling, C. S., 16–18

Homeland Security, Department of, 37, 97–98, 100, 210, 289n11

Honduras, 210

Honoré, Russell, 103

hospitals, 156; bombing victims in, 150, 153; in pandemics, 183, 187

Hungary, 216

Hunt, Jim, 123

hurricanes, 111, 117, 122; Congress focusing on relief *vs.* mitigation for, 115–18, 117; Florida policies for, 118–23; mitigation for, 114, 123–25; North Carolina policies for, 118–19, 123–25. *See also* specific hurricanes

Hutchins, E., 277

Hyogo Framework for Action, 225, 230–31, 242

ideational factors, in cooperation, 207–8, 217–19

improvisation, 23, 74; in immediate aftermath of disasters, 11, 150; importance of, 11, 176–77; luck and, 171–72; promoting, 72, 140, 175–76; in resilient systems, 134, 138

income, maintaining in pandemics, 183

individual assistance program, FEMA's, 110–11

individuals, 194; mitigation efforts by, 124–25, 241; resilience and resourcefulness of, 148, 285n2; resilient, 14–16, 142

Indonesia, 229; international aid for, 221, 230, 235; not prepared for disaster, 232–33; response to tsunami, 232–34, 242; in search for tsunami early warning system, 246

Indonesian Chamber of Commerce, in tsunami response, 239–40

information: collective wisdom, 288n13; in communication of risk, 37–39; correcting, 278; difficulty in underground events, 153–54; in disaster management, 51, 134–35, 230–31, 242–43, 288n3;

information: *(cont.)*
  from early warning systems, 244–45;
  exchange of, 34, 202, 223, 242–43,
  277–78; intelligence in war, 286n2; lack
  of, 42, 59, 133, 148; to make common
  knowledge base, 35–36, 42; managing,
  29–30, 37, 59, 140; from media, 88–89,
  288n3; public given, 151, 156–57, 192–93,
  288n1; transforming events into crises,
  86, 88–89
information age, risks and benefits of,
  29–30
information-processing system, in tsunami
  early warning, 247–48
information technology, 60, 288n8; effects
  of development of, 36–37, 87–93, 156;
  increasing capacity to act, 35, 40
infosphere, 89, 91, 93, 157
injuries: from bombs, 147–50, 153–54; in
  L'Aquila earthquake, 220
innovation, in response to surprise, 74
institutions: cooperation and, 205–7, 214–
  17; Indonesia's, 233
insurance: assessment for emergency-
  management costs, 120–21; for earthquakes *vs.* hurricanes, 117; National
  Flood Insurance Program (NFIP), 114;
  rationalizing: as process-oriented mitigation, 113; shifting federal disaster policies away from payouts, 111–12
Insurrection Act, on military in disaster
  response, 102–3, 289n15
intelligence, 286n2; British, 154; U.S., 85,
  98–99
interdependence, 183, 219; effects of, 5–6,
  197; spread of disasters transborder and,
  274–75
interests, as factor in cooperation, 204,
  212–13
Intergovernmental Oceanographic Commission (IOC), of UN, 246
intergovernmental response system, Gulf
  Coast, 51–58, 60
interjurisdictional disasters, 35; blending
  organizations' own missions in, 39–40;
  communication of risk among organizations, 45–47; management of, 51–58, 60,
  231; response *vs.* prevention of, 219
intermestic territory, U.S. and Canada
  sharing, 217
International Decade for Natural Disaster
  Reduction, UN, 222–24, 241

International Federation of Red Cross and
  Red Crescent Societies, 218, 220, 229
international relations literature, 291n5; cooperation and, 203–4, 217–19; cooperation studies in, 197, 200; on distribution
  of intellectual resources, 202
International Strategy for Disaster Reduction (ISDR), 224
Internet, 135, 151, 157; in changing infosphere, 89–90; pressure on government
  in crises on, 92–93
interpersonal relations, 201–3, 206, 287n12
Iraq War, 97, 102
"Irreversible Harm Precautionary Principle" (Sunstein), 64
Israel, 210
Italy, 210; earthquake in L'Aquila of,
  220–21
Ivan, Hurricane, 122

Jamaica, 210
Japan, 287n7; helping after Katrina, 210,
  216; international disaster planning in,
  223–25, 230–31, 242
Joint Atrium. *See* Atrium model
joint operations, military, 74, 215–16

Kalla, Jusuf, 235
Katrina, Hurricane, 35; analysis of LOHSEP
  situation reports after, 41–58; Bush's
  response to, 102, 288n3; casualties and
  damage from, 60, 196; cooperation
  successes and failures after, 197–98,
  208–19; crisis management failures
  in, 58–59, 129, 155, 196; criticisms of
  response to, 85, 93, 100, 288n3; effectiveness of decentralized response to,
  27; federal government held responsible
  for response to, 85, 93, 288n3; FEMA
  in, 96–97, 122; lack of preparation for,
  96–98, 133; media coverage of, 1–2,
  92–93, 210; public response to, 92–93;
  vulnerability in, 1–2, 28, 36, 40
Keegan, J., 286n2
Kendra, J. M., 158
Keohane, R. O., 198–99, 201, 291n5
knowledge: absorbing, forecasting, and
  adapting to, 67–68, 71, 83; collective,
  73, 288n13; development of, 73–76,
  80–82; effects of lack of, 63, 65–67, 71;
  military failures and, 83; military needs
  for, 64–65; relation to outcomes, 69–72;

sharing, 63, 76–80; surprises *vs.*, 63, 79; tacit, 73–74, 76–78, 81–82; valuing unusual sources of, 73
knowledge burden, 69, 71; Atrium preparing military for larger, 74–75; complexity and, 62, 72
Kobe, Japan, 224
Kouzmin, A., 158–59
KPN Mobile,: resilience in, 160, 173–77

Landreneau, Bennett, 103
Landrieu, Mary, 92–93
land use, control of, 113, 118
land-use planning, 115, 122–24
L'Aquila, Italy, earthquake in, 220–21
law enforcement, by military, 103
lawlessness, in New Orleans, 92–93
leaders: disasters as betrayal of public trust in, 157; errors in public instructions by, 157; expectations of, 280; getting information from media, 288n3; giving rationale for crisis: sense-making, 137, 192–93; helplessness in immediate aftermath, 11; public expectations of, 137; resilience as hard sell for, 280
leadership: blaming citizens, 136; constraints on disaster preparation by, 141–42; constructive activities by, 136–37; correcting weaknesses in crises, 140–41; disconnect from citizens, 133; expectations of top-down, 141; helplessness in immediate aftermath, 11, 134, 137; in HROs, 281; need in disaster preparation, 133; pathologies to avoid, 134–36; public expectations of, 133–34; relations with media, 133–34, 136, 140; resilience-oriented: need for more research on, 281; role in nurturing resilience, 138–42. *See also* government
learning, 278; with Atrium model, 75, 79–80; from briefings after events, 149, 155; collaborative, 73; from experience, 23–24, 67, 79–80; feedback loops in, 231; from gaming exercises in water-system management, 164; instrumental policy, 112, 125; from natural disasters, 60, 106, 120–23; political, 113; resilience as outcome of, 23, 276; social policy, 112–13; trial-and-error, 23–24, 161–62, 166. *See also* training
Lewis, Philip D., 120
Lewis Committee (Florida), 120–21

Lisbon, Portugal, earthquake and tsunami in, 222
local level, 27–28, 71, 145, 221. *See also* government, local
logistics: after tsunami, 237–38; breakdowns in, 64–65, 202
London: aborted second wave of bombings in, 143, 154; bombings in, 138, 143, 151, 153–54; bomb on bus, 149–50; bombs on Underground trains, 147–49; emergency planning in, 143, 145, 152; emergency response to bombings in, 144–45, 150, 154–56; size and diversity of, 144
London Ambulance Service, 145
London Assembly, investigating emergency services after bombings, 154–56, 289n3
London Emergency Services Liaison Panel (LESLP), 145
London Fire Brigade, 145, 151
London Mass Fatality Plan, 155
London Resilience organization, 145; evaluating response to bombings, 149, 155, 289n3; Web site of, 157
London Underground system, 146; bombs on, 147–48; emergency response in, 148–50
losses: affected by competence of response, 228; assessment of, 237; from Katrina, 60, 196
Louisiana, waiving standards for foreign doctors, 216
Louisiana National Guard, 55–56
Louisiana Office of Homeland Security and Emergency Preparedness (LOHSEP), analysis of situation reports by, 41–58
Louisiana State Police, 55–56, 218

Madrid, bombings in, 146, 151
management studies, on cooperation, 208
maps, military failures due to lack of, 66, 286n2
May, Peter, 112
McDonald, N., 286n8
MCEER (Multidisciplinary Center for Earthquake Engineering Research), 108
media: changing ethos of, 89, 91–92; coverage of Katrina and aftermath, 92, 102–3, 210; creating common operating picture, 93; effects on leadership in crises, 133–34; increasing speed of news dissemination by, 90–91; leaders' relations with, 136, 140, 288n3;

Canada helping with search-and-rescue in, 217–18; flooding of, 246; Hurricane Rita hitting, 213–14; lack of resilience in, 2, 138, 272; media criticisms on, 92–93; military in, 102; vulnerability of underrated, 36, 42–43. *See also* Katrina, Hurricane

9/11 Commission, 98

9/11 terrorist attacks, 3; British response to, 145; bureaucratic reorganizations following, 98; Bush militarizing response to, 102; effectiveness of decentralized response to, 27; federal government handling of criticized, 85; increasing crisis awareness, 132–33; knowability of attack on, 71; not stopping pressure to cut taxes, 97; public response to, 91–92; slowness of response to, 144; strategy of anticipation in responses to, 279; TV coverage of, 91–92

Nonaka, I., 287n7

nongovernmental organizations (NGOs), 6, 229. *See also* organizations

NORAD (North American Aerospace Defense Command), 215–16

North Africa, Rommel's failures in, 65

North Carolina: hurricane policies of, 114, 118–19, 123–25; mitigation efforts by, 114, 123–26

North Carolina Disaster Recovery Task Force, 123

North Carolina Division of Emergency Management, Mitigation Section of, 123

Northern Ireland, and Britain's terrorism experience, 144, 152

Nye, J. S., 199, 201, 291n5

Office of Foreign Disaster Assistance, U.S., 210

operational indicators, of resilience, 20

optimization, resilience as antithetical to, 285n5

Oren, S., 168

organizational studies, 197

organization and management sciences, 21–25, 31–32

Organization of American States, 226

organizations: being overwhelmed, 58–59, 71, 178–79; case studies of resilient, 159–60, 177–79; of civil society, 183, 189–90; collaboration of, 39–40, 73–74, 203–8; in disaster management,

39–40, 54–58, 221, 228–30; exchange of information among, 34, 63; involved in tsunami response, 233–34, 236–41; knowledge and, 63, 69, 75; networks of, 24, 56–59, 141; relations of civilian agencies, 87, 97–99, 104–5; resilience held as ideal for, 158–59, 178; resilience of, 138, 178–79; resilient, 9–10, 13; resistance to change, 84–85; responses to surprise, 79–80; in search for early warning system for tsunamis, 245–46; technology's interactions with, 29–30; in tsunami response, 234, 234–41. *See also* specific organizations

organization theory and policy studies, 11–12

outcomes: communities' resilience judged on, 272–73; knowledge's relation to, 69–72; rogue, 70, 72, 287n6

outside assistance: coordination of, 137; resilient systems not waiting for, 134–35

Padang, West Sumatra, 246–47

pandemics: phases of, 185; uncertainty in, 186, 192; vulnerability to, 195. *See also* avian flu pandemic

panic, minimal, 148–49, 154

Pearl Harbor, attack on, 71, 88

Perrow, C., 287n4

planning: by California Independent Operator, 168–69; effects of reliability demands on, 166, 178. *See also* disaster planning

police: in efforts to contain avian flu risks, 185; as lead in British emergencies, 144

policy implementation: coordination in, 201–2; of Hyogo Framework for Action, 225

politics: Atrium as neutral, 81; of building regulation in Florida, 121–22; of crisis management, 142; influence on communities' resilience, 108; resilience as hard sell for, 141; in staffing federal agencies, 99–101; use of disaster declarations and relief in, 96, 113, 126

Posse Comitatus Act, forbidding domestic law enforcement by military, 103

preparedness, for disasters, 110, 118, 133; constraints on, 96–97, 141–42; costs of, 189; in disaster cycle, 3–4, 109, 223; in disaster management policies, 111–12, 120, 126, 225; focus on, 106, 111–12,

simulations, in Atrium model, 79–80
Singapore Air Force, helping after Katrina, 218
situation reports (LOHSEP), during Katrina, 41–58
slack. *See* redundancy
Small Business Administration, disaster loan program, 110–11
smoke, in London Underground emergencies, 147
social capital, cooperation increasing, 202–3
social engineering, on organizations' resistance to change, 84–85
social life, during pandemics, 183
social organizations, technology's impact on, 12
social psychology, cooperation studies in, 197, 199–200
social sciences, studies of resilience in, 21–30
social systems, resilience in, 19
societies, vulnerability of, 132, 184
sociotechnical systems: Atrium as, 63; benefits of, 37, 159, 222, 242, 282; building infrastructure, 278–79; components of, 62, 71, 72, 81; research on, 29–30; resilience and, 242, 273, 279–80, 282; in underwater sensor networks for early warning of tsunamis, 246–47, 265
South Florida Water Management District (SFWMD), 161, 163
Spanish flu epidemic (1918–20), 182
Speaker's Task Force on Emergency Preparedness (Florida), 119–20
Special Operations-13 (Britain), 150
St. John's Ambulance Brigade, 145
stability, *vs.* bounce back, 17–18, 25–26
Stafford Act (1988). *See* Robert T. Stafford Disaster Relief and Emergency Assistance Act of 1988
stamina, 11, 138
standards, shared, 215
State Department, U.S., 212, 214
State Ministry of Research and Technology, Indonesia, 247
state of emergency, difficulty maintaining, 187, 191
strategies, for resilience, 21–23, 22
stress, effects on leadership, 133, 135
subsidies, 110, 117
Sumatra: field study of underwater sensor

networks in, 246–47. *See also* tsunami, Indian Ocean
Sunstein, C. R., 64
surface buoys, and underwater sensor networks, 252
Surowiecki, James, 288n13
surprise: ecological resilience and, 19–20; effects of, 64–65, 286n1; as inevitable, 273, 284; knowability of, 69–71; military and, 63, 65, 67, 286n1; responses to, 63, 74, 79–80, 82; rogue outcomes and, 70, 72; suddenness *vs.*, 73
survival, resilience in, 16
Sutcliffe, K., 158
Sweden, offering help after Katrina, 196–97, 214

Takeuchi, H., 287n7
task forces, experimenting with Atrium model, 82
Tavistock Institute for Social Research, 12, 29
taxes, pressure to cut, 96–97
technology, 12, 23, 151, 223, 288n8; in early warning systems, 227–28, 244–45; risk and, 223, 276, 278–79; in sociotechnical systems, 29–30, 282
telecommunication. *See* cellular telephone systems; mobile telecommunication systems
television: coverage of 9/11, 91–92; coverage of Katrina, 92. *See also* media
terrorism: in Britain, 152, 154; natural disasters *vs.*, 108; responses to, 279. *See also* London, bombings in; 9/11 attacks
top-down orientation, 3, 141
trade, pandemics and, 181, 183, 185
training: education *vs.* on-the-job, 175–76; of first responders, 139; joint exercises for, 139–40, 215–16. *See also* learning
Transatlantic Business Dialogue, 214
transboundary disasters, 5
Transportation Safety Administration (TSA), 97
transportation systems: in pandemics, 187; vulnerability of, 146–47
treaties, 213, 242
trust, 81, 100, 208; cooperation increasing, 202–3; exercises to build, 82, 139–40, 164; in institutions, 139
tsunami, Indian Ocean, 2, 155; Indonesia's response to, 221, 232–34, 242; interac-

tions among organizations involved in, 198, 236–41; organizations responding to, 229, 232–41; response showing lack of international resilience, 241–42; spurring search for early warning system, 244, 246

tsunami, in Lisbon, Portugal, 222

Tsunami Research Program, NOAA, 245

tsunamis, search for early warning system for, 244–46

2000 bug, 189–90, 289n2

UK Emergency Planning Society, 144

uncertainty: in crises, 181, 286n6; measures to reduce, 192–93; in pandemics, 186, 192

underwater sensor networks (UWSNs): data collected by, 248; in early warning system for tsunamis, 246–66; other uses of, 246, 249; out-of-range information in location of, 254–66

United Kingdom: helping after Katrina, 197, 210, 215, 217; spending on security, 152. *See also* Britain

United Nations, 246; coordinating international disaster aid, 197; International Decade for Natural Disaster Reduction of, 222–24, 241; promoting international cooperation in disaster management, 223–25

United States: collaborating in search for early warning system, 246; cooperation during the Cold War, 201, 291nn4, 6; cooperation with Canada, 201, 215–17; inexperience receiving aid, 210, 214; international aid after Katrina, 196–97, 209; military operations of, 66–67; overwhelmed by Katrina and aftermath, 210; role reversal in aid after Katrina, 196, 209, 212

unknowns: knowable *vs.* unknowable, 69–70, 72, 287n4; preparation for, 4, 279–80

USSR, cooperation with U.S., 201, 291n6

Van de Ven, A. H., 208

Venezuela, 210, 213

Vickers, M. H., 158–59

victims: in flu pandemic, 187; of London bombings, 155–57; of tsunami, 242. *See also* casualties; injuries

virtuality, 287n8

Vogus, T. J., 158

volunteers, in plan for avian flu pandemic, 190

vulnerability, 1–2, 13, 108; of California Independent Operator, 170–71; of large-scale systems, 129, 132, 141; to pandemics, 181, 183–84, 195; promoting reduction of, 223, 225; in risk detection, 36, 42–43; of transportation systems, 146–47

Wachtendorf, T., 158

Wal-Mart, success in maintaining supply chains, 202

war model, classical approach to crisis management as, 189

War on Terror, as response to 9/11, 102

water columns, tsunami early warning system monitoring, 247–48

water-management systems, U.S., 159–66

water policies, popularity of flood-control projects in, 113

Water Resources, California Department of (DWA), 161, 163

wave speed, tsunami early warning system monitoring, 247–48

Weick, K. E., 158

Westrum, R., 25

Wildavsky, Aaron, 201, 279; development of resilience concept by, 7, 21–23, 31

Winham, Gilbert R., 290n2

Witt, James Lee, 100, 110, 114

workplaces, sociotechnical systems in, 29

World Conference on Disaster Reduction, 224–25

World Food Program, 240

World Health Organization (WHO), 180, 185, 235

World Trade Center attacks. *See* 9/11 terrorist attacks

World War II, 145–46, 287n12

Yokohama Strategy and Plan of Action for a Safer World, 223

Designing Resilience: Preparing for Extreme Events was designed in Scala Pro and Scala Sans and typeset by Kachergis Book Design of Pittsboro, North Carolina.